# "VIRGINIA MAKES THE POOREST FIGURE OF ANY STATE"

*The Virginia Infantry at the Valley Forge Encampment* 1777-1778

Volume I

Joseph Lee Boyle

CLEARFIELD

Copyright © 2019 by
Joseph Lee Boyle

All Rights Reserved.

Printed for Clearfield Company by
Genealogical Publishing Company
Baltimore, Maryland
2019

ISBN 9780806358901

## TABLE OF CONTENTS

Preface..................................................................................iv

Introduction.........................................................................viii

Glossary..............................................................................xiii

Locations Mentioned............................................................xix

Name Index............................................................................1

Bibliography.......................................................................365

## Preface

While the six month encampment of the Continental Army at Valley Forge in 1777-1778 has been part of America's folklore for generations, most of the men who served there have remained anonymous. The names of over 30,000 men of all ranks appear on the surviving monthly muster and payroll records. This compilation is the second volume of an effort to recognize some of these heroes of the Revolutionary War.

The information in the Name Index has been abstracted from Record Group 93, "Revolutionary War Rolls, 1775-1783," at the National Archives in Washington, D.C. Microfilm copies can be found at the branches of the National Archives and at some larger libraries. Microfilm rolls 92-113 cover various infantry regiments from Virginia. There is also an online subscription service, fold3.com, which contains all the muster rolls as well as other information.

It must be noted that men were not required to enlist in a regiment from their home state. There was always competition for recruits, and as the Virginia regiments were in Delaware, Maryland, New York, and Pennsylvania for various times before Valley Forge, some men in those states would have been enticed to join Virginia units. A payment for twenty-six men recruited by Captain Thomas Lucas of the Eleventh Virginia in 1777, shows twelve were from Harford County, Maryland, thirteen from various places in Pennsylvania, and one from Cumberland County, which could be in several states.[i]

This compilation includes information from the muster and pay rolls for ten of the Virginia infantry regiments at the Valley Forge Encampment. They were in four difference brigades, each known by the name of the brigade commander. This includes the First (Muhlenberg), First State (Weedon), Second (Weedon), Second State (Muhlenberg), Third (Woodford), Sixth (Weedon), Seventh, (Woodford) Twelfth (Scott), Fourteenth (Weedon), and Fifteenth (Woodford) regiments from Virginia. The other Virginia regiments, and Additional Continental regiments will be included in another volume. The First Artillery (Harrison's) will be included in a volume of the artillery units.

Each regiment was supposed to have both monthly muster and payroll for each company, and one for the senior officers and staff. The muster rolls are where the comments on a soldier's status such as "sick absent" are likely to be found, It should be noted that in many cases not all the rolls survived, particularly for June 1778. For example only payrolls for the seven months survive from Meriwether's Company of the First Virginia State. No June rolls at all survive for the Twelfth Virginia.

The information which follows in the Name Index has been taken from the muster and payrolls. Though the reports are for the preceding month, it cannot be assumed that a man who appears as "on command" for example, was in that status for an entire month. Such annotation indicates a soldier's status on the day a given roll was compiled. As these were current status reports, a man who appears as "sick absent" on a June roll may not have been sick at all in June, but become sick in July.

The payrolls were derived from the muster rolls. These were also kept on a monthly basis and ideally, though rarely, the men were paid on a monthly basis for the preceding month. In practice, the pay was usually several months behind and the non-financial notations on payrolls may be less accurate. Where discrepancies are noted on the date a man enters or leaves the service, the payroll is probably more accurate than the muster roll, as the regimental paymaster was audited on his disbursements.

The companies are known by the name of the company captain, though this does not mean the captain was ever present at Valley Forge. Captain Matthew Jouett of the Seventh died on November 15, 1777, but his company, commanded by Second Lieutenant Tarpley White, continued to be shown as Jouett's. A company of the Second Virginia Regiment is listed as Captain James Upshaw's, however Upshaw himself does not appear on any of the rolls. Captain John Willis of the Second was captured at the Battle of Brandywine on September 11, 1777, and though absent as a POW, the company continued to be shown by his name. Captain William H./Billey Haley Avery of the Twelfth was on furlough December 1777, through May 1778, and appears as resigned on July 28.

For the most part the original rolls are reasonably legible. However in some cases they are extremely poor. Brackets indicate illegible or questionable words. The reader should be very much aware that many of the names on the original lists have multiple spellings. For last and first names, the two most common spellings are presented here. However, some names appear with more than two variations. Examples include:

    Aldmon/Almond/Alman Allman/ Taltern/Talton, Philip;
    Reisor/Reysor/Ryzer/Rizor, Thomas ;
    Keaton/Keyton/Keating/Ketton/Katon, Thomas;
    Caufield/Cawfield/Coffold/Coffeld, James;
    Patillo/Pattillo/Pittlo/Pittillo/Patillar/Pettillo/Portillon etc.

Trying to present all the variations would be far too confusing to keep up with. Even a simple name such as Harris became Horrace in one case. In some cases names are so variously spelled, that John Gauman/Gawmon/Ganmon/Gawmon of the Fourteenth Virgina, could be the same man as John Goudman of the same regiment. For the person doing ancestry research even simple names that are spelled the same might create a challenge. For example there were two men named Thomas Holt who held the rank of lieutenant at Valley Forge.

There are probably other variations for the time periods before and after Valley Forge. In cases where no dominant spelling appears, the rolls have been checked forwards or backwards from the Valley Forge time period to find the most common variations. Additional variations can be found for some men on the rolls before and after the Valley Forge period. In these cases only the names shown on the rolls from December 1777 through June 1778 inclusive are used.

A common problem was that the record keeping was often months behind for men who had been sent to distant hospitals or were left behind on special duty. Some men were fortunate in being resurrected from the grave by the Army's paperwork. Archer Toney of the Fourteenth was sick absent in the early months but the March roll reads that he "returned dead 20 Jany but found out he was sick absent." He served through the end of the Encampment.

The entries for men who were not physically present often lagged months behind reality. Lewis Brown of the Twelfth was carried on the rolls through March 1778 as in the hospital. But the April roll shows he died on December 28, 1777. Bartholomew Vauter/Vawer appears as sick at Valley Forge from June-September 1778, but the October 1778 rolls show he died on July 10, 1778. Richard Crook of the Fifteenth had deserted on September 8, 1777, but this is not reported until the February 1778, muster roll.

Some of the comments are extremely cryptic. In the Seventh Regiment Edward Brooks, Alexander Gilliland, John Oneel, and Peter Waldron all have "In Room of John Long" listed for May 1778. "In Room of" was used for a man taking another's place, but it is unknown why the four have this listing for John Long. Bookkeeping errors were not uncommon. Private Josiah Blankinship/Blankenship of the Fourteenth Virginia, died on April 24, according to the payroll, but the muster roll shows he deserted the same day.

A number of men appear as deserting and then returning. This may account for some of the gaps in the records for other men. Some may have deserted for a month or two, then returned, and the non-com or officer preparing the roll never noted the soldier's absence. Those who are interested in a particular individual before or after the Valley Forge Encampment should check the rolls for the months before or after Valley Forge or request a copy of the soldier's service record from the National Archives in Washington.

Fathers and sons may have served together. Sergeant John Bourn/Bourne served in Captain Taylor's company of the Second Virginia. A John Bourn was drafted from Culpepper in February 10, 1778, and served in the same company. Other men are struck off the rolls and reappear without explanation. Sergeant John Copin/Coppin/Copen/ Coppen/Cowpen/Cowpens is shown as having deserted on February 9, 1778, but reappears on the rolls from April through June. Other men appear on the rolls but were never at Valley Forge. John Staples of the Fourteenth enlisted on February 15, 1778, but does not appear on a roll until August 1778.

In some cases the muster roll shows only part of the story and the researcher needs to look at for more detail in orderly books, and other sources. There is a short entry for John Riley/Reily of the Second Virginia being executed on January 10. Other sources show he "was tried at court martial on January 4, 1778 "charged with deserting from his guard, and taking with him Two prisoners in irons—was tried, and found guilty of the crime wherewith he was charged and Sentenced therefor to suffer Death—The Commander-in-Chief approves the sentence; and orders that it be put in execution next Friday at Ten Oclock in the forenoon near the grand parade."[ii]

First Lieutenant John Green of the First is simply listed as died on April 29. The rest of the story is that he was killed a duel (strictly forbidden by military law) with Elisha White, and on April 30 "he was Interred with the honours of War he was a Gentlemen of an Amiable disposition, who unfortunately got mortally wounded in a Deuel with L$^t$. White, our procession was honourable being accompanied by the most of the Officers in Gen$^l$. Greens Division."[iii]

---

[i] Signed by Christian Febiger as former Lt. Col. of the regiment, 21 May 1778, RG 93, M 246, Roll 109, f207, National Archives.
[ii] General Orders, 6 January 1778, https://founders.archives.gov.
[iii] James McMichael Diary, de Coppet Collection, Princeton University Library.

## INTRODUCTION

There are few regimental histories for units in the Revolutionary War. In several cases there are histories of the regulars, then called the Continental Line, of a given state. Several individual Virginia regiments have had histories compiled which are listed in the bibliography. The best single source remains Robert K. Wright's *The Continental Army*. This gives a short sketch of each regiment with an excellent bibliography for further reading.

In June 1775, the Continental Congress adopted the army of New Englanders besieging the British in Boston and appointed George Washington of Virginia as Commander in Chief on the Continental Army. Washington inherited what were essentially state armies with short terms of enlistment. Throughout the Fall of 1775 into the Spring of 1776, Congress authorized the formation of various regiments by the states in a piecemeal fashion while Washington and his officers strove to establish a coherent organization.

At the end of 1776, most of the enlistments for Continental troops expired. Congress had anticipated the problem of a disappearing army and had passed a resolve for eighty-eight battalions, or regiments, on September 16, 1776. This was intended to be an army for the duration of the war. However, efforts to recruit the new organization were ineffectual, and in January 1777 Washington was left with only a small cadre of veterans.

Virginia's quota for the new army in 1777 was fifteen Continental regiments, all which were with Washington for the 1777 campaign. The Virginia legislature reorganized its officer corps and made strenuous efforts to fill the regiments. However, most of the regiments did not achieve substantial numbers until April and May 1777. Each regiment was to have ten companies of sixty-four men, commanded by a captain, with all ranks included, the regiment was to have 792 men. Virginia also raised two "State Regiments" intended for home defense. The First State Regiment joined Washington during the summer of 1777.[i]

On December 27, 1776, Congress authorized "sixteen additional regiments" to be organized directly by Continental authority instead of by the state governments. Three of these were to be raised by William Grayson, Nathaniel Gist, and Charles Thurston, veteran leaders in Virginia. Thurston's never came into being, Gist's was used on the frontiers, and only Grayson's served with the main army in 1777-1778, though well below full strength.

Virginia, and several other states, were chronically short of their regiments quotas. At the end of March, 1777, Governor Patrick Henry complained that:

"Enlisting goes on badly. Terrors of the small-pox added to the Lies of Deserters &c, &c, deter but too many. Indeed the obstacles & discouragements are great."[ii]

The major British initiative of the year against the middle states, found General William Howe in late August with a British fleet at the head of the Chesapeake Bay. Howe landed in Cecil County, Maryland, and began the advance which would lead to the capture of the American capital of Philadelphia a month later.

All sixteen of the regiments of Virginia men were with George Washington's "Grand Army" for the entire campaign. They were in four named brigades under Generals John Peter Gabriel Muhlenberg, Charles Scott, George Weedon, and William Woodford, under the overall command of Major General Adam Stephen, also from Virginia.

These men fought at the Battle of Brandywine and were part of those who attacked the British right wing at Germantown on October 4. In an audacious surprise attack on the encampment of the British Army, the Americans initially routed the Redcoats but lost momentum and cohesiveness and were forced to retreat. Despite the losses, Washington's men were in high spirits from having initially rocked the British back on their heels. But the Ninth Virginia penetrated so deeply into the enemy lines that most of the men were captured. [iii]

After Germantown, the opposing armies licked their wounds. The British withdrew and fortified themselves in Philadelphia. They also began their "river assault" of nearly six weeks to clear the Delaware of obstructions and subdue the American strong points of Fort Mifflin south of Philadelphia and Fort Mercer on the New Jersey side of the river. This was critical for the British to be able to communicate with their fleet and bring up supplies and reinforcements.[iv]

In the aftermath of the Germantown battle, the Virginia regiments lost their overall commander. Major General Stephen was tried in a court-martial in November and decided that "he is guilty of unofficerlike behaviour, in the retreat from Germantown, owing to inattention, or want of judgement; and that he has been frequently intoxicated since in the service....Therefore sentence him to be dismissed the service—" General Washington approved the sentence.[v] This vacancy led to a months long dispute between Brigadier Generals Muhlenberg, Scott, Weedon, and Woodford, as to who was the most senior, important to them, as the most senior expected to be promoted to major general. Weedon left Valley Forge in February 1778, and never returned to the Continental Army when it was determined by a board of general officers, and approved by Congress, that Woodford was the most senior brigadier.

On December 4, General Howe led his army out of Philadelphia to confront Washington. By this time the Americans were well fortified on the hills at White Marsh in present day Montgomery County. They had also been reinforced by four more brigades of men, fresh from victory over Burgoyne at Saratoga. Howe looked things over for three days, and tried to maneuver for an engagement, but Washington was too wise to leave his stronghold and engage the British in the open field.

After the British retired to Philadelphia, Washington remained at White Marsh until December 11. The army crossed the Schuylkill River to a place called the Gulph and remained there from December 12 until December 19. Exactly when it was decided to encamp the army at Valley Forge for the winter is not certain, but it was on December 17 that Washington told the men in General Orders that the army would take post in the neighborhood. On December 19 the Continental Army marched into Valley Forge.

Some idea of the rigors of the campaign can be gained by the December strength return of the nine Virginia regiments that marched into Valley Forge on December 19. Each regiment was supposed to have 640 privates, for a total of 5,706 soldiers. Yet the nine regiments could only show 627 privates present fit for duty.[vi] This was less than a single regiment was supposed to muster. Many more men were present in camp. For example the Second only mustered eighty men fit for duty, but 139 more were sick present.

Washington warned repeatedly of his manpower shortages. He wrote to the Board on War on December 14, 1777, reporting that "most of the Men of the Nine eldest Virginia Regiments whose time would have expired in February have been permitted to go home upon Furlough, to induce them to reenlist for the War...." More enlistments ended in early January, and General Weedon wrote to Paymaster William Palfrey that he hoped money could be found to pay his men as he wanted "to leave the Service perfectly satisfied, as have hopes of their re-enlisting after a while provided they can be paid up to the time of their Dismission, and not kept in Service longer than they Contracted for." [vii]

The tale of the Continental Army at Valley Forge has often been told. The most thorough recent study is Wayne K. Bodle, *The Valley Forge Winter: Civilians and Soldiers in War*. University Park, Pa: Penn State University Press, 2002. Other studies are listed in the bibliography. However, a body folklore and myth has so encompassed the six-month encampment that the historical facts are sometimes difficult to discern.

The first few days of the Valley Forge Encampment and mid February 1778 were the hardest times for the troops. Worn out after a hard campaign, they had to build log huts for their winter lodging. At the same time a food shortage so severe occurred that Washington wrote to the President of Congress on December 22 that if something was not done immediately "this Army must dissolve."[viii] The General was forced to send details out from the camp to take food from the citizenry to feed his men. Thousands of other troops were too ill-clad to be out of doors or participate in any work details.

Many Virginians left the Army in January and February 1778 as their terms of service were up. For the next few months few new enlistments appear. However, by April the number of recruits began to increase. Some historians have remarked that General Howe missed a golden opportunity to attack Washington at Valley Forge when the Continental Army was at a low ebb. This might be so, but even if Washington could have kept a full complement of men at Valley Forge, there would have been no chance of feeding them.

There were few opportunities for glory or excitement at Valley Forge. After the huts were constructed, many of the soldiers were given the opportunity to go home on furlough. Those who remained stood guard duty, cut firewood, drilled, and were sometimes sent out of camp "on command." This catchall term might mean guarding stores at an outlying post, collecting forage for the army's horses, or guarding prisoners. Throughout the six months the British were in Philadelphia and the Continental Army at Valley Forge, detachments were rotated to the "lines"–the area close to the British fortifications to stop civilians going into the city and harass enemy patrols. These assignments were probably a welcome break from the tedium of camp, but they were not without risk as men were killed, wounded, or captured in skirmishes.

All of the regiments listed, except the Second State, were at Valley Forge during the entire encampment. The Second State marched from Fredericksburg on March 30, 1778, arrived at Valley Forge on April 22, and was added to Muhlenberg's Brigade by Washington's orders of May 31.

In March the arrival of "Baron" Frederick von Steuben brought a new drill+ for the army. The Commander-in-Chief's guard, then composed of Virginians, was enlarged to serve as the model company. A hundred men from other states were transferred to the guard at this time. Steuben introduced a simple but highly efficient drill which was critical to the success of American arms.[ix]

The high point of the Encampment was reached on May 6, 1778. Word of the American alliance with France was announced a few days before, and the entire army celebrated with an orchestrated *feude de joie*. Further good news arrived shortly after when it became certain that the British were preparing to evacuate Philadelphia. No one knew what the new British commander Henry Clinton was planning to do, but the simple fact that the American capital would be free was enough reason for joy.

Though still pathetically understrength, the Virginia regiments included in this work were able to muster 1275 men present fit for duty at the end of May. By June the the Fourth, Eighth and Twelfth regiments had been combined, as had the First, Fifth, and Ninth regiments. David Griffith of the Third wrote on June 3, that "Virginia makes the poorest figure of any State in the recruiting way. People from other States do not forget to tell us of it."[x]

Philadelphia was evacuated on June 18, and the Continental Army left Valley Forge the next day. At the Battle of Monmouth on June 28, fought under their various generals but Washington had to settle for a drawn battle when he might have had a clear victory, though the British viewed things differently

The Virginia regiments in the Continental Line were reorganized and consolidated in several more times. In 1780 they were all marched south in the doomed effort to defend Charleston, South Carolina, and were taken prisoners at the surrender there on May 12, 1780.

---

[i] Robert K. Wright, Jr., *The Continental Army,* (Washington: Government Printing Office, 1986), 108.
[ii] Patrick Henry to Adam Stephen, 31 March 1777, H. R. McIlwaine, ed. *Official Letters of the Governors of Virginia, Vol II: Letters of Patrick Henry.* (Richmond,: Virginia State Library, 1926), 133.
[iii] General Orders, 3 October 1777, *Writings of George Washington*, 9:307.
[iv] John F. Reed, *Campaign to Valley Forge*, (Pioneer Press, 1965), 269-87.
[v] General Orders, 20 November 1777, founders.archives.gov/documents.
[vi] Charles H. Lesser, ed. *The Sinews of Independence: Monthly Strength Reports of the Continental Army* (Chicago: University of Chicago Press, 19760, 61-62.
[vii] Washington to the Board of War, 14 December 1777, *WGW*, 10:152-53; Weedon to William Palfrey, 31 January 1778, John Reed Collection, Valley Forge National Historical Park.
[viii] Washington to Henry Laurens, 22 December 1777, *WGW*, 10:183.
[ix] Bodle, Wayne K. The *Valley Forge Winter: Civilians and Soldiers in War.* University Park, Pa: Penn State University Press, 2002.
[x] David Griffith to Leven Powell, 3 June 1778, "Correspondence of Revolutionary Leaders," *The John P. Branch Historical Papers of Randolph-Macon College* (June 1901), 53.

## GLOSSARY

| Absent Without Leave | Missing from his regiment without authorization. |
|---|---|
| Ammunition Guard | Assigned to guard ammunition supplies |
| A. G. | The Adjutant General was responsible for directing and organizing the administrative paperwork of the Army. |
| Armorer | Armorers were responsible for repairing weapons and keeping them in service. |
| Artificer | Artificer was a generic term for skilled specialists such as blacksmiths, carpenters, and leather workers who made and repaired articles required by the army. |
| Baggage | The clothes, tents, provisions, cooking equipment, and other stores and supplies. |
| Baker | A man detailed to bake bread for the Army. |
| Barren Hill/Barren Hill Church | This refers to the "Barren Hill Expedition" of May 18-22, in which Lafayette was sent out with several thousand men to scout towards Philadelphia. The enemy came out of the city with a much larger force and nearly caught the Marquis. Barren Hill Church still stands in Montgomery County, Pennsylvania. |
| Brigade Commissary | The officer assigned to each brigade to obtain food from the army's commissary and deliver it to each regiment. |
| Brigade Hospital | In January 1778, each brigade was ordered to build a log hut to serve as a hospital for the men of the brigade. |
| Brigade Major | An officer in each brigade who was in charge of the unit's paperwork. This was a staff, not a command position. |
| Bullock Guard | A soldier assigned to watch over the livestock kept for slaughter. |
| Butcher | A soldier assigned to cut up livestock in order to feed the men. |
| Cadet | A soldier who was in training to become an officer. |

| | |
|---|---|
| Cashiered | The term applied to an officer who was dismissed from the Army for incompetence or misconduct. |
| C. C. Man | Short for Camp Color Man, individuals assigned to sanitary duties, such as caring for looking after the "vaults" or latrines. |
| Clothier General | The official in charge of obtaining clothing for and delivering it to the army. |
| Commander-in-Chief's Guard/Comr. Guard | See General Washington's Guard. |
| Commissary/Comsy. Department | The department responsible for obtaining food and delivering it to the army. |
| Commissary Guard | Guarding the camp's food supplies. |
| Confined | Under arrest for one or more infractions of the army's regulations. |
| Corps of Invalids/Invaleds | See Invalids. |
| Court Martial | Military court of officers to try men of all ranks for misconduct and infractions |
| Deserter/Deserted | A man who left his regiment without authorization and may have gone over to the enemy or left for his home. |
| Discharged | Released from the army either due to a physical infirmity or completion of the required term of service. |
| Drafted | A man chosen by lot in Virginia, to serve in the army. |
| Drum Major | The lead drummer in a regiment who teaches the other drummers the proper drum calls and their usage. |
| Enlisted | The man has joined the army as a private or non-commissioned officer. |
| Ensign | The lowest ranking officer, who carried the colors or ensign into battle. |
| Exchanged | An exchange was the trading of prisoners with the enemy for those of equal rank or a trade based on a mutually agreed on set of values by rank. |
| Fatigue/On Fatigue | Assigned to a work detail in camp such as building fortifications or cleaning the encampment. |

| | |
|---|---|
| Fife Major | The lead fifer in a regiment who teaches the other fifers the proper calls and their usage. |
| Furlough | See on furlough. |
| Forage Guard | Assigned to guard the grain and hay used to feed horses and other livestock |
| Gallies/Rogaley/Roe Galley | On temporary duty in a galley on the Delaware River. |
| Generals Guard/On Genl. Guard | Each general officer was entitled to a small personal guard detail, the men of which usually rotated. |
| Genl Woodford's Guard | On the guard detail for Brigadier General William Woodford of Virginia. |
| His Excellency's Guard/General Washington's Guard | Washington's personal guard, usually called the Commander in Chief's guard. Originally all Virginians, in March 1778, one hundred men from the other ten states represented at Valley Forge were added. These men protected Washington's person, the official papers, and the army's cash. |
| Horse service | Light Dragoon cavalry. |
| Impressing/Impressed | Out of camp on a detail seizing supplies from the civilian population |
| In/On Command Row Boat | In service in a small boat on the Schuylkill River, bringing food, forage, or other supplies to Valley Forge. |
| In his room/In place of | A man serving as a substitute for another. |
| In inoculation/under inoculation | Under inoculation for smallpox. |
| In R. Bat./In R. Regt. | A soldier assigned to the special rifle unit under Colonel Daniel Morgan. |
| Inlisted with Major Washington | William Augustus Washington was Major of the Fourth Dragoon Regiment. |
| Invalids | A special unit of men who were physically unfit for field duty but who were capable enough to serve as guards for prisoners and supplies. |
| In General Washington's Guard | See His Excellency's Guard. |
| In the Train | On temporary service with an artillery unit. |

| | |
|---|---|
| Joined | The date the man reported to his regiment at camp. |
| Joined since last muster | The muster roll was usually done early in a given month. This means the man had joined in that month, after the muster roll was completed. |
| Left on the road/Left behind | Unable to keep up with the line of march due to physical problems. |
| Life Guards | See His Excellency's Guards. |
| Light Dragoons/Light Horse | The army's cavalry. |
| M. Gard | Probably the main guard, which was the daily guard detail for the encampment. |
| Not Joined | The soldier has not joined his regiment. This is usually noted when he has not reported when expected. |
| Oath | On February 3, 1778, Congress resolved that every officer who held a commission from Congress was required to take an oath of allegiance. Many of oaths do not survive. Details on the oaths can be found in Waldenmaier, *Some of the Earliest Oaths of Allegiance*. |
| On Clothier General guard | Serving as a guard for the man who headed the department that purchased and distributed clothing to the army. |
| On Command | On assignment outside the camp for periods of a day up to several months. Frequently where, or what the assignment was, does not appear in the records. |
| On command at the Bridge | A few days after the army arrived at Valley Forge, work was started by the soldiers on a bridge across the Schuylkill River. The bridge was not completed until March 1778. |
| On command coaler/collier | On detail outside the camp making charcoal for the use of the artificers. |

| | |
|---|---|
| On command on the lines | On assignment with other soldiers close to the British line of fortifications at Philadelphia. Men on the lines were to harass British patrols and stop civilians from carrying supplies into Philadelphia for sale to the enemy. |
| On command thrashing | On assignment outside of camp threshing grain to be used as food by the army. |
| On command to the Adjutant General | On temporary assignment to the Adjutant General of the Army. |
| On command with sick | Serving outside the main camp at one of the hospitals. |
| On court martial | An officer serving as one of the judges at a military trial. |
| On Detachment | A variable number of men sent out of camp on a particular task or assignment. Detachments could last for days or months. |
| On guard with the A.G. | On assignment in the personal guard of the Adjutant General. |
| On main guard | The regular daily guard detailed to protect the encampment. Several hundred men were assigned to this task each day. |
| On parole/parole | A soldier who had been captured by the enemy, but released pending a prisoner exchange, but was not supposed to do military service until exchanged. |
| On picket/picquet/picquett | An advanced guard posted at various points outside the camp to keep watch for the approach of the enemy. |
| On present duty | In camp on some undifferentiated military assignment. |
| On quarter guard | On duty guarding the quarters of a unit. |
| Paymaster servant | Serving as the personal servant to the Paymaster General. |
| Picket | See on picquet/picquett. |
| P. M. G. Guard | Serving as a guard for the Paymaster General. |
| Pioneer | Assigned to duty such as road construction and repair, or building fortifications. |
| Prisoner | A soldier held captive by the enemy. |

| | |
|---|---|
| Prisoner in camp | A soldier under guard in camp for one or more violations of army regulations. |
| Provost guard | Assigned to guard military prisoners and keep order in camp. |
| Q.M.G. | Quartermaster General |
| Quartermaster | The department responsible for setting up encampments, supplying wagons for transportation, and providing items such as tents, knapsacks, and tools for an army |
| Reduced | Lowered in rank due to incompetence or an infraction of regulations. |
| Redeemed from prison | Exchanged from captivity with the enemy. |
| Resigned | Officers could resign from the army without completing a specific term of service. However they could not do so without approval from their superiors. |
| Returned from captivity and joined since last muster | Refers to a man who had been taken prisoner by the enemy and returned to his unit at some time during previous month. |
| S. H. | Probably Sick Hospital. |
| Sick Absent | Sick at an unspecified location outside the camp. |
| Sick Present | Sick in a hut or tent at camp. |
| Sick Quarters | Sick in a hut or tent at camp. |
| Superceded | A staff officer, such as a doctor, being replaced. |
| Surgeon General | The doctor at the head of the army's medical department. |
| Taking smallpox/smallpox | Under inoculation for smallpox. |
| Taylor/Tayloring | Making up clothing for the soldiers. |
| Time out | The end of a soldier's enlistment period. |
| Under Guard | A man who faced charges for an infraction of army regulations. |
| Virginia State Store | Several states set up special shops to supply only soldiers from that state. |
| Waggoner/Wagoner | Driving a wagon for the army. |
| Waiter/waiting | An enlisted man detailed to look after the needs of an officer |
| Waiting on General Porteel | Brigadier General Le Bégue Du Portail was the chief engineer of the army. |
| With butchers | Detailed to slaughter and process the livestock brought to feed the army. |

## LOCATIONS MENTIONED

Counties listed are those which are on current maps. Many of the counties that existed in 1777-1778 are now much smaller, as they were broken up to form new counties. For example, all the land which forms the current Delaware County, Pennsylvania, was then part of Chester County. Some of the locations are not certain:

| | |
|---|---|
| Albany | Albany, New York. |
| Alexandria | Alexandria, Virginia. |
| Allentown | Allentown, Lehigh County, Pennsylvania, or Allentown, Monmouth County, New Jersey. |
| Amwell | Amwell Township, Hunterdon County, New Jersey. |
| Baltimore | Baltimore, Maryland. |
| Barren Hill/Barren Hill Church | Montgomery County, Pennsylvania. |
| Bethlehem | Northampton County, Pennsylvania. |
| Billett | Crooked Billet, now Hatboro, Montgomery County, Pennsylvania. |
| Bristol | Bucks County, Pennsylvania. |
| Brunswick | New Brunswick, New Jersey. |
| Burlington | Burlington, Burlington County, New Jersey |
| C. Billet/Crooked Billett | See Billett. |
| Church Hospital | Any one of a number of churches that were used as hospitals. |
| Corryell's/Correls/Carrells Ferry | This ferry crossed the Delaware River between what is now New Hope, Bucks County, Pennsylvania and Lambertville, Hunterdon County, New Jersey. |
| Cross Road | Now Hartsville, Bucks County, Pennsylvania Chester County, Pennsylvania. |
| Cuckoldstown | Now Berwyn, Chester County, Pennsylvania |
| Downingtown | Chester County, Pennsylvania. |
| Dumfries | Prince William County, Virginia |
| Dunkers Town/Dunkerstown | Now Ephrata, Lancaster County, Pennsylvania. |
| Englishtown/English Town | Monmouth County, New Jersey. |
| Fishwater Mills | Probably Fitzwater Mill, Montgomery Couunty, Pennsylvania |
| French Creek/French Creek Hospital | East Vincent and East Whiteland Townships, Chester County, Pennsylvania. |
| Fort Pitt | Now Pittsburgh, Pennsylvania. |

| | |
|---|---|
| George Town | George Town, Washington, D.C. |
| Greenswick | Probably Greenwich Township, Cumberland County, New Jersey. |
| Gulph | Montgomery County, Pennsylvania. |
| Heidle | Probably Heidleberg Township, Berks County, Pennsylvania. |
| Hopewell | Mercer County or Cumberland County, New Jersey. |
| Jersey/Jerseys/Jersies | New Jersey had been divided into the colonies of East and West Jersey. Well before of the Revolution it had been unified into one colony, but was still frequently called the "Jersies" or "Jerseys." |
| Lancaster | Lancaster County, Pennsylvania. |
| Lititz/Lidice | Lititz, Lancaster County, Pennsylvania. |
| Little York | May be a reference to York, York County, Pennsylvania. |
| Mendham/Mendum | Mendham, Morris County, New Jersey. |
| Monmouth | Battle of Monmouth, on June 28, 1778, in Monmouth County, New Jersey. |
| Morristown | Morris County, New Jersey. |
| New Brunswick | New Brunswick, New Jersey. |
| Newtown | Bucks County, Pennsylvania. |
| New Providence New Jersey | Essex County, New Jersey. |
| Potts Grove | Now Pottstown, Montgomery County, Pennsylvania. |
| Princeton/Princetown | Mercer County, New Jersey. |
| Q. Meeting House | Quaker Meeting House, many Quaker meeting houses were used as hospitals, this may refer to Valley Friends Meeting House, Wayne, Delaware County, Pennsylvania. |
| Readner/Radnor | Delaware County, New Jersey. |
| Reading/Reding | Probably Reading, Berks County, Pennsylvania. |
| Red Lyon/Red Lyons/Red Lion | Now Uwchlan, Chester County, Pennsylvania. |
| Rocky Hill/R. Hill | Middlesex County, New Jersey. |
| R. Hospital | May mean regimental hospital, or Reading Hospital. |

| | |
|---|---|
| Swedes Ford/Sweds Fort | Swede's Ford crossed the Schuylkill River at what is now Norristown, Montgomery County, Pennsylvania. |
| Shaefferstown/Shaferstown | Schaefferstown, Lebanon County, Pennsylvania. |
| Slotterdam | Now Elmwood Park, Bergen County, New Jersey. |
| Three Churches | Elizabeth Township, Lancaster County, Pennsylvania. |
| Trenton/Trentown | Mercer County, New Jersey. |
| Uynkland | Probably Uwchlan Township, Chester County, Pennsylvania. |
| White Marsh | Montgomery County, Pennsylvania. |
| Wilmington | Wilmington, Delaware. |
| Yellow Springs/Y.S.H | Now Chester Springs, Chester County, Pennsylvania. |

| Name | Rank | Regiment/Company | Remarks |
|---|---|---|---|
| Abbey, Edward | Private | Third, Arell | Dec 23, 1777 discharged. |
| Abbott, Benjamin | Corporal | Seventh, Moseley | Dec 1777-Jan 1778 in R. Reg't; Feb 19, 1778 discharged. |
| Abbott/Abbett, Daniel | Sergeant | First State, Hoffler | Dec 1777-June 1778. |
| Abbott, George/Geo. | Private | Third, Powell | Feb 12, 1778 enlisted; June 1778 sick Valley Forge. |
| Abbott/Abott, Randill/Randell | Private | Second, Taylor, F. | Dec 1777 on furlough; Jan-May 1778; June-July 1778 sick at Valley Forge. |
| Abner, Pail | Private | Fourteenth, Marks | Dec 1777-Feb 1778; March 1778 sick present; April 1778 sick; May-June 1778. |
| Abner, Simon | Private | Fourteenth, Marks | Dec 1777 in hospital; Jan 1778; Feb 1778 sick present; March-May 1778. |
| Abrahams/Abrams, Levi/Lewis | Private | Seventh/Third, Posey/Powell | Feb 27, 1778 enlisted; April 1778; May 1778 on guard; In June 1778 he is listed in Powell's Company, Third Virginia. |
| Absolam/Absolem, Edmond | Private | Fifteenth, Gray | Dec 1777-Jan 1778 sick absent; Feb 1778 sick; March 1778 on command; April 1778-May 1778. |
| Abud/Abeet, Thomas | Private | Fourteenth, Thweatt | Dec 1777; Jan 1778 sick at hospital; Feb 1778 on command; March-June 1778. |
| Acrey/Acre, Ambrose | Drummer/Private | Seventh, Lipscomb | Dec 1777-Jan 1778 on furlough; April 1778 on furlough; May 1, 1778 reduced to Private. |
| Acrey/Acree, William | Private | Seventh, Lipscomb | Dec 1777 hospital; Jan 1778; Feb 2, 1778 discharged. |
| Adamas, George | Private | Seventh, Lipscomb | Feb 14, 1778 enlisted; April-May 1778. |
| Adams, Benjamin | Private | Seventh, Spencer | Dec 1777; Jan 1778 on guard; Feb 17, 1778 discharged. |

| | | | |
|---|---|---|---|
| Adams/Addams, Cornelius | Private | First, Cummings/ Mennis | Dec 1777; Jan-Feb 1778 on furlough; March 1778 on furlough Virginia; April 1778 on furlough; May 1778 on command; June 1778 transferred to Mennis' Co., sick Valley Forge. |
| Adams, Ellison | Private | Seventh, Lipscomb | Dec 1777 roll shows he was left in Virginia in July 1777. |
| Adams/Addams, Gavin/Gavan | Private | Third, Blackwell | Dec 1777-Jan 1778 on furlough; Feb 14, 1778 discharged. |
| Adams, George | Private | Seventh, Lipscomb | Feb 14, 1778 enlisted; June 1778. |
| Adams, Gregory | Private | Fifteenth, Harris | Jan 1778 sick; Feb 23, 1778 dead. |
| Adams, John | Private | First, Cunningham | February 14, 1778 enlisted; April 1778 under inoculation; May 1778 sick in the hospital; June 1778 sick at Valley Forge. |
| Adams, John | Private | First State, Brown | Dec 1777-May 1778; July 1778 sick at Valley Forge. |
| Adams, John | Private | Twelfth, Bowyer, T. | Dec 1777; Jan 1778 on guard; Feb 1778-April 1778; May 3, 1778 deserted. |
| Adams, Littleton | Private | Third, Peyton, V. | Feb 1778 sick in hospital; Feb 12, 1778 discharged. |
| Adams/Addams, Malory/ Malleroy | Private | Third, Mercer/ Powell | Dec 1777-March 1778; April 1778 sick in camp; May 1778 sick present; June-July 1778 sick Valley Forge, listed in Powell's Company. |
| Adams, Richard | Private | Seventh, Lipscomb | Dec 1777-Jan 1778; Feb 21, 1778 discharged. |
| Adams, Robert | Private | Seventh, Jouett | Dec 1777 sick in hospital; Jan 1778; Feb 8, 1778 discharged. |
| Adams/Addams, Thomas | Private | Seventh/ Third, Crockett/ Young | Dec 1777-Jan 1778 on furlough; Feb-May 1778; June 1778 in Young's Company. |

| Name | Rank | Regiment, Company | Notes |
|---|---|---|---|
| Adams, William/Wm. | Private | First, Cunningham | February 17, 1778 enlisted April 1778 under inoculation; May 1778 sick in the hospital; June 1778 sick Valley Forge. |
| Adams, William | Private | Third, Briscoe | Dec 1777; Feb 5, 1778 discharged. |
| Adams, William | Private | Seventh, Jouett | Dec 1777 on furlough Virginia; Jan 1778 on furlough; Feb 7, 1778 discharged. |
| Adams, William | Private | Seventh, Lipscomb | Dec 1777 hospital; Jan 31, 1778 discharged. |
| Adams, William | Private | Seventh, Lipscomb | June 1778. |
| Adams, William | Private | Fifteenth, Gregory | June 1778 sick Correls Ferry. |
| Adams, William/Wm. | Private | Fifteenth, Mason | Dec 1777 sick absent; Jan 1778-May 1778 hospital Lancaster. |
| Adamson, Andrew | Private | Sixth, Hockaday | Feb 10, 1778 drafted; April 1778; May 1778 on command; June 1778 |
| Adcock, William | Drummer | Fourteenth, Marks | Dec 1777-March 1778; April-June 1778 on command. |
| Adkerson/Atkinson, Thomas | Private | Seventh, Spencer/Lipscomb | Feb 13, 1778 enlisted; April 1778; June 1778 in Lipscomb's Company. |
| Adkins/Atkins, Edward/Eadward | Private | Seventh, Spencer/Lipscomb | Feb 13, 1778 enlisted for 1 year; April-May 1778. June 1778 in Lipscomb's Company. |
| Adkins/Atkins, John | Private | Sixth, Avery | Dec 1777; Jan 21, 1778 discharged. |
| Adkins, Phillip | Private | Sixth, Apperson | Dec 1777 left at Alexandria; Jan-Feb 1778. |
| Adkinson, Isick/Isaac | Private/Drummer | Twelfth, Madison | Dec 1777-March 1778; April 1778 reduced to private, April 1778 on guard; May 1778. |
| Agee, Jacob | Private | Seventh/Third, Fleming/Heth | Feb 19, 1778 enlisted; April 1778 sick present; May 1778; June 1778 on guard in Heth's Company. |
| Ager, John | Private | Seventh, Posey | Dec 1777 sick Reading; Jan 1778 sick in hospital. |

| Name | Rank | Regiment | Service |
|---|---|---|---|
| Agnue, John | Private | Seventh, Crockett | Dec 1777-Jan 1778. |
| Aikin, Jacob | Private | Seventh/Third, Fleming | Feb 13, 1778 enlisted; April 1778 sick present; May 1778; June 1778 in Heth's Company; sick Valley Forge. |
| Aikin/Aiken, George/Geo. | Sergeant | First, Cunningham | Feb 1778 enlisted; April-May 1778; June 1778 on furlough. |
| Ailsworth, George | Private | Sixth, Massie | Dec 1777 in hospital; Feb 10, 1778 discharged. |
| Aires/Ayres, John | Private/Sergeant | Third, Mercer/Powell | Dec 1777; Jan-March 1778 on furlough; April promoted to Sergeant; April-May 1778; June 1778 on guard. |
| Airey, Ambros | Private | Seventh, Lipscomb | June 1778. |
| Akin/Aiken, Joel | Private | Second State, Dudley | March 15-May 1, 1778; May-June 1778. |
| Albert/Abert, Jacob | Private | Twelfth, Casey | Dec 1777-Jan 1778; Feb 20, 1778 discharged. |
| Alday, Peter | Private | Second State, Lewis | July 1778 shows pay for 1 ½ months. |
| Alderson, Richard | Private | Second, Taylor, W. | Dec 1777-Jan 1778; Feb 14, 1778 discharged. |
| Aldey, Benjamin | Private/Fifer/Private | Second, Taylor, W | Dec 1777; Jan 1778; Jan promoted to Fifer; Feb-May 1778; May reduced to Private; June 1778. |
| Aldmon/Allman, Taltern/Talton | Private | Fifteenth, Gregory | Dec 1777; Jan 1778 on guard; Feb 1778 sick present; March 1778 on command; April 1778; May 1778 Yellow Springs; June 1778. |
| Aldridge, James | Private | Second, Calmes | Dec 1777-May 1778; June 30, 1778 deserted. |
| Albridge/Aldrige, Richard | Private | Fourteenth, Lambert | Dec 1777; Jan 1778 sick in country; Feb-March 1778 hospital; April-May 1778; June 1778 sick Valley Forge. |

| Name | Rank | Regiment/Company | Notes |
|---|---|---|---|
| Alderson, Amos | Private | Seventh, Fleming | Dec 1777 sick in hospital; Jan 1778 hospital; Feb 15, 1778 discharged. |
| Alexander, Andrew | Private | Third, Arell/Briscoe | Dec 1777 Jan 1778; Feb 1778 sick absent; March-June 1778. In June he is in Briscoe's company. |
| Alexander, William | Private | Seventh, Spencer | Enlisted for 3 years. Dec 1777-Jan 1778 on furlough. |
| Alford/Alferd, Jacob | Private | Seventh/Third, Fleming/Heth | Dec 1777 sick Princetown hospital; Jan 1778 hospital; Feb-March 1778 on furlough; April 1778 on furlough Virginia; June 1778 in Heth's Company, wounded Virginia |
| Alford/Aford, John | Private | Twelfth, Casey | Dec 1777-May 1778. |
| Alfriend, Francis | Private | Second State, Spiller | June 1778 sick Valley Forge. |
| Alison see Ellison | | | |
| Allan, Benjamin | Corporal | Seventh, Fleming | Dec 1777 sick present; Jan 1778; Feb 13, 1778 discharged. |
| Allan, Robert | Sergeant | Seventh, Jouett | Dec 1777-Jan 1778; Feb 7, 1778 discharged. |
| Allan/Allen, Richard | Private | Seventh, Jouett | Dec 1777-Jan 1778; Feb 14, 1778 discharged. |
| Allen/Allin, David | Corporal | First, Lawson | Dec 1777-Feb 1778; March 1778 on command; April 1778 on guard; May-June 1778. |
| Allen, David | Private | Seventh, Posey/Sayers | Feb 27, 1778 enlisted; April 1778; May 1778 on guard; June 1778 in Sayers' Company. |
| Allen/Allin, Hamlin/Thomas H. | Corporal | Sixth, Fox | Dec 1777 on furlough; Jan 1778 absent in Virginia; Feb 11, 1778 discharged. |
| Allen/Allin, Isick/Isaac | Private | Sixth, Avery | Dec 1777-Jan 1778; Feb 15, 1778 discharged. |
| Allen, John | Private | First, Taylor | Dec 1777. |

| | | | |
|---|---|---|---|
| Allen, John | Sergeant | Seventh, Lipscomb | Dec 1777-Jan 1778; Feb 2, 1778 discharged. |
| Allen/Allan, Moses | Corporal/ Sergeant | Third, Blackwell | Dec 1777-March 1778 on furlough; April 1778 sick present; April promoted to Sergeant; May-June 1778. |
| Allen, Reuben/ Rueben | Private | Second, Upshaw | Dec 1777-Jan 1778; April 1778; June 1778. |
| Allen, Richd. | Private | Sixth, Fox | Dec 1777-Jan 1778; Feb 11, 1778 discharged. |
| Allen/Allin, Robert | Private | Third, Arell/ Briscoe | Dec 1777-Jan 1778; Feb 1778 sick absent; March-April 1778; May 1778 sick present; June 1778 sick Greenswick. In June he is in Briscoe's company. |
| Allen, Thomas | Sergeant | Seventh, Webb | Enlisted for 3 years. Jan-Feb 1778 on furlough; April-May 1778. |
| Allen, Thomas | Sergeant | Third, Young | June 1778. |
| Allen/Allin, William/Wm. | Private | Sixth, Avery | Dec 1777-Jan 1778; Feb 15, 1778 discharged. |
| Allexon, Thomas | Private | First State, Hamilton | Dec 1777-Jan 1778. |
| Allexon/Alexon, William | Private | First State, Hamilton | Dec 1777-March 1778. |
| Allgood/ Algood, John | Private | Fifteenth, Harris | Jan 1778-Feb 1778 on guard; March 1778 on command; April 1778-May 1778 sick present; June-July 1778 sick Valley Forge. |
| Allid, Solomon | Private | Twelfth, Casey | May 1778 "in room of Benjamin Bullet." See Bullet. |
| Allin, Hamlin | Private | Sixth, Hockaday | Feb 1778 in Virginia. |
| Allison, George | Private | Second, Sanford/ Lawson, | Dec 1777-April; June 1778. From April on he appears in Lawson's company. |
| Allison, John | Major/ Lt. Col. | First State | Jan-June 1778; June 1, 1778 promoted to Lt. Col. Oath at Valley Forge on May 12, 1778, witnessed by Muhlenberg. |

| Name | Rank | Regiment, Company | Notes |
|---|---|---|---|
| Almond, John | Private | Second, Taylor, F. | Dec 1777 left sick Virginia. |
| Almond/Allmond, John | Private | Seventh, Hill | Dec 1777; Jan 25, 1778 discharged. |
| Almond, William | Corporal | First, Cummings | Dec 1777. |
| Alsop, Benjamin | Sergeant | Sixth, Avery | Dec 1777 sick in hospital; Jan 31, 1778 discharged. |
| Alvey/Alva, John | Private | Third, Lee | Dec 1777-Jan 1778; Feb 14, 1778 discharged. |
| Alvey/Olway, Robert | Private | Third, Mercer/Powell | Dec 1777-Jan 1778; Feb 1778 on forage guard; March-May 1778; June 1778 sick at Valley Forge. |
| Alverson/Olverson, James | Private | Third, Arell | Dec 1777-March 1778; April-May 1778 on command; June 1778, in Briscoe's company. |
| Alvis/Olvis, Jon | Sergeant | Fourteenth, Winston | Dec 1777 sick Virginia; Jan 1778 sick absent; Feb 1778 Virginia. |
| Amory/Emmore, William | Corporal | Seventh, Young | Feb 16, 1778 enlisted; April-June 1778. |
| Anderson, Arthur | Private | First, Scott/Pelham | Feb 1778 enlisted; May 1778; June 1778 in Pelham's Company. |
| Anderson, Charles | Private | First, Scott | May 1778. |
| Anderson, Charles | Sergeant | Fourteenth, Winston | Dec 1777; Jan 1778 sick Bethlehem; Feb 1778 sick in hospital. |
| Anderson, Henry | Corporal | Twelfth, Bowyer, T. | Dec 1777-March 1778; April 1778 sick in camp; May 1778; June 1778 sick in camp. |
| Anderson, Henry | Corporal | Twelfth, Vause | Dec 1777 on guard; Jan 1778; Feb 1778 on command; March-May 1778. |
| Anderson, Isick/Isaac | Private | First State, Hamilton | Jan 1778-June 1778. On the March 1778 payroll he was paid for Dec 1777 as well as March. |

| | | | |
|---|---|---|---|
| Anderson, James | Private | Sixth, Fox | March 1778; April 21, 1778 deserted. He is advertised as a "black soldier" in the *Pennsylvania Packet*, May 13, 1778. |
| Anderson, James | Private | Twelfth, Waggener | Dec 1777; Jan 1778-March 1778 hospital; April 10, 1778 discharged. |
| Anderson, John | Drummer | Second, Sanford/ Lawson | Dec 1777-March 1778; April 1778; June 1778. From April on he appears in Lawson's company. |
| Anderson, Joseph | Private | Seventh, Posey | Dec 1777-Jan 1778 in Rifle Battn.; Feb 13, 1778 discharged. |
| Anderson, Richard | Private | First State, Nicholas | Dec 1777; Jan 1778 sick; Feb-March 1778; April 1778 on guard; May-June 1778. |
| Anderson, Richard | Private | Seventh/ Third, Young | Jan 1778 joined since mustered last; Feb-March 1778 sick present; May 1778; June-July 1778 sick at Valley Forge. |
| Anderson, Saml. | Private | Sixth, Fox | April 21, 1778 deserted. |
| Anderson, Spencer | Private | Third, Lee | Dec 23, 1777 enlisted in Light Horse. |
| Anderson/ Anddison, William | Private | First State, Ewell, T. | Dec 1777; Jan-Feb 1778 on command. |
| Anderson, William | Private | Seventh, Hill | Dec 1777 on furlough Virginia; Jan 1778 on furlough; Feb 14, 1778 discharged. |
| Anderson, William | Private | Seventh, Moseley | Dec 1777-March 1778 on furlough; May 1778. |
| Anderson, William | Private | Fourteenth, Conway | Dec 1777-Jan 1778 waggoner; Feb 1778; March-June 1778 waggoner, |
| Anderson, William | Corporal | Fourteenth, Winston | Dec 1777; Jan 1778 on guard; Feb-March 1778; April 1778 sick Yellow Springs; May 1778; June 1778 on duty. |
| Andrews, Adam | Private | Fifteenth, Harris | April 1778 sick present; May 1778 sick absent; June 1778 sick Yellow Springs. |

| Name | Rank | Regiment/Company | Service |
|---|---|---|---|
| Andrews, James | Private | Fourteenth, Thweatt | Dec 1777-Jan 1778; Feb 1778 sick present; March-April 1778; May 1778 on command; June 1778. |
| Andrews, John | Private | Seventh/Third, Posey/Hill | Feb 27, 1778 enlisted; April 1778; May 1778 on command; June 1778 in Hill's Company. |
| Andrews, John | Private | Twelfth, Casey | Dec 1777 sent to hospital; Jan-March 1778 at hospital; April 1778 supposed to be at hospital Reading; May 1778 at hospital near Camp; June 1778 sick at Readner. |
| Andrews, Robert/Robt. | Private | Sixth, Fox | Dec 1777-Jan 1778; Feb 11, 1778 discharged. |
| Andrews/Andrew, William | Sergeant | Seventh/Third, Fleming/Heth | Dec 1, 1777 appointed; April-May 1778; June 1778 in Heth's Company. |
| Andrews, William | Private | Seventh, Fleming | Dec 1777 on furlough in Virginia; Jan-March 1778 on furlough. |
| Angel/Angell, John | Private | Second State, Spiller | May-June 1778. |
| Angell, James | Musician | Third, Young | June 1778. |
| Angell/Angel, Robert | Drummer | Seventh, Young | Dec 1777 Light Horse Dec 21, 1777; April-May 1778; pay begins April 11. |
| Angel/Angell, William | Private | Second State, Bernard | April-June 1778. |
| Annen/Annon, Robert | Private | Second, Calmes | March 1778 paid back to March 24, 1777; April-June 1778. |
| Anthony, Nathan | Private | Fourteenth, Overton | Dec 1777 sick in hospital; Jan 1778 sick absent; Feb 1778; March 1778 sick absent; April 1778; May 1778 on duty; June 1778. |
| Antill/Antil, Jacob | Private | Second, Calmes | Dec 1777-June 1778. |

| Name | Rank | Company | Notes |
|---|---|---|---|
| Apperson/ Epperson, David | Private | Fourteenth, Marks | Dec 1777 on guard; Jan 1778; Feb 9, 1778 died. |
| Apperson, Richard | 1st. Lt./ Captain | Sixth, Rose/ Apperson | Dec 1777 in Rose's company; Jan 1778 appears as a Captain in command of the deceased Dunn's company; Jan-April 1778 on furlough; June 1778 on command. Oath at Valley Forge on May 12, 1778, witnessed by Muhlenberg. |
| Apping, Thomas | Private | Seventh, Posey | Feb 27, 1778 enlisted; April-May 1778 |
| Archdeacon, Edmund/ Edmond | Private | Seventh/ Third, Fleming/ Heth | Feb 13, 1778 enlisted; April-May 1778; June 1778 in Heth's Company, sick at Valley Forge. |
| Archdeacon, James | Private | Seventh, Fleming | Feb 13, 1778 enlisted; April 1778 sick present; May 1778; June 1778 sick at Valley Forge. |
| Archer, Isick/Isaac | Private | Seventh, Crockett/ Sayers | March 19, 1778 enlisted for the war; April-May 1778. June 1778 in Sayers' Company. |
| Arell/Arrell, David | Captain | Third, Arell | Dec 1777-Jan 1778 sick absent; Feb 14, 1778 resigned. Ensign Arthur Lind was then senior officer in the company. |
| Armistead/ Armstead, Thomas | 1st Lt./ Captain | First State, Crump | Dec 1777-May 1778; June 1778 promoted to Captain of Lee's former company. Oath at Valley Forge on May 12, 1778, witnessed by Muhlenberg. |
| Armistead/ Armstead, William | Drummer | Second State, Garnett | March 15-May 1, 1778; May 1778; June 1778. |
| Armstead/ Armistead, Adam | Fifer | First State, Camp/ Valentine | Dec 1777; Jan-Feb 1778 sick present; March-June 1778. |
| Armstead, Edward | Private | First, Cummings | Dec 1777. |
| Armstead, Samuel | Sergeant | First, Pelham | Dec 1777 on furlough; Feb 15, 1778 discharged. |
| Armstrong, George | Private | Third, Mercer | Dec 1777-March 1778 on furlough; April 24, 1778 died. |

| | | | |
|---|---|---|---|
| Armstrong, George | Private | Third, Powell | Feb 12, 1778 enlisted; First appears on roll for June 1778. |
| Armstrong, James | Private | Second State, Bressie | March 15-May 1, 1778; May 1778; June 1778. |
| Armstrong, James | Private/ Sergeant | Third, Powell | Dec 1777-Feb 1778; Feb promoted to Sergeant; March-April 1778; June 1778. |
| Armstrong, John | Private | First, Cunningham | Dec 1777. |
| Armstrong, John | Corporal | Second State, Bressie | March 15-May 1, 1778; May 1778; June 1778. |
| Armstrong, Robert | Private | Third, Lee/ Peyton, J. | Feb 27, 1778 enlisted; April 1778; May 1778 on command; June 1778 in Peyton's Company. |
| Arnold, Anthony | Private | Fourteenth, Winston | Oct 1, 1777 drafted; March 1778 has joined the regiment; April 1778; May 1778 sick present; June 8, 1778 died. |
| Arnold, Charles | Private | Twelfth, Ashby | Dec 1777; Jan 1778 sick in hospital; March 1778 sick in hospital; April-May 1778. |
| Arnold, David | Private | Seventh, Lipscomb | Dec 1777; Jan 31, 1778 discharged. |
| Arnold, Elisha | Private | Sixth, Avery | Dec 1777 sick in hospital; Jan 1778; Feb 15, 1778 discharged. |
| Arnold, Francis | Private | Second State, Quarles | June 26, 1778 died. |
| Arnold, Richard | Private/ Fifer | Fourteenth, Reid | Dec 1777 hospital; Jan 1778 sick hospital; Feb 1778 sick absent. |
| Arnold, Samuel | Private | First State, Camp/ Valentine | Dec 1777 sick in the country; Jan 1778; Feb 1778 on guard; March-June 1778. |
| Arresmith, James | Private | Third, Mercer | Dec 1777-Jan 1778 sick absent. |
| Arrington/ Arington, William | Private | First State, Hamilton | Dec 1777-June 1778. |
| Arthen see Earthen | | | |

Artherton see Etherington

| Name | Rank | Regiment | Notes |
|---|---|---|---|
| Arthur/Aathur, John | Private | Seventh/Third, Fleming/Heth | Feb 10, 1778 enlisted; April-May 1778; June 1778 in Heth's combined Company. |
| Arvin/Arvan, James | Private | Sixth, Avery | Dec 1777-Jan 1778; Feb 19, 1778 discharged. |

Ash see Osh

| Name | Rank | Regiment | Notes |
|---|---|---|---|
| Ash, Benjamin/Benjm. | Private | Fifteenth, Edmunds | Dec 1777 "Bowman"; Jan 1778 sick present. |
| Ash, Benjamin | Private | Fifteenth, Wills | Jan 1778 sick present; Feb 1778-April 1778. |
| Ash, Elvin | Private | Fifteenth, Harris | Jan 1778 sick; Feb 1778 sick present; March 15, 1778 dead. |
| Ashbey/Ashby Thomas | Private | Second State, Bernard | April-June 1778. |
| Ashbrook, Joseph | Private | Fifteenth, Gibbs | Jan 1778 on guard; Feb 1778; March 1778 on command; April 1778 sick present; May 1778; June-Sept sick Valley Forge; Oct 1778 dead. |
| Ashby, John | Private | First State, Brown | Dec 1777-April 1778. |
| Ashby/Ashbey, John | Private | Second, Calmes | Dec 1777-Feb 1778. |
| Ashby, John/Jno | Private | Sixth, Massie | Dec 1777 inoculated; Jan 1778; on command; Feb 1778 absent with leave; March-June 1778. |
| Ashby/Ashbey, Stephen | Captain | Twelfth, Ashby | Dec 1777-Feb 1778 on furlough Virginia; March 1778-May 1778. |
| Asher, Anthony | Private | Fourteenth, Thweatt | Feb 14, 1778 enlisted; April 1778 lately joined the regiment; May 1778; June 1778 sick Valley Forge. |
| Asher, Levi | Private | Seventh, Posey/Sayers | March 13, 1778 enlisted; April 1778 sick; May 1778; July 7, 1778 discharged from Sayers' Company. |
| Asherst/Ashurst, Francis | Private | Fifteenth, Harris | Jan 1778-Feb 1778; March 1778 on guard; April 1778. |

| Name | Rank | Regiment, Company | Notes |
|---|---|---|---|
| Ashford, William | Private | Second, Willis | Dec 3, 1777 deserted. |
| Ashlock, James | Private | Seventh, Moseley | Dec 1777 sick in hospital; Jan 1778 on fatigue; Feb 20, 1778 discharged. |
| Ashlock, William | Private | Seventh, Moseley | Dec 1777 on fatigue; Jan 1778; Feb 21, 1778 discharged. |
| Ashton, James | Private | Fourteenth, Conway | Feb 23, 1778 enlisted; June 1778 lately joined. |
| Ashton/Aston, Richard | Private | Second, Willis | Dec 1777 hospital; Jan-June 1778. |
| Ashton, Wm | Private | Sixth, Massie | Feb 1778-March 1778 sick absent; April 1778 not to be found in hospital returns. |
| Askew/Ascue, James | Private | Seventh/Third, Jouett/Young | Dec 1777 on furlough Virginia; Jan-April 1778 on furlough; May 1778 transferred to Young's company; June-July 1778 sick Valley Forge. |
| Askin, Obadiah | Private | Seventh, Jouett | Dec 1777 sick in hospital; Jan 3, 1778 discharged. |
| Askin/Askins, William | Corporal | Twelfth, Vause | Dec 1777-May 1778. |
| Asling/Oslin, Thomas | Sergeant | Fourteenth, Jones | Jan 1778 on duty; Feb-April 1778; May 1778 sick present. |
| Atchinson, David | Private | Twelfth, Waggener | Dec 1777-May 1778. |
| Atherly/Atherley, Thomas | Private | Second, Harrison | Dec 1777 hospital; Jan-June 1778. |
| Athey, James | Private | Twelfth, Ashby | Feb 10, 1778 drafted; May 1778; June 1778 sick Valley Forge. |
| Athey, John | Corporal | Third, Lee | Dec 1777; Jan 31, 1778 time out. |
| Athey/Athe, Robert | Private | First State, Lee/Meriwether | Dec 1777 sick present; Jan-Feb 1778; March 1778 on command; April 1778. |
| Atkins, Bartlet | Private | Fourteenth, Conway | Dec 1777; Jan 1778 on command; Feb 1778; March 1778 on guard; April-June 1778. |

Atkinson see Adkerson

| | | | | |
|---|---|---|---|---|
| Atkinson, John | Private | First State, Hamilton | Dec 1777-Jan 1778. | |
| Atkinson, John | Private | Third, Arell/ Briscoe | Dec 1777-March 1778; April-May 1778 on command. In June he is in Briscoe's company. | |
| Atkinson, Thomas | Private | Seventh, Spencer | Feb 13, 1778 enlisted for 1 year; April-May 1778 | |
| Atwood, Benjamin | Private | Twelfth, Bowyer, T. | Enlisted Aug 1, 1777; March 1778 joined; April 1778 sick in camp; March 1778 sick in hospital. | |
| Auber, John | Drummer | Third, Blackwell | Dec 15, 1777 discharged. | |
| Auber/Obarr, Peter | Private | Twelfth, Vause | Dec 1777; Jan 1778 on furlough; Feb-May 1778. | |
| Aubony/Abony, Thomas | Private | Second, Sanford/ Parker | Dec 1777 hospital; Jan-March 1778; April 1778; June 1778. From April on he appears in Parker's company. | |
| Aubray/Aubry, William | Private | Second State, Spiller | March 15-May 1, 1778; May 1778; June 1778 sick Monmouth. | |
| Augustus, David | Private | Fifteenth, Wills | June 25, 1777 enlisted; Feb 1778 roll shows he deserted on June 30. | |
| Austian, Henry | Private | First, Taylor | Dec 1777-Jan 1778. | |
| Austin, Isick/Isaac | Private | First State, Hoffler | April-May 1778; June 1778 sick absent. | |
| Austin, Henry | Drummer | First, Scott | Dec 1777 orderly to [     ] Morristown; Jan-May 1778; June 1778 absent. | |
| Austin, Walter | Private | Fourteenth, Winston | Feb 17, 1778 drafted; May-June 1778. | |
| Austin/Austen, John Wilson | Sergeant/ Sergeant Major | First State, Ewell, T./Lee | Dec 1777 present in Ewell's company; Jan-April 1778 in Lee's Company; May promoted to Sergeant Major; May-June 1778. | |
| Austin, Wm. | Private | First Cummings/ Mennis | Jan 1778 pay omitted; Feb 1778 on furlough; March-May 1778; June 1778 in Mennis' Company. | |
| Austin/Austian, William | Fifer | First, Lawson | Dec 1777; Jan 1778 sick present; Feb-June 1778; June 1778 sick at Valley Forge. | |

| Name | Rank | Company | Service |
|---|---|---|---|
| Avery, Billey Haley/ William H. | Captain | Sixth, Avery | Dec 1777-May 1778 on furlough; June 28, 1778 resigned. |
| Aylor/Ayler, Abraham/ Abram | Private | First State, Nicholas | Dec 1777-Feb 1778 on furlough in Virginia. |
| Ayres/Eyres, Henry | Private | First State, Hoffler | Dec 1777-June 1778. |
| Ayres, Joseph | Private | Twelfth, Bowyer, T. | Dec 1777; Jan 1778 on fatigue; Feb 1778-May 1778; June 28, 1778 killed. |
| Baber, Thomas | Sergeant | First State, Nicholas | Dec 1777-Jan 1778; Feb 7, 1778 discharged. |
| Badgett, John | Private | Seventh, Jouett | Dec 1777-Jan 1778; Feb 10, 1778 discharged. |
| Bacoman, James | Private | Sixth | June 1778 sick Valley Forge. |
| Baghal, Wm. | Private | Fifteenth, Wills | Aug 21, 1777 enlisted; Dec 4, 1777 deserted. |
| Bagill, Thomas | Private | Seventh, Fleming | Dec 1777-Jan 1778; Feb 28, 1778 discharged. |
| Bailey, Anselm/ Ansulumn | Private | First State, Crump | Dec 15, 1777 deserted; April-June 1778. |
| Bailey, Charles | Private | Fourteenth, Winston | Feb 18, 1778 enlisted; June 1778 sick Valley Forge. |
| Bailey/Bayley, Daniel | Private | Fifteenth, Hull | Dec 1777 sick absent; Jan-Feb 1778 sick in hospital; March-April 1778 sick present; May 6, 1778 discharged. |
| Bailey, Ismmal | Private | Seventh, Fleming | Dec 1777; Jan 1778 sick present; Feb 17, 1778 discharged. |
| Bailey, James | Private | Third, Blackwell | Feb 14, 1778 discharged. |
| Bailey/Baley, James | Private | First State, Ewell, T. | Dec 1777; Jan 1778 on guard; Feb 1778; April 1778; May 1778 sick Yellow Springs; June 1778 sick Valley Forge. |
| Bailey/Baley, James | Private | First State, Lee | Dec 1777 sick; Jan-Feb 1778 sick absent; April-June 1778. |
| Bailey, John | Private | Sixth, Avery | Dec 1777 waggoner; Jan 1778; Feb 8, 1778 discharged. |
| Bailey, John | Private | Fourteenth, Winston | Oct 1, 1777 enlisted; May 17, 1778 deceased. |

| | | | |
|---|---|---|---|
| Bailey/Baley, Richard/Richd. | Private | Fifteenth, Harris | Jan 1778 on guard; Feb 1778 sick present; March 15, 1778 deserted. |
| Bailey, Rueben | Private | Seventh, Fleming | Dec 1777 sick in hospital; Jan 1778 hospital; Feb 7, 1778 discharged. |
| Bailey/Baily, William | Private | First State, Payne | Dec 1777-April 1778; May 1778 on guard; June 1778. |
| Bailey/Baley, William | Private | Second State, Bernard | April-May 1778; June 1778 on guard. |
| Bailey, William | Private | Third, Peyton, J. | Dec 1777-Jan 1778; Feb 5, 1778 discharged. |
| Bailey/Beiley, William/Wm | Private | Sixth, Fox | Dec 2, 1777 reenlisted; Jan-April 1778 on furlough; June 1778. |
| Bailis/Bayles, Jesse/Jessy | Private | Second, Calmes | Dec 1777-June 1778. |
| Bails, Thom | Private | Third, Blackwell | Dec 23, 1777 discharged. |
| Baines, John | Private | Fourteenth, Marks | Dec 1777 supposed to be dead. |
| Baker, Caleb | Private | First, Taylor | Dec 1777. |
| Baker, David | Private | Third, Peyton, V. | Dec 1777-Jan 1778 wagoner; Feb 12, 1778 discharged. |
| Baker, Finnel | Private | Fifteenth, Gregory | June 1778. |
| Baker, James | Sergeant | Second State, Garnett | April 15-May 30, 1778; June 1778. |
| Baker, James | Private | Second State, Bernard | May-June 1778. |
| Baker, John | Private | Second State, Quarles | April-June 1778. |
| Baker, Moses | Private | Second, Calmes | Dec 1777-June 1778. |
| Baker, Moses | Private | Third, Mercer | Dec 1777-Jan 1778. |
| Baker/Bacor, Reuben/Rubin | Private | First, Taylor/Payne | Dec 1777-May 1778; June 1778 in Payne's Company. |

| | | | |
|---|---|---|---|
| Baker, Roland/ Rowland | Private | Twelfth, Ashby | Dec 1777; Jan 1778 sick hospital; March 1778 at hospital. |
| Baker, William | Private | Second State, Garnett | March 15-May 1, 1778; May 1778; June 1778 sick Valley Forge. |
| Baker, William | Private | Twelfth, Madison | Dec 1777-Jan 1778 sick in country; Feb 1778 sick hospital; March-April 1778. |
| Baley/Bailey, James | Private | Third, Blackwell | Dec 1777-Jan 1778; Feb 14, 1778 discharged. |
| Baley/Bailey, North | Private | First State, Nicholas | Dec 1777; Jan-March 1778 on command; April 1778 Yellow Springs hospital; May 1778 sick present; June 1778 sick Yellow Springs. |
| Balf, Peter | Private | First, Payne | Dec 1777-March 1778 on furlough; April 1778 on guard; June 1778 Light Infantry. |
| Balf/Balfe, Nicholas | Private | First State, Camp | Dec 1777 sick in the country; Jan 5, 1778 died. |
| Ball, David | Private | Third, Blackwell | Feb 18, 1778 drafted; May 1778 joined; June 1778. |
| Ball, James | Private | Twelfth, Vause | Dec 1777 on command; Jan-Feb 1778 on furlough; March-April 1778; May 1778 waiting on Brigade Major Johnson. |
| Ball, Nicholas | Corporal | Third, Peyton, V. | Dec 23, 1777 discharged. |
| Ballance, Henry | Sergeant | Second State, Bressie | March 15-May 1, 1778; May 1778; June 1778. |
| Ballance/ Balance, Willis | Corporal | Second State, Bressie | March 15-May 1, 1778; May 1778; June 1778. |
| Ballard, Dudley | Private | Fourteenth, Lambert | April-May 1778; June 1778 sick Valley Forge. |
| Ballard, John | Private | Fourteenth, Marks | Dec 1777-May 1778; June 1778 sick Valley Forge. |

| Name | Rank | Regiment/Company | Notes |
|---|---|---|---|
| Ballard/Balard, Robert | Lt. Col. | First | Dec 1777 absent with leave; Jan 1778 on command; Feb 1778 absent sick; March 1778 on command; April 1778 on furlough; May 1778; June 1778 Virginia recruiting. |
| Ballew/Balew, David | 2nd. Lt. | Second State, Bernard | April 1778; May 13, 1778 died. |
| Ballenger/Balenge, Samuel/Sam | Sergeant | Third, Peyton, V./Peyton, J. | Feb 14, 1778 drafted; April-May 1778; June 1778 sick Princeton |
| Ballow/Ballou, Charles | Sergeant | First, Cunningham | Enlisted Aug 1776 for 3 years; Dec 1777 sick at Bethlehem Hospital; Jan 1778 sick at hospital; Feb 1778 sick present; March-April 1778 sick at hospital; May-June 1778. |
| Ballow, Thomas | Corporal | Seventh, Fleming | Dec 1777 sick in hospital; Jan 1778; Feb 10, 1778 discharged. |
| Ballow, William | Sergeant | First, Cunningham | Feb 12, 1778 enlisted for 1 year; April-June 1778. |
| Bane/Baine, Lewis | Private | Seventh/Third, Young | Feb 16, 1778 enlisted; April 1778 sick present; May-June 1778 |
| Banks, James | Private | First State, Ewell, T. | Dec 1777; Jan 1778 dead. |
| Banks, Joshua | Private | Seventh/Third, Young/Hill | Feb 16, 1778 enlisted; April 1778 sick present; May 1778 on guard. |
| Banks, Josiah/Joshua | Private | Seventh/Third, Young | Dec 1777-April 1778 on furlough; May-June 1778 |
| Banks/Blanks, Thomas | Private | First, Mennis | April-June 1778. |
| Banks, Thomas | Private | Fifteenth, Grimes | Dec 1777-Jan 1778 on guard; Feb-May 1778; June 1778 sick Valley Forge. |
| Banks/Bank, William | Private | Seventh, Jouett | Dec 1777 sick in hospital, Dec 5, 1777 discharged. |
| Banks, William | Private | Seventh, Young | Dec 1777-Jan 1778 sick in Virginia; Feb 3, 1778 discharged. |

| Name | Rank | Regiment, Company | Service |
|---|---|---|---|
| Banks, William | Private | Fourteenth, Thweatt | Dec 1777-Jan 1778; Feb 1778 sick present; March-April 1778; May 1778 sick present; June 1778 sick Valley Forge; July 1778 dead. |
| Barbee, Daniel/Danl/ | Sergeant | First, Taylor/Payne | Dec 1777-Feb 1778; April-May 1778; June 1778 in Payne's Company. |
| Barbee/Barby, Francis | Private | Second, Willis | Dec 1777-Feb 1778; March 1778 deserted, date not stated. |
| Barbee, John/Jno. | Sergeant | First, Taylor/Payne | Dec 1777-Jan 1778; Feb-March 1778 on furlough; April 1778 in Jersey; May 1778 on command; June 1778 in Payne's Company. |
| Barbee, John | Corporal | Second, Willis | Dec 1777 on furlough; Feb 1778; May 1778 "Pay not drawn since Nov 1777." June 1778. |
| Barber, Elisha | Private | Seventh, Jouett | Dec 1777; Jan 6, 1778 discharged. |
| Barber, John | Private | Second, Calmes | Dec 1777-June 1778. |
| Barber, Willis/Willes | Sergeant | First, Lewis | Dec 1777-April 1778; May 1778 on command; June 1778 on command Valley Forge. |
| Barham, Hartwell | Private | Fifteenth, Mason/Gregory | Feb 1, 1778 drafted; May 1778; June 1778 in Gregory's Company. |
| Barker, Charles | Private | Third, Peyton, V./Peyton J. | Dec 1777; Jan-May 1778 wagoner; June 1778 wagoner, in J. Peyton's Company. |
| Barker, Henry | Private | Second, Jones | Dec 1777-June 1778. |
| Barker, John | Fifer | Fifteenth, Gray | Dec 1777-Jan 1778 sick absent; Feb 1778 sick; March 1778; April 1778 sick Lancaster; May-June 1778 hospital Lancaster. |
| Barker, Jonathan | Private | First State, Payne | Dec 1777-Jan 1778 sick George Town; Feb 1778 sick absent. |
| Barkley, Joseph | Private | Fourteenth, Reid | Sept 13, 1777 enlisted; April 1778; May 1778 sick present; June 1778 sick Valley Forge. |
| Barksdale, Daniel | Private | Second State, Quarles | April-June 1778. |

| | | | |
|---|---|---|---|
| Barley, James | Private | First State, Ewell, T. | April-May 1778 sick at Yellow Springs. |
| Barlow/Barlon, Lewis | Private | Twelfth, Bowyer, M. | Dec 1777-Feb 1778; March 1778 on guard; April-May 1778. |
| Barlow, Richard | Private | Twelfth, Wallace | Dec 1777-May 1778; June 1778 sick Valley Forge. |
| Barnard, Thomas | Corporal | Seventh, Fleming | Dec 1777-March 1778 on furlough; April 1778; May-June 1778 on guard. |
| Barnes/Barns, John | Private | First State, Hoffler | Dec 1777-June 1778. |
| Barnes, John | Private | Sixth, Avery | Dec 28, 1777 enlisted in the Light Dragoons. |
| Barnes/Barns, Robert/Robt | Private | Sixth, Hockaday | Dec 1777 on furlough in Virginia; Jan-May 1778 on furlough; June 1778. |
| Barnes, Thomas | Sergeant | First State, Crump | Dec 1777-Feb 1778; June 1778 pay roll states he was omitted for pay for March, April and May. June 18 he was paid for 3 months and 18 days. |
| Barnes, William | Drummer | First State, Meriwether | Dec 1777-June 1778. |
| Barnet/Barnit, Ambrose/Ambros | Private | Fourteenth, Overton | Dec 1777-Jan 1778 sick absent; Feb-April 1778; May 1778 sick present; June 1778 sick at Valley Forge. |
| Barnett/Barnet, Henry | Private | Second, Taylor, F. | Dec 1777-Feb 1778. |
| Barnett, James | 1st. Lt. | Sixth, Apperson | Dec 1777; Jan-May 1778 recruiting; Oath at Valley Forge on May 28, 1778, witnessed by Muhlenberg; June 1778. |
| Barnett, John | Private | Fourteenth, Marks | Dec 1777; Jan 1778 C. C. man; Feb 19, 1778 died. |
| Barns, Armsted/Armstad | Private | Seventh, Spencer | Dec 1777-Jan 1778 on command; Feb 17, 1778 discharged. |
| Barns, John | Private | Sixth | May 1778 on furlough; June 1778. |
| Barns, Robert | Private | Twelfth, Wallace | Feb 28, 1778; May 1778. |
| Barr, Isick/Isaac | Private | Third, Peyton, V. | Dec 23, 1777 discharged. |

| | | | |
|---|---|---|---|
| Barrett/Barret, Edward | Private | Twelfth, Wallace | Dec 1777-Jan 1778; Feb 4, 1778 deserted. |
| Barrom, Peter | Private | Sixth, Hobson | Dec 1777 sick Princetown. |
| Barron, Joseph | Private | Second, Taylor, W. | Dec 1777-Jan 1778. |
| Barrs, Thomas | Private | Second State, Bernard | April-June 1778. |
| Barry/Berray, Thomas | Private | Third, Lee/ Peyton, J. | Feb 27, 1778 enlisted; April-May 1778; June 1778 in Peyton's Company. |
| Bartlett/Bartlate, Benjamin/ Benjm. | Private | Fifteenth, Harris | Jan 1778 on guard; Feb-March 1778; April 1778 sick present; May 1778. |
| Bartlett, James | Private | Fifteenth, Harris | Jan 1778 on guard; Feb 15, 1778 deserted. |
| Bartley/Bartlett, Alexander | Private | Second State, Lewis | March 15-May 1, 1778; May-June 1778. |
| Bartley, John | Private | Fifteenth. Grimes | Feb 11, 1778 drafted; April-May 1778; June 3, 1778 died. |
| Barton, Henry | Private | Twelfth, Wallace | Dec 1777-March 1778; April 1778 weeks command; May 1778. |
| Barton, James | Private | Fourteenth, Reid | Dec 1777 hospital; Jan 1778 sick Reading; Feb 1778 sick absent; March 1778; May 1778; June 1778 sick Princetown. |
| Barton, Samuel | Sergeant | Seventh, Posey | Dec 1777-Jan 1778 on furlough. |
| Basey/Basie, Richard | Private | Third, Blackwell | Dec 1777-Jan 1778; Feb 14, 1778 discharged. |
| Basham, Jeremiah | Private | Fifteenth, Foster/Gray | Dec 1777-March 1778; April 1778 sick present; May 1778. |
| Baston/Buston, George | Private | Sixth, Massie | Dec 1777 innoculated. |
| Bateman, John | Private | First, Taylor/ Payne | Dec 1777-May 1778; June 1778 in Payne's Company. |
| Bates/Beates, James | Private | Fifteenth, Harris | March 1778; April 1778 sick; May 1778 sick absent; June-Aug 1778 sick at Yellow Springs; Sept 1778 "Said to be dead". |

| Name | Rank | Company | Notes |
|---|---|---|---|
| Bates, Jesse | Private | First, Cunningham | Feb 13, 1778 enlisted; July 1778 absent sick Valley Forge. |
| Bates, John | Drummer | Third, Arell/Briscoe | Dec 1777-June 1778. In June he is in Briscoe's company. |
| Bates, Thomas | Private | First, Pelham/Lawson | Feb 1778 enlisted; April 1778 under inoculation; May 1778; June 1778 sick on the road, in Lawson's Company. |
| Batson, Mordecai/Mordekey | Private | Twelfth, Ashby | Dec 1777; Jan 1778 sick in hospital; March-May 1778. |
| Baucutt/Bawcutt, William | Private/Sergeant | Third, Blackwell | Dec 1777; Jan 1778 promoted to Sergeant; Jan-June 1778. |
| Baughan, Aries | Corporal | Second State, Dudley | March 15-May 1, 1778; May 1778; June 1778 sick absent. |
| Baughan/Boughan, Richard | Private | Seventh/Third, Hill | Dec 1777-Jan 1778 on furlough; April 1778; May 1778 on guard; June 1778. |
| Bawney/Barney, Joseph | Private | Second, Sanford/Lawson | Dec 1777-June 1778. From April on he appears in Lawson's company. |
| Baxter, James | Private | Second, Upshaw | Dec 1777 hospital; Jan 1778. |
| Bayley, James | Private | First State, Lee/Meriwether | Dec 1777-March 1778 sick absent; April-June 1778. |
| Bayley, Joseph | Private | Seventh, Posey | Dec 1777-Jan 1778 on furlough; Feb 29, 1778 discharged. |
| Bayley/Baley, William | Private | Third, Blackwell | Dec 1777-March 1778 sick at hospital; April-June 1778 sick Lancaster; |
| Bayley, William | Private | Twelfth, Casey | Feb 28, 1778 drafted; May 1778. |
| Baylis, William | Paymaster | Twelfth | Dec 1777-May 1778. |
| Bayoner/Banyer, Peter | Private | First State, Meriwether | Dec 1777-May 1778; June 1778 sick absent. |
| Baytop, James | 1st Lt. Captain-Lieutenant | Seventh/Third, Young/Heth | Dec 1777-March 1778 on furlough; April-May 1778; June 1778 is listed as Captain-Lieutenant of Heth's Company. |

| Name | Rank | Regiment | Notes |
|---|---|---|---|
| Baytop, John | Cadet/Ensign | Second State | March 15-May 1, 1778; May-June 1778; June 1, 1778 commissioned Ensign. Oath at Valley Forge on June 1, 1778, witnessed by Muhlenberg. |
| Bazwell/ Bizwell, John/Jno | Corporal | Sixth, Apperson | Dec 1777 left at Alexandrey; Jan-Feb 1778 on command; March 9, 1778, discharged. |
| Beach/Beech, James | Private | First State, Payner | Dec 1777 sick Meeting House; Jan 1778 sick absent; Feb 1778 deceased. |
| Beacom/ Beecom, Robert | Private | Twelfth, Waggener | Dec 1777-March 1778 hospital; April 1778 sick Lancaster; May 1778 hospital. |
| Beal/Beale, Richard | Sergeant Major | Third | Feb 14, 1778 discharged. |
| Beal/Beel, William | Private | Twelfth, Waggener | Dec 1777-May 1778. |
| Bean, Joseph | Sergeant | Twelfth, Wallace | Dec 1777-Jan 1778; Feb 4, 1778 deserted. |
| Beanham/ Baynham, Joseph | 2nd. Lt. | Third, Peyton, V. | Dec 31, 1778 resigned. |
| Beard, Thomas | Private | Second State, Taliaferro | March 15-May 1, 1778; May-June 1778. |
| Beasley/Beasly, Larkin/Larken | Private | Seventh/ Third, Webb/ Young | April 1778 sick present; May 1778 on command; June 1778 in Young's Company. |
| Beasley, Richard | Private | Second State, Garnett | April 15-June 1, 1778; June 1778. |
| Beaty/Baty, George | Private | Third, Briscoe | March 2, 1778 drafted; April-May 1778; June-Aug 1778 sick at Valley Forge. |
| Beaty/Baty, John | Private | Third, Briscoe | April 1778 "not mustered in April;" May 1778 sick present; June-Aug 1778 sick at Valley Forge. |
| Beaver, Ambrose | Private | Seventh, Fleming | Dec 1777 on furlough Virginia; Jan 1778 Virginia; Feb 20, 1778 discharged. |

| Name | Rank | Regiment, Company | Service |
|---|---|---|---|
| Beavers, Benjamin | Sergeant | First State Ewell, T., | Dec 1777-June 1778 |
| Beavers/Beaver, Samuel | Private | First State, Ewell, T. | Dec 1777 on command, Jan-June 1778. |
| Beazley, James | Private | Second, Taylor, F. | Dec 1777-Feb 1778; March 12, 1778 discharged. |
| Bebey, Joseph | Private | Seventh, Jouett | Dec 21, 1777 discharged. |
| Beck, John | Private | First, Cunningham | March 1777 enlisted for 3 years; Dec 1777 deserted. |
| Beckam/Beckum, James | Private | Second, Harrison | Dec 1777-June 1778. |
| Bedford, James | Private/Corporal | Seventh/Third, Fleming/Heth | Feb 11, 1778 enlisted; Feb 20, 1778 promoted to Corporal; April-May 1778; June 1778 in Heth's Company. |
| Bedgood, James | Private | First, Lewis | Dec 1777 sick; Jan 1778 sick hospital; Feb 1778 dead. |
| Bedleston/Beddleston, John | Private | Fourteenth, Marks | Dec 1777; Jan 1778 "Deserted Jan, 19, 1778, Accot against him." |
| Bedworth, William | Corporal | Twelfth, Madison | Dec 1777-Feb 1778 sick in hospital; March-April 1778. |
| Beets see Botts | | | |
| Belcher, Geo. | Private | Fifteenth, Foster/Gray | Dec 1777-Feb 1778; March 1778 on command; April 1778 sick present; May 1778. |
| Belcher, Robert/Robt. | Private | Fifteenth, Foster/Gray | Dec 1777-March 1778; April-May 1778 sick present. |
| Belcher, Stephen | Private | Fifteenth, Gray | April 1778 sick present. |
| Belcher/Bellcher, William/Wm. | Private | Fifteenth, Harris | Jan 1778; Feb-April 1778 sick present; May 1778. |
| Belemor/Bellemore, Daniel | Private | Second State, Spiller | April 1778; June 1778 sick Valley Forge. |
| Bell, James | Private | Sixth, Rose | Dec 1777-Jan 1778; Feb 28, 1778 discharged. |
| Bell, John | Private | First, Mennis | Dec 1, 1777 enlisted; Dec 1777-June 1778 on furlough; July 1, 1778 deserted. |

| Name | Rank | Company | Service |
|---|---|---|---|
| Bell/Jno, John | 1st. Lt. | Sixth, Hockaday | Dec 1777; Jan 1778 recruiting in Virginia; Feb-May 1778 recruiting; June 1778. |
| Bell, Peter | Private | Second State, Bernard | Stationed in York garrison March 15-April 15, 1778. |
| Bell, Richard | Private | Second State, Dudley | March 15-May 1, 1778; May 1778; June 1778 sick absent. |
| Bell, Thomas | Private | First State, Brown | Dec 1777-May 1778. |
| Bell/Beall, Thomas | Sergeant | Twelfth, Bowyer, T. | Enlisted Aug 15, 1777. Jan 1778 joined; Jan-Feb 1778; March-April 1778 sick in camp; May 1778. |
| Bell, William | Private | First State, Crump | Dec 1777-March 1778. |
| Bell, William/Wm. | Private | Third, Peyton, V./ Peyton, J. | Dec 1777 on furlough Virginia; Jan-March 1778 on furlough; April-May 1778; June 1778 in J. Peyton's company. |
| Bell/Beall, William | Private | Twelfth, Bowyer, T. | Dec 1777-Jan 1778; Feb-April 1778 on command; May 1778; June-Aug 1778 sick Valley Forge. |
| Bellamy/ Belemy, William | Drummer | Third, Peyton, V./ Peyton, J. | April 1, 1778 enlisted; April-May 1778; June 1778 sick Brunswick, in J. Peyton's company. |
| Bellew/Bellow, Solomon | Private | Second, Taylor, F. | Feb 13, 1778 drafted from Orange; April-June 1778. |
| Bellwood, Robert | Private | Twelfth, Bowyer, M. | May 1778 drafted one year; sick in camp. |
| Belsher, Edward | Private | Second, Taylor, W. | Dec 1777-Jan 1778; Feb 14, 1778 discharged. |
| Belsher, Jacob | Private | Second, Taylor, W. | Dec 1777-Jan 1778; Feb 21, 1778 discharged. |
| Belsher, Joel | Private | Second, Taylor, W. | Dec 1777-Jan 1778; Feb 21, 1778 discharged. |
| Belsher, Thomas | Private | Second, Taylor, W. | Dec 1777-Jan 1778; Feb 5, 1778 discharged. |
| Belsher, William | Private | Second, Taylor, W. | Dec 1777 guard; Jan 1778; Feb 5, 1778 discharged. |
| Belvin, Aaron | Private | Seventh, Young | Dec 1777-Jan 1778; Feb 3, 1778 discharged. |

| Name | Rank | Company | Notes |
|---|---|---|---|
| Belvin, George | Private | Seventh, Young | Dec 1777-Jan 1778; Feb 3, 1778 discharged. |
| Belvin, John | Private | Seventh, Young | Dec 1777-Jan 1778; Feb 3, 1778 discharged. |
| Belvin, Lewis | Private | Seventh, Young | Dec 21, 1777 to Light Horse |
| Belvin, Thomas | Private | Seventh/Third, Young | Dec 1777-April 1778 on furlough; May-June 1778 |
| Benge/Berge, Will Lewis/William Lewis | Private | Seventh/Third, Jouett/Hill | Feb 16, 1778 enlisted; April-May 1778; June 1778 in Hill's Company. |
| Bennett/Bennitt, Richard | Private | Seventh, Lipscomb | Dec 1777; Jan 31, 1778 discharged. |
| Berger/Burga, Nicholas | Private | Seventh, Hill | June 1778. |
| Benham/Bonham, Peter | Sergeant | Third, Briscoe | Dec 1777; Feb 2, 1778 discharged; Feb 1778 payroll shows discharge date of Feb 5. |
| Bentley, Jeremiah/Jerh. | Private | Fifteenth, Foster/Gray | Aug 28, 1777 enlisted; Jan-Feb 1778; March 1778 sick in camp; April 1778 sick present; May-June 1778 hospital Yellow Springs. |
| Bernard, Peter | Captain | Second State, Bernard | May-June 1778. |
| Bernard, Robert | Private | Seventh, Fleming | Dec 1777 with Rifle Regt.; Jan 1778 R. Regimt; Feb 5, 1778 discharged. |
| Bernard, Thomas | Private/Corporal | Seventh/Third, Fleming/Heth | Dec 1777 on furlough Virginia; Jan-March 1778 on furlough; Feb 11, 1778 promoted to Corporal; April 1778; May-June 1778 on guard, in Heth's Company. |
| Berry, Daniel | Private | Fourteenth, Reid | Dec 1777 on duty; Jan 1778 on command; Feb 1778 on guard; April 1778 on command; May 1778 sick present; June 1778 sick Valley Forge; Later roll shows he died June 30, 1778. |
| Berry, James | Private | Fourteenth, Reid | May-June 1778. "In Room of Joseph Infett deserted Returned 23 May 78." |

| Name | Rank | Regiment | Service |
|---|---|---|---|
| Berry, John | Sergeant | First State, Lee | Dec 1777 sick; Jan 1778 deceased. |
| Berry/Berrey, Joshua | Private | Fifteenth, Gregory | Dec 1777-March 1778 hospital. |
| Berry, Nathaniel | Private | First State, Nicholas | Dec 1777-Feb 1778; March-April 1778 on command; May-June 1778. |
| Berry, William | Ensign | Twelfth, Vause | Dec 9, 1777 resigned. |
| Berryn, John | Private | Fourteenth, Lambert | Feb 23, 1778 enlisted; June 1778 sick Valley Forge. |
| Best, John | Ensign | First State, Hoffler | Dec 1777-Feb 1778. |
| Best, Lewis | Sergeant | Fifteenth, Gregory | Dec 1777-March 1778 hospital; April-May 1778 sick Princeton; June 1778 sick Valley Forge. |
| Best, Malachi/Malicha | Corporal | First State, Hoffler | Dec 1777-May 1778. |
| Best, Tucker | Sergeant | First State, Hoffler | Dec 1777-June 1778. |
| Beswick, John | Private | Second, Willis | Dec 1777-Feb 1778. |
| Bettisworth/Bitsworth, William | Private | First State, Lee | Dec 1777 sick; Jan 1778 sick at Lancaster; Feb 1778 sick absent; March 1778 Yellow Springs hospital. |
| Bettysworth/Betsworth, Charles | Private | Third, Briscoe | Feb 10, 1778 drafted; June 1778. |
| Beverly/Belvey, Sylvester | Private | First State, Nicholas | Dec 1777-Feb 1778; March 1778 on command; April-June 1778. |
| Bevin, Robert | Private | Third, Mercer | May 1778 sick present. |
| Bibby, John | Private | Fifteenth, Grimes | Dec 1777-Feb 1778; March 1778 on guard; April 1778; May 1778 on picquet. |
| Bidder/Bebber, Daniel | Private | Seventh/Third, Crockett/Young | Dec 1777-Jan 1778 on furlough; Feb-May 1778; June 1778 sick Corrells Ferry, in Young's Company. |
| Biddlecomb, William | Private | Fifteenth, Mason | Feb 11, 1778 drafted; April 1778. He and Wm. Bilgum may be the same individual |

| | | | |
|---|---|---|---|
| Biggs, John | Private | First State, Lee | Dec 1777 sick at Bethlehem; Jan 14, 1778 died. |
| Biggs, Ranoll/ Randolph | Private | First State, Brown | Dec 1777-May 1778; June 1778 Yellow Springs sick. |
| Bilgum, William See Biddlecomb | Private | Fifteenth, Mason | April-May 1778; about June 1, 1778 died. |
| Billings, John | Private | First State, Camp/ Valentine | Dec 1777 on guard; Jan 1778; Feb-March 1778 sick present; April-June 1778. |
| Billups, George | Sergeant | Seventh, Young | Dec 21, 1777 to Light Horse. |
| Billups, Joseph | Sergeant | Seventh, Young | Dec 1777 sick in hospital; Jan 1778 hospital; Feb 7, 1778 discharged. |
| Bingley, Lewis | Private | Second State, Dudley | March 15-May 1, 1778; May 1778; June 1778 sick absent. |
| Binns, William | Private | First, Mennis | Feb 11, 1778 enlisted for 1 year; April 1778; May 1778 sick present; June-July 1778 sick Valley Forge. |
| Bird/Byard, John | Sergeant | Second State, Quarles | April-June 1778. |
| Bird, Richard | Private | First State, Meriwether | Dec 1777-March 1778. |
| Bird, Richard | Private | Second State, Taliaferro | March 15-May 1, 1778; May-June 1778. |
| Bird/Byrd, Robert | Private | Second, Jones | Dec 1777-Feb 1778; March 15, 1778 dead. |
| Bird/Birds, Thomas | Private | First State, Brown | Dec 1777-May 1778. |
| Bird, William | Private | Seventh, Hill | Dec 1777; Jan 28, 1778 discharged. |
| Bishop, Jones | Private | First, Lawson | June 1777 deserted; March 1778 omitted whilst in Virginia; April 1778 on command; May-June 1778. |
| Bishop, Marks | Private | Fifteenth, Grimes | Dec 1777-March 1778 sick absent; April 1778 muster roll shows he died on Jan 30, 1778. |

| Name | Rank | Company | Service |
|---|---|---|---|
| Bishop, Solomon | Private/Corporal | Second, Calmes | Dec 1777-Feb 1778; March promoted to Corporal; March-June 1778. |
| Bishop, Thomas | Private | Second, Calmes | Dec 1777-June 1778. |
| Bivins/Bivens, John | Drummer | Second, Jones | Dec 1777-Jan 1778 hospital; Feb-June 1778. |
| Black, George | Private | Twelfth, Bowyer, T. | Sept 11, 1777 taken prisoner; March 28, 1778 joined; March 1778; April 1778 lame in camp; May 1778 lame in camp on parole; June 1778 a prisoner on parole. |
| Black, Robert | Private | Twelfth, Waggener | Dec 1777-March 1778 hospital; April-May 1778. |
| Black, Thomas | Private | Twelfth, Bowyer, T. | Dec 1777-Jan 1778; Feb 1778 on guard; March-April 1778; May 1778 on guard. |
| Blackborne, James | Private | Seventh, Fleming | Jan 1778 with Rifle Regt.; Jan 1778 R. Regimt; Feb 5, 1778 discharged. |
| Blackmore/Blakemore, George | Corporal/Sergeant | Second, Calmes | Dec 1777-Feb 1778; March promoted to Sergeant; March-May 1778; June 1778 sick Valley Forge. |
| Blacknall/Blacknell, Thomas | Private | Seventh, Young | Dec 1777-Feb 1778; March 7, 1778 discharged. |
| Blackwell, John | Captain | Third, Blackwell | Dec 1777 on court martial; Jan-March 1778; April 1778 on furlough; May 1778 on furlough in Virginia; June 1778. |
| Blackwell, Joseph | 2nd. Lt. | Third, Blackwell | Dec 1777-Feb 1778; March 1778 on command in Virginia; April 20, 1778 resigned. |
| Blair, John | Private | Sixth | Feb 11, 1778, enlisted; June 1778. |
| Blair, John Neel/John N. | Private | Twelfth, Bowyer, M. | Dec 1777-Jan 1778 on guard; Feb-May 1778. |
| Blair/Blar, Samuel | Sergeant | Twelfth, Bowyer, T. | Dec 1777 sick at hospital; Jan-March 1778 sick absent. |
| Blair, William | Private | Second, Taylor, F. | April-June 1778. |
| Blair, William | Private | Seventh, Spencer | Dec 1777 hospital; Jan 1778. |

| | | | |
|---|---|---|---|
| Blake, Edward | Private | Fifteenth, Hull | Dec 1777; Jan 6, 1778 discharged. |
| Blake, John | Private | Second, Harrison | Dec 1777-Feb 1778. |
| Blakey/ Blackeye, John | Private | First State, Lee/ Meriwether | Dec 1777 sick; Jan 1778 on command; Feb-June 1778. |
| Blanch, John | Private | Twelfth, Bowyer, M. | Dec 1777; Jan 1778 orderly at hospital; Feb 1778 on command; March-May 1778. |
| Bland, George | Private | First State, Hamilton | Dec 1777-March 1778. |
| Bland, James | Private | Second State, Quarles | April-June 1778. |
| Bland, John | Private | Second State, Taliaferro | March 15-May 1, 1778; May-June 1778. |
| Bland, John/Jno. | Private | Sixth, Massie | Dec 1777 innoculated; Jan-May 1778; June 1778 on guard. |
| Bland, William | Private | Third, Mercer | Dec 1777-Jan 1778; Feb 1778 on command; March 15, 1778 deserted. |
| Blankinship, Geo. | Private | Fifteenth, Harris | May 1778. |
| Blankinship/ Blankenship, Josiah | Private | Fourteenth, Conway | Feb 1778 came to the regiment Feb. 25, 1778; March 1778 sick present; Payroll shows he died April 24, 1778, but the Muster Roll shows he deserted on that date. |
| Blankinship/ Blankingship, Wamach/ Womack | Corporal | First, Cunningham | Enlisted August 1776 for 3 years; Dec 1777-Jan 1778 sick at hospital; Feb-June 1778. |
| Blanks, Jesse | Private | Sixth, Avery | Dec 27, 1777, reenlisted in the Light Dragoons. |
| Blanks/Banks, Thomas | Private | First, Mennis | Feb 9, 1778 enlisted; April-June 1778. |
| Blann/Bland, Thomas | Private/ Corporal | First, Mennis | Dec 1777; Jan 1778-May 1778 on furlough; June promoted to Corporal; June 1778. |

| Name | Rank | Regiment/Company | Notes |
|---|---|---|---|
| Blatchford/ Blachford, Michael | Sergeant | First, Scott/ Lawson | Dec 1777-Feb 1778; March 1778 sick present; April-May 1778; June 1778 in Lawson's Company. |
| Blazenham/ Blasinghem, Morris/Moris | Private | Third, Blackwell | Feb 18, 1778 drafted; March 1778 lately joined; April 1778; May 1778 on command; June 1778. |
| Bledsoe, Miller/Millar | Private | Second State, Spiller | March 15-May 1, 1778; May 1778; June 1778 sick Valley Forge. |
| Bledsoe, Peachy/Pechy | Corporal | Second State, Bernard | April-May 1778; June 1778 sick Valley Forge. |
| Bleshford, John | Private | First, Lawson | Dec 1777 on command; Jan 1778 sick present |
| Blies/Blize, William | Private | Fourteenth, Reid | Jan-Feb 1778 sick at York; March 1778 orderly Little York; April 1778 at Lancaster; May-June 1778. |
| Block, Thomas | Private | Second State, Bressie | March 15-May 1, 1778; May 1778; June 1778 wounded Valley Forge. |
| Blondon, Joseph | Private | First State, Crump | Dec 1777-Feb 1778. |
| Bluford, William/Willm. | Private | Fifteenth, Hull | Dec 1777 sick absent; Jan 1778 sick in hospital; Feb-May 1778. |
| Blundell/ Blundle, Elijah | Private | Fifteenth, Hull | Dec 1777 on guard; Jan-April 1778 on command; May 1778 on guard. |
| Blundell/ Blundle, Saml. | Private/Fifer | Fifteenth, Hull | Dec 1777 sick absent; Jan 1778 sick at hospital; Feb 1778; March 1778 promoted to Fifer; March-April 1778; May 1778 sick in camp; June 1778; July 1778 sick at Valley Forge. |
| Blunder, Charles | Private | Third, Powell | Dec 1777-May 1778; June 1778 sick Brunswick. |
| Blunt, William | Private/ Corporal | First, Lawson | Dec 1777; Jan 1778 sick present; Feb-March 1778 sick hospital; April 1778 at Princeton; May 1778 promoted to Corporal, on command; June 1778. |

| | | | |
|---|---|---|---|
| Blyth/Blitch, Jacob | Sergeant | Fifteenth, Wills | Jan 13, 1778 enlisted, York; Feb 1778; March-April 1778 sick present; May 1778; June 1778 sick Valley Forge. |
| Boady/Body, Will | Private | Twelfth. Bowyer, M. | Dec 1777-May 1778. |
| Boaz/Boze, Abednego/ Ebednego | Private | First, Cunningham | Feb 19, 1778 enlisted for 1 year; April 1778 under inoculation; May 1778; June 1778 sick at Princeton. |
| Bodwin/Bodin, William | Private | Second State, Spiller | March 15-May 1, 1778; May-June 1778. |
| Boen/Bowen, John | Private | Second, Calmes | Dec 1777-May 1778; June 1778 sick absent. |
| Bogard, Cornelius | Private | Twelfth, Bowyer, T. | Dec 1777; Jan 1778 sick in camp; Feb-April 1778; May 1778 sick hospital. |
| Boggs, Robert | Private | Twelfth, Wallace | Feb 28, 1778 drafted; May 1778. |
| Bogguarder/ Bogger, Nicholas | Private | Third, Mercer | Dec 1777-Jan 1778. |
| Bon guards, Robert | Private | Twelfth, Wallace | Feb 28, 1778 drafted; May 1778. |
| Bohanon/ Bohanan, John | Private | Second, Upshaw | Dec 1777-Jan 1778. |
| Bohanan/ Bohanon, Joseph | Private | Sixth, Avery | Dec 1777-Jan 1778; Feb 8, 1778 discharged. |
| Bollen/Boling, Edmond | Private | Third. Mercer | Dec 1777 on duty; Jan 1778 on guard. |
| Bolling/Bolin, Joseph | Private | Third, Peyton, V./ Peyton, J. | April 1778 inoculated; May-June 1778. |
| Bolton, William | Private | Seventh, Lipscomb | Dec 1777-Jan 1778 hospital; Feb 2, 1778 discharged. |
| Bonner, Richard | Corporal/ Sergeant | Second, Jones | Dec 1777-April 1778; April 15, 1778 promoted to Sergeant; May-June 1778. |
| Bonny/Bennyer, Alexander | Private | First State, Meriwether | Dec 1777-April 1778. |
| Booker, Edward | Private | Second, Taylor, W. | Dec 1777-Jan 1778; Feb 14, 1778 discharged. |

| | | | |
|---|---|---|---|
| Booker, Richard | Sergeant | First, Cummings | Feb 17, 1778 enlisted; April 1778 pay omitted; May-June 1778. |
| Booker, Richeson/ Rickason | Sergeant | Fifteenth, Foster/ Gray | Dec 1777-May 1778. |
| Booker, Samuel/Saml. | 1st. Lt. | Fifteenth, Foster/ Gray | Dec 1777; Jan 1778; on command at Ladetz; Feb 1778 on command, in Gray's company; March 1778 on command Laditz; April 1778 on command; May 1778. |
| Booth, Michael | Private | Fifteenth, Gregory | June 1778 on guard. |
| Booth, Michael/Michal | Private | Fifteenth, Mason | Dec 1777-Jan 1778; Feb-April 1778 sick in camp; May 1778. |
| Booth, William | Private | Fourteenth, Overton | Dec 1777 sick in hospital; Jan 1778 sick absent; Feb 1778; March 1778 sick present; April-May 1778; June 1778 sick Princeton. |
| Boquett see Baucutt | | | |
| Borne/Bourne, Thomas | Private | Second State, Quarles | April-May 1778; June 1778 sick Princeton. |
| Borroughs/ Burris, Dobson | Private | Sixth, Rose | Dec 1777-Jan 1778; Feb 10, 1778 discharged. |
| Boston/Bootin/ Booton, Joshua | Private | Seventh, Webb/ Young | Enlisted for 3 years. April-May 1778; June 1778 in Young's company. |
| Boswell, John | Sergeant | First State, Crump | Dec 1777-June 1778. |
| Boswell, Machen | 1st. Lt. | Second State, Taliaferro | March 15-May 1, 1778; May-June 1778. Oath at Valley Forge on June 1, 1778, witnessed by Muhlenberg. |
| Boswell/ Bozwell, Robert | Private | First State, Payne | Dec 1777 on guard; Jan-June 1778. |
| Botts/Beets, Joseph | Private | Fifteenth, Wills | Aug 21, 1777 enlisted; Jan-Feb 1778 sick Virginia; March 1778 sick absent. |
| Bouch, John | Private | Seventh, Posey | Feb 27, 1778 enlisted; April 1778 on command; May 1778 deserted near the last of May. |

| | | | |
|---|---|---|---|
| Bouldin/ Boulding, Wood | 1st. Lt. | Fourteenth, Lambert | Dec 1777-Jan 1778; Feb 1778 on guard; March 1778 absent with leave; April-May 1778; June 1778 sick Valley Forge. |
| Boulware/ Bolware, Mark | Private | Second, Upshaw | Dec 1777 sick hospital; Jan 1778. |
| Bourn/Boarn, Francis | Sergeant | Fourteenth, Overton | Dec 1777 sick in hospital; Jan 1778 sick absent; Feb 1778; March 1778 sick absent; April-May 1778; June 1778 sick at Valley Forge. |
| Bourn/Bourne, John | Sergeant | Second, Taylor, F. | Dec 1777 on furlough; Jan-June 1778. |
| Bourn, John | Private | Second, Taylor, F. | Feb 10, 1778 drafted from Culpepper; April-June 1778. |
| Bourn, Reuben | Private | Second, Taylor, F. | Feb 10, 1778 drafted from Orange; April-June 1778. |
| Boutell/Bouttell, James | Private | First, Cunningham | June 1777 enlisted for 3 years; Dec 1777-Feb 1778; March 1778 sick present; April 1778; May 1778 sick present; June 1778 sick Valley Forge. |
| Bouton/ Boughton, William | Private | Second, Jones | Dec 1777-June 1778. |
| Boutwell, Samuel | Corporal | Second, Upshaw | Dec 1777-Jan 1778. |
| Bowden William | Private | Second State, Taliaferro | March 15-May 1, 1778; May-June 1778. |
| Bowen, John | 2nd. Lt. | Twelfth, Wallace | Dec 1777-May 1778. |
| Bowen/Boen, Joseph | Private | Third, Arell/ Briscoe | Dec 1777-March 1778 sick absent; April-June 1778. In June he is in Briscoe's company. |
| Bowers/Bowen, George | Private | Second State, Spiller | March 15-May 1, 1778; May 1778; June 1778 sick Monmouth. |
| Bowers, Phill | Private | Seventh, Lipscomb | Dec 1777-Jan 1778 hospital; Feb 2, 1778 discharged. |
| Bowes/Bowers James | Corporal | First State, Crump | April-June 1778. |

| Name | Rank | Regiment, Company | Dates |
|---|---|---|---|
| Bowers, John | Private | Third, Arell | Dec 1777-Feb 1778; March 1778 sick in camp; April 1778 waggons; May 1778 wagoner. |
| Bowers, John | Private | Fourteenth, Conway | June 1778 drafted Feb 16, 1778 for one year, then enrolled June 16 for three years. |
| Bowers, Thomas | Private | Second, Taylor, W. | Dec 1777-June 1778. |
| Bowers, William | Private | First State, Nicholas | Dec 1, 1777 deceased. |
| Bowers, William | Private | Second, Taylor, W. | Feb 16, 1778 drafted; April-June 1778. |
| Bowes/Booze, John | Private | Fourteenth, Winston | Dec 1777 absent without leave; Jan-May 1778; June 1778 sick Valley Forge. |
| Bowin/Bowen, William | Private | Twelfth, Bowyer, T. | Dec 1777-April 1778; May 1778 on command. |
| Bowler, Obediah | Private | Second State, Garnett | April 15-May 30, 1778. This man and the man below are probably the same individual. |
| Bowler, Obediah | Drummer | Second State, Quarles | June 1778. |
| Bowles/Boles, Peter | Private | Second State, Taliaferro | March 15-May 1, 1778; May-June 1778. |
| Bowles/Bowler, Samuel | Private | Second State, Garnett | April 15-June 1, 1778; June 1778. |
| Bowling, Edmund | Private | Third, Mercer | Feb 1778 discharged. |
| Bowling/Bolan, Jesse | Private | Second, Jones | Dec 1777-June 1778. |
| Bowling/Bolen, Robert | Private | Third, Arell/Briscoe | Dec 1777-June 1778. In June he is in Briscoe's company. |
| Bowling, Thornberry/T'Bery | Private | Second State, Quarles | April-June 1778. |
| Bowling/Bolden, William | Private | Second State, Bernard | April-May 1778; June 1778 sick Valley Forge. |

| Name | Rank | Regiment/Company | Notes |
|---|---|---|---|
| Bowling, William | Private | Fourteenth, Conway | Jan 1778 sick in camp; Feb 1778 sick hospital; March 11, 1778 deceased. |
| Bowman, James | Private | Sixth | June 1778 "Omitted since Feb. 1, 1778, sick Valley Forge." |
| Bowman/Boman, Samuel | Private | Second, Harrison | Dec 1777 on guard; Jan-June 1778. |
| Bowman, William | Private | Second, Upshaw | Feb 14, 1778 drafted; April 1778; June 1778. |
| Bowne/Boune, Thomas | Adjutant/2nd. Lt. | First, Pelham/Payne | Dec 1777 in Pelham's Company; Jan-Feb 1778 on command; March 1778 on command in Virginia; March 1778 promoted to 2nd. Lt. of Payne's Company; April-June 1778. He appears as Adjutant on the regimental rolls, as well as a company officer on company rolls. Oath at Valley Forge on May 11, 1778, witnessed by Muhlenberg. |
| Bowrey/Boury, Giles | Private | Fifteenth, Edmunds/Wills | Dec 1777 Camp Colorman; Jan 1778 in Wills' Company; Feb 1778; March 1778 sick present; April 1778; May 1778 on duty. |
| Bowyer, Henry | Cadet | Twelfth, Bowyer, T. | Dec 1777. Probably the same man as the one listed below. |
| Bowyer, Henry | Adjutant | Twelfth | Appointed Jan 1, 1778; Jan-May 1778. |
| Bowyer/Bower, Jacob | Private | Twelfth, Casey | Dec 1777 sent to hospital; Jan-March 1778 at hospital; April 1778 no account of. |
| Bowyer, Michael | Captain | Twelfth, Bowyer, M | Dec 1777-March 1778 on furlough; April-May 1778. |
| Bowyer, Thomas | Captain | Twelfth, Bowyer, T | Dec 1777-Feb 1778 on command; March 1778; April 1778; on command; May 1778. |
| Boyce/Boice, John | Private | Fourteenth, Thweatt | Dec 1777-March 1778; April 1778 on guard; May-June 1778. |
| Boyd, James | Private | First, Cunningham | Aug 1776 enlisted for 3 years; Dec 1777 on command; Jan-May 1778; June 1778 waggoner. |
| Boyd, James | Private | Fifteenth, Harris | Feb 1778; March-May 1778 sick present. |

| Name | Rank | Regiment, Company | Notes |
|---|---|---|---|
| Boyers/Boyars, Jacob | Private | Fourteenth, Reid | Sept 18, 1777 enlisted; April-June 1778. |
| Boyes see Byas | | | |
| Boyle/Boile, George | Private | Third, Mercer | Dec 1777 sick absent; Jan 1778. |
| Boyles/Byles, Charles | Private | Fourteenth, Thweatt | Dec 1777-Feb 1778 sick at hospital; March 1778; April 1778 Y. S. H.; May 1778 sick Yellow Springs; June 1778. |
| Boylin/Boylen, John | Private | Twelfth, Madison | Dec 1777-Jan 1778; Feb 1778 on command; March 1778 guard. |
| Brabston/Bratston, William | Sergeant/Private | Twelfth, Ashby | Dec 1777-Feb 1778; March 1778 at hospital; April 1778 reduced to Private; April-May 1778. |
| Bradberry, James | Private | Fourteenth, Jones | Feb 12, 1778 drafted; April-May 1778; June 1778 sick Carrell's Ferry. |
| Bradly, Richard | Private | Second, Harrison | December 18, 1778 deserted. |
| Bradford, Henry | Sergeant | Third, Blackwell | Dec 23, 1777 discharged. |
| Bradford, William | Private | Third, Blackwell | Dec 1777-Feb 1778; March 1778 on command; April-May 1778; June 1778 on guard. |
| Bradley, David | Private | Seventh/Third, Fleming/Heth | Dec 1777 on furlough Virginia; Jan-March 1778 on furlough; April-May 1778; June 1778 in Heth's Company. |
| Bradley/Bradly, Hinche/Hinckly | Private | Fifteenth, Wills | Feb 14, 1778 enlisted; April-May 1778 sick present. |
| Bradley/Bradlay, John | Sergeant | Third/Seventh, Crockett/Sayers | Dec 1777; Jan 1778 sick in hospital; Feb-May 1778; June 1778 in Sayers' Company. |
| Bradley, William | Private/Sergeant | Seventh/Third, Posey/Sayers | Dec 1777-Jan 1778 on furlough; April-May 1778 on command, In April he appears as a Sergeant; June 1778 in Sayers' Company. |
| Bradshaw, Robert | Corporal | Fourteenth, Overton | Dec 1777; Jan 1778 sick present; Feb-April 1778; May 1778 on command; June 1778. |
| Brady, John | Private | Seventh, Spencer | Dec 1777-Jan 1778; Feb 11, 1778 discharged. |

| Name | Rank | Regiment | Notes |
|---|---|---|---|
| Brady/Braday, Luke | Private | Third, Peyton, J. | Dec 1777-March 1778 sick absent; April-May 1778 sick absent Reading; June 1778 sick Reading, in J. Peyton's Company. |
| Brady/Bready, Michael | Private | Twelfth, Waggener | Dec 1777-May 1778. |
| Brafford/Braford, John | Private | Fourteenth, Reid | Dec 1777-Feb 1778; March 1778 sick present; April 10, 1778 discharged. |
| Bragg, John | Private/Corporal | First State, Lee | Dec 1777 on duty; Jan 1778 on command; Feb 1778 on guard; March-June 1778. In May he was promoted to Corporal. |
| Bragg, William | Private | First State, Camp/Valentine | Dec 1777-May 1778; June 1778 with Col. Morgan |
| Branch, John | Private | Fourteenth, Conway | Feb 23, 1778 enlisted; June 1778 sick Valley Forge. |
| Brander/Brandor, Robert | Private | First, Jones/Hoomes | Dec 1777 on command; Jan 1778 on furlough; Feb-June 1778. |
| Brandom, John | Private | Second State, Dudley | March 15-May 1, 1778; May-June 1778. |
| Brandom, Rhode | Private | Second State, Dudley | March 15-May 1, 1778; May-June 1778. |
| Branham, Eben/Evan | Private | Second, Harrison | Dec 1777 on furlough; Jan-June 1778. |
| Branham/Brannan, John | Private | Second, Harrison | Dec 1777-May 1778; June 1778 sick Valley Forge. |
| Branham/Brannan, James | Private | Fourteenth, Conway | Aug 28, 1777 enlisted; Jan 1778 has joined the regiment lately, on command; March-May 1778; June 1778 left at Valley Forge. |
| Brann, Thomas/Thos. | Private | Fifteenth, Foster/Gray | Dec 1777-Jan 1778 sick absent; Feb 1778 dead time uncertain. |
| Brannan/Brannen, Jas. | Sergeant | Third, Powell | June 1778. |
| Branson/Bransom, John | Private/Fifer | Seventh/Third, Webb/Young | Feb 16, 1778 enlisted; June 1778 promoted to Fifer, in Young's Company. |

| Name | Rank | Regiment/Company | Service |
|---|---|---|---|
| Brantley, William/Wm. | Private | Fifteenth, Edmunds/Wills | Dec 1777; Jan 1778 in Will's Company, on guard; Feb 1778 on duty; March-April 1778; May 16, 1778 dead. |
| Branum, James | Sergeant | Third, Mercer/Powell | Feb 12, 1778 enlisted; April-May 1778. |
| Brasey/Bercy, John | Private | Fifteenth, Wills | Aug 21, 1777 enlisted; Jan 1778 on guard; Feb 1778; March 1778 on command; April-May 1778; June-Aug sick Valley Forge. |
| Brasington, Samuel | Private | Fourteenth, Jones | Jan 1778 deserted in Virginia. |
| Brathwate, John | Private | Fourteenth, Reid | Dec 1777. |
| Brawner, Johnathan | Private | Fifteenth, Hull | May 1778 sick at Leditz Hospital. |
| Bray, John | Private | Twelfth, Vause | Dec 1777 sick in camp; Jan-May 1778. |
| Bray, Martin | Private | Third, Young | June 1778. |
| Bray, Winter | Private | Seventh/Third, Webb/Young | Feb 16, 1778 enlisted; April-June 1778. |
| Breedin/Breadan, Berryman/Berreman | Private | Seventh, Posey | April 1, 1778 enlisted; April 1778 sick; May 1778 sick in camp |
| Breeding Breading, Abraham | Private | Sixth, Fox | April-May 1778; June 1778 sick Valley Forge. |
| Breedlove/Breadlove, James | Private | Sixth, Hockaday | Feb 17, 1778 drafted; April 1778; May 1778 on fatigue; June 1778 sick at Valley Forge. |
| Breedlove, John | Private | Second, Calmes | Dec 26, 1777 discharged. |
| Breedlove, Thomas | Private | Second, Taylor, F. | Dec 1777-Feb 1778; March 4, 1778 discharged. |
| Breedlove/Bridlove, William | Private | First State, Nicholas | Dec 1777-June 1778. |

| | | | |
|---|---|---|---|
| Breedlove/ Breadlove, William | Private | Third, Powell | Dec 1777; Jan-March 1778 on furlough; April-May 1778; June 1778 on guard. |
| Breedy, John | Private | Fourteenth, Thweatt | Sept 5, 1777 enlisted; Jan-April 1778; May 1778 sick present; June 1778 sick Carrells. |
| Brelsford/ Bleshford, John | Private | First, Lawson | Nov 1777 sick Princeton; Dec 1777 on command; Jan 1778 sick present; Feb 1778; March-April 1778; May 1778; June 1778 sick present. |
| Brent, George | Sergeant | Second State, Garnett | March 15, 1778-May 1, 1778; May-June 1778. |
| Brent, John | Private | Second, Calmes | Dec 1777-June 1778. |
| Brent, William | Lt. Col./ Colonel | First State/ Second State | Jan 1778-Feb 1778; March 1778 on command in Virginia; April-May 1778; June promoted to Colonel of Second Virginia State Regiment. Oath at Valley Forge on May 12, 1778, witnessed by Muhlenberg. |
| Brentle/Brintle, Jas. | Private | Fifteenth, Foster/ Gray | Dec 1777; Jan 1778 sick absent; Feb 1778 dead time uncertain. |
| Bressie, Thomas | Captain | Second State | May-June 1778. Oath at Valley Forge on May 18, 1778, witnessed by Muhlenberg. |
| Bressie/Bresie, William | Private | Seventh/ Third, Fleming/ Heth | Feb 13, 1778 enlisted; April 1778 sick present; May 1778; June 1778 in Heth's Company. |
| Brewer, Henry | Drummer | Sixth, Massie | Dec 1777-March 1778 on furlough; May-June 1778. |
| Brewer, John | Private/ Sergeant/ Private | Fourteenth, Reid | Dec 1777; Jan 1778 sick in camp; Feb-March 1778; April 1778 promoted to Sergeant; April 1778; May 17, 1778 reduced to Private; May-June 1778. |
| Briant/Brient, James | Private | Second State, Quarles | April-June 1778. |

| Name | Rank | Regiment/Company | Service |
|---|---|---|---|
| Briant, James | Private | Twelfth, Wallace | Dec 1777-Feb 1778; March 1778 sick in camp; April-May 1778. |
| Briant/Bryant, John | Private | First State, Meriwether | Dec 1777-April 1778; June 1778. |
| Briant/Brian, Thomas | Private | First State, Meriwether | Dec 1777-June 1778. |
| Briant/Bryant William | Private | Twelfth, Wallace | Dec 1777-Feb 1778; March 1778 sick in camp; April-May 1778. |
| Brice/Brier, John | Private | First State, Payne | Dec 1777 sick in hospital; Jan 1778 sick Reading; Feb 1778 sick absent. |
| Bricken/Bricksen, James | Private | Second, Taylor, W. | Dec 1777 hospital; Jan-Feb 1778. |
| Brickle, Richard | Private | Seventh/Third, Crockett/Sayers | Dec 1777-Jan 1778 on furlough; Feb-May 1778; June 1778 in Sayers' Company. |
| Bridgen, Charles | Private | Seventh, Spencer | Dec 1777 hospital; Jan 1, 1778 died. |
| Bridges, George | Private | Seventh, Young | Dec 1777-April 1778 on furlough; April 17, 1778 deserted. |
| Bridges, John | Private | Third, Mercer/Powell | Dec 1777-March 1778; April 1778 sick at Church Hospital; May 1778 sick present; June 1778, in Powell's Company. |
| Bridges, Ransome/Randsom | Private | Seventh, Young | Dec 1777-April 1778 on furlough; May 13, 1778 deserted. |
| Bridges, James | Private | Fifteenth, Gray | April-May 1778 "in room of Thomas Simons Sergt under inoculation." June 14, 1778 died. |
| Bridgman/Bridgeman, Hezekiah/Kiah | Private | First State, Hoffler | Dec 1777-June 1778. |
| Bridgman/Bridman, Thomas/Thos. | Private | Fifteenth, Hull | Dec 1777-Jan 1778; Feb-May 1778 sick present; June-July 1778 sick Valley Forge. |
| Brient, Jeremiah | Private | Second, Sanford | Dec 1777-Jan 1778; Feb 20, 1778 deserted. |
| Bright, John | Private | Second State, Bressie | March 15-May 1, 1778; May 1778; June 1778. |

| Name | Rank | Regiment | Notes |
|---|---|---|---|
| Bright, Willis | Private | Fifteenth, Grimes | Dec 1777-Jan 1778 sick absent; Feb 1778 died some time ago in the hospital. |
| Brightmore, Robert | Private | Twelfth, Wallace | March 20, 1778 joined; March-May 1778. |
| Brightwell, John | Private | Seventh, Lipscomb | Dec 1, 1777 enlisted, Dec 1777-Jan 1778 on furlough; April 1778 on furlough; May 1778 Virginia with Col. Richardson; June 1778. |
| Brightwell, William | Private | Seventh, Lipscomb | Dec 1777; Jan 31, 1778 discharged. |
| Brimm/Brim, Josiah | Private | First State, Lee | Dec 1777 sick; Jan 1778 deceased. |
| Brimm, Richard | Private | First State, Crump | Dec 1777; Jan 1778 deceased. |
| Brimm, Thomas | Private | First State, Crump | Dec 1777; Jan 2, 1778 deceased. |
| Brinson, Henry | Private | Sixth | June 1778. |
| Briscoe, Reubin/Reuben | Captain | Third, Briscoe | Dec 1777; Jan 1778 sick in the country; Feb 1778; March-April 1778 on command; May 1778 on command Virginia; June 1778. |
| Brister, Charles | Private | Second, Upshaw | Feb 18, 1778 drafted; April; 1778; June 1778 sick Valley Forge. |
| Bristol, Sandirs/Saunders | Private | First State, Brown | Dec 1777-May 1778. |
| Bristow, Alexander | Private | Seventh, Webb | Jan 1778; Feb 14, 1778 discharged. |
| Britt, John | Private | First State, Hamilton | April-June 1778. |
| Britt, John | Private | Fourteenth, Marks | Drafted Feb 16, 1778; April 1778; May 1778 on command; June 1778 sick Valley Forge. |
| Britt, William/Wm. | Private | Fifteenth, Mason | Dec 1777-March 1778 sick in the hospital; April 1778 muster roll shows he died Jan 18, 1778. |
| Britton, John | Private | Fourteenth, Thweatt | Aug 27, 1777 enlisted; Jan-June 1778. |

| Name | Rank | Regiment/Company | Service |
|---|---|---|---|
| Broadas/ Broadus, Robert | Private/ Corporal | Seventh/ Third, Jouett/Hill | Dec 1777 on furlough Virginia; Jan-Feb 1778 on command; May 1778 sick in camp; April-May 1778; June 1778 promoted to Corporal; in Hill's Company. |
| Broaddus/ Broddis, William | Sergeant | First State, Hamilton | Dec 1777-June 1778. |
| Broadfield/ Broadfill, Charles/Chas. | Private/ Musician | Fifteenth, Edmunds/ Wills | Dec 1777 on guard; Jan 1778 in Wills' Company, on guard; Feb 1778 sick present; March 1778 promoted to Musician; April-June 1778 sick Yellow Springs. |
| Broadrib, John | Private | Fifteenth, Harris | Jan 1778 artificer; Feb 1778 sick present; March 20, 1778 dead. |
| Broadus/ Braddus, James | Sergeant | Second, Taylor, F. | Dec 1777 on furlough; Jan-May 1778; June-July 1778 sick Valley Forge. |
| Broadway, John | Private | First, Pelham/ Lawson | Feb 1778 enlisted; April 1778 under inoculation; May 1778 sick present; June 1778 sick at Valley Forge, in Lawson's Company. |
| Brock, Elias | Private | Second State, Bressie | March 15-May 1, 1778; May 1778; June 1778. |
| Brock, Henry | Quartermaster Sergeant | Sixth | Feb 8, 1778 discharged. |
| Brock/ Brockman, John | Private | Seventh, Spencer/ Lipscomb | Feb 13, 1778 enlisted for 1 yeqr; April-May 1778; June 1778 to Lipscomb's company. |
| Brockhouse/ Brockus, John | Private | Third, Peyton, J. | Dec 1777; Jan 31, 1778 discharged. |
| Brockman, Jesse | Private | Seventh, Spencer | Feb 13, 1778 enlisted for 1 year; April 1778 sick in camp; May 1778 |
| Brockman, Thomas | Private | Fourteenth, Marks | Dec 1777; Jan 1778 sick in hospital; Feb 1778 sick absent; April-June 1778. |
| Brockmart, Major | Private | Seventh, Lipscomb | June 1778. |

| Name | Rank | Regiment/Company | Notes |
|---|---|---|---|
| Brodie/Broady, Lodowick | Surgeon's Mate | Second State | First appears on May 1778 roll with time of service as 2 months, 18 days with remark "March 12"; June 1778. Oath at Valley Forge on May 18, 1778, witnessed by Muhlenberg. |
| Broils, Daniel | Private | Twelfth, Bowyer, M. | Dec 1777-Jan 1778 sick in country; Feb-March 1778 sick in hospital; April 1778 sick in some hospital. |
| Bromeger/Bromager, Patrick/Partrick | Private | Second, Calmes | Dec 1777-June 1778. |
| Bronough/Burnaugh, Henry | Private | First State, Payne | Dec 1777-Jan 1778 sick George Town; Feb 1778 sick absent. |
| Brooke, Thomas | Private | Seventh, Webb | Jan 1778 hospital; Feb 1778 deceased. |
| Brooker, Richard | Private | Fifteenth, Wills | Feb 1778 returned from desertion; March-April 1778; May 1778 on command. |
| Brookes, James | Private | Seventh, Moseley | Dec 1777-Jan 1778 sick in hospital; Feb 1778; March 7, 1778 discharged. |
| Brooks/Brooxe, David | Private | Twelfth, Bowyer, T. | Enlisted Aug 8, 1777. March 1778 joined April; April-May 1778; June 1778 sick Valley Forge. |
| Brooks, Edmond | Private | Seventh, Crockett/Sayers | March 8, 1778 enlisted; April 1778 sick in Virginia; May 1778 in room of John Long; June 1778 sick Virginia, in Sayers' Company. |
| Brooks, George/Geo. | Private | First, Mennis | Dec 1777 Jan 1778 on furlough; Feb 1778; March 1778 on fatigue; April 1778; May 1778 on furlough; June 1778. |
| Brooks/Brook, George | Private | Second, Taylor, F. | Dec 1777 hospital; Jan-Feb 1778; March 12, 1778 discharged. |
| Brooks, Nathaniel | Private | First, Pelham | April 1778; May 1778 on guard; June 1778. |
| Brooks, Richard/Richd | Private | Sixth, Avery | Dec 1777-Jan 1778; Feb 18, 1778 discharged. |

| Name | Rank | Unit | Notes |
|---|---|---|---|
| Brooks, Robert | Private | Seventh. Hill | Dec 1777-Jan 1778 sick in hospital; Jan 31, 1778 discharged. |
| Brooks, Thomas | Private | Second, Taylor, W. | Dec 1777-Jan 1778; Feb 5, 1778 discharged. |
| Broom, John | Corporal/ Sergeant | Twelfth, Vause | Dec 1777-March 1778; April 1, 1778 promoted to sergeant; April 1778 on picket; May 1778. |
| Browder/ Bronder, Frederick | Private | Fourteenth, Jones | Jan-Feb 1778 sick in Lancaster; Feb 28, 1778 died. |
| Browder, Harrison | Private | Fourteenth, Jones | Jan-Feb 1778 sick York; March-May 1778. |
| Browder, Isham | Private | Second, Jones | Dec 1777-June 1778. |
| Browder, Samuel | Private | Fourteenth, Jones | Jan-Feb 1778 sick at Lancaster. |
| Brown, Andrew | Private | Second, Willis | Dec 1777; Jan 7, 1778 deserted. |
| Brown, Aris/Aries | Corporal | Second State, Bernard | April-May 1778; June 1778 sick Valley Forge. |
| Brown, Augustin | Private | Twelfth, Bowyer, T. | Dec 1777-Jan 1778; Feb 1778 on guard; March-May 1778. |
| Brown/Browne, Charles | Private | Second, Jones | Dec 1777-June 1778 |
| Brown, Charles | Private | Second, Upshaw | Dec 1777-sick hospital. |
| Brown, Daniel | Surgeon | Fourteenth | Dec 1777-Feb 1778; April-May 1778 absent without leave; June 1778 superceded by Doctor Spencer. |
| Brown, Duncan/Dunkin | Private | First State, Ewell, T. | Dec 1777-Feb 1778; March 1778 sick present; April-May 1778; June 1778 sick R. Hill |
| Brown, George | Private | First State, Camp/ Valentine | Dec 1777-June 1778. |
| Brown, George | Corporal/ Sergeant | Twelfth, Waggner | Dec 1777-Jan 1778; Feb1778 on command; March 1778; April 10, 1778 promoted to Sergeant; April-May 1778. |

| | | | |
|---|---|---|---|
| Brown, Henry | Private | First State, Camp/Valentine | Dec 1777-Jan 1778; Feb 1778 on guard; March-June 1778. |
| Brown, James | Private | First, Lewis/Lawson | Dec 1777; Jan 1778 on command; Feb-May 1778; June 1778 sick Valley Forge, in Lawson's Company. |
| Brown, James | Private | Second, Calmes | Dec 1777-June 1778. |
| Brown, James | Private | Twelfth, Wallace | Dec 1777; Jan 1778 sick in camp; Feb-May 1778. |
| Brown, John | Private | First, Cummings | Dec 1777; Jan-April 1778 on furlough; May 1778. |
| Brown, John | Private | First, Mennis | June 1778 on furlough. |
| Brown, John | Private | Third, Blackwell | Feb 17, 1778 drafted; June 1778. |
| Brown, John | Private | Third, Lee | Dec 1777-Jan 1778 sick at Mendham/Mendum. |
| Brown, John | Corporal | Sixth, Hockaday | Dec 1777 sick in the country; Jan 1778; Feb 10, 1778 discharged. |
| Brown, John | Private | Seventh, Crockett | March 19, 1778 enlisted; April-May 1778 |
| Brown, John | Private | Seventh/Third, Hill | June 1778. |
| Brown, John | Private | Seventh, Spencer | Dec 1777 hospital. |
| Brown, Lewis | Private | Twelfth, Wallace | Dec 1777 hospital; Jan 1778 sent to hospital; Feb-March 1778 hospital; April 1778 roll shows he was deceased on Dec 28, 1777. |
| Brown, Moses | Private | Twelfth, Bowyer, M. | Dec 1777-Jan 1778; Feb 1778 on command; March 1778; April-May 1778 on command. |
| Brown, Philip | Private | Third, Peyton, V. | Dec 23, 1777 discharged. |
| Brown, Reuben | Private | First State, Lee | Dec 1777 sick; Jan 1778 at Yellow Springs; Feb 1778 roll states he died sometime in January. |
| Brown, Robert/Robt. | Private | First, Pelham | Dec 1777-Jan 1778; Feb 15, 1778 discharged. |

| Name | Rank | Regiment | Service |
|---|---|---|---|
| Brown, Robert | Private | First State, Lee | Dec 1777; Jan 1778 at Yellow Springs hospital; Feb 1778 sick present; March 1778 on guard; April-June 1778. |
| Brown, Stephen | Private | Sixth, Avery | Dec 1777-Jan 1778; Feb 8, 1778 discharged. |
| Brown, Thomas | Private | Third, Powell | Dec 1777-April 1778; May 1778 sick present; June 1778. |
| Brown, Wm. | Private | Sixth, Avery | Dec 1777-Jan 1778; Feb 8, 1778 discharged. |
| Brown, William | Private | Sixth, Fox | Jan 1778-May 1778; June 1778 sick Coryell's Ferry. |
| Brown, William | Private | Seventh/Third, Fleming/Young | Feb 13, 1778 enlisted; April-June 1778 Unchland hospital; June in Young's Company. |
| Brown, William | Private | Seventh, Lipscomb | June 1778. |
| Brown, William | Private | Seventh, Spencer | Feb 10, 1778 enlisted for 1 year; April-May 1778 |
| Brown, William | Private/Corporal | Twelfth, Wallace | Dec 1777-April 1778; May 1778 on guard. |
| Brown, William | Private | Fourteenth, Reid | Dec 1777; Jan 1778 on command; Feb 1778; March 1, 1778 deserted. |
| Brown, William | Private | Fourteenth, Marks | Dec 1777-Jan 1778; Feb 1778 on guard; April 30, 1778 died. |
| Brown, Windsor | Private | First State, Brown | Dec 1777-May 1778. |
| Browning, Daniel/Danl. | Private | First, Payne | Feb 5, 1778 enlisted; April-June 1778. |
| Browning, William | Corporal | Second State, Taliaferro | March 15-May 1, 1778; May 1778; June 1778 sick Valley Forge. |
| Browing, Williamson/Wm. Som | Private | First, Taylor/Payne | Feb 5, 1778 enlisted April-May 1778; June 1778 in Payne's Company. |
| Bruce, George | Corporal | Fourteenth, Marks | Dec 1777-June 1778. |
| Bruce, William | Sergeant | Second. Willis | Dec 1777-June 1778. |
| Bruker, Richd. | Private | Fifteenth, Wills | March-April 1778; May 1778 on command. |

| Name | Rank | Regiment | Notes |
|---|---|---|---|
| Brumfields, Isick/Isaac | Private | Fifteenth, Wills | Feb 17, 1778 enlisted; April-May 1778 sick present. |
| Brunch, John | Private | Fourteenth, Lambert | Feb 23, 1778 enlisted; June 1778. |
| Brunt, William/Wm. | Corporal | First, Lawson | June 1778. |
| Bruton, William | Private | Third, Briscoe | Dec 1777; Feb 5, 1778 discharged. |
| Bryan, Jesse | Private | Fifteenth, Foster/ Gray | Dec 1777 confined; Jan 1778; Feb 1778 on guard; March 1778 on command; April 1778; May 1778 sick present; June 1778 waiting on sick at Valley Forge. |
| Bryant, Augustine | Private | Seventh, Fleming/ Heth | Feb 19, 1778 enlisted; April 1778 sick present; May 1778; June 1778 in Heth's company |
| Bryant/Briant, James/Jas. | Private | Fifteenth, Gregory | Dec 1777; Jan 1778 on command; Feb-April 1778; May 1778 on guard; June 1778. |
| Bryant/Briant, John | Private | Fifteenth, Gregory | Dec 1777-Jan 1778; Feb 1778 sick present; March 1778 hospital; April-June 1778 sick Yellow Springs. |
| Bryant/Bryan, Patrick/Partrick | Private | Second, Willis | Dec 1777-June 1778. |
| Bryant, Reuben | Private | Third, Peyton, V. | Dec 1777 Rifleman on command with Col. Morgan; Jan 1778 with Col. Morgan. |
| Bryant, William | Private | Third, Arell | Dec 1777-Jan 1778; Feb 1778 sick absent; March 15, 1778 dead. |
| Bryant/Bryent, William | Private | Fourteenth, Lambert | Dec 1777-April 1778; May 1778 on guard; June 1778. |
| Buchanan/ Buchanon, Ezekiel | Sergeant | Seventh/ Third, Crockett/ Sayers | March 12, 1778 enlisted; April-May 1778; June 1778 to the Major's company. |
| Buckingham, William | Private | Fourteenth, Conway | Dec 1777 absent without leave. |
| Buckner, Thomas | 1st. Lt. | Seventh, Hill | Dec 1777; Jan-Feb 1778 on furlough; April 1778 on furlough Virginia; June 1778. |
| Buffin, John | Sergeant Major | First State, Payne | Dec 1, 1777 died. |

| Name | Rank | Regiment | Notes |
|---|---|---|---|
| Buffin/Buffen, John | Private | Second State, Garnett | March 15-May 1, 1778; May 1778; June 1778. |
| Buford/Beuford, Abraham | Lt. Col. | Fourteenth | Dec 1777-Feb 1778; April-June 1778. Oath at Valley Forge on May 28, 1778, witnessed by Muhlenberg. |
| Bull, Samuel | Private | Twelfth, Casey | Dec 1777 left with baggage; Jan 1778 deserted Dec 7, 1777; May 1778 deserted December and since joined. |
| Bull, Thomas | Private | Twelfth, Waggener | Dec 1777-March 1778 at the hospital; April 10, 1778 discharged. |
| Bullet, Benjamin | Private | Twelfth, Casey | Dec 1777-Jan 1778; Feb 1778-April 1778 off; May 1778. See Solomon Allid. |
| Bullifant/Bellifant, James/Jas. | Private | Sixth, Hockaday | Dec 1777 sick at Princetown; Jan 1778; Feb 10, 1778 discharged. |
| Bullin, William | Private | Seventh/Third, Heth | June 1778. |
| Bullington, John | Private | First State, Crump | Dec 1777; Jan 24, 1778 deceased. |
| Bullock/Bulluck, Obediah/Obedier | Private | Fifteenth, Wills | Feb 19, 1778 enlisted; April 1778; May 1778 sick present. |
| Bullock, Rice | Quartermaster | Fifteenth | Dec 1777-April 1778 on furlough; May 6, 1778 superseded. |
| Bumpass/Bumpas, Job | Private | Seventh, Crockett | March 19, 1778 enlisted; April 1778; May 1778 "Room of John Long"; June-July 1778 sick at Valley Forge. |
| Bumper, Joseph | Private | Third, Briscoe | June 1778 sick at Valley Forge. |
| Bunn, Daniel/Danl. | Private | Sixth, Fox | Dec 28, 1777 reenlisted in the Light Dragoons. |
| Buns, John | Drummer | Second State, Taliaferro | March 15-April 15, 1778. |

| Name | Rank | Regiment | Notes |
|---|---|---|---|
| Buntin, Thacker/Tracker | Private | Second State, Dudley | March 15-May 1, 1778; May-June 1778. |
| Burch/Birch, Thomas | Private | Fourteenth, Winston | Feb 17, 1778 drafted; May 1778; June 1778 sick near English Town. |
| Burchett/Burchet, Burwell | Private | Fourteenth, Jones | Dec 1777 deserted in Virginia; June 1778 lately joined regiment. |
| Burchett/Burckett, David | Private | Fourteenth, Thweatt | Sept 10, 1777 enlisted; Jan 1778 lately joined regiment, sick in hospital; Feb 1778 sick present; April-June 1778 sick Y. S. H. |
| Burfoot, Thomas | Adjutant | Fourteenth | Appointed Jan 12, 1778; Jan-Feb 1778; April-June 1778. Oath at Valley Forge on May 12, 1778, witnessed by Muhlenberg. |
| Burford, William | Private | Fourteenth, Marks | Jan 8, 1778 enlisted; Jan-April 1778 on furlough; May-June 1778. |
| Burge/Burg, Henry | Sergeant | Second State, Dudley | March 15-May 1, 1778; May-June 1778. |
| Burge/Burgey, Nicholas | Private | Seventh, Jouett | Feb 16, 1778 enlisted; April 1778 sick in camp; May 1778. |
| Burge, Wooden | Corporal | Second State, Lewis | Roll for July 1778 shows "Omitted half June." |
| Burger/Burge | Sergeant Major | Seventh/Third | Dec 1777 on furlough; March-April 1778 on furlough; May-June 1778. |
| Buris/Burris, James | Private | Twelfth, Casey | Dec 1777-May 1778. |
| Burk, James | Private | Seventh, Crockett | Dec 1777-Jan 1778 on furlough; March 1, 1778 deserted; June 1778 guard. |
| Burk, James B. | Private | Seventh, Lipscomb | June 1778. |
| Burk, John | Private | First State, Brown | Dec 1777-Feb 1778. |
| Burk, John | Fifer | Twelfth, Bowyer, T. | Dec 1777-April 1778; May 1778 sick hospital. |
| Burk/Burke, Richard | Private | Seventh, Hill | Feb 1778; May 1778; June 1778 on guard. |

| Name | Rank | Regiment, Company | Notes |
|---|---|---|---|
| Burk, Thomas | Private | Seventh, Lipscomb | June 1778. |
| Burk, Thomas | Private | Seventh, Spencer | Enlisted for 3 years; Dec 1777-Jan 1778 on furlough; April-June 1778. |
| Burk, William | Private | Seventh/Third, Webb/Young | Feb 16, 1778 enlisted; April-May 1778; June 1778 in Young's company. |
| Burke/Burk, Richard | Private | Seventh, Hill | Dec 1777 on fatigue; Feb 1, 1778 discharged. |
| Burks/Buks, Christopher | Private | Twelfth, Ashby | Dec 1777-Feb 1778; March-April 1778 at hospital; May 1778 on guard. |
| Burks, Samuel | Corporal | Seventh, Posey | Dec 1777-Jan 1778 on furlough. |
| Burley, James | Private | Fourteenth, Overton | Dec 1777; Jan 1778 sick absent; Feb-June 1778. |
| Burnet, Midleton | Private/Corporal | Second State, Spiller | March 15-May 1, 1778; May-June 1778; June 1778 appears as a Corporal. |
| Burnett, Bond | Private | Sixth, Massie | Dec 1777 in hospital; Feb 1778. |
| Burnett see Bennett | | | |
| Burnett/Bennet, Elisha | Private | Sixth, Massie | Dec 1777 in hospital; Jan 1778-March 1778 sick absent; April 1778 not to be found in hospital returns, supposed to be dead. |
| Burnett/Burnitt, Rubin/Rewbin | Private | First, Lewis | Dec 1777 sick; Jan 1778 sick hospital; Feb 1778 dead. |
| Burn, Robert/Robt. | Private | Third, Mercer/Powell | Dec 1777-March 1778 on furlough; April 1778; May 1778 sick present; June 1778 in Powell's Company. |
| Burne/Burn, Christopher | Private | Third, Peyton, V./Peyton J. | Dec 1777 on furlough in Virginia; Jan-March 1778 on furlough; April-May 1778; June 1778 in J. Peyton's Company. |
| Burnet, James | Private | Fourteenth, Marks | Nov 30, 1777 deceased. |

| Name | Rank | Regiment/Company | Service |
|---|---|---|---|
| Burnham/ Bearnam, Thomas | Private | First State, Lee | Dec 1777 sick; Jan 15, 1778 deceased. |
| Burnley, Garland | 1st. Lt. | Seventh, Spencer | Commissioned May 6, 1776. Dec 1777-Jan 1778; April-May 1778. He was the senior officer in Spencer's company on all the rolls. |
| Burns/Burnes, John | Private | First State, Hamilton | Dec 1777-June 1778 |
| Burns, John | Private | First State, Lee | June 1778. |
| Burns, John | Drummer | Second State, Taliaferro | Appears only on roll from March 15-April 15, 1778. |
| Burns/Burnes, John | Private | Third, Briscoe | June 1778. |
| Burns, John | Private | Seventh, Posey | Feb 27, 1778 enlisted; April-May 1778 on command. |
| Burns, William | Private | Twelfth, Wallace | Dec 1777 on command; Jan 1778 roll shows he deserted about Dec 23, 1777. |
| Burris/Burriss, Frederick | Private | Second State, Bressie | March 15-May 1, 1778; May 1778; June 1778. |
| Burris/Burrows, Thomas | Corporal | Third, Mercer/ Powell | Dec 1777-March 1778 on furlough; April 1778; June 1778 in Powell's Company, on detachment. |
| Burroughs, George | Quartermaster | Second | Jan-Feb 1778. |
| Burrus/ Burroughs, Jacob | Private | Second, Taylor, F. | Dec 1777-Feb 1778; March 4, 1778 discharged. |
| Burten/Burtin, Marshal/ Marchel | Private | Twelfth, Casey | Dec 1777 sent to hospital; Jan 1778 at hospital; Feb 1778 on duty; March-April 1778 on command. |
| Burton, George | Private | Third, Lee/ Peyton, J. | Feb 27, 1778 enlisted; April-May 1778. |
| Burton, James | 2nd Lt. | Second, Taylor, F. | Dec 1777-June 1778. |

| | | | | |
|---|---|---|---|---|
| Burton, James | Private | Second State, Taliaferro | March 15-May 1, 1778; May-June 1778. |
| Burton, Thomas | Private | Second, Taylor, W. | Dec 1777 on guard; Jan 1778; Feb 21, 1778 discharged. |
| Burton, William A./ Wm. Allen | Private | First, Cunningham | Feb 12, 1778 enlisted for 1 year; April 1778 under inoculation; May-June 1778. |
| Burwell/ Berwell, John | Private | Second, Taylor, F. | Feb 17, 1778 drafted from Fauquier; April-May 1778; June-June 1778 sick Valley Forge. |
| Bush, Francis | Private | Second, Upshaw | Feb 14, 1778 drafted; April 1778; June 1778 sick at Valley Forge. |
| Bush, James | Private | First State, Hamilton | Dec 1777 Jan 1778; died about Feb 15, 1778. |
| Bush, John | Private | Seventh, Spencer | Enlisted for 3 years; Dec 1777-Jan 1778 hospital |
| Butler, Henry | Private | Twelfth, Waggener | Dec 1777-March 1778 sick at the hospital; April 1778 "Sepos to be Dead." |
| Butler, Jacob | Private | Second, Harrison | May-June 1778. |
| Butler, James | Private | Second, Willis | Dec 1777-June 1778. |
| Butler, James | Private | Fifteenth, Hull | Dec 1777 sick absent; Jan 1778 sick in hospital; Feb 1778 sick absent; March 1778 on command; April 1778; May-June 1778 hospital Yellow Springs. |
| Butler, Jesse | Private | Second, Taylor | Dec 1777-Feb 1778. |
| Butler, Joshua/Joseph | Private | Fourteenth, Jones | Sept 18, 1777 drafted; April-May 1778. |
| Butler, Laurence | 1st. Lt. | Fifteenth, Hull | Dec 1777-May 1778. |
| Butler, Shadrock/ Shadrach | Private | Third, Peyton, V. | Dec 1777 Rifleman on command with Col. Morgan; Jan 1778 with Col. Morgan. |
| Butler, William | Private | Second State, Garnett | April 15-June 1, 1778; June 1778. |
| Butler, William | Private | Seventh, Fleming | Dec 22, 1777 enlisted in the Light Horse. |

| Name | Rank | Regiment | Service |
|---|---|---|---|
| Butt/Butts, Simon | Corporal | Fifteenth, Grimes | Dec 1777-Feb 1778; March 1778 on command; April-May 1778. |
| Butterworth, Nicholas | Private | Fourteenth, Jones | Drafted Feb 12, 1778; April 1778; May 1778 on duty. |
| Buzan/Busan, John | Private | Twelfth, Waggener | Dec 1777-March 1778; April 10, 1778 discharged. |
| Byas/Boyes, Adam | Private | Second, Calmes | Dec 1777-June 1778. |
| Byas, John | Private | First, Scott | Feb 1778 waggoner Morristown; April-May 1778 waggoner. |
| Byram, Peter | Private | Third, Mercer | Dec 1777-Jan 1778. |
| Byrd/Bird, Henry | Private | Fifteenth | Jan 1778 sick; Feb 1778; March-April 1778 sick present; May 1778; June 1778 sick Valley Forge. |
| Byrne, Charles | Corporal | Seventh, Crockett | Dec 1, 1777 appointed; Dec 1777-Jan 1778. |
| Bryom/Birum, Henry | Private | Seventh, Webb | Jan 1778 hospital; Feb 1778 deceased. |
| Cabell, Samuel Jordan | Major | Sixth/Fourteenth, Cabell | Dec 23, 1777, promoted from Captain, Sixth Virgina; Jan 1778 command; Feb 1778; April-June 1778. |
| Caddell/Caddle, John | Private | Second, Harrison | Dec 1777-May 1778; June 1778 hospital. |
| Caer, John | Private | Second, Spencer | Dec 1777. |
| Cain/Keane, James | Private | Third, Mercer/Powell | Dec 1777; Jan 1778 sick present; Feb 1778 on guard; March 1778 on command; April 1778 on guard; May 1778 sick present; June-July 1778 sick at Valley Forge, in Powell's Company. |
| Cair, David | Private | Fourteenth, Marks | Feb 12, 1778 enlisted; April 1778. |
| Caldwell/Caldwill, David | Private | Seventh/Third Fleming/Heth | April 1778 sick present; May 1778 on command; June 1778 on furlough Springfield, in Heth's Company. |

| Name | Rank | Regiment/Company | Notes |
|---|---|---|---|
| Caldwell/ Caldwill, John | Private | Seventh Third, Fleming/ Heth | Feb 17, 1778 enlisted; April 1778 sick present; May 1778 on command; June 1778 in Heth's Company, on furlough Springfield. |
| Caldwell/ Calwell, William | Private | Fourteenth, Reid | Dec 1777-March 1778; April 1778 sick present; May 1778; June 1778 left sick at Valley Forge. |
| Callahan/ Callihan, David | Private | Sixth, Hockaday | Feb 17, 1778 drafted; April 1778; May 1778 on fatigue; June 1778. |
| Calmes, Marquis/Marcus | Captain | Second, Calmes | Dec 1777-June 1778. Oath at Valley Forge on May 12, 1778, witnessed by Muhlenberg. |
| Calor/Caylor, Mathew | Private | First State, Meriwether | Dec 1777-June 1778. |
| Calvert, Zelia/ Zely | Private | Third, Peyton, J. | Dec 1777; Jan 1778 on guard; Feb 5, 1778 discharged. |
| Cambell/Campbell, Robert | Private | Twelfth, Wallace | Drafted February 28, 1778; May 1778. |
| Cambow see Cumbo | | | |
| Cameron/ Camron, John | Private | Twelfth, Waggener | Dec 1777; Jan-Feb 1778 on command; March-May 1778. |
| Cammell/ Camell, Alexander/ Alexr. | Private | Fifteenth, Harris | Jan 1778 on guard; Feb 1778 sick present; March-April 1778 on command; May 1778 sick present; June 1778 sick Yellow Springs. |
| Camp see Kemp | | | |
| Camp, James | Private | Second State, Taliaferro | Appears only on roll for March 15-April 15, 1778. |
| Camp, John | Captain | First State, Camp/ Valentine | Dec 1777 at home; Jan-March 1778 off in Virginia; April 8, 1778 resigned. Jacob Valentine assumed command of the company. |
| Camp, Thomas | Private | Second State, Taliaferro | March 15-May 1, 1778; May-June 1778. |
| Campbell, David | Sergeant | Second State, Bressie | March 15-May 1, 1778; May-June 1778 sick Valley Forge. |

| Name | Rank | Regiment | Service |
|---|---|---|---|
| Campbell/ Cambell, John | Private | First, Scott | Dec 1777-Feb 1778; March 1778 on guard; April-May 1778; June 1778 detached with Col. Morgan. |
| Campbell, John | Sergeant | Second State, Taliaferro | March 15-May 1, 1778; May-June 1778. |
| Campbell/ Cambell, John | Sergeant | Second State, Lewis | March 15-May 1, 1778; May-June 1778. |
| Campbell, Samuel | 1st. Lt. | Fourteenth, Conway | Sept 3, 1777 appointed; April 1778 on command; May-June 1778. Oath at Valley Forge on May 12, 1778, witnessed by Muhlenberg. |
| Campbell, William | 1st. Lt. | First State, Hamilton | Dec 1777-June 1778. Oath at Valley Forge on May 12, 1778, witnessed by Muhlenberg. |
| Campbell/ Campble, William | Private | Fourteenth, Marks | Dec 1777; June 1778 on duty; Feb 1778; March 1778 on command; April-May 1778. |
| Canafax/ Cannafax, Edward | Private | First, Cunningham | August 1776 enlisted for 3 years; Dec 1777 sick present; Jan 1778 sick at hospital; Feb-April 1778; May 1778; June 1778 sick Valley Forge. |
| Canary, William | Private | Second, Harrison | Dec 1777 on command; Jan-June 1778. |
| Cannaday see Kennedy | | | |
| Cannady/ Kennody, John | Private | Second, Willis | Dec 1777-April 1778. |
| Cannahan/ Canahan, John | Private | Twelfth, Bowyer, T. | Dec 1777; Jan 1778 on command; Feb-April 1778; March 1778 on guard. |
| Cannefax/ Cannifax, John | Private | First, Cunningham | Feb 11, 1778 enlisted for 1 year; April 1778 under inoculation; May 1778 sick present; June 1778 sick at Valley Forge; July roll shows he died on June 28. |
| Cannisare, Edward | Private | First, Cunningham | June 1778 sick Valley Forge. |
| Cannon, Luke | Ensign | Fifteenth, Wills | Feb 1778 on command; March-May 1778. |

| Name | Rank | Regiment/Company | Notes |
|---|---|---|---|
| Cannon, Michael | Private | First State, Meriwether | Dec 1777-Feb 1778. |
| Carabine/Carbine, Henry | Corporal | Twelfth, Bowyer, T. | Dec 1777-May 1778. |
| Cardwell, John | Private | Seventh/Third, Hill | Feb 1778; May 1778; June 1778 on guard, in Hill's Company. |
| Cardwell, William | Private/Corporal | Seventh/Third, Hill | Dec 1777-Jan 1778; April 1, 1778 promoted to Corporal; April-May 1778; June 1778 sick present. |
| Care see Kerr | | | |
| Carey/Cary, James | Private | First, Lewis | Dec 1777-Jan 1778; Feb 1778 sick hospital; March 1778 sick hospital; April-June 1778. |
| Carfree/Caffery, Peter | Private | Twelfth, Casey | Feb 28, 1778 drafted; May 1778. |
| Carless, William | Private | Fourteenth, Conway | Dec 1777. |
| Carlton, James | Private | Seventh, Hill | Dec 1777-Jan 1778 sick in hospital |
| Carlton, Joseph | Private | First, Cummings | Dec 1777. |
| Carlton, William | Private | First, Lawson | Dec 1777; Jan 1778 sick hospital; Feb-June 1778. |
| Carnell, John | Corporal | First State, Meriwether | Dec 1777-Feb 1778. |
| Carney/Carny, Anthony | Corporal | Second, Calmes | Dec 1777-June 1778. |
| Carney, John | Private | Second, Harrison | May-June 1778. |
| Carpenter, John | Private | First, Lawson | Dec 1777-Feb 1778; March 1778 on fatigue; April-June 1778. |
| Carpenter, John | Private | Seventh, Lipscomb | Dec 1777; Jan 1778 hospital; Feb 5, 1778 discharged. |
| Carpenter, Thomas | Private | Fifteenth, Wills | Aug 21, 1777 enlisted; Feb 1778 sick Lancaster; March 1778 sick absent; April muster roll shows he died on March 13, 1778. |
| Carr/Kerr, John | Private | First State, Ewell, T. | Dec 1777; Jan 1778 sick Yellow Springs; Feb 1778 at Yellow Springs hospital; April 1778; May 1778; June 1778 sick Yellow Springs. |

| | | | |
|---|---|---|---|
| Carr, John | Sergeant | Seventh, Briscoe | June 1778. |
| Carr, John | Private | Twelfth, Vause | Dec 1777-March 1778 sick at Trenton; April 1778 waits on French engineer; May 1778 waits on French Colonel; May 10, 1778 discharged. |
| Carr/Car, William | Private | First State, Lee | Dec 1777 sick; Jan 1778 sick absent; Feb 1778 Yellow Springs hospital; March 1778 roll shows he deserted in February 1778. |
| Carrell/Carroll, Berry | Private | Second State, Spiller | May-June 1778. |
| Carrigin/ Carriggin, Michael | Private | Twelfth, Madison | Dec 1777-March 1778 sick hospital; April 1778 sick in camp; May 1778 sick Yellow Springs. |
| Carrington, Mayo | 2nd. Lt. | Seventh/ Third, Fleming/Hill | Dec 1777-March 1778 on furlough; April-May 1778; June 1778 in Hill's Company. |
| Carroll/Carrol, John | Private | Second, Calmes | Dec 1777-June 1778. |
| Carroll/Carrole, John/Jno | Private | Sixth, Garland | Dec 1, 1777 reenlisted; Dec 1777-June 1778. |
| Carroll/Carrol, John | Corporal/ Sergeant | Seventh, Spencer/ Lipscomb | Dec 22, 1777 enlisted in Light Horse; Feb 13, 1778 enlisted; April-May 1778; May 1778 promoted to Sergeant; June 1778 in Lipscomb's company. |
| Carroll/Carrole, Joseph | Private | First State, Brown | Dec 1777-May 1778; July 1778 sick Valley Forge. |
| Carroll/Carrole, Thomas | Private | First State, Brown | Dec 1777-May 1778. |
| Carroll/Carrill, William/Wm | Private | Sixth, Hockaday | Feb 10, 1778 drafted; April 1778; May 19, 1778 decd. |
| Carter, Armistead/ Armsted | Private | First, Mennis | Dec 1777 sick Bethlehem; Jan 1778 sick in the hospital; Feb 1778; March 1778 on fatigue; April 1778; May 1778 on furlough; June 1778. |

| Name | Rank | Company/Regiment | Service |
|---|---|---|---|
| Carter/Cartor Charles | Private | First, Cunningham | March 1777 enlisted for 3 years; Dec 1777 sick at Trenton; Jan-Feb 1778; March 1778 on fatigue; April 1778; May 1778 on command; June 1778. |
| Carter, Charles | Private | First State, Hoffler | Dec 1777-Feb 1778. |
| Carter, Charles | Private | Second State, Garnett | April 15-June 1, 1778; June 1778. |
| Carter, George | Private | Second State, Dudley | March 15-May 1, 1778; May 1778. This man and the man below may be the same individual. |
| Carter, George | Private | Second State, Spiller | June 1778 sick Valley Forge. |
| Carter, Henry | Private | Twelfth, Waggener | Dec 1777-March 1778; April 10, 1778 discharged. |
| Carter, James | Corporal | Seventh, Posey | Dec 1777-Jan 1778; Feb 12, 1778 discharged. |
| Carter, James | Private | Fourteenth, Winston | Feb 17, 1778 drafted; May 1778 on guard; June 1778. |
| Carter/Cartor, Jesse | Private | Sixth, Garland | Dec 1777-Jan 1778; Feb 23, 1778 discharged. |
| Carter, John | Private | First, Pelham | Feb 7, 1778 enlisted; April 1778 sick at camp; May-June 1778. |
| Carter, John | Corporal | First State, Meriwether | Dec 1777-June 1778. |
| Carter, John | Private | Second, Upshaw | Dec 1777-Jan 1778. |
| Carter, Joseph | Private | First, Lewis | Dec 1777-June 1778 on command. |
| Carter, Joseph | Private | Fifteenth, Harris | Jan 1778 on command; Feb 1778; March-May 1778 sick present; June-Aug 1778 sick Valley Forge. |
| Carter, Landon/Landern | Private | Second, Upshaw | Dec 1777 sick hospital; Jan 1778. |
| Carter, Obediah | Private | Second, Upshaw | Dec 30, 1777 inlisted in the Horse Service. |
| Carter, Robert | Sergeant | Fourteenth, Winston | Dec 1777-Feb 1778 sick in hospital; March-June 1778. |
| Carter, William | Corporal | Second, Upshaw | Dec 30, 1777 enlisted in the Horse Service. |

| Name | Rank | Regiment/Company | Notes |
|---|---|---|---|
| Carter, William | Drummer | Fourteenth, Conway | Dec 1777-Feb 1778; March 1778 absent with leave; April 1778 on command; May-June 1778. |
| Cartright, Jese/Jesse | Private | Twelfth, Bowyer, T. | Dec 1777-May 1778. |
| Cartright, Thomas | Private | Seventh/Third, Webb/Young | Feb 16, 1778 enlisted; April-May 1778; June 1778 to Young's company. |
| Cartwright, James | Private | Seventh, Fleming | Dec 1777 sick in hospital; Jan 1778 hospital; Feb 26, 1778 discharged. |
| Cartwrite, James | Private | Seventh, Crockett | Dec 1777-Jan 1778 in R. Bat. |
| Carver, Henry/Harry | Private | Twelfth, Casey | Dec 1777-Feb 1778 on command; March 31, 1778 died. |
| Carver, John | Private | Seventh/Third, Jouett/Hill | Feb 16, 1778 enlisted; April-May 1778; June 1778 in Hill's Company. |
| Cary, Samuel | Adjutant | Second State | May-June 1778. |
| Case/Cayse, John | Private | Twelfth, Madison | Dec 1777-Feb 1778; March-April 1778 on guard. |
| Casey, Archibald | Private | Second State, Bernard | April-May 1778; June 1778 sick Correll's Ferry. |
| Casey, Benjamin | Captain | Twelfth, Casey | Dec 1777 on command; Jan-April 1778; May 1778 on command. |
| Casey/Casee, James | Private | Fifteenth, Edmunds | Dec 1777. Probably the same man as shown below. |
| Casey, James | Private | Fifteenth, Wills | Jan-March 1778; April-June 1778 on command. |
| Cash, Archdell/Archdall | Private | First State, Lee | Dec 1777 sick; Jan 1778 deserted. |
| Cash, David | Private | Fourteenth, Conway | Feb 23, 1778 enlisted; June 1778 sick Valley Forge. |
| Cash, Paul | Private | Twelfth, Wallace | Dec 1777; Jan 1778 wounded absent; Feb 1778 roll shows he died about Jan 15, 1778. |
| Cash, Warren | Private | Seventh/Third, Jouett/Hill | Dec 1777 on furlough Virginia; Jan-April 1778 on furlough; May 1778 on guard; June 1778 in Hills Company. |

| Name | Rank | Regiment/Company | Service |
|---|---|---|---|
| Casky/Caskey, John/Jno | Private | Sixth, Avery | Dec 1777 reenlisted; Dec 1777-May 1778 on furlough; June 1778 deserted. |
| Casle, Thomas | Private | Fifteenth, Edmunds | Feb 1778 muster shows he died on March 5, 1778. |
| Casley/Casely Robert | Drummer | Seventh/Third, Jouett/Hill | Dec 23, 1777 enlisted; April-May 1778; June 1778 in Hill's Company. |
| Caslin, John | Private | Fourteenth, Winston | May-June 1778. |
| Cason/Casen, James | Private | Second State, Quarles | April-June 1778. |
| Cason/Casen, John | Corporal | Second State, Quarles | April-June 1778. |
| Cason, John | Private | Fifteenth, Gregory | Dec 1777-March 1778 sick in hospital; April 1778 muster roll shows he died Dec 28, 1778. [sic] |
| Cason/Casen, William | Private | Second State, Quarles | April-June 1778. |
| Cassady/Cassidy, John | Private | First, Mennis | Dec 1777 on command; Jan 1778 on furlough; Feb-March 1778; April 1778 on command; May-June 1778 |
| Casson, John | Private | Fifteenth, Gregory | Dec 1777-March 1778 hospital; April 1778 muster roll shows he died on Dec 28, 1777. |
| Casson, Wm. | Private | Fifteenth, Grimes | Dec 1777-Feb 1778 sick absent; March 1778 roll shows he "died some time ago in the hospital." |
| Castle, Ben | Private | Seventh, Crockett | Dec 1777-Jan 1778 on furlough. |
| Castlen, John | Private | Fourteenth, Winston | Feb 17, 1778 drafted; June 1778. |
| Catlett, James | Private | Second, Willis | Dec 20, 1777 deserted. |
| Catlett, Thomas | 1st. Lt. | Second, Calmes | Dec 1777-June 1778. |
| Caton, William | Private | Second State, Bressie | March 15-May 1, 1778; May 1778; June 1778. |

| Name | Rank | Regiment | Notes |
|---|---|---|---|
| Caufield/ Coffeld, James | Private | Twelfth, Waggener | Dec 1777-May 1778. |
| Cave, James | Private | Seventh/ Third, Jouett/Hill | Dec 1777 on furlough Virginia; Jan-March 1778 on furlough; April 1778 sick in camp; May 1778; June 1778 sick Valley Forge, in Hill's Company. |
| Cave, John | Private | Second, Sanford | Dec 1777. |
| Cave/Kave, Peter | Private | Fifteenth, Hull | Dec 1777 sick absent; Jan 1778 sick in hospital; Feb 1778 sick absent; March 7, 1778 deceased. |
| Cave, Reuben | Private | Second State, Bernard | First appears on May roll "from April 15, 1778."; June 1778. |
| Cavender/ Ceavender, John | Private | Second, Taylor, W. | Dec 1777 sick absent; Jan-Feb 1778. |
| Cavender, Jos./Joseph | Private | Fifteenth, Foster | Dec 1777-Feb 1778; March-May 1778 on command. |
| Caves, John | Private | Second, Parker | Dec 28, 1777 deserted. |
| Cawley/Cauley, Asa/Asia | Private | Fifteenth, Foster/ Gray | Dec 1777 on guard; Jan 1778 on command; Feb 1778 sick; March 1778; April 1778 sick present; May 1778 on guard. |
| Cearnell, John | Corporal | First State, Meriwether | Dec 1777-Feb 1778. |
| Chace, John | Private | Seventh, Posey | Dec 1777-Jan 1778 left sick in Virginia; Feb 15, 1778 discharged. |
| Chaddock see Shaddock | | | |
| Chaffin/ Chappin, John | Private | Fifteenth, Foster | Dec 1777-Feb 1778 on guard; March 1778 on command; April 1778 sick present; May 1778; June-July sick present. |
| Challiss, Robert/Robt. | Private | First, Pelham | Dec 1777-Jan 1778; Feb 15, 1778 discharged. |
| Chamberlain, Joseph | Private | First State, Hamilton | Dec 1777-Feb 1778. |
| Chambers, Alexander | Private | Seventh/ Third, Crockett/ Sayers | Dec 1777-Jan 1778 on furlough; Feb-May 1778; June 1778 in Sayers' Company. |

| Name | Rank | Regiment, Company | Notes |
|---|---|---|---|
| Chambers, Henry | Private | Fourteenth, Thweatt | Feb 14, 1778 enlisted; April 1778 lately joined regiment; May 1778; June 1778 sick Carrells. |
| Chambers/Chaimbers, James | Private | Twelfth, Bowyer, M. | Dec 1777-May 1778. |
| Chambers, John | Private | Fourteenth, Conway | Feb 23, 1778 enlisted; June 1778 sick Valley Forge. |
| Chambers, John | Private | Fourteenth, Thweatt | Feb 14, 1778 enlisted; April 1778 lately joined regiment; June 1778. |
| Chambers, Thorow Good/Thoroughgood | Private/Corporal | Seventh, Hill | Dec 1777-Jan 1778; April 1, 1778 promoted to Corporal; April-June 1778. |
| Chambers, Travis | Corporal | Twelfth, Wallace | Dec 1777-March 1778 on command; April-May 1778. |
| Chandler, Robert | Private | Second, Taylor, F. | Dec 1777 left sick Virginia. |
| Chapman, Cager | Private | Second, Upshaw | Dec 30, 1777 enlisted in horse service. |
| Chapman, Jacob | Private | Fourteenth, Conway | Jan 1778 joined regiment lately; on command; Feb-March 1778 sick at Little York; April-May 1778; June 1778 on command. |
| Chapman, Robert | Sergeant | Seventh, Hill | Dec 1777 on guard; Jan 26, 1778 discharged. |
| Chappel/Chapple, Benjamin/Benjn. | Private | First, Mennis | Dec 1777; Jan 1778 sick in the hospital; Feb-June 1778. |
| Chappel, David | Private | Fifteenth, Mason | Dec 1777; Jan 1778 sick present; Feb 27, 1778 died. |
| Chappel/Chappell, James | Private | Second, Taylor, W. | Dec 1777 guard; Jan 1778; Feb 21, 1778 discharged. |
| Chappell/Chapell, David | Private | First State, Crump | Dec 1777-Feb 1778. |
| Chappell, David | Private | Fifteenth, Mason | Jan 1778 sick present; Feb 27, 1778 died. |
| Chappell/Chapple, John | Private | First State, Ewell, T. | Dec 1777; Jan-March 1778 sick at Yellow Springs hospital; May 1778 Yellow Springs; June 1778. |
| Charles, William | Private | Second State, Dudley | June 1778. |

| | | | |
|---|---|---|---|
| Charlton, Joseph | Private | First, Cummings | December 1777. |
| Chase/Chaice, James | Private | Third, Powell | Dec 1777-Jan 1778; Feb 17, 1778 discharged. |
| Chavaus/ Chavus, James | Private | Second State, Dudley | March 15-May 1, 1778; May-June 1778. |
| Chavier, Adam | Private | First, Mennis | April 1778. |
| Chavis/Shavis, Shadrach | Private | Second, Upshaw/ Taylor, W. | Feb 14, 1778 drafted; April-May 1778; June 1778 sick Valley Forge. In June he is in Taylor's Company. |
| Chavos/Chavas John | Private | Seventh/ Third, Fleming/ Heth | Feb 13, 1778 enlisted; April 1778 sick present; May 1778; June 1778 in Heth's Company. |
| Chavoure/ Chavours, Isick/Isaac | Private | Fourteenth, Reid | Dec 1777-Jan 1778; Feb 1778 sick in camp; March 1778 sick present; April-May 1778; June 1778 sick Valley Forge. |
| Chavoures/ Cheavours, Edward | Private | Fourteenth, Reid | Aug 28, 1777 drafted; March-May 1778; June 1778 sick Valley Forge. |
| Chavoures/ Cheavours, Samuel/Samuell | Private | Fourteenth, Reid | August 28, 1777 drafted; March 1778; May 1778 sick present; June 1778 sick Valley Forge. |
| Cheatham, William | Private | Seventh/ Third, Fleming/ Heth | Feb 10, 1778 enlisted; April 1778 sick present; May 1778; June 1778 in Heth's company. |
| Cheatwood/ Chitwood, Elias | Private | First, Cunningham | Feb 14, 1778 enlisted for 1 year; April 1778 under inoculation; May 1778 sick present; June 1778 sick at Princetown. |
| Cheeke/ Cheekes, Thomas | Sergeant | Fourteenth, Lambert | Sept 9, 1777 enlisted; April 1778 lately joined regiment; May-June 1778. |
| Chenam, James | Private | First, Cunningham | Feb 23, 1778 enlisted; July 1778 sick at Valley Forge. |
| Chenning/ Chewning, Richard | Private | Second, Upshaw | Dec 1777-Jan 1778. |

| Name | Rank | Regiment | Notes |
|---|---|---|---|
| Chew, Robert B. | 1st. Lt. | First State, Brown | Dec 1777-Feb 1778; March-June 1778 on furlough to Virginia. |
| Chewning, Harden/Hardin | Private | Second, Upshaw | Dec 1777 hospital; Jan 1778. |
| Chewning, John | Private | Third, Hill | June 1778. |
| Chiely/Cheley, Joseph | Private | Fourteenth, Jones | Feb 14, 1778 enlisted; May 1778 left out in April, sick present. |
| Chihew/Cyhue, Peter | Private | Twelfth, Vause | April 1778 on weeks command; May 1778 waiting on General Porteel. |
| Childers/Childress, John | Sergeant | Second, Jones/Hoomes | Feb 1778; March 1778 payroll states he drew no pay from July 1, 1777 to Feb 1, 1778; May 1778 discharged. |
| Childress, Henry | Private | Fourteenth, Lambert | Oct 7, 1777 enlisted; April 1778 lately joined regiment; May 1778 sick in camp; June 1778 sick Valley Forge. |
| Childress/Childress, Mosby | Private | Seventh/Third, Hill | Dec 1777 on furlough Virginia; Jan 1778-March 1778 on furlough; April 1778; May 1778 on guard; June 1778 |
| Chilton/Chelton, Henry | Private | Second, Sanford/Parker | Dec 1777-April 1778; June 1778. From April on he appears in Parker's company. |
| Chisham/Chisholm James | Private | Second State, Dudley | March 15-May 1, 1778; May 1778; June 1778 sick absent. |
| Chisnell/Chisneel, Peter | Private | First State, Hoffler | Dec 1777-June 1778. |
| Chissum/Chisum, George | Sergeant | Seventh, Spencer | Enlisted for 3 years; Dec 1777-Jan 1778 on furlough Virginia; April-May 1778; June 1778 on guard, in Lipscomb's Company. |
| Chissum, William | Private | Seventh, Spencer | Jan 4, 1778 discharged. |
| Chitwood, John | Private | Seventh, Fleming | Dec 1777 with Rifle Regt.; Jan 1778 R. Regimt; Feb 16, 1778 discharged. |
| Choney, Joseph M. | Private | Second, Sanford | Dec 1777-Jan 1778. |

| Name | Rank | Company | Notes |
|---|---|---|---|
| Chowning, John | Private | Seventh, Hill | Dec 1777-Jan 1778; April-June 1778. |
| Chrisell/Chrisil, William | Private | Third, Briscoe | Feb 10, 1778 drafted; June-Sept 1778 sick Valley Forge. |
| Christian, James | Corporal | Sixth, Hockaday | Jan 1778; Feb 10, 1778 discharged. This man and the one below may be the same individual. |
| Christian, James | Private | Sixth, Hockaday | Feb-May 1778 on furlough; June 1778. |
| Christian, James | Corporal | Sixth, Garland | March 1778 payroll only. |
| Christian, Joseph/Joel | Private | Sixth, Massie | Dec 1777-Jan 1778; Feb 15, 1778 discharged. |
| Christian, Richard/Richd. | Corporal | Sixth, Massie | Dec 1777-Jan 1778; Feb 12, 1778 discharged. |
| Christian, Dan | Private | Seventh, Gray | Dec 1777 dead. |
| Chun/Chunn, Sylvester/Silvester | Fifer/Private | Fourteenth, Thweatt | Dec 1777-April 1778; April 1778 reduced to Private; May-June 1778 on command. |
| Chuning, John | Private | Second, Taylor, F. | Dec 1777 left sick Virginia. |
| Church, Scarlet | Private | First State, Payne | Dec 1777 sick Burlington hospital; Jan 1778 sick Princeton; Feb 1778 deceased. |
| Churchwell/Churchill, Chs. | Private | Twelfth, Waggener | Dec 1777; Jan 1778 on guard; Feb-April 1778; May 1778 on command. |
| Cipes, John | Private | Third, Mercer | Dec 1777 on furlough. |
| Clack, Thomas | Sergeant | Third, Arell | Dec 1777-Jan 1778; Feb 1778 sick present; March 1778 sick in camp; April 15, 1778 dead. |
| Clamount/Clarmount, John | Private | Third, Lee/Peyton, J. | Feb 27, 1778 enlisted; April-May 1778; June 1778 in J. Peyton's Company. |
| Clanton/Lanthon, Mark | Private | Sixth, Rose | Dec 1777; Jan 1778 "Time to serve March 2." Feb 1778. |
| Clardy, John | Private | Seventh, Moseley | Dec 1777-Jan 1778 sick in Virginia. |

| | | | |
|---|---|---|---|
| Clardy, Joseph | Private | Seventh, Moseley | Dec 1777 on guard; Jan 1778 on command; Feb 22, 1778 discharged. |
| Clark/Clarke, Henry | Sergeant | Twelfth, Ashby | Dec 1777-Jan 1778; March-May 1778. |
| Clark, James | Sergeant | Second State, Garnett | April 15, 1778- June 1, 1778; June 1778. |
| Clark, John | Private | First, Lewis | Feb 7, 1778 enlisted April-June 1778. |
| Clark/Clerk, John | Private | First State, Brown | Dec 1777-May 1778. |
| Clark/Clarke, John | Private | Second, Upshaw | Feb 14, 1778 drafted; April 1778; June 1778. |
| Clark, John | Private | Twelfth, Bowyer, T. | Dec 1777-Jan 1778; Feb-March 1778; April 1778 on guard; May 1778 confined. |
| Clark, John | Private | Fourteenth, Conway | Dec 1777 orderly to sick; Jan 1778 attending hospital; Feb 1778 on command; March-April 1778; May 1778 on duty; June 1778. |
| Clark, John | Corporal/ Sergeant | Fifteenth, Edmunds | Dec 1777; Jan 1778 promoted to Sergeant; Feb 1778 on command; March 1778; April 1778 sick in camp. |
| Clark/Clerk, Lewin | Private | Fifteenth, Hull | Dec 1777-Jan 1778 on guard; Feb-May 1778 sick present; June 1778 sick Yellow Spring. |
| Clark/Clarke, Thomas | Private | First State, Payne | Dec 1777-Jan 1778; Feb 1778 on guard; March-May 1778; June 1778 sick Valley Forge. |
| Clark, Thomas | Private | Twelfth, Ashby | Dec 26, 1777 missing. |
| Clark, Wm. | Private | Fifteenth, Edmunds | Dec 1777 sick absent. This man and the one below are probably the same individual. |
| Clark, Wm. | Private | Fifteenth, Wills | Jan-March 1778 sick absent; April 1778 Lancaster, May 1778 "waiting on the Clothier General as I have been informed at Lancaster." |
| Clarke, John | Private | First State, Camp | Dec 1777 on command; Jan-June 1778. |

| | | | |
|---|---|---|---|
| Clarke, John | Private | Second State, Taliaferro | Appears only on roll for March 15-April 15, 1778. |
| Clarke, Robert | Private | First State, Crump | April-June 1778. |
| Clarke/Clark, Thomas | Private | Seventh, Webb | Jan 1778; Feb 19, 1778 discharged. |
| Clarkson, William | Private | First State, Crump | March-June 1778. |
| Clary, John | Private | Second State, Lewis | March 15-May 1, 1778; May-June 1778. |
| Clay, John | Private | Fourteenth, Jones | Drafted Feb 12, 1778; May 1778; June 1778 on command. |
| Clay, Shadrach | Private | Second, Taylor, W. | Dec 1777-Jan 1778; Feb 21, 1778 discharged. |
| Claybrook, Anderson | Private | Seventh, Lipscomb | Dec 1777; Jan 31, 1778 discharged. |
| Clayton, Daniel | Sergeant | Sixth, Hockaday | Jan 1778. |
| Cleavland/ Cleaveland, John | Private | Fifteenth, Gregory | Feb 1778 joined; March-April sick in camp; June 1778. |
| Clements/ Clemens, Edmund/Edmd. | Private | Fifteenth | Dec 1777-Jan 1778 sick absent; March 1778 sick absent; April 1778 sick Lancaster; May 1778; June 1778 guard. |
| Clements, Mace | Surgeon's Mate | Third/ Seventh | June 1778 roll shows he served from Jan 1 to May 1, 1778, as temporary [    ]. Same man as below? |
| Clements, Mace | Surgeon | Fifteenth | Dec 1777-May 1778. |
| Clements, Stephen | Corporal | Second, Upshaw | Feb 14, 1778 drafted; April 1778; June 1778. |
| Clements, William | Sergeant | Second, Upshaw | Feb 14, 1778 drafted; April 1778; June 1778; July 1778 sick at Valley Forge. |
| Clements/ Clemmings, William | Private | Second State, Lewis | March 15-May 1, 1778; May-June 1778. |
| Clemons/ Clemmons, John | Private | First State, Hoffler | Dec 1777-June 1778. |

| Name | Rank | Company | Notes |
|---|---|---|---|
| Clemonts, Thomas | Private | Seventh, Jouett | Dec 1777 on furlough Virginia; Jan 1778 on furlough; Feb 12, 1778 discharged. |
| Clewley/ Clewly, Joseph | Private | First, Pelham | Dec 1777 sick hospital; Jan-Feb 1778 sick at Bethlehem; March 26, 1778 discharged. |
| Clifton, John | Private | Twelfth, Wallace | Dec 1777-March 1778 sent to hospital; April 1778 muster roll shows him as deceased on Feb 9, 1778. |
| Clifton, Thomas | Private | Seventh, Spencer/ Lipscomb | Feb 27, 1778 enlisted for 1 year; April 1778 Scout; May 1778 hospital; June 1778 in Lipscomb's Company; July 15, 1778 died. |
| Clifton, William | Private | Second, Harrison | Dec 1777-June 1778. |
| Clod/Clodd, Robert | Corporal | First State, Ewell, T. | Dec 1777-June 1778. |
| Clopton, David | Private | Sixth, Apperson | Feb 18, 1778 drafted; April-May 1778; June 1778 sick at Valley Forge. |
| Clunt/Clount, Jacob | Private | First State, Meriwether | Dec 1777-June 1778. |
| Cluverius/ Cleaveares, James | Corporal | Seventh, Young | Dec 1777-April 1778 on furlough; May 1778 discharged by Col. Richardson. |
| Clyne/Cline, John | Private | Twelfth, Ashby | Dec 1777; Jan 1778 on guard; March-April 1778; May 1778 sick in camp. |
| Coates/Coats, James | Private | Third, Peyton, J. | Dec 1777-Jan 1778; Feb 1778 baker to the Brigade; March 1778; April 30, 1778 died. |
| Coats, George | Private | Fourteenth, Marks | Jan 6, 1778 enlisted; Jan-May 1778 on furlough; June 1778 |
| Coats/Couts, Jacob | Private | Twelfth, Casey | Dec 1777 sent to hospital; Jan-March 1778 at hospital; April-May 1778. |
| Coats/Coates, William | Private | Second, Upshaw | Dec 1777 on furlough; Jan 1778; April 1778; June 1778 sick Coryell's Ferry. |
| Cobb, Howell | Private | Sixth, Avery | Dec 1777-Feb 1778; March 20, 1778 discharged. |

| Name | Rank | Company | Notes |
|---|---|---|---|
| Cobbitt, John | Corporal | Seventh, Lipscomb | Dec 1777-Jan 1778; Feb 8, 1778 discharged. |
| Cobbs, Samuel | 1st. Lt. | Second, Upshaw | April 1778. Oath at Valley Forge on May 12, 1778, witnessed by Muhlenberg. |
| Cochran/ Cocran, Henry | Private | Second State, Spiller | March 15-May 1, 1778; May 1778; June 1778 sick Valley Forge. |
| Cochran, Obediah | Private | Seventh, Fleming | Feb 13, 1778 enlisted; May 1778 sick present. |
| Cochran, Wm. | Private | First, Cunningham | Enlisted for 1 year; April 1778 under inoculation; May 1778 sick present; June 1778 sick Valley Forge. |
| Cochran, William | Sergeant | Seventh, Posey | Dec 1777-Jan 1778 on furlough. |
| Cochrom/ Cochran, Daniel | Private | Seventh, Lipscomb | Dec 1777 hospital; Jan 31, 1778 discharged. |
| Cochron/ Cochran, Samuel | Sergeant | Second State, Lewis | May 1778; June 1778 sick absent. |
| Cocke, Collin/Colin | 2nd. Lt. | Sixth, Fox | Dec 1777 recruiting; Jan 1778 recruiting in Virginia; Feb-May 1778 recruiting; June 1778 recruiting Virginia. |
| Cocke, John | Private | Seventh, Fleming | Dec 1777 on furlough Virginia; Jan 1778 on furlough; Feb 5, 1778 discharged. |
| Cocke, William | Ensign | First, Lawson | Dec 1777; Jan 5, 1778 cashiered. |
| Cocke, Wm. | Sergeant | Fifteenth, Harris | Sept 5, 1777 enlisted; Jan-Feb 1778; March 1778 on command; April 1778 sick; May 1778. |
| Cockram/ Cochran, Samuel | Private | Fourteenth, Conway | Dec 1777 hospital; Jan-Feb 1778 sick in hospital; March 1778 sick at Reading; April-May 1778; June 1778 sick in camp. |
| Cockram/ Cochran, William | Sergeant | Fourteenth, Conway | Dec 1777; Jan 1778 hospital; Feb 1778 sick in hospital; March 1778 sick at Reading; April-May 1778; June 1778 sick camp. |

| Name | Rank | Regiment | Service |
|---|---|---|---|
| Cockram/ Cochran, William | Sergeant | Fourteenth, Conway | Dec 1777; Jan 1778 hospital; Feb 1778 sick in hospital; March 1778 sick at Reading; April-May 1778; June 1778 sick camp. |
| Cockran, William | Private | First, Cunningham | Feb 1778 enlisted; April 1778 under inoculation; May 1778 sick present; June 1778 sick at Valley Forge. |
| Cockron, Obadiah | Private | Seventh/ Third, Fleming/ Heth | Feb 13, 1778 enlisted; April 1778 sick present; May 1778; June 1778 on guard; in Heth's Company. |
| Cofer/Coffer, George | Corporal | First State, Nicholas | Dec 1777-March 1778; April 1778 on command; May-June 1778. |
| Coghill, Frederick | Private | Second State, Dudley | March 15, 1778-May 1, 1778; May 1778; June 1778 sick absent. |
| Coghill, James | Private | Seventh, Spencer | Dec 1777-Jan 1778 hospital; Feb 20, 1778 discharged. |
| Coholon/ Coholn, John | Private | Seventh, Young | Dec 1777-Feb 1778 on furlough; March 1778 muster roll shows him discharged on March 1, payroll shows the discharge date as March 7. |
| Coins, Samuel | Private | Twelfth, Casey | Dec 1777. |
| Colbert/Colburt, John | Private | Seventh/ Third, Crockett/ Sayers | Dec 1, 1777; April 1778; May 1778 "in Room of Willm"; June 1778 in Sayers' Company. |
| Colden/Coldin, James | Private | First State, Hoffler | Dec 1777-June 1778. |
| Colden, Jonathan | Private | Fifteenth, Wills | Feb 19, 1778 enlisted; April 1778 sick present; May 16, 1778 dead. |
| Cole, Hamlin/ Hamblen | Sergeant | Second, Taylor, W. | Dec 1777-June 1778. |
| Cole/Coll, John | Private | First, Cunningham | Aug 1777 enlisted for 3 years; Dec 1777-Jan 1778; Feb-March 1778 on command; April 1778; May 1778 on command; June 28, 1778 dead. |

| Name | Rank | Regiment, Company | Service |
|---|---|---|---|
| Cole, John | 2nd. Lt. | Second, Jones | Dec 1777-June 1778. Oath at Valley Forge on May 12, 1778, witnessed by Muhlenberg. |
| Cole, John | Private | Seventh, Crockett | Dec 1777-Jan 1778 on furlough; April 1, 1778 deserted. |
| Cole, Walter King | Surgeon | First State | Jan-Feb 1778; March 1778 attending on a Sick Officer; April-June 1778 on furlough in Virginia. |
| Cole, William | Private/Drummer | Second, Taylor, W. | Dec 1777-Feb 1778; February promoted to Drummer; March-June 1778. |
| Coleman, Humphrey | Private | Seventh, Fleming | Nov 1777 Reading sick; Dec 1777 sick in hospital; Dec 23, 1777 died. |
| Coleman, Isham | Private | Sixth, Rose | Dec 1777-Jan 1778; Feb 19, 1778 discharged. |
| Coleman, Levi/Levy | Private | Second State, Dudley | March 15-May 1, 1778; May-June 1778. |
| Coleman, Naniad/Nat | Private | Third, Peyton, V. | Dec 1777; Jan 1778 on guard; Feb-April 1778; May 1778 sick present. |
| Coleman/Colman, Peter | Private | Second, Harrison | Dec 1777-Feb 1778; March 1778 deserted while on furlough. |
| Coleman, Richard | Private | Second State, Taliaferro | March 15-May 1, 1778; May-June 1778. |
| Coleman, Richard | 2nd. Lt. | Seventh, Young/Blackwell | Dec 1777-May 1778; Blackwell's Company in June. |
| Coleman, Samuel | Private | Fourteenth, Marks | Dec 1777; Jan 1778 on duty; March 1778 on command; May 1778 confined; June 1778 on command. |
| Coleman, Thomas | Private | Second State, Taliaferro | March 15-May 1, 1778; May-June 1778. |
| Coleman, Uriah/Uria | Private | Third, Peyton, J. | June-Aug 1778 sick at Valley Forge. |
| Coleman, William | Private | Fourteenth, Marks | Dec 1777 hospital; Jan 1778 sick in hospital; Feb 1778; March 24, 1778 discharged. |

| Name | Rank | Regiment | Service |
|---|---|---|---|
| Coleman, Wyatt | Ensign | First State, Camp | Dec 1777 sick in the Jersies; Jan 1778; Feb 1778 in ye country; March-June 1778. Oath at Valley Forge on May 12, 1778, witnessed by Muhlenberg. |
| Colley, Charles | Private | Third, Powell | Dec 23, 1777 discharged. |
| Colley, Maniard/Mainyard | Private | Fourteenth, Marks | Dec 1777 hospital; Jan 1778 on duty; Feb-April 1778; May 1778 confined; June 1778 sick Valley Forge. |
| Colley, William/Wm. | Private | Sixth, Avery | Dec 1777-Jan 1778; Feb 13, 1778 discharged. |
| Collier, James | Private | Second State, Taliaferro | Appears only on roll for March 15-April 15, 1778. |
| Collier, John | Private | Seventh/Third, Hill | Dec 1777-Jan 1778; April-June 1778. |
| Collier, Thomas | Sergeant | Second State, Taliaferro | March 15-May 1, 1778; May 1778. This man and the one below are probably the same individual. |
| Collier, Thomas | Quartermaster | Second State | June 1778. |
| Collier/Culliar, Wiat/Wiatt | Sergeant | Fourteenth, Reid | Dec 1777-Feb 1778; March 1778 sick present; April-June 1778. |
| Collier, William/Wm. | Private | Sixth, Garland | Dec 1777-Jan 1778; Feb 19, 1778 discharged. |
| Collins, Bartlet/Bartlett | Quartermaster and Ensign | Second State, Garnett | April 15-June 1, 1778; June 1778. Oath at Valley Forge on May 18, 1778, witnessed by Muhlenberg. |
| Collins, George | Private | First State, Ewell, T. | May 1778 on command; June 1778. |
| Collins, George | Private | Seventh, Hill | Dec 1777; Jan 31, 1778 discharged. |
| Collins, James | Private | Twelfth, Bowyer, T. | Dec 1777-Jan 1778; Feb 1778 on guard; March 1778 on command; April 1778 bullock guard; May 1778. |
| Collins/Collens, John | Private | First, Lawson | Dec 1777; Jan 1778 guard; Feb-March 1778; April 1778 on command; May-June 1778. |
| Collins, John | Private | Twelfth, Bowyer, T. | Jan-March 1778; April-May 1778 tayloring Lancaster. |

| Name | Rank | Regiment | Service |
|---|---|---|---|
| Collins, Julius | Private | Fifteenth, Gray | Dec 1777 on furlough; Jan-May 1778 on command; June 1778 waiting on Col. Innis. |
| Collins, Major | Private | Fifteenth, Gray | Dec 1777 dead. |
| Collins, Richard | Private | Second State, Spiller | March 15-May 1, 1778; May 1778; June 1778 sick Monmouth. |
| Collins/Collens, Thomas | Sergeant | First, Lawson | Dec 1777; Jan 1778 hospital; Feb-April 1778; May 1778 on guard; June 1778. |
| Collins, William | Private | Third, Briscoe | Dec 1777; Jan 1778 butcher; Feb-Junr 1778 butcher to the Brigade. |
| Collinsworth, Edmund/Edmond | Private | First State, Hoffler | Dec 1777-June 1778. |
| Collinsworth, John | Private | First State, Hoffler | May-June 1778. In June he was paid back to January 1778. |
| Collop/Callop, George | Private | Third, Mercer | Dec 1777; Jan 1778 on guard; Feb 1778 on command; March 15, 1778 deserted. |
| Colman, Samuel | Private | Twelfth, Wallace | Dec 1777-Jan 1778; Feb 1778 absent with leave; March 1778 on guard; April-May 1778. |
| Colquett, William | Private | Seventh, Fleming | Feb 12, 1778 enlisted; April 7, 1778 died. |
| Combs/Combes, John | Private | Twelfth, Casey | Dec 1777 sent to hospital; Jan-April 1778. |
| Combs, Michael | Private | Sixth, Fox | March-April 1778. |
| Combs, Richard | Private | Sixth, Fox | March-April 1778. |
| Comer, Augusteen/Augustin | Private | Twelfth, Casey | Dec 1777; Jan-Feb 1778 at hospital; Feb-May 1778. |
| Comer/Conner, Thomas | Private | Seventh, Lipscomb | Dec 1777; Jan 31, 1778 discharged. |
| Compton, Reuben | Private | Second, Taylor, W. | Dec 1777-Jan 1778; Feb 21, 1778 discharged. |
| Coneley/Conley, Philip | Private | Twelfth, Madison | Dec 1777-Jan 1778; Feb 1778 hospital; March 1778 on guard; April 1778; June 6, 1778 died. |

| Name | Rank | Regiment | Notes |
|---|---|---|---|
| Connant, John | Private | Fifteenth, Edmunds | Dec 1777. This man and the one below are probably the same individual. |
| Connant/Cannant, John | Private | Fifteenth, Wills | Jan-Feb 1778; March 1778 sick present; April-May 1778. |
| Connell, Thomas | Private | Sixth, West | Feb 20, 1778 enlisted; April-June 1778. |
| Conner, Daniel | Private | Sixth, West | May-June 1778 |
| Conner/Connor, John | Private | First State, Meriwether | Dec 1777-June 1778. |
| Conner, John | Private | Seventh, Posey | Feb 28, 1777 enlisted; April 1778; May 1778 on guard. |
| Conner, Michael | Private | First, Lawson | Dec 1777 sick Princeton; Jan-Feb 1778 sick absent; March-April 1778; June 1778 sick at Lancaster. |
| Conner/Coner, Patrick | Private | Seventh/Third, Posey/Sayers | Dec 1777 on furlough; Jan 1778; April-May 1778; June 1778 in Sayers's Company. |
| Conner, Phillip/Phill | Private/Corporal/Sergeant | Third, Briscoe | Dec 1777-Jan 1778 on furlough; Feb-April 1778; April promoted to Corporal; May-June 1778; June promoted to Sergeant. |
| Conner, William | Private | Third, Peyton, J. | Dec-Jan 1778; Feb 5, 1778 enlisted. Apparently reenlisted. |
| Connery, John | Fifer | Sixth, Rose | Dec 31, 1777 reenlisted in Light Horse. |
| Connolly, Andrew | Private | First State, Brown | Dec 1777-May 1778; June 1778 sick at Valley Forge. |
| Connor/Conner, Laurence | Private | Twelfth, Wallace | Dec 1777-May 1778. |
| Connor/Conner, Owen/Owin | Private | Fourteenth, Winston | Dec 1777; Jan 1778 sick present; Feb-May 1778; June 1778 sick Coryell Ferry. |
| Connors, James | Private | Twelfth, Wallace | March 10, 1778 joined; March-May 1778. |
| Consolver, John/Jno. | Private | Sixth, Avery | Jan-Feb 1778 absent with leave; March-June 1778. |
| Conway/Coniway, George | Private | Twelfth, Bowyer, T. | Dec 1777; Jan 1778 on detachment; Feb 5, 1778 missing. |

| | | | |
|---|---|---|---|
| Conway, Henry | Captain | Fourteenth, Conway | Dec 1777-Jan 1778; Feb-April 1778 on furlough; May-June 1778 on command. |
| Conway, James | Private | Fourteenth, Lambert | Dec 1777 hospital; Jan 1778; Feb 8, 1778 discharged. |
| Conway, Joseph | Ensign | Fourteenth, Conway | Jan 1778 on command; Feb-March 1778; April 1778 on command; May-June 1778. Oath at Valley Forge on May 18, 1778, witnessed by Muhlenberg. |
| Cook, Giles | Cadet | Second State, Taliaferro | Appears only on roll for March 15-April 15, 1778. |
| Cook, Henry | Private | Seventh, Hill | April 1778 on furlough Virginia; May 1778 deserted. |
| Cook, John | Private | Second, Upshaw | Feb 14, 1778 drafted; April 1778; June-July 1778 sick Valley Forge. |
| Cook, John | Private | Twelfth, Wallace | Dec 1777; Jan 23, 1778 deserted; May 1778. |
| Cook, Joseph | Private | First, Taylor | Dec 1777-Jan 1778. |
| Cook, Lewis | Private | Seventh, Spencer | Dec 22, 1777 enlisted in Light Horse. |
| Cooke/Cook, John | Private | First State, Camp | Dec 1777 sick Meeting House; Jan-Feb 1778 sick absent. June 1778 payroll reads "Struck out of 2 last M. Rolls Agreeable to Orders. Therefore omitted in 2 last P. Rolls." |
| Cooke, Henry | Private | Seventh, Hill | Dec 1777-Jan 1778 on furlough. |
| Coony/Cooney, Mat/Matthew | Private | Twelfth, Bowyer, M. | Dec 1777-Jan 1778; Feb 1778 on command; March-April 1778; May 1778 on command. |
| Cooper, Charles | Private | Fourteenth, Winston | Dec 1777 sick in hospital; Jan 1778 sick at Reading; Feb 1778; March 1778 S. H.; April-June 1778. |
| Cooper, Ephraim | Private | Fourteenth, Thweatt | Dec 1777 sick in hospital; Jan 1Sa778; Feb 1778 sick present; March-June 1778. |

| Name | Rank | Company | Notes |
|---|---|---|---|
| Cooper, Hillary/Hilrey | Private/ Corporal | First, Lewis | Dec 1777-Feb 1778; March 1778 fatigue; April promoted to corporal; April 1778-June 1778. |
| Cooper, Peter | Private | Twelfth, Madison | Dec 1777; Jan 1778 Generals guard; Feb 1778 sick in hospital; March-April 1778. |
| Cooper, Reubin/Reuben | Sergeant Major | Fourteenth, Winston | Dec 1777-June 1778. |
| Cooper, Richard | Private | Seventh/ Third, Webb/ Young | Enlisted for 3 years; Jan-Feb 1778 on furlough; April-May 1778; June 1778 in Young's Company. |
| Cooper, Samuel/Saml. | Ensign | Fifteenth, Gray | Dec 1777-May 1778. |
| Cooper, Sterling | Private | Fourteenth, Winston | Feb 17, 1778 enlisted; April-June 1778. |
| Cooper, Thomas | Private | Fourteenth, Reid | Sept 1, 1777 enlisted; Dec 1777 on command at York; March-April 1778 orderly Little York; May-June 1778 sick hospital Little York. |
| Copin/Cowpen, John | Sergeant | Third, Peyton, J. | Dec 1777-Jan 1778; Feb 9, 1778 deserted; April-June 1778. |
| Coppage, John | Private | Third, Peyton, V./ Peyton, J. | Dec 1777 on furlough Virginia; Jan-March 1778 on furlough; April 1778 sick Virginia; May 1778 sick absent; June 1778 sick at Valley Forge, in J. Peyton's Company. |
| Corbet, John | Private | Seventh, Crockett | Dec 1, 1777 enlisted "in room of Willaim Strawton, deserter". |
| Cord/Coard, Abraham/ Abram | Corporal/ Sergeant | Seventh, Spencer | Enlisted for 3 years; Dec 1777-Jan 1778 on furlough in Virginia; April-May 1778; May 1778 promoted to Sergeant |
| Core, Ralph | Private | Sixth, Garland/ Rose | April-June 1778. In April only he is listed in both Garland's and Rose's companies. |
| Corkin/Corken, John | Private | Second, Calmes | Dec 1777-May 1778; June 1778 sick at Coryell's Ferry. |
| Corn, Jesse | Private | Seventh, Jouett | Dec 1777-Jan 1778; Feb 7, 1778 discharged. |

| | | | |
|---|---|---|---|
| Corn, Peter | Private | Seventh, Jouett | Dec 1777-Jan 1778; Feb 7, 1778 discharged. |
| Cornelius, George | Private | First State, Camp | Dec 1777 sick in hospital; Dec 1777 payroll shows he died on Dec 16, 1777. |
| Cornelus/Cornelius, Jese/Jesse | Private | Twelfth, Bowyer, T. | Dec 1777-April 1778 on furlough; May 1778; June-July 1778 sick at Valley Forge. Died about Aug 20, 1778. |
| Corner, William | Private | Third, Peyton, J. | Dec 1777-March 1778. |
| Corriwell, Luke | Private | Twelfth, Madison | Dec 1777 sick in hospital. |
| Corse, Charles William/Wm. | Sergeant | Fifteenth, | Dec 1777-Feb 1778 sick absent; March 19, 1778 died. |
| Cosby, Charles | Private | Third, Briscoe | May 1778. |
| Cosby, Hickason/Hick | Sergeant | Third, Peyton, V. | Dec 1777 on furlough Virginia Jan-March 1778 on furlough; April 1778 on furlough Virginia; May 1778 transferred in the Artillery Virginia. |
| Cosby, Thomas | Private | Third, Powell | Dec 23, 1777 discharged. |
| Cotton, Frederick/Fredk. | Fifer | Fifteenth, Edmunds/Gregory | Dec 1777-April 1778; May 1778 sick absent; June 1778 in Gregory's Company, sick Yellow Springs. |
| Cotton/Cotten, Michael | Private | Third, Peyton, V./Peyton, J. | Dec 1777-Jan 1778 sick in hospital; Feb 1778 sick absent; March-April 1778; May-June 1778 on guard; June 1778 on J. Peyton's Company. |
| Cottrill/Cotrill, Richard | Private | Twelfth, Bowyer, M. | Dec 1777 in hospital; Jan 1778 sick in camp; Feb 1778; March 1778 on command; April 1778 on two weeks command; May 1778. |
| Coulter/Coalter, Uriah | Private | Second, Jones/Hoomes | Dec 1777-June 1778. |

| Name | Rank | Regiment/Company | Notes |
|---|---|---|---|
| Coupland, John | Private | Seventh/ Third, Fleming/ Heth | Feb 10, 1778 enlisted; April 1778 sick present; May 1778; June 1778 in Heth's Company. |
| Cousins/ Cussins, Austin | Private | Second State, Bernard | April-May 1778; June 1778 sick Valley Forge. |
| Cousins, James | Private | Second State, Lewis | March 15-May 1, 1778; May-June 1778. |
| Cousins, John | Private | Second, Taylor, W. | Dec 1777-March 1778. |
| Courtney/ Coatney, Philip | Sergeant | First, Lawson | Dec 1777 orderly headquarters; January-June 1778. |
| Coventry, William | Drum Major | Twelfth | Dec 1777-May 1778. |
| Covington/ Covonton, William | Sergeant | Third, Peyton, V. | Dec 1777; Jan 1778 on command; Feb 10, 1778 discharged. |
| Cowan/Cowen, Henry | Private | Fourteenth, Lambert | Dec 1777-March 1778 hospital. |
| Cowherd, Francis | 1st. Lt./ Adjutant | Second, Taylor, F. | Dec 1777; Jan-March 1778; April-June 1778. He appears as Adjutant in Jan-March 1778, and as 1st. Lt. of Taylor's Company for the other months. Oath at Valley Forge on May 12, 1778, witnessed by Muhlenberg. |
| Cowley/Cowler, William | Private | Seventh/ Third, Fleming/ Heth | Feb 13, 1778 enlisted; April 1778 sick present; May 1778; June 1778 in Heth's Company. |
| Cowling/ Cawling, George | Private | Third, Blackwell | Feb 18, 1778 drafted; April-May 1778; June 1778 sick Princetown. |
| Cox, George | Private | Fourteenth, Reid | Sept 13, 1777 drafted; May 1778 sick present; June 1778 sick Valley Forge. |
| Cox, Henry | Private | First, Cunningham | Feb 14, 1778 enlisted for 1 year; April 1778 under inoculation; May 1778 sick present; June 1778 sick at Valley Forge. |

| | | | |
|---|---|---|---|
| Cox, Jeremiah | Drummer | Second, Taylor, F. | Dec 1777 on furlough; Jan-June 1778. |
| Cox, Presley | Private | Second, Upshaw | Dec 1777. |
| Cox, Radford/ Redford | Corporal | Fifteenth, Harris | Jan 1778; Feb 1778 on guard; March-April 1778; May 1778 sick near camp. |
| Cox/Coxe, Wm. | Corporal/ Sergeant | Fifteenth, Harris | Sept 5, 1777 enlisted; Jan 1778 on command; Feb 1778; March 1778 promoted to Sergeant; April-May 1778. |
| Cox, Samuel | Private | Third, Peyton, V./ Peyton, J. | Dec 1777 on furlough in Virginia; Jan-March 1778 on furlough; April-May 1778; June 1778 he is in J. Peyton's Company. |
| Cox, William | Private | Second, Willis | Dec 1777 muster roll shows he deserted, but the payroll shows full pay for the month. Dec 1777-June 1778. |
| Cox, William | Corporal | Fifteenth, Harris | Jan 1778 on command. |
| Coxson, Joseph | Private | Second, Sanford | Dec 1777. |
| Coyle, John | Private | First, Lawson | Dec 1777; Jan-Feb 1778 sick hospital; March 1778 on guard; April-May 1778; June 1778 sick at Valley Forge. |
| Craddock, Robert/Robt. | Sergeant | Fifteenth, Foster/Gray | Dec 1777-Feb 1778; March 1778 sick absent; April-May 1778. |
| Craddock, Henry | Private | Fifteenth, Foster/Gray | Dec 1777-Jan 1778 on guard; Feb 1778; March 1778 sick in camp; April 1778 sick present; May 1778. |
| Craft, John | Private | First State, Nicholas | Dec 1777-Jan 1778; Feb 1778 on guard; March 1778 on command; April-June 1778. |
| Crafton, James | Private | Seventh/ Third, Hill | Feb 16, 1778 enlisted; June 1778. |
| Crafton, Richard | Private | Seventh, Lipscomb | Dec 1777 hospital; Jan 31, 1778 discharged. |

| Name | Rank | Regiment/Company | Service |
|---|---|---|---|
| Cragan/Crigon, James | Private | Seventh/Third, Crockett/Sayers | Dec 1777-May 1778; June 1778 sick on march; in Sayers' Company. |
| Cragwall, James | Private | Fourteenth, Overton | Dec 1777 sick in country; Jan 1778 sick absent; Feb 1778; March 20, 1778 died. |
| Craig/Cragg, John | Private | Fourteenth, Lambert | Dec 1777-Feb 1778 hospital; March-May 1778 on guard; June 1778. |
| Craig/Crag, Thomas | Sergant Major | Fourteenth | Jan 16, 1778 appointed; Jan-Feb 1778. |
| Craig, Thomas | Sergeant | Fourteenth, Marks | Dec 1777; Jan 1778 hospital; Feb-June 1778. |
| Crain, Aaron/Aron | Private | Seventh, Spencer/Lipscomb | Feb 11, 1778 enlisted for 1 year; May 1778; June 1778 in Lipscomb's Company. |
| Crain/Craine, James | 2nd. Lt. | Fifteenth, Hull | Dec 1777-March 1778 on furlough; April-May 1778. |
| Crain, Thomas | Private | Seventh, Spencer/Lipscomb | Feb 13, 1778 enlisted for 1 year; May 1778; June 1778 in Lipscomb's Company. |
| Crane/Crain, Joshua | Private | Seventh/Third, Hill | Dec 1777-Jan 1778 on furlough; April 1778; May 1778 on command; June 1778. |
| Cranmore, John | Private | Twelfth, Waggener | Dec 1777-March 1778 hospital; April 1778 deserted from the hospital. |
| Crawford, Andrew | Private | Seventh, Posey | Dec 1777-Jan 1778 in Rifle Battn; Feb 24, 1778 discharged. |
| Craton/Crayton, Wm. | Private | Fifteenth, Harris | Jan 1778 sick; Feb-March 1778; April-May 1778 sick present. |
| Crawford, John | 2nd. Lt. | Second, Willis | Dec 1777-June 1778. |
| Crawford, John | Sergeant | Seventh, Posey | Dec 1777-Jan 1778 in Rifle Battn.; Feb 24, 1778 discharged. |
| Crawford/Crewford, Peter | Fife Major/Private | Seventh, Crockett/Briscoe | Dec 1777-Jan 1778 on furlough; April 1, 1778 reduced to Private. In June he appears in Briscoe's Company. |

| | | | |
|---|---|---|---|
| Crawley, James | Private | Twelfth, Madison | Dec 1777 B. guard; Jan 1778 on bullock guard; Feb 1778 on command; March 1778 on guard; April 1778 on command. |
| Cray, Thomas | Private | Seventh, Young | Dec 1777; Jan 1778 on guard; Feb 7, 1778 discharged. |
| Creamour/ Cramour, Wm. | Private | Fifteenth, Grimes | Dec 1777-Jan 1778 on guard; Feb-March 1778 on command; April 1778 on bullock guard; May 1778 sick present; June 1778 sick Valley Forge. |
| Credille/ Criddile, Moses | Sergeant | Sixth, Rose | Feb 13, 1778 drafted; April-June 1778. |
| Creed, Thomas | Drill Sergeant | Twelfth | Dec 1777-May 1778. |
| Creel/Creell, John | Private | Twelfth, Waggener | Dec 1777-Feb 1778 hospital; March 1778; April 10, 1778 discharged. |
| Creighton/ Creghton, Daniel | Sergeant | Sixth, Hockaday | Dec 1777; Jan 1778 discharged. |
| Crenshaw, Daniel | Private | Sixth, Hockaday | Feb 17, 1778 drafted; April-June 1778. |
| Crenshaw, Nathaniel/ Nathanial | Private | Sixth, Hockaday | Feb 17, 1778 drafted; April-June 1778. |
| Crews, Joseph | Private | Fourteenth, Reid | Aug 14, 1777 enlisted; Jan 1778 payroll "never was drawn for before." |
| Crews, Obediah | Private | Fourteenth, Reid | Aug 11, 1777 enlisted; Jan 1778; Feb 1778; March 1778 on command; April-May 1778; June 1778 left at Coryell's Ferry. |
| Crickmore/ Creekmore, William | Private | First State, Hoffler | Dec 1777-May 1778; June 1778 sick absent. |
| Criddle/Creddle, James | Private | First, Cunningham | Feb 14, 1778 enlisted for 1 year; April 1778 under inoculation; May-June 1778. |
| Cridenton/ Crodinton, Christopher | Private | First State, Brown | Dec 1777-Jan 1778; Feb 1778 died. |
| Crisley, Henry/Heny | Private | Twelfth, Ashby | Dec 1777-Jan 1778; March 1778 confined; April-May 1778. |

| Name | Rank | Regiment | Notes |
|---|---|---|---|
| Crittenden, John | 2nd. Lt. | Fifteenth, Wills | Feb-May 1778. |
| Crockett, Anthony | Private | Seventh, Posey | Dec 1777-Jan 1778 on furlough; Feb 24, 1778 discharged. |
| Crockett, Joseph | Captain | Seventh, Crockett | Dec 1777-Jan 1778 on furlough; Feb-May 1778. |
| Crodey, John | Private | Seventh, Posey | Dec 1777-Jan 1778 in Rifle Battn; Feb 22, 1778 discharged. |
| Croker, William | Drum Major | Sixth, Avery | Dec 1777-Jan 1778; Feb 8, 1778 discharged. |
| Cromwell/Crumwell, Joseph | Private | Third, Peyton, V. | Dec 1777 on command with Col. Morgan; Jan 1778 with Col. Morgan. |
| Crone/Crow, Thomas | Private | Second, Parker | April 1778. |
| Crook, James | Private | Fifteenth, Wills | May 1778 muster roll reads "Empld. as a waggoner at Williamsburg have heard he was discharged." |
| Crook/Crooke, Jonathan | Private | Third, Blackwell | Dec 1777-March 1778 on furlough; April-June 1778. |
| Crook, Joseph | Sergeant | Second, Jones | Dec 1777-June 1778. |
| Crook, Richd. | Private | Fifteenth, Wills | July 30, 1777 enlisted; Feb 1778 muster roll shows he deserted on September 8, 1777. |
| Cropper, John | Major | Third | Dec 1777 sick Bethlehem; Jan 1778 on command; Feb-April 1778 |
| Crosby/Cozby, Charles | Private | Seventh, Crockett | Dec 1777-Jan 1778 sick in hospital; Feb-May 1778. |
| Crosly, Thomas | Private | Second, Willis | Dec 1777 hospital. |
| Cross, Charles | Private | Fourteenth, Winston | Dec 1777 on command; Jan-March 1778. |
| Cross, John | Private | Twelfth, Casey | Dec 15, 1777 deserted; April 1778 supposed to be deserted and since joined; April-May 1778. |
| Cross, Richard | Corporal | Fourteenth, Jones | Jan 1778 on duty; Feb-May 1778. |

| | | | |
|---|---|---|---|
| Crossett/ Croswit, Thomas | Private | First State, Lee/ Meriwether | Dec 1777 sick; Jan-Feb 1778 sick absent; March-May 1778; June 1778 sick absent. |
| Croston/Croson, Gustavus/ Gustavos | Private | First State, Hamilton | Dec 1777-May 1778; June 1778 sick absent. |
| Crouch, Jacob | Private | Fourteenth, Reid | April 28, 1777 enlisted; Jan 1778 sick at York; Feb 1778 sick absent; March 1, 1778 died. |
| Croucher/ Croutcher, James | Private | Second, Upshaw | Dec 1777-Jan 1778. |
| Crow, Dennis | Private | Third, Peyton, V. | Dec 1777-on command with Col. Morgan; Jan 1778 with Col. Morgan. |
| Crow, John | Private | Third, Peyton, V. | Dec 1777 on command with Col. Morgan; Jan 1778 with Col. Morgan. |
| Crow, Robert | Private | Seventh/ Third, Crockett/ Sayers | Feb 8, 1778 enlisted; April-June 1778 waggoner; June 1778 in Sayers' Company. |
| Crow, Thomas/Thos. | Private | First, Mennis | Feb 7, 1778 enlisted; April-June 1778. |
| Crow, Thomas | Private | Second, Sanford | Dec 1777 hospital; Jan-Feb 1778; March 24, 1778 deserted. |
| Crowden/ Crowdan, Abraham/ Abrihim | Private | First State, Ewell, T./ Nicholas | April 1778; May 1778 transferred to Nicholas' Company; June 1778 sick Valley Forge. |
| Crowder, Matthew | Private | Second, | Dec 1777 hospital; Jan-April 1778; June 1778 hospital. From April on he appears in Parker's company. |
| Crowder, Sterling | Private | Fourteenth, Reid | Dec 1777-May 1778; June 1778 on guard. |
| Crowley, David | Private | Second, Calmes | Dec 1777-June 1778. |
| Croxton/ Crexton, John | Private | Seventh/ Third, Webb/ Young | Enlisted for 3 years; Jan-Feb 1778 on furlough; April-June 1778 on command Lancaster; June 1778 in Young's Company. |

| Name | Rank | Regiment/Company | Service |
|---|---|---|---|
| Crump, Abner | Captain | First State, Crump | Dec 1777-June 1778. Oath at Valley Forge on May 12, 1778, witnessed by Muhlenberg. |
| Crump, Antipas/Antipass | Corporal | Second State, Quarles | April-June 1778. |
| Crump, Benjamin | Private | First State, Lee | Dec 1777 sick; Jan-Feb 1778 sick at Yellow Springs; March 1778 Red Lion hospital; April-May 1778; June 1778 sick absent. |
| Crump, Jesse | Private | Seventh, Lipscomb | Dec 22, 1777 enlisted in the Light Horse. |
| Crump/Crumps, John | Private | First State, Payne | Dec 1777-Jan 1778 sick George Town, Feb 1778 sick absent. |
| Crump, John | Private | Seventh, Lipscomb | Feb 14, 1778 enlisted; April 1778; May 1778 sick in camp; June 1778 hospital. |
| Crumpton, Thomas | Private | Fourteenth, Winston | Feb 17, 1778 drafted; May-June 1778. |
| Cruse/Scrus, John | Private | Fifteenth, Wills | Dec 1777-Feb 1778 on furlough; March-May 1778. |
| Crutchfield/Cruchfield, John | Private | Fourteenth, Jones | Drafted Feb 12, 1778; April-May 1778. |
| Crute/Cruit, John | Sergeant Major | Fifteenth | Dec 1777-May 1778. |
| Crutchfield/Cunkerville, John | Private | Seventh/Third, Webb/Young | April 1778; June 1778 in Young's Company. |
| Crutchfield, Cruchfield, Lewis | Private | Fourteenth, Jones | Drafted Feb 12, 1778; April-May 1778. |
| Crutchfield/Cruchfield, Ralph/Ralf | Private | First State, Lee | Dec 1777 sick; Jan-Feb 1778 at Yellow Springs Hospital; March 1778 at Red Lyon Hospital; April-June 1778. |
| Crutchfield, Stapleton | Private | Fourteenth, Overton | Dec 1777-April 1778; May 1778 on duty; June 1778. |
| Cuff see Goph | | | |
| Culbertson, Samuel | Surgeon | Twelfth | Dec 1777-April 1778; April 21, 1778 superseded. |
| Cullin/Cullins, John | Corporal | Third, Peyton, J. | Dec 1777-Jan 1778 wagoner; Feb 5, 1778 discharged. |

| Name | Rank | Company | Notes |
|---|---|---|---|
| Cumbo/Cambow, Daniel | Private | First, Cunningham | March 1777 enlisted for 3 years; Dec 1777-March 1778 on furlough; April 1778; May 1778 sick hospital; June 1778. |
| Cumbo/Cumlio, Michael | Private | Sixth, Fox | Sept 5, 1777 enlisted; March-April 1778; May-June 1778 at the ys hospital. |
| Cumbo/Cuambo, Peter | Private | Third, Lee/Peyton, J. | Feb 14, 1778 enlisted; April-May 1778; June 1778, in J. Peyton's Company; |
| Cumbo/Cumlio, Richard | Private | Sixth, Fox | Sept 5, 1777 enlisted; March-April 1778; May-June 1778 at the Yellow Springs hospital. |
| Cummerford/Cummrford, James | Private | Twelfth, Waggener | Dec 24, 1777 deserted. |
| Cummings/Cummins, Alexander/Alex. | Captain | First, Cummings | Dec 1777; March 1778 on command; April on furlough. |
| Cummins, Daniel | Private | Twelfth, Waggener | Dec 1777-May 1778. |
| Cummings, George | Private | Second State, Lewis | May-June 1778. |
| Cummings, Thomas | Private | Second State, Lewis | March 15-May 1, 1778; May-June 1778. |
| Cunningham, Jacob | Private | First, Cunningham | Feb 12, 1778 enlisted for 1 year; April 1778 under inoculation; May 1778 sick present; June 1778 sick at Valley Forge. |
| Cunningham., Nathaniel | Private/Sergeant | First, Cunningham | Enlisted for 3 years; May 1778; June 1778 he is shown as a sergeant. |
| Cunningham, Valentine/Vall | Private | First, Cunningham | Feb 13, 1778 enlisted for 1 year; April 1778 under inoculation; May-June 1778. |

| Name | Rank | Regiment, Company | Notes |
|---|---|---|---|
| Cunningham, William | Captain | First, Cunningham | Dec 1777 in Virginia; Jan 1778 on furlough in Virginia; Feb-March 1778 on furlough; April-May 1778; June 1778 in Virginia recruiting. Oath at Valley Forge on May 28, 1778, witnessed by Muhlenberg. |
| Curdess, Abram | Private | First State, Ewell, T. | April-May 1778. |
| Curl/Carrell, Dudly | Private | Twelfth, Vause | Dec 1777 sent sick with baggage; Jan-Feb 1778 sick Reading; March 3, 1778 died. |
| Curle, Thomas | Private | Fifteenth, Edmunds | March 5, 1778 died. |
| Curle/Cronle, John/Jno | Private | Sixth, Massie | Dec 1777; Jan 1778 roll shows he was discharged on Feb 16, 1778. |
| Currol/Carrell, James | Private | Twelfth, Vause | Dec 1777-March 1778 sick Mendum. |
| Curry/Currile, Richard | Private | Seventh/Third, Young | Feb 16, 1778 enlisted; April 1778 sick present; May-June 1778 |
| Curtin/Curtain, Joseph | Private | Second, Jones | Dec 1777-June 1778. |
| Curtis, Charles | Private | Second State, Taliaferro | March 15-May 1, 1778; May-June 1778. |
| Curtis/Curtice, James | Drummer | Fifteenth, Gray | Dec 1777-May 1778. |
| Curtis/Curtice, Thomas | Private | Third, Peyton, V./Peyton, J. | March 27, 1778 drafted; April-May 1778; June 1778 sick at Valley Forge, in J. Peyton's Company. |
| Curtis/Curtice, Wm. | Private | Fifteenth, Hull | Dec 1777 sick absent; Jan 1778 sick in hospital; Feb-March 1778 sick absent; April-May 1778 sick hospital Yellow Springs. |
| Cuts/Cutts, Zachariah/Zackh. | Fifer | First, Cunningham | Dec 1777-Feb 1778 sick at Trenton. |
| Cyphers/Syphers, Andrew | Private | Twelfth, Waggener | Dec 1777-March 1778 hospital; April 1778; May 1778 on command. |

| | | | |
|---|---|---|---|
| Cyrus/Syrus, Bartholomew/ Barthw. | Musician | Fifteenth, Harris | Feb-May 1778. |
| Dabney, Charles | Lt. Col. | Second State | May-June 1778. |
| Dagger/Daggar, Peter | Private | Twelfth, Casey | Dec 1777 sent to hospital; Jan-March 1778 at hospital; April 1778 supposed to be deserted. |
| Dagnal, Stephen | Private | Seventh, Fleming | Dec 1777 on furlough Virginia; Jan 1778 Virginia; Deb 17, 1778 discharged. |
| Dalby, William | Private | Fourteenth, Winston | Feb 17, 1778 drafted; May-June 1778. |
| Dale, Daniel/Danl. | Private | Fifteenth, Gregory | Dec 1777-May 1778 hospital; June 1778 unknown where. |
| Daley, Wm. | Private | Fifteenth, Gregory | June 1778 sick Valley Forge. |
| Dallis, James | Corporal | Second, Harrison | Dec 1777. |
| Dame, John | Private | Seventh, Hill | Dec 1777-Jan 1778; Feb 2, 1778 discharged. |
| Damron/ Dameron, John | Private | Second State, Dudley | March 15, 1778-May 1, 1778; May 1778; June 1778 sick absent. |
| Damwood, Boston | Private | Seventh, Posey | Dec 1777-Jan 1778 on furlough; Feb 22, 1778 discharged. |
| Dangerfield, William | Private | First State, Hoffler | Dec 1777-June 1778. |
| Daniel, Christopher | Private | Fourteenth, Jones | Jan 1778 on command; Feb 1778; March 1778 sick present; May 1778 sick present. |
| Daniel, George | Corporal | Second, Willis | Dec 20, 1777 deserted. |
| Daniel, John | Private | First State, Crump | April-June 1778. |
| Daniel, Oliver | Corporal | Seventh, Webb | Jan 1778 hospital; Feb 3, 1778 discharged. |
| Daniel, Richard | Private | Fifteenth, Hull | April 1778; May 1778 sick present; June 9, 1778 deserted. |
| Danks, William | Private | Fifteenth, Hull | Feb-March 1778 sick present; April 25, 1778 died. |
| Dansford, William | Private | First, Mennis | June 1778 on furlough. |

| | | | |
|---|---|---|---|
| Darnold/ Darnald, Adam/Addam | Private | Third, Blackwell | Feb 18, 1778 drafted; May 1778 joined since last muster; June 1778. |
| Datring/Detran, Jacob | Private | Seventh/ Third, Crockett/ Sayers | Dec 1777-Jan 1778 on furlough; April 1778 sick in Virginia; May 1778; June 1778 sick Virginia, in Sayers' Company. |
| Daubins/ Dobbins, William | Private | Seventh, Webb | Dec 1777-Jan 1778; Feb 2, 1778 discharged. |
| Daulen, Moses | Sergeant | Third, Peyton, J. | Dec 23, 1777 Reenlisted in the Light Horse. |
| Davenport/ Deavenport, Claiborne/ Clayborn | Private | Seventh/ Third, Fleming/ Heth | Dec 1777 on furlough Virginia; Jan-March 1778 on furlough; April-May 1778; June 1778 on Heth's Company. |
| Davenport/ Devenport, Joell/Joel | Private | Fourteenth, Jones | Dec 1777; Jan 1778 on guard; Feb-April 1778; May 1778 sick present; June 1778. |
| Davenport/ Devenport, Joseph | Private | Fourteenth, Lambert | Dec 1777-Jan 1778 hospital; Feb 1778; March 1778 hospital; April-May 1778; June 1778 on furlough. |
| Davenport/ Devenport, Moses | Fifer | Fourteenth, Lambert | Dec 1777 sick in hospital; Jan 1778; Feb-March 1778 hospital; April-May 1778. |
| Davidson/ Davison, Edward/Edwd, | Private | Sixth, Hockaday | Jan 1778; Feb 10, 1778 discharged. |
| Davidson, Philemon/ Philmon | Private | Seventh/ Third, Fleming/ Heth | Feb 19, 1778 enlisted; April 1778 sick present; May 1778; June 1778 sick Valley Forge, in Heth's Company. |
| Davidson, William | Private | Third, Blackwell | Dec 1777-April 1778 on furlough; May 1778; July 1, 1778 deserted. |
| David, Abram | Private | First State, Hamilton | Dec 1777. |
| Davice, Thomas | Private | Seventh, Posey | Dec 1777-Jan 1778 on furlough. |
| Davie/Davey, Peter | Quartermaster | Fourteenth | Dec 1777-Feb 1778; April-June 1778. |

| | | | |
|---|---|---|---|
| Davies, William | Lieut. Col./ Colonel | Fifth/ Fourteenth | March 20, 1778 promoted to Colonel of the Fourteenth Virginia; April-June 1778. Oath at Valley Forge on May 12, 1778, witnessed by Muhlenberg. |
| Davis, Asolam | Private | Fifteenth, Gray | Feb 10, 1778 drafted; April 1778 under inoculation; May 1778. |
| Davis, Benjamin | Private | Twelfth, Ashby | Dec 1777-Jan 1778 sick in hospital; March-May 1778; June-Aug 1778 sick Valley Forge. |
| Davis, George | Private | Seventh, Lipscomb | Feb 14, 1778 enlisted for 1 year; April-June 1778 |
| Davis, Humphrey | Private | Second, Upshaw | Dec 1777 hospital; Jan 1778. |
| Davis, Humphrey/ Humphris | Private | Second State, Lewis | June 1778; July 1778 payroll states he was omitted from the 15th of March to the 1st of July, and he was then paid for 4 ½ months. |
| Davis/Davies, Ishmael/Isml. | Private | Second, Taylor, W. | Dec 1777-April 1778; May 19, 1778 died. |
| Davis, Jacob | Private | Second, Taylor, W. | Dec 1777-Jan 1778; Feb 5, 1778 discharged. |
| Davis, Jacob | Private | Seventh, Webb | Jan 1778 Feb 5, 1778 discharged. |
| Davis, James | Private | First, Lawson | Dec 1777 sick Princeton; Jan-Feb 1778 sick hospital; March 1778 "time expired but not discharged"; April 1778 "Omitted March April May & June 1778 whilst in Va. & now dischd." |
| Davis, James | Private | First, Mennis | Dec 1777-March 1778 on furlough; April-June 1778. |
| Davis, James | Private | Second, Willis | Dec 1777-June 1778. |
| Davis, James | 2nd. Lt. | Third, Powell/ Lee/ Peyton, J. | Dec 1777; Jan 1778 on command; February 1778; March 1778 on picket; April 1778; May 1778 in Lee's Company; June 1778 in J. Peyton's Company. |
| Davis, James | Private | Third, Powell | Jan 1778 on command; March 1778 on picquette |

90

| Name | Rank | Regiment/Company | Dates |
|---|---|---|---|
| Davis, Jeremiah/Jerry | Private | Seventh/Third, Crockett/Powell | Dec 1777-Jan 1778; April-May 1778; June 1778 in Powell's Company. |
| Davis, John | Drummer | First, Mennis | Dec 1777 on command; Jan-April 1778; May 1778 sick present; June 1778 absent sick. |
| Davis, John | Sergeant | Second State, Dudley | March 15, 1778-May 1, 1778; May 1778; June 1778 sick absent. |
| Davis, John | Private | Second State, Quarles | April-June 1778. |
| Davis, John | Private | Seventh, Crockett | Dec 1777-Jan 1778 on furlough. |
| Davis, John | Private | Seventh, Lipscomb | Dec 1777-Jan 1778 waggoner; Feb 24, 1778 discharged. |
| Davis, John | Private | Seventh, Lipscomb | June 1778. |
| Davis, John, Jr. | Private | Seventh, Lipscomb | June 1778. |
| Davis, John | Private/Corporal | Seventh, Young | Dec 1777 on furlough; Jan 1, 1778 promoted to Corporal; Jan-April 1778 on furlough; May 1778 sick Virginia; June 1778. |
| Davis, Joseph | Private | Fifteenth, Harris | Jan 1778; Feb 1778 on command; March-April 1778 sick present; May 1778; June 1778 orderly at Valley Forge. |
| Davis/Davies, Lewis | Private | First State, Brown | Dec 1777-May 1778. |
| Davis, Nicholas | Private | First, Cunningham | Feb 23, 1778 enlisted; July 1778 sick in hospital. |
| Davis, Robert | Private | Seventh, Lipscomb | Dec 1777 hospital; Jan 31, 1778 discharged. |
| Davis, Richard | Private | Seventh, Lipscomb | Dec 22, 1777 enlisted in the Light Horse. |
| Davis, Simon | Private | Fourteenth, Reid | Sept 18, 1777 enlisted; April 1778 lately joined regiment; May-June 1778. |
| Davis, Thomas | Private | Second State, Spiller | March 15, 1778-May 1, 1778; May-June 1778. |

| Name | Rank | Company | Service |
|---|---|---|---|
| Davis, William | Private | Second, Taylor, F. | Dec 1777-Feb 1778; March 4, 1778 discharged. |
| Davis, William | Private | Second, Upshaw | Dec 1777-Jan 1778. |
| Davis, William | Private | Second, Calmes | Dec 1777-March 1778. |
| Davis/Davies, William | Private | Third, Blackwell | Dec 1777-March 1778 sick in hospital; April 1778 sick at Lancaster; May 1778 on guard; June 1778. |
| Davis, William | Private | Third, Mercer | Dec 1777-Jan 1778 sick present. |
| Davis, William | Private | Fourteenth, Jones | Jan-May 1778; June 1778 on duty. |
| Davison, Adonijah | Private | Second, Harrison | Dec 1777-May 1778; June 1778 sick at Valley Forge. |
| Davison, Ambrose/ Ambruss | Private | First, Cunningham | Feb 1777 enlisted for 3 years; Dec 1777-Feb 1778; March 1778 sick hospital; April 1778; May 1778 sick present; June 1778 sick at Valley Forge. |
| Davison/ Davidson, Edwd | Private | Sixth, Hockaday | Dec 1777-Jan 1778; Feb 10, 1778 discharged. |
| Davison, Joseph | Private | First, Cunningham | Feb 1777 enlisted for 3 years; Dec 1777-Feb 1778; March 1778 sick hospital; April-May 1778; June 1778 sick at Valley Forge. |
| Davison, Joshua/ Joseah | Private | First, Cunningham | Feb 19, 1778 enlisted for 1 year; April 1778 under inoculation; May 1778 sick in the hospital; June 1778 sick at Valley Forge. |
| Davison, Josiah | Private | First, Cunningham | Feb 19, 1778 enlisted for 1 year; April 1778 under inoculation; May 1778 sick in the hospital; June 1778 sick at Valley Forge. |
| Davison, William/Wm. | Private | First, Cunningham | Dec 1777; Jan 1778 sick hospital; Feb 1778 sick present; March-June 1778. |
| Dawson, Benjamin | Private | Second, Taylor, F. | Dec 1777-March 1778; April 10, 1778 discharged, time of service expired. |

| Name | Rank | Regiment | Service |
|---|---|---|---|
| Dawson, Francis | Private | First, Lawson | January-April 1778; May-June 1778 on guard. |
| Dawson, James | Private | Fourteenth, Reid | March 12, 1778 drafted; May 1778 joined lately; June 1778. |
| Dawson, Robert | Sergeant | Second, Taylor, F. | Dec 1777 on command; Jan-Feb 1778. |
| Dawson, Thomas | Private | First State, Hamilton | Dec 1777-June 1778. |
| Dawson, Thomas | Drummer | Second State, Dudley | March 15, 1778-May 1, 1778; May-June 1778. |
| Day, James | Private | Sixth, Massie | Dec 1777 in hospital; Jan 1778. |
| Day/Dea, John | Private | Second, Jones | Dec 1777-June 1778. |
| Day, Richard/Richd. | Private | Fifteenth, Foster/Gray | Dec 1777-Jan 1778; Feb 1778 on guard, in Gray's Company; March 1778 sick in camp; April-May 1778. |
| Day, Samuel | Private | Fourteenth, Winston | Feb 17, 1778 drafted; May-June 1778. |
| Dayley/Dayly, Daniel | Private | Twelfth, Wallace | Dec 1777-Jan 1778; Feb 1778 on command; March-May 1778. |
| Deacon/Dacon, Peter | Private | Third, Blackwell | Feb 18, 1778 drafted; March-May 1778; June-Nov 1778 sick at Valley Forge. |
| Deadman/Dedman, Samuel | Sergeant | Fourteenth | Dec 1777-Feb 1778; March 1778 on furlough; April-June 1778. |
| Deady/Dady, Jerry | Private | Twelfth, Bowyer, M. | Dec 1777; Jan 1778 on command; Feb 24, 1778 deserted. |
| Deagles, Emanuel/Eamuel | Private | Fourteenth, Winston | Dec 1777 on command; Jan 1778 at R. hospital; Feb 1778; March 8, 1778 died. |
| Dean, Benjamin | Private | Seventh/Third, Webb/Young | June sick Valley Forge, in Young's Company; July 1778 sick at Valley Forge; Aug 14, 1778 died. |
| Dean, Daniel | Corporal | Second State, Lewis | March 15-May 1, 1778; May 1778; June 1778 sick absent. |
| Dean/Deane, Jesse | Private | First State, Ewell, T. | Dec 1777; Jan 1778 sick Yellow Springs; Feb 1778 Yellow Springs hospital; March-June 1778. |

| | | | |
|---|---|---|---|
| Dean, John | Private | Second State, Spiller | March 15-May 1, 1778; May 1778; June 1778 sick Valley Forge. |
| Dean/Deane, Joshua/Joshia | Private | Seventh/Third, Moseley/Blackwell | Dec 1777-May 1778 on furlough; April 1778 on guard; May 1778 sick at Yellow Springs; June-July 1778 sick Valley Forge. |
| Dean, Matt. | Private | Fifteenth, Gregory | June 1778 sick Valley Forge. |
| Dean/Deane, Peter | Private | Second, Jones | Dec 1777-June 1778. |
| Deane, John | Private | First State, Crump | April-May 1778; June 1778 sick absent. |
| Deane, John | Private | Third, Blackwell | Dec 1777-Jan 1778; Feb 14, 1778 discharged. |
| Dearing, Edward | Private | First State, Brown | Dec 1777-Feb 1778. |
| Dearman, Harrison | Private | Sixth, Garland | Only record is the April 1778 payroll which shows he enlisted on Sept 22, 1777. |
| Dearner/Dearener, Michael | Private | Twelfth, Waggener | Dec 1777; Jan 1778 on command; Feb 1778 on duty; March-May 1778. |
| Death/Deeth, Randal | Private | Twelfth, Waggener | Dec 1777-Jan 1778; Feb 1778 on duty; March 1778; April 1778 on guard; May 1778. |
| Deaton, George | Private | Second, Taylor, W. | Dec 1777-Feb 1778; March 5, 1778 discharged. |
| Deaton, Jaby/Eaby | Private | Second, Taylor, W. | Dec 1777 sick absent; Jan-Feb 1778. |
| Deavenport, James | Private | Seventh, Jouett | Dec 1777 sick in hospital; Feb 3, 1778 discharged. |
| Deavenport, John | Corporal | Seventh, Jouett | Dec 1777; Feb 3, 1778 discharged. |
| Deavenport, William | Private | Seventh, Fleming | Dec 1777 sick in hospital; Jan 1778; Feb 9, 1778 discharged. |
| Debord, James | Private | First State, Brown | Dec 1777-Feb 1778. |
| Decharoe/Decharo, William | Private | Second State, Dudley | March 15, 1778-May 1, 1778; May-June 1778. |
| Decker, Samuel | Private | Twelfth, Vause | Dec 1777-May 1778. |

| Name | Rank | Regiment, Officer | Service |
|---|---|---|---|
| Deering, James | Private | Second, Taylor, F. | Dec 1777-Feb 1778. |
| Delany, Anthony/ Anthoney | Private | Third, Peyton, V. | Dec 1777-Jan 1778; Feb 12, 1778 discharged. |
| Delaney/ Delany, Thomas | Private | First State, Ewell, T. | Dec 1777; Jan-Feb 1778 sick at Yellow Springs hospital; March-June 1778. |
| Dellis/Ellison, Robert | Private | Fourteenth, Lambert | Dec 1777; Jan 1778 artificer; Feb 1778; March 1778 on furlough; April-June 1778. |
| Delozier, Richard | Sergeant | Fifteenth, Hull | Dec 1777-March 1778 sick in the hospital; Feb 1778 payroll shows he died on Feb 15, 1778. |
| Demoss/Demos, John | Private | Twelfth, Waggener | Dec 1777-March 1778 on command; April-May 1778 waggoner |
| Denby/Derby, Jonathan | Drummer | Seventh/ Third, Fleming/ Heth | Dec 1777 on furlough Virginia; Jan-March 1778 on furlough; May 1778; June 1778 in Heth's Company. |
| Denby, Samuel | Private | Second State, Bressie | March 15, 1778-May 1, 1778; May-June 1778. |
| Dener/Dereal, John | Private | First State, Camp | Dec 1777 sick in hospital; Jan-Feb 1778 sick absent; March 1778 hospital, Red Lyon; April-May 1778; June 1778 discharged. |
| Denholm/ Denholme, Archibald/ Archd. | 1st. Lt. | First, Lawson | Dec 1777 Virginia recruiting; Jan 1778; Feb 1778 absent with leave; March 1778; April-May 1778 on command; June 1778. |
| Denna/Denny, Henry | Private | Twelfth, Waggener | Dec 1777; Jan 1778 on guard; Feb-April 1778; May 1778 picket. |
| Dennis/ Dennison, Briant/Bryan | Private | First, Mennis | March 1778 on furlough; April-June 1778. |
| Denton, David | Private | Seventh/ Third, Jouett/Hill | Feb 16, 1778 enlisted; April-May 1778; June 1778 in Hill's Company. |
| Deremiah, John | Private | Twelfth, Waggener | Dec 1777-March 1778; April 10, 1778 discharged. |

| | | | |
|---|---|---|---|
| Derry, John | Private | Fifteenth, Hull | Dec 1777-March 1778 on command; April 1778 on guard; May 1778; June-July sick Valley Forge. |
| Derwin, John | Private | Third, Powell | Dec 1777. |
| Devenport/ Devinport, Reuben | Private | Seventh, Lipscomb | Dec 1777; Feb 2, 1778 discharged. |
| Devorix/ Devereux, Joseph | Private | Third, Lee/ Peyton J. | Feb 27, 1778 enlisted; April-May; June 1778 on command, in J. Peyton's Company. |
| Dewalt, Thomas | Private | Twelfth, Bowyer, M. | Dec 1777 leg broke in Virginia. |
| Dewitt/Duwitt, Henry/Henery | Private | Twelfth, Vause | Dec 1777; Jan 1778 sick in camp; Feb-March 1778 on command; April-May 1778. |
| Dewitt/Duwitt, Peter | Private | Twelfth, Vause | Dec 1777 sent sick with baggage; Jan-March 1778 sick Reading; April-May 1778. |
| Diamond, James | Private | First State, Brown | Dec 1777-May 1778. |
| Dian, Benjamin | Private | Seventh, Webb | April-May 1778 |
| Dick, James/Jas. | Private | Fifteenth, Gregory | June 1778. |
| Dickens/ Dickins, George | Private | Twelfth, Ashby | Dec 1777-Jan 1778; March 1778 on guard; April 1778 on command; May 1778 on command at the post. |
| Dickens/ Deekins, James | Private | Third, Arell | Dec 1777-Jan 1778; Feb 1778 sick absent; March 15, 1778 dead. |
| Dickerson, Nathaniel/Nathl | Sergeant | Sixth, Avery | Dec 1777; Jan 31, 1778 discharged. |
| Dickerson, Robert | Private | Second, Jones | Dec 1777-June 1778. |
| Dickerson, William/Wm | Private | Sixth, Avery | Dec 26, 1777 discharged. |
| Dickinson, Edmund B. | Major | First | Dec 1777 absent with leave; Jan-March 1778 on furlough in Virginia; April-May 1778; June 28, 1778 killed. |

| Name | Rank | Regiment | Service |
|---|---|---|---|
| Didlake, John | Corporal/ Sergeant | Second State, Taliaferro | March 15, 1778-May 1, 1778; May-June 1778. |
| Dillard/Dillyard, Edward | Private | Fourteenth, Jones | Jan 1778 on command; Feb-March 1778; May 1778. |
| Dillard, Thomas | Corporal | Fourteenth, Conway | Dec 1777; Jan-Feb 1778 on command; March 1778 orderly at hospital; April 1, 1778 deceased. |
| Dillian/Dillion, William | Fleming | Second, Jones | Dec 1777-June 1778. |
| Dillimore/ Dillemor, Robert/Robt. | Drummer | Sixth, Hockaday | Dec 1777 wounded, in hospital; Jan 1778; Feb 19, 1778 discharged. |
| Dimery, James | Private | Fifteenth, Gray | Feb 10, 1778 drafted to serve one year; April 1778 under inoculation; May 1778 sick present; June 1778 sick at Valley Forge; July 9, 1778 died. |
| Dison, Robt. | Private | Fifteenth, Harris | March 1778; April 1778 sick; May 1778. |
| Dison, Stephen | Private | Fifteenth, Harris | Feb-April 1778 sick absent; May 1778. |
| Diven/Divin, Robert | Private | Fourteenth, Conway | Dec 1777; Jan 1778 on command; Feb 1778; March 1778 sick present; April-June 1778. |
| Diven/Divin, William | Sergeant | Fourteenth, Conway | Dec 1777-Jan 1778; Feb 1778 sick in camp; March 1778 sick present; April-May 1778; June 1778 left at Valley Forge to wait on sick. |
| Diweas, Lewis | Private | Seventh, Posey | Dec 1777; Jan 1778 on command; Feb 24, 1778 discharged. |
| Dixon/Dickson, Edward | Private | First State, Hoffler | Dec 1777-June 1778. |
| Dixon, James | Private | First State, Crump | Dec 1777-May 1778; June 1778 sick absent. |
| Dixon/Dixson, Thomas | Private | Twelfth, Bowyer, M. | Dec 1777-Jan 1778; Feb 1778 on command; March 1778 on guard; April-May 1778. |
| Dobbs, Keader | Private | Fifteenth, Grimes | Feb 1778 sick present; March-May 1778; June 1778 sick Valley Forge. |
| Doblin, Robert | Private | Twelfth, Bowyer, T. | April 1778. |

| Name | Rank | Regiment/Company | Service |
|---|---|---|---|
| Dockerty/ Docherty, Patrick/Pattrick | Private | Third, Lee | Feb 14, 1778 discharged. |
| Dodd, Drury | Private | Second State, Spiller | March 15, 1778-May 1, 1778; May-June 1778. |
| Dodd, Simon | Private | Second, Willis | Dec 1777-June 1778. |
| Dogan/ Don guardon, Wilford | Private/ Corporal | First State, Payne | Dec 1777-Jan 1778 sick Bethlehem; Feb-May 1778; June 1778 guard. He is listed as a Corporal for the month of April only. |
| Dogin/Dogan, William | Private | Third, Peyton, V./ Peyton, J. | Dec 1777-Jan 1778; Feb 1778 sick present; March 1778; April 1778 sick in camp; May 1778 sick present; June 1778 sick at Valley Forge, in J. Peyton's Company; July 13, 1778 discharged. |
| Doggins, Samuel | Corporal | Seventh, Webb | Jan 1778; Feb 3, 1778 discharged. |
| Dogherty/ Dority, John | Private | Twelfth, Ashby | Dec 1777-Jan 1778; February 22, 1778 deserted. |
| Doland, Midal | Private | Fourteenth, Overton | Dec 1777; Jan 1778 waggoner; Feb 1778; March 10, 1778 deserted. |
| Dolby, William/ Willm. | Private | First, Lewis | Dec 1777-Jan 1778; Feb 1778 on guard; March 1778 on fatigue; April-June 1778. |
| Dollar, William | Private | Second, Calmes | Dec 1777-May 1778; June 1778 sick Valley Forge. |
| Donalon, Michael | Private | Fourteenth, Overton | Feb 1778 waggoner; March 10, 1778 deserted. |
| Doney, Francis | Private | First, Lawson | Feb 1778. |
| Donaghu/ Donohugh, John | Private | Twelfth, Bowyer, T. | Jan 1778 joined; Jan-March 1778 on command; April-June 1778 waggoner. |
| Donalson/ Donilson, William/Will. | Private | Twelfth, Bowyer, M. | Dec 1777 on guard; Jan-Feb 1778 on command; March-May 1778. |
| Donge, Nathan | Private | Fifteenth, Wills | Sept 10, 1777 enlisted; Feb-May 1778; June 15, 1778 deserted. |

| Name | Rank | Regiment/Company | Service |
|---|---|---|---|
| Doniphan, Jarrard | Private | Second State, Garnett | May-June 1778. |
| Donlevy, John | Ensign | First State, Crump | Dec 1777-Feb 1778; March 15, 1778 resigned. |
| Dorridon/ Dorodon, Patrick | Private | First State, Brown | Dec 1777-April 1778. |
| Doswell, James | Private | Fourteenth, Winston | Feb 17, 1778 drafted; May-June 1778. |
| Dougherty/ Doyerty, Charles | Private | Twelfth, Vause | Dec 1777-April 1778; May 1778 on guard. |
| Dougherty, John | Private | Twelfth, Ashby | Dec 1777-Jan 1778; Feb 22, 1778 deserted. |
| Doughty/Doty, Daniel | Private | Second, Jones | Dec 1777; Jan-Feb 1778 hospital; March 15, 1778 discharged. |
| Douglass, John | Private | Seventh, Moseley | Dec-Jan 1778 in R. Regt; Feb 20, 1778 discharged. |
| Dountron, George | Private | Second State, Spiller | March 15, 1778-May 1, 1778; May-June 1778. |
| Dowden, John | Private | Fourteenth, Jones | Jan-Feb 1778 sick Lancaster; Feb-March 1778; April 1778 sick present; May 1778. |
| Dowden, Thomas | Private | Fourteenth, Jones | Jan-Feb 1778 sick Lancaster; Feb-May 1778; June 1778 on duty. |
| Dowel/Dowell, George | Private | Fourteenth, Marks | Dec 1777; Jan 1778 on duty; Feb-April 1778; May 1778 sick present; June 1778. |
| Downey/ Downy, John | Sergeant | Second State, Dudley | March 15, 1778-May 1, 1778; May-June 1778. |
| Downey, Michael | Private | Second State, Dudley | March 15, 1778-May 1, 1778; May-June 1778. |
| Doyel/Doyle, John | Private | Twelfth, Madison | March 1778. |
| Doyl, Lawrence | Private | Twelfth, Waggener | Dec 1777 dead. |
| Doyle, Robert/ Robt. | Private | Third, Blackwell | Dec 1777-March 1778 on furlough; April 1778 on guard; May-June 1778. |

| | | | |
|---|---|---|---|
| Doyle/Doyal, Thomas | Private | Seventh/ Third, Posey/ Sayers | Dec 1777-Jan 1778 on furlough; April 1778 sick Lancaster; May 1778; Jan 1778 sick Lancaster, in Sayers' Company. |
| Dragoe/Dragoo, William | Private | Twelfth, Waggener | Dec 1777-Jan 1778 hospital; Feb 1778; March 1778 sick in camp; April 10, 1778 discharged. |
| Drake, Joel | Private | Seventh, Fleming | Dec 1777 sick in hospital; Jan 1778 hospital; Feb 7, 1778 discharged. |
| Drake, Michael | Private | Third, Arell/ Briscoe | Dec 1777-Jan 1778; Feb-March 1778 sick absent; April 1778 sick Lancaster; May 1778 sick absent; June 1778 in Briscoe's Company. |
| Drake, William/Wm. | Private | Fifteenth, Harris | Jan 1778 on command; Feb 5, 1778 deserted. |
| Draper/Dreaper, Robert | Private | Twelfth, Casey | Dec 1777 sent to hospital; Jan-Feb 1778 at hospital; March-April 1778; May 1778 on guard. |
| Dreskile, Florence | Private | Fourteenth, Conway | Feb 13, 1778 enlisted; April 1778 lately joined regiment; May 1778 on command. |
| Drinker, Joseph | Private | Second, Calmes | Dec 1777-June 1778. |
| Driskill/ Driskale, Dennis | Private | Second State, Lewis | March 15, 1778-May 1, 1778; May 1778; June 1778 sick absent; July 1778 sick Valley Forge. |
| Driskill/ Dreskill, Michael | Private | Second State, Bernard | May 1778; June 1778 sick Corrells Ferry. |
| Driskill/Driskle, Timothy | Private | Second, Willis | Dec 1777-June 1778. |
| Driver, Edward | Private | Second, Willis | Dec 1777-June 1778. |
| Driver, Emanuel/Man | Private | Second State, Bernard | May-June 1778. |
| Driver, Francis | Private | First, Cunningham | Dec 1777. |
| Driver, William | Private | Second State, Bernard | May-June 1778. |

| | | | |
|---|---|---|---|
| Drury, James | Private | Second State, Bernard | April-June 1778. |
| Drury/Drewry, John | Ensign/ 2nd. Lt. | First, Cunningham | Dec 1777 in Virginia recruiting; Jan 1778 present sick; Feb-May 1778; June 1778 in Virginia recruiting. Oath at Valley Forge on May 11, 1778, witnessed by Muhlenberg. |
| Duck, Samuel | Private | Third, Lee/ Peyton J. | Feb 27, 1778 enlisted; April-May 1778; June 1778 in J. Peyton's Company. |
| Dudley, Banks | Sergeant/ 2nd/ Lt. | Seventh, Hill | Dec 1777-Jan 1778 on furlough; April 1778; Promoted to Second Lieutenant in April; June 1778. |
| Dudley, Harry | Captain | Second State, Dudley | March 15, 1778-May 1, 1778; May-June 1778. Oath at Valley Forge on May 18, 1778, witnessed by Muhlenberg. |
| Dudley, John | 1st. Lt | Second State, Dudley | March 15, 1778-May 1, 1778; May-June 1778. Oath at Valley Forge on May 12, 1778, witnessed by Muhlenberg. |
| Duffel, James | Corporal | Fifteenth, Grimes | Dec 1777-June 1778. |
| Dugan/Dugin, William | Private | Twelfth, Vause | Dec 1777 on guard; Jan 1778; Feb 1778 on command; March-May 1778. |
| Dugas, Robert | Corporal | Seventh, Lipscomb | Dec 22, 1777 enlisted in the Light Horse. |
| Duglas/Dugles, Adam | Private | Second State, Garnett | March 15, 1778-May 1, 1778; May 13, 1778 died. |
| Duglass, Archibald | Corporal | Fifteenth, Hull | Dec 20, 1777 died. |
| Duglass/ Douglass, George | Private | Seventh, Spencer | Dec 1777-Jan 1778 hospital; March 7, 1778 discharged. |
| Dugmore, John | Drummer/ Private | First State, Hamilton | Dec 1777-March 1778; April 1778 reduced to Private; April 1778-Jan 1778. |
| Duke, Clevaes/ Clevears | Private | Fourteenth, Winston | Feb 17, 1778 drafted; May-June 1778 |

| Name | Rank | Regiment | Notes |
|---|---|---|---|
| Duke, John | Corporal | Twelfth, Casey | Dec 15, 1777 deserted. |
| Dunavant/ Dunavt., Daniel | Corporal | Second, Taylor, W. | Dec 1777-Jan 1778; Feb 5, 1778 discharged. |
| Dunavant/ Dunavt., Leonard/Leono. | Private | Second, Taylor, W. | Dec 1777-Feb 1778; March 1778 died at the hospital, no date given. |
| Dunavant/ Dunavante, Philip | Private | Second, Taylor, W. | Dec 1777-Feb 1778. |
| Dunaway, John | Private | Second, Sanford/ Parker | Dec 1777-June 1778. In April Captain Parker took command of the company. |
| Dunaway, John | Private | Fifteenth, Hull | Dec 1777-March 1778 sick absent or sick in hospital; April 1778; May 1778 sick present. |
| Dunbarr/ Dunbar, Hamilton | Private/ Sergeant | Twelfth, Waggener | Dec 1777-Feb 1778; March 1778 promoted to Sergeant; March 1778; April 1778 sick in camp; May 1778. |
| Duncan, James | Sergeant | Twelfth, Waggener | Dec 31, 1777 enlisted in light horse. |
| Duncan/ Duncum, John | Private | First State, Lee | Dec 1777; Jan 1778 on guard; Feb-May 1778; June 1778 sick absent. |
| Duncan, John | Private | Seventh, Crockett | Dec 1777-Jan 1778. |
| Duncan, Joseph | Sergeant | Seventh, Crockett | Dec 1777-Jan 1778 on furlough. |
| Dunlap, John | Private | Second, Harrison | Dec 1777-June 1778. |
| Dunlap, Samuel | Private | Second, Harrison | Dec 1777-June 1778. |
| Dunn, David | Private | Fifteenth, Gregory | June 1778 at hospital. |
| Dunn, James | Private | Seventh/ Third, Posey/ Sayers | Feb 28, 1778 enlisted; April-May 1778; June 1778 in Sayers' Company. |
| Dunn, James | Private | Fourteenth, Lambert | Oct 1, 1777 enlisted; April 1778 lately joined regiment; May 1778; June 1778 on guard. |

| Name | Rank | Regiment, Company | Notes |
|---|---|---|---|
| Dunn/Dun, John | Private | First State, Payne | Dec 1777-Jan 1778 sick Bethlehem; Feb 1778 deceased. |
| Dunn, John | Private | Fifteenth, Foster | Dec 1777 in Virginia; Jan 11, 1778 discharged. |
| Dunn, Patrick | Private | Twelfth, Madison | Dec 1777 on guard; Jan-April 1778. |
| Dunn/Dun, Peter | Captain | Sixth, Dunn/Apperson | Heitman shows that Captain Dunn was killed on September 26, 1777. During the start of the Valley Forge period it was still called Dunn's company, though commanded by Captain Apperson. |
| Dunn, Richard | Private | First State, Hoffler | Dec 1777-June 1778. |
| Dunn, Robert | Private | Twelfth, Bowyer, T. | Dec 1777-March 1778; April 1778 on guard; May 1778 confined. |
| Dunn, Thomas | Private | Fourteenth, Marks | Dec 1777-Jan 1778 sick in hospital; Feb 1778 sick absent; March 1778 sick in hospital. Sept 8, 1778 supposed dead. |
| Dunn/Donn, William | Private | Twelfth, Wallace | Dec 1777-May 1778. |
| Dunnacan, Daniel | Private | Seventh, Crockett | Dec 1777-Jan 1778 on furlough. |
| Dunstead, John | Private | Sixth, Massie | Feb-March 1778. |
| Dunston, Almond/Almon | Private | Second State, Taliaferro | March 15-May 1, 1778; May-June 1778. |
| Dunston, Warner | Private | Second State, Taliaferro | March 25-May 1, 1778; May-June 1778. |
| Dunton, Steven/Stephen | Private | Second State, Garnett | March 15-May 1, 1778; May-June 1778. |
| Durham/Durrum, William | Private | Fourteenth, Winston | Feb 17, 1778 drafted; May 1778 sick in camp; June 1778 on duty. |
| Durmey/Durmmey, Daniel | Private | First State, Hoffler | Dec 1777-May 1778; June 1778 sick absent. |
| Durrah, Ephraim | Private | Second, Calmes | Dec 1777; Jan 1778 deserted. |

| | | | |
|---|---|---|---|
| Durrett/Durritt, Claiborne/ Clayborne | Private | Second, Upshaw | Dec 1777-Jan 1778. |
| Dust, Samuel | Private | First State, Camp | Dec 1777 sick Fishwater Mills; Jan 12, 1778 died. |
| Duvall/Devall, Jeremiah | Private | Twelfth, Ashby | Dec 1777 sick in hospital; Feb 1778 sick in hospital; March 1778 dead. |
| Dyer, Robert | Private | Fourteenth, Thweatt | Dec 1777-Feb 1778 sick in hospital; March 12, 1778 died. |
| Ealey, John | Private | Fifteenth, Gregory | June 1778 sick [ ]. |
| Eanes/Enas, Druary/Drury | Private | Fifteenth, Harris | Jan 1778 on guard; Feb 1778 sick present; March 1778 on command; April-May 1778 sick present. |
| Eanes/Enos, Josiah | Private | Fifteenth, Harris | Jan 1778 sick; Feb-March 1778 sick present; April 1778; May 17, 1778 died. |
| Earles, John | Private | Fourteenth, Conway | Dec 1777; Jan-Feb 1778 on command; March-June 1778. |
| Earthen/Arthen, Ruben/Reuben | Private | Third, Powell | Dec 1777; Jan-Feb 1778 on furlough; April 1778. |
| Eastes, Abraham | Private | Seventh, Moseley | Dec 1777 waggoner; Jan 1778 sick present; Feb 21, 1778 discharged. |
| Eastes, John | Private | Seventh, Moseley | Dec 1777 on fatigue; Jan 1778; Feb 20, 1778 discharged. |
| Eastes/Thomas | Private | Seventh, Moseley | Dec 1777-Jan 1778 sick in hospital; Feb 19, 1778 discharged. |
| Eastin/Easten, Philip | Private | Seventh, Spencer | Enlisted for 3 years; Dec 1777; Jan 1778 on command; April-June 1778 waggoner. |
| Eastman, Edward | Private | Fourteenth, Reid | Sept 18, 1777 enlisted; April 1778 lately joined regiment; May-June 1778. |
| Eastwood, Charles | Private | Seventh, Spencer/ Lipscomb | Feb 13, 1778 enlisted for 1 year; April-June 1778. |
| Eastwood, Demey/Dimey | Private | First State, Hoffler | Dec 1777-June 1778. |

| | | | |
|---|---|---|---|
| Eatkins/Eakins, Samuel | Private | Twelfth, Bowyer, T. | Dec 1777-Jan 1778 sick in camp; Jan-Feb 1778; March 1778 on command; April 1778 on guard; May 1778. |
| Edgar, John | Fourteenth | Fourteenth, Lambert | Feb 23, 1778 enlisted; June 1778 sick Valley Forge. |
| Edmonds/ Edmons, Daniel | Private | Second State, Spiller | March 15, 1778-May 1, 1778; May-June 1778. |
| Edmonds/ Edmunds, Richard | Private | Fifteenth, Gregory | Dec 1777; Jan 1778 sick present; Feb-June 1778. |
| Edmonds/ Edmos, Robert | Corporal | Fifteenth, Hull | Dec 1777-April 1778 on furlough. |
| Edmondson, Benjamin | Ensign | Second State, Quarles/ Dudley | May-June 1778. In June he transferred to Dudley's Company. |
| Edmunds, Thomas | Captain | Fifteenth, Edmunds | Nov-Dec 1777 wounded; Jan-May 1778 on furlough. |
| Edmundson, Joseph | Private | Fourteenth, Overton | Dec 1777 sick in hospital; Jan 1778 sick absent; Feb 20, 1778 died. |
| Edwards, Andrew | Private | Seventh, Fleming | Dec 1777 sick in hospital; Jan 1778 hospital; Feb 7, 1778 discharged. |
| Edwards, Charles | Private | Fifteenth, Hull | Dec 1777-June 1778 on command. |
| Edwards, Edmund/ Edmond | Fifer | Fifteenth, Gregory | June 1778. This man and the individual below are probably the same individual. |
| Edwards, Edmund | Fifer | Fifteenth, Mason | Dec 1777-April 1778; May 1778 sick in camp. |
| Edwards, Edward | Corporal | Seventh, Crockett | Dec 1777-Jan 1778 in Rifle Bat. |
| Edwards, Henry | Drummer | First State, Lee | Dec 1777 sick; Jan-June 1778. |
| Edwards, James | Private | First State, Hamilton | Dec 1777-June 1778. May 1778 payroll states he was omitted for March and April, and was then paid for three months. |
| Edwards, John | Private | First State, Crump | Dec 1777-June 1778. |

| | | | |
|---|---|---|---|
| Edwards, John | Private | Fifteenth, Wills | March-May 1778. |
| Edwards, Richard | Private | Twelfth, Vause | Dec 1777; Jan 1778 on guard; Feb 1778 on command; March 1778; April 1778 taylor Headquarters; May 1778. |
| Edwards, Richard | Private | Twelfth, Wallace | Dec 1777-May 1778. |
| Edwards, Robert | Private | Second, Jones | Dec 1777-Jan 1778; Feb 1778 deserted when on command. |
| Edwards, William | Private | First, Lawson | Jan-Feb 1778 on command. |
| Edwards, William | Private | Third, Powell | June 1778 sick at Valley Forge. |
| Eel, Gasper | Private | Twelfth, Waggener | Dec 25, 1777 discharged. |
| Egliston/ Egloston, William Cary | Private | Fourteenth, Winston | Drafted Feb 15, 1778; May-June 1778. |
| Elam, Alexander | Private | Second State, Spiller | March 15, 1778-May 1, 1778; May 1778. This man and the man below are probably the same individual. |
| Elam, Alexander | Private | Second State, Dudley | June 1778. |
| Elam, Josiah | Private | Seventh, Fleming | Dec 1777-Jan 1778; Feb 25, 1778 discharged. |
| Elcock/Ellocks, John | Private | Third, Peyton, V. | Dec 1777 on furlough Virginia; Jan-March 1778 on furlough; April 1778 sick in camp; May 1778 sick absent; June 1778 Yellow Springs. |
| Elder, Andrew | Private | Seventh, Posey | Dec 1777-Jan 1778 on furlough. |
| Elder, Charles | Private | Fourteenth, Jones | Jan-Feb 1778 sick in Alexandria, Virginia; April-May 1778. |
| Elder/Eldor, Newman | Private | Sixth, Rose | Dec 1777-Feb 1778; March 4, 1778 discharged. |
| Eleazor/Eliazer, Jacob | Private | Second State, Lewis | March 15, 1778-May 1, 1778; May 1778; June 1778; July 1778 sick Valley Forge. |

| Name | Rank | Regiment/Company | Notes |
|---|---|---|---|
| Elgee, John | Corporal | Third/Seventh, Sayers | June 1778 with Col. Morgan, in Sayers' Company. |
| Ellett, William/Will | Private | Second, Harrison | Dec 1777-June 1778. |
| Eliock, John | Private | Third, Peyton, V. | June 1778 sick Yellow Springs. |
| Eliot/Elliott, William | Private | Twelfth, Wallace | On scout and missing December 20, 1777. |
| Elliott, Edward | Private | Fourteenth, Jones | Jan-Feb 1778 sick Lancaster; Feb 28, 1778 died. |
| Elliott/Elliot, John | Private | Second State, Dudley | March 15, 1778-May 1, 1778; May-June 1778. |
| Elliott, Robert | 2nd. Lt. | Twelfth, Madison | Dec 1777-Jan 1778; Feb 1778 on command; March-May 1778. |
| Elliott/Elliot, William | Private | Second State, Dudley | March 15, 1778-May 1, 1778; May-June 1778. |
| Elliott, Wyatt | Sergeant | Second State, Garnett | May-June 1778. |
| Ellis/Elise, Jesse | Private | Twelfth, Wallace | Dec 1777-March 1778 sent to hospital; April 1778 roll shows him deceased December 16, 1777. |
| Ellis/Ellise, Samuel | Private | Twelfth, Wallace | Dec 1777-March 1778 sent to hospital; April 1778 roll shows him deceased Feb 10, 1778. |
| Ellison see Dellis | | | |
| Ellison, Robert | Private | Fourteenth, Roberts | Jan 1778. |
| Ellison, William | Private | Fourteenth, Conway | Dec 1777. This man and the man below are probably the same individual. |
| Ellison/Alison, William | Private | Fourteenth, Jones | Jan 1778 on command; Feb-May 1778. |
| Ellmore/Elsmore, John | Sergeant | Third/Seventh, Briscoe | Dec 1777-March 1778 on furlough; April-May 1778; June 1778 on guard. |

| Name | Rank | Company | Service |
|---|---|---|---|
| Ellsmore/Elsmore, Willam | Private | Third, Peyton, V./ Peyton, J. | Dec 1777 on furlough Virginia; Jan-March 1778 on furlough; April 1778 sick in camp; May 1778; June 1778 in J. Peyton's Company. |
| Elmore, Thomas | Private | Second, Taylor, W. | Dec 1777 on guard; Jan 1778; Feb 14, 1778 discharged. |
| Elmore/Elmoore, William | Private/Sergeant | First State, Hoffler | Dec 1777-March 1778; March 1778 promoted to Sergeant; April-June 1778. |
| Elsmore, Moses | Private | Third, Peyton, V./ Peyton, J. | Dec 1777; Jan 1778 on command; February 1778 on guard; March-April 1778; May 1778 on command; June 1778 in J. Peyton's Company. |
| Elsey/Elsay, John | Corporal | Seventh, Posey | Feb 28, 1778 enlisted; April-May 1778 |
| Elynne, John | Private | Twelfth, Ashby | March-April 1778. |
| Emberson/Emerson, Henry | Private | Sixth, Avery | Dec 28, 1777 enlisted into the Light Dragoons. |
| Emerson/Emmerson, Elliot | Private | First State, Lee | Dec 1777 sick; Jan 1778 sick absent; Feb 1778 roll states he died sometime in January. |
| Emerson, Henry | Private | Sixth, Avery | Dec 18, 1777 enlisted into the Light Dragoons. |
| Emery, Drury | Private | Second State, Bressie | May 1778 "Virga. last Pay roll now sick Valley Forge;" June 1778. |
| Emmore see Amory | | | |
| English see Inglish | | | |
| English/Inglish, John | Private | Third, Blackwell | Feb 12, 1778 drafted; March 1778; April 1778; May 1778 on guard; June 1778. |
| English, Robert | Private | Third, Blackwell | Feb 14, 1778 discharged. |
| English/Inglish, Samuel | Private | Fifteenth, Hull | April-May 1778. |
| Ennis/Innis, Robert | Private | Fourteenth, Jones | Jan-April 1778; May 1778 on command. |

| Name | Rank | Regiment | Notes |
|---|---|---|---|
| Epperson see Apperson | | | |
| Epperson/ Eperson, Peter | Private | First State, Meriwether | Dec 1777-June 1778. |
| Eppes, Peter | Private/ Sergeant | Sixth, Rose | Dec 1777; Jan 1778 promoted to Sergeant; Feb 1778; March 26, 1778 discharged. |
| Eppes/Epps, Richard | Sergeant | Fourteenth, Jones | Jan-April 1778. |
| Eppes/Epps, William | 1st. Lt. | Fourteenth, Jones | Jan-May 1778. Oath at Valley Forge on May 28, 1778, witnessed by Muhlenberg. |
| Eppes/Epps, Wyatt | Sergeant | Fourteenth, Jones | Sept 18, 1777 enlisted; Jan 1778 on command; Feb 1778 sick present; March 1778; May 1778 sick present; June 1778 sick Valley Forge. |
| Erskine, Charles | Quartermaster Sergeant | Fifteenth | Dec 1777-May 1778. |
| Erskine/Erskin, Robt | Private | Sixth, Garland | Dec 1777 on command; Jan 1778 sick absent; Feb 1778 hospital. |
| Erwin, Edward | Private | Twelfth, Waggener | Dec 1777-Feb 1778 hospital; March 1778 muster roll shows he deserted on Jan 22, 1778. |
| Erwin, Robert | Corporal | Twelfth, Bowyer, M. | Dec 1777-May 1778. |
| Erwin, William | Sergeant | Twelfth, Bowyer, M. | Dec 1777-March 1778; April 1778 on guard; May 1778. |
| Esdale, James | Private | First State, Hoffler | May 1778. |
| Eskridge/ Eskrige, George | Sergeant | Twelfth, Casey | Dec 1777-May 1778. |
| Eskridge/ Eshridge, Joseph | Private | Second, Taylor, W. | Dec 1777-Jan 1778; Feb 5, 1778 discharged. |
| Eskridge/ Eshridge, William | 2nd. Lt. | Second, Sandford/ Parker | Dec 1777-June 1778. From April on he appears in Parker's company. |
| Estes see Eastes | | | |
| Estes, Elisha | Private | First, Pelham | April 1778 under inoculation; May-June 1778. |
| Estes, Elisha | Private | Second, Taylor, F. | Dec 1777-Feb 1778. |

| | | | |
|---|---|---|---|
| Estes, James | Private | First, Pelham | Feb 1778 enlisted; April 1778 under inoculation; May-June 1778. |
| Estes/Estis, Elijah | Private | Sixth, Avery | Dec 20, 1777 discharged. |
| Estes/Eastes, George/Geo | Private | Sixth, Hockaday | Dec 1777 on command; Jan 1778 on guard; Feb 1778; March-June 1778. |
| Estes/Eastes, William/Wm. | Private/ Corporal | Sixth, Hockaday | Dec 1777-June 1778; April 1, 1778 promoted to Corporal. |
| Etheredge, John | Private | Fifteenth, Grimes | Dec 1777-Jan 1778 sick absent. |
| Etherington/ Artherton, John, Sr. | Private | Third/ Seventh, Mercer/ Powell | Dec 1777 sick absent; Jan 1778 on command; Feb-March 1778; April 1778 on command at the Lines; May 1778; June 1778 sick Brunswick, in Powell's Company. |
| Etherington/ Artherton, John, Jr. | Private | Third, Mercer | Dec 1777-Jan 1778; Feb sick present; March-April 1778; May 1778 sick present. |
| Eubank, John | Private | Seventh, Hill | Dec 22, 1777 enlisted in Light Dragoons. |
| Eubanks/ Ewbanks, Richard | Sergeant | Fourteenth, Marks | Dec 1777-March 1778; April 1778 Uynkland hospital; May-June 1778. |
| Eubanks/ Ewbanks, William | Private | Fourteenth, Marks | Feb 16, 1778 enlisted; April-June 1778. |
| Evans, Henry | Private | Sixth, Avery | March-April 1778; May 1778 on command; June 1778 sick Princetown. |
| Evans, Henry | Private | Sixth, Rose | April 1778. |
| Evans/Evins, James | Private | Twelfth, Casey | Dec 1777; Jan 1778 on command; Feb-March 1778 at hospital; April-May 1778 at hospital near camp; June 1778 sick at Yellow Springs. |
| Evans, Joseph | Sergeant | Seventh, Crockett | Dec 1777-Jan 1778 on furlough. |
| Evans/Evance, Richard | Private | Second, Jones | Dec 1777-June 1778. |

| Name | Rank | Regiment | Notes |
|---|---|---|---|
| Evans/Evens, Thomas | Private | Second State, Dudley | March 15, 1778-May 1, 1778; May-June 1778. |
| Evans, Vincent | Private | Third, Powell | Feb 10, 1778 enlisted; June 1778. |
| Evans, Williams | Private | Twelfth, Bowyer, M. | Dec 1777-Jan 1778 sick at Allentown; Jan 1778 dead. |
| Evans/Evins, William | Private | Twelfth, Waggener | Dec 1777-Jan 1778; Feb 1778 on command; March roll shows he was taken prisoner Feb 7, 1778. |
| Eversage, Michael | Private | Second State, Garnett | June 1778 sick Valley Forge. |
| Everitt, John | Private | Fifteenth, Wills | Feb 19, 1778 enlisted; April-May 1778. |
| Evins, David | Private | Fifteenth, Gray | Dec 1777-April 1778; May 1778 on guard. |
| Ewell, Charles | 1st. Lt./ Captain | First State, Ewell, T./ Ewell, C. | Dec 1777-Jan 1778; Feb-March 1778 on furlough in Virginia; April-May 1778; June 1, 1778 he was promoted to Captain and transferred to command William Payne's former company. |
| Ewell, Thomas W. | Captain | First State, Ewell, T. | Dec 1777; Jan-March 1778 on command Virginia; April-June 1778. Oath at Valley Forge on May 12, 1778, witnessed by Muhlenberg. |
| Ewing, Alexander | 2nd. Lt./ 1st. Lt. | Fourteenth, Lambert | Sept 3, 1777 appointed; April-June 1778. Oath at Valley Forge on May 12, 1778, witnessed by Muhlenberg. He signs the oath as a 1st. Lt. |
| Ewing, Rawly | Private | Third, Powell | May 1778. |
| Eyres see Ayres | | | |
| Eyres/Ears, Joseph | Private | Twelfth, Casey | Dec 1777; Jan 1778 on fatigue; Feb 1778 on duty; March-May 1778. |
| Fagg, John | Private | Fifteenth, Grimes | Feb 11, 1778 drafted; May 1778 sick present. |

| Name | Rank | Regiment/Company | Service |
|---|---|---|---|
| Falkner/Faulkner, Ralph/Rudolph | Major | Second | April 1778; June 1778. Oath at Valley Forge on May 12, 1778, witnessed by Muhlenberg. |
| Falknor/Faulkner, Spencer | Private | Seventh, Spencer/Lipscomb | Feb 13, 1778 enlisted for 1 year; April-May 1778; June 1778 on guard, in Lipscomb's Company. |
| Fambrough, Benjamin | Private | Seventh, Moseley | Dec 1777 sick in hospital; Jan 24, 1778 deceased. |
| Fambrough, Thomas | Private | Seventh, Moseley | Dec 1777-Jan 1778 sick in hospital; Feb 22, 1778 discharged. |
| Fanjoy/Panjay, William | Private | Second, Willis | Dec 28, 1777 deserted. |
| Fancher see Fenshire | | | |
| Fanning, Michael | Private | Twelfth, Vause | Dec 1777 on guard; Jan-April 1778; May 1778 on guard. |
| Farey/Fary, Beverly | Private | Seventh/Third, Hill | Dec 1777-Jan 1778 on furlough; April-May 1778; June 1778 sick present. |
| Farguson/Ferguson, William | Private | Fourteenth, Thweatt | Feb 15, 1778 drafted; June 1778. |
| Faris/Pharis, William | Private | Third, Powell | Dec 1777-Jan 1778; February 1778 on furlough; June 1778. |
| Fariss, Andrew | Private | Seventh, Posey | Dec 1777-Jan 1778 in Rifle Battn. |
| Farmer, Jesse | Private | Seventh/Third, Fleming/Heth | Dec 1777 sick in hospital; Jan-March 1778 on furlough; April-June 1778. |
| Farnbrow/Fambrough, John | Private | Sixth, Apperson | Dec 1777-Jan 1778 hospital; Feb 28, 1778 discharged. |
| Farrol, John | Drummer/Private | Seventh, Crockett | Dec 1777-March 1778; April 1, 1778 reduced to private; April-May 1778. |
| Farrow, James | Private | Second, Harrison | Dec 1777-June 1778. |
| Farrow, William | Private | Second, Harrison | Dec 1777 hospital; Jan-June 1778. |
| Farough see Pharoah | | | |

| Name | Rank | Regiment | Service |
|---|---|---|---|
| Faucett/Faucitt, Obediah | Private | Seventh, Webb | Jan 1778 sick present; Feb 14, 1778 discharged. |
| Faucett, Richard | Private | Seventh, Webb | Jan 1778; Feb 1, 1778 discharged. |
| Fears, Edmond | Private | Twelfth, Bowyer, T. | August 18, 1777 enlisted; Jan 1778 joined; Jan-May 1778. |
| Febiger/Febigar, Christian | Colonel | Second | Dec 1777-June 1778. Oath at Valley Forge on May 11, 1778, witnessed by Muhlenberg. |
| Feesel/Fesel, Michael | Private | Twelfth, Casey | Dec 1777-Jan 1778; Feb 1778 on command; March-April 1778; May 1778 on guard. |
| Feld, John | Private | Seventh, Crockett | Dec 1777-Jan 1778 on furlough; April 10, 1778 discharged. |
| Felkins, John | Private | Third, Peyton, V. | Dec 1777; Jan 1778 on command; February 1778; March-April 1778 on command; May 1778 on guard; June-Aug 1778 sick at Valley Forge. |
| Felton, Thomas | Drummer/ Private | First State, Ewell, T. | Dec 1777; Jan-Feb 1778 sick at Yellow Springs Feb 1778 reduced to Private; March-April 1778; May 1778 on command; June 1, 1778 deserted. |
| Felts/Fetts, Isham | Sergeant | Fifteenth, Mason/ Gregory | Dec 1777 on guard; Jan 1778; Feb 1778 on command; March 1778; April 1778 sick in camp; May 1778; June 1778 in Gregory's Company, sick Valley Forge. |
| Fenley, Charles | Sergeant | Third, Arell | Dec 1777-Jan 1778. |
| Fenlton, John | Private | First, Cummings | Dec 1777. |
| Fennell/Fennel, Reuben/Reubin | Private | First, Taylor | Dec 1777-April 1778; May 1778 sick present; June 1778. |
| Fenshire/ Fancher, Isick/Isaac | Private | Twelfth, Bowyer, T. | Dec 1777-Jan 1778; Feb 1778 sick absent; March 1778 sick in hospital; April-June 1778. |
| Ferell, Benjm. See Fowell. | Private | Fifteenth, Wills | Feb 1778 on guard. |
| Ferguson/ Farguson, John | Private | Second State, Dudley | March 15, 1778-May 1, 1778; May-June 1778. |

| | | | |
|---|---|---|---|
| Ferguson/ Farguson, Larkin | Private | Second State, Dudley | March 15, 1778-May 1, 1778; May-June 1778. |
| Ferguson/ Furguson, Robert | Private | Second, Taylor, W. | Dec 1777-Jan 1778; Feb 5 1778 discharged. |
| Ferguson/ Forguson, Thomas | Private | Second State, Spiller | March 15, 1778-May 1, 1778; May-June 1778. |
| Feris, William | Private | Third, Powell | Jan-March 1778 on furlough; April 1778 on detachment |
| Ferril/Ferrill, Edmund | Private | Second State, Quarles/ Garrett | April-June 1778. In June he transferred to Garrett's company. |
| Ferril/Ferrell, John | Drummer/ Private | Seventh/ Third, Crockett/ Sayers | Dec 1777-Jan 1778 on furlough; April 1, 1778 reduced to Private; April-May 1778; June 1778 in Sayers' Company. |
| Ferril/Ferrill, Thomas | Private | Second State, Quarles/ Garrett | April-June 1778. In June he transferred to Garrett's company. |
| Fers, Jonathan | Sergeant | Sixth, Apperson | Feb 1778. |
| Fevell, Benjamin/Ben | Private | Fifteenth, Wills | Feb 1778 on guard; March-April 1778 sick present; May 1778; June 18, 1778 deserted. |
| Fidler/Fidlar, William | Private | Fourteenth, Thweatt | Aug 30, 1777 inlisted; Jan 1778 lately joined regiment; Feb 1778 on command; March 1778; April 1778 sick Yellow Springs hospital. |
| Field, John | Private | Second State, Bressie | May 1778 "Virginia last payroll;" June 1778 "draws pay in Morgans Corps." |
| Fielder/Feelder, Abraham | Private | Fourteenth, Reid | Dec 1777; Jan 1778 sick in camp; Feb-March 1778; April-June 1778 sick Yellow Springs hospital. |
| Fielder, Charles | Private | Seventh/ Third, Crockett/ Sayers | March 19, 1778 enlisted; April-May 1778; June 1778 in Sayers' Company. |

| | | | |
|---|---|---|---|
| Fielder, David | Private | Second State/ Dudley | March 15-May 1, 1778; May 1778; June 1778 sick absent. |
| Fielder, George/Geo. | Private | Seventh/ Third, Crockett/ Sayers | Dec 1777-Jan 1778 on furlough; April-June 1778 sick in Virginia; June in Sayers' Company. |
| Fields, Simon | Private | Twelfth, Ashby | Dec 1777; Jan 1778 on furlough; March 1778 on furlough; April-May 1778. |
| Fielding/ Felding, James | Private | Sixth, Fox | Dec 1777-Jan 1778; Feb 7, 1778 discharged. |
| Fierse see Phears | | | |
| Fife, William | Private | Twelfth, Waggener | Dec 1777-March 1778; April 10, 1778 discharged. |
| Fillyoung see Phillyoung | | | |
| Finnell, John | Private | Second, Taylor, F. | Dec 1777 hospital; Jan-Feb 1778. |
| Finney/Finnay, John | Private | Seventh/ Third, Crockett/ Sayers | Dec 1777 on guard; Jan 1778; April-May 1778; June 1778 sick Valley Forge. |
| Fish, Thomas | Private | Twelfth, Vause | Dec 1777-Jan 1778; Feb 1778 on command; March-May 1778. |
| Fisher, Richard | Private | Seventh, Webb | Jan 1778; Feb 1778 discharged. |
| Fisher, Thomas | Private | Second, Jones/ Hoomes | Dec 1777-Feb 1778 hospital. |
| Fisher/Fishar, William | Corporal | Twelfth, Ashby | Dec 1777; Jan 1778 sick in hospital; March 1778 at hospital; April-May 1778; June 1778 sick Valley Forge. |
| Fitch, Daniel | Private | First, Scott | Dec 1777 with Colonel Morgan. |
| Fitchsimons/ Fitchsimmon, Thomas/Thos. | Private | First, Cunningham | Feb 14, 1778 enlisted; for 1 year; April 1778 under inoculation; May 1778; June 1778 sick at Valley Forge. |

| Name | Rank | Regiment, Company | Notes |
|---|---|---|---|
| Fitzgerald/ Fitzgarrald, John | Private | Sixth, Massie | May 1778; June 1778 on command. |
| Fitzhugh, John | Private | Fourteenth, Lambert | Dec 1777; Jan 1778 on command; Feb 1778; March 1778 on command; April-June 1778. |
| Fitzpartrick/ Fitspartrick, William | Private | Third, Peyton, J. | Dec 1777-Jan 1778 sick present. |
| Fitzpatrick James | Private | Twelfth, Ashby | March 1778; April 1778 on furlough; May 1778. |
| Fitzpatrick, James | Private | Twelfth, Vause | Dec 1777; Jan 1778 on guard; Feb-May 1778. |
| Fitzsimons/ Fitsimmons, Nicholas | Private | Twelfth, Waggener | Dec 1777-March 1778 hospital; April 1778 deserted at hospital. |
| Flagua/Fluva, Henry | Private | First, Cummings | Feb 7, 1778 enlisted; April-May 1778; June 1778 sick Valley Forge. |
| Flatford, Robert | Drummer | First State, Payne | Dec 1777-June 1778. |
| Flatford, Thomas | Private | Second State, Spiller | March 15-May 1, 1778; May-June 1778. |
| Flax, George/Geo. | Private | First, Cummings | Dec 1777. |
| Fleaman/ Fleeman, Thomas | Private | First, Taylor, F. | Dec 1777-Feb 1778; March 12, 1778 discharged. |
| Fleet, Benjamin/ Benjm. | Private | Fifteenth, Gray | Dec 1777-Feb 1778 on command; March 1778 sick absent; April 1778; May 1778 on command; June 1778 missing at Monmouth. |
| Fleet/Flut, John | Ensign/ 2nd. Lt. | Second State, Dudley/ Taliaferro | April-June 1778. On June 1 he was promoted to 2nd. Lt. and transferred to Taliaferro's company. Oath at Valley Forge in June, 1778, witnessed by Muhlenberg. |
| Flemister/ Flemester, James | Private | Seventh/ Third, Moseley/ Blackwell | Dec 1777-March 1778 on furlough; April 1778; May 1778 on command; June 1778 waggoner, in Blackwell's Company. |

| Name | Rank | Regiment | Service |
|---|---|---|---|
| Fleming, Bernat/Bernett | Private | Second State, Taliaferro | March 15, 1778-May 1, 1778; May-June 1778. |
| Fleming, Charles | Captain | Seventh, Fleming | Dec 1777 on furlough Virginia; Jan-May 1778 on furlough; April 1778 on furlough Virginia; May 1778. |
| Fleming/Flemming, James | Private | Third, Peyton, V./Peyton, J. | Dec 1777 on furlough Virginia; Jan-March 1778 on furlough; April-May 1778; June 1778 in J. Peyton's Company. |
| Fleming, Ludwell C. | Private | Second State, Taliaferro | March 15, 1778-May 1, 1778; May-June 1778. |
| Fleming, William | Private | Second State, Taliaferro | March 15, 1778-May 1, 1778; May-June 1778. |
| Flesher, Henry | Sergeant | Twelfth, Bowyer, T. | Dec 1777-Jan 1778. |
| Fletcher/Flecher, William | Private | Twelfth, Bowyer, T. | Dec 1777-May 1778 on command. |
| Flin/Fling, Thomas | Private | Fourteenth, Jones | Dec 1777; Jan-March 1778 on command; April-May 1778; June 1778 on command. |
| Fling, Edward | Sergeant | Second, Jones | Dec 1777-March 1778. |
| Fling/Flyng, John | Corporal | Seventh, Webb | Jan 1778 sick present; Feb 3, 1778 discharged. |
| Flippin, Robert | Private | First, Cunningham | Feb 12, 1778 enlisted; May-June 1778. |
| Flippo/Flipper, Joseph | Private | Second, Jones | Feb 1778 on furlough; March 1778. |
| Flippo/Fhlipper, Joseph | Private | Second, Upshaw | Dec 1777 on furlough; Jan 1778; April 1778; June 1778. |
| Flood, Henry | Private | Second, Jones | Dec 1777-Feb 1778 hospital; March-June 1778. |
| Flora, William/Wm. | Private | Fifteenth, Grimes | Dec 1777-May 1778. |
| Florance/Florence, George | Private | Third, Lee | Dec 1777 on command; Jan 1778; Feb 14, 1778 discharged. |

| | | | |
|---|---|---|---|
| Flourney/Flournoy, Samuel | Sergeant | First State, Crump | Dec 1777-June 1778. |
| Flowers, James | Private | Seventh, Fleming | Dec 1777-Jan 1778; Feb 26, 1778 discharged. |
| Floyd, Mitchell | Private | Sixth | Feb 28, 1778 drafted; May 1778; June 3, 1778 deceased. |
| Floyd, William | Private/Drummer | Second, Taylor, W. | Dec 1777-Jan 1778; Jan 1778 promoted to Drummer; Feb 17, 1778 died. |
| Flud/Flued, Burrell/Burwel | Private | Fifteenth, Wills | August 21, 1777 enlisted; Jan 1778 on guard; Feb-May 1778. |
| Flynn/Flinn, Daniel | Private | Twelfth, Ashby | Dec 1777; Jan 1778 waggoner; March 1778 on command; April-May 1778. |
| Foot, Ewin/Youen | Private | Second, Parker | April-June 1778. |
| Forbes, James | Private | First, Lawson | Dec 1777 sick Princeton; Jan-Feb 1778 sick hospital; March-April 1778 hospital Lancaster; May 1778 muster roll shows he died June 1, payroll shows he died on June 2. |
| Forester/Forister, Samuel | Private | Twelfth, Waggener | Dec 1777-May 1778. |
| Forguson/Farguson, Hugh | Private | Third, Lee/Peyton J. | Feb 14, 1778 enlisted; April-May 1778; June 1778 on command. |
| Forrest/Forrist, Edmond | Private | Seventh, Young | Dec 1777-Jan 1778 sick in Virginia; Feb 3, 1778 discharged. |
| Forrest, George, Jr. | Private | Seventh, Young | Dec 21, 1777 to Light Horse. |
| Forrest/Forrist, George, Sr. | Private | Seventh, Young | Dec 1777 sick Virginia; Feb 3, 1778 discharged. |
| Forrest, Thomas | Private/Quartermaster Sergeant | Seventh/Third, Crockett | March 19, 1778 enlisted; April-May 1778; May 27, 1778 promoted to Quartermaster Sergeant; June-Aug 1778 sick at Valley Forge. |
| Forrester, James | Private | First State, Hoffler | Dec 17, 1777 deceased. |

| Name | Rank | Company | Notes |
|---|---|---|---|
| Forsythe, Hugh | Private | Twelfth, Bowyer, T. | August 30, 1777 enlisted; Jan 1778 joined; Jan-April 1778; May 1778 on guard. |
| Fortune, Gardner/ Guardner | Private | First State, Lee | Dec 1777-Jan 1778; Feb 1778 on guard; March-Jan 1778. |
| Foss, Mark | Private | Twelfth, Madison | Dec 1777 on guard; Jan 1778 sick in camp; Feb-March 1778; April 1778 on guard; "Labertery Gud". |
| Foster, Achilles | Quartermaster | Twelfth | Dec 1777-May 1778. |
| Foster, Edmond/ Edmund | Private/ Corporal | Fourteenth, Marks | Dec 1777-Jan 1778; Jan 1778 promoted to Corporal; Feb-June 1778. |
| Foster/Fouster, James | Private | Fourteenth, Lambert | Dec 1777; Jan-Feb 1778 artificer; March-May 1778; June 1778 on command. |
| Foster, James | Captain | Fifteenth, Foster | Nov 15, 1777 died. In Feb 1778 his entire company was joined to Captain James Gray's. |
| Foster/Fostor, Joel | Private | Second, Taylor, F. | Dec 1777 hospital; Jan-Feb 1778; March 12, 1778 discharged. |
| Foster, John | Sergeant | Second State, Spiller | March 15, 1778-May 1, 1778; May-June 1778. |
| Foster, Peter | Quartermaster Sergeant/ Sergeant | First State, Meriwether | Feb 1778 Quartermaster Sergeant; June 1778 Sergeant. |
| Foster, Robert | Ensign | Fifteenth, Foster/ Gray | Dec 1777-Jan 1778; Feb 1778 in Gray's Company; March 1778; April 24, 1778 taken prisoner at Barren Hill Church. |
| Foster, Simson/ Simpson | Sergeant/ Sergeant Major | Fourteenth, Marks | Dec 1777-Feb 1778; March 1778 promoted to Sergeant Major; March-June 1778. Company roll shows promotion on March 14, Field and Staff roll shows March 18. |
| Foster, William | Private | First, Taylor/ Lawson | Dec 1777-Jan 1778; Feb-March 1778 wagoner; April-May 1778; June 1778 on command, in Lawson's Company. |
| Foster, William | Private | Seventh/ Third, Jouett/Hill | Dec 1, 1777 enlisted; Jan-April 1778 on furlough; May 1778; June 1778 on guard. |

| | | | |
|---|---|---|---|
| Foushee/Foshee, William/Wm. | Private | First, Payne | Feb 5, 1778 enlisted; May 1778 sick present; June 1778 sick at Valley Forge. |
| Fowell/Fewell, Benjn. See Ferell. | Corporal | Fifteenth, Wills | March-April 1778 sick present; May 1778. This man and Benjm. Ferrll may be the same individual. |
| Fowler, Charles | Private | Second, Sanford/ Parker | Dec 1777-June 1778. From April on he appears in Parker's company. |
| Fowler, Micajah/ Mccajia | Private | First, Cummings | May 14, 1778 joined, sick present; June 1778 sick at Valley Forge. |
| Fox, Adam | Private | Fifteenth/ Wills | Aug 18, 1777 enlisted; Feb 1778 sick in Virginia; March 1778 sick absent; April 1778; May 1778 sick present; June-July 1778 sick Valley Forge; Aug 1778 dead. |
| Fox, Lewis/Lewes | Private/ Sergeant/ Quartermaster Sergeant | Sixth, Massie | Dec 1777 innoculated; Jan 1778 promoted to Sergeant; Feb 1778; March 1778 promoted to Quartermaster Sergeant; March-June 1778. |
| Fox, Nathaniel/Nathl. | Captain | Sixth, Fox | Dec 1777-Jan 1778 sick at Trenton; Feb-June 1778 on furlough. |
| Fox, Martin | Private | Fifteenth, Wills | Aug 18, 1777 enlisted; Feb 1778; March-April 1778 sick present; May 1778: June 1778 sick absent. |
| Fox, Thomas | Private | Third, Peyton, V./ Peyton, J. | Dec 1777 on furlough Virginia; Jan-March 1778 on furlough; April 1778 sick in camp; May 1778; June 1778 in J. Peyton's Company. |
| Fox, William | Private | Second State, Dudley | March 15, 1778-May 1, 1778; May-June 1778; July 26, 1778 died. |
| Francis, Rubin/Reubin | Private | Sixth, Hockaday | Dec 1777 sick Princetown; Jan 15, 1778 died at Princetown. |
| Francis, Thomas/Thos | Private | Sixth, Massie | Dec 1777-Jan 1778; Feb 12, 1778 discharged. |
| Franklin, Henry | Private | Second State, Lewis | March 15, 1778-May 1, 1778; May-June 1778. |

| Name | Rank | Regiment | Service |
|---|---|---|---|
| Franklin, John | Private | Fourteenth, Thweatt | Dec 18, 1777 died. |
| Franklin, Joseph | Corporal | Second, Willis | Dec 1777-May 1778; June-July 1778 sick at Valley Forge. |
| Franklin, Samuel | Private | Twelfth, Madison | Dec 1777; Jan 1778 on bullock guard; Feb 1778 on command; March-April 1778 on guard. |
| Frazer/Frazier, John | Private | Twelfth, Waggener | Dec 1777; Jan 1778 on guard; Feb-March 1778; April 1778 sick in camp; May 1778 on guard. |
| Frazier, Anthony | 2nd. Lt. | First State, Camp | Dec 1777 sick in ye country; Jan 1778; Feb 12, 1778 resigned. |
| Frazier, James | Sergeant/ Private | Fifteenth, Hull | Dec 26, 1777 reduced to Private; Dec 1777-Feb 1778; March-April 1778 on command; May 1778 sick present. |
| Frazier, Thomas | Private | Second, Willis | Dec 1777-March 1778. |
| Freeman/ Freaman, Colsup/Calsup | Private | Fourteenth, Winston | Dec 1777; Jan 1778 on guard; Feb-April 1778; May 1778 sick present; June 1778 sick Valley Forge. |
| Freeman, Charles | Private | First State, Meriwether | Dec 1777-March 1778. |
| Freeman, Hezekiah/ Hezekia | Private | First State, Crump | Dec 1777-June 1778. |
| Freeman, John | Private | First, Cunningham | Feb 17, 1778 enlisted for 1 year; April 1778 under inoculation; May 9, 1778 died. |
| Freeman, John | Private | Fifteenth, Gray | Dec 1777 G. Washn. Gd.; Jan 1778; Feb 1778 deserted; March 1778 sick camp; April 10, 1778 dead. |
| Freeman, Stephen/ Stephan | Private | Fifteenth, Gray | Dec 1777-Jan 1778; Feb 1778 on guard; March 1778 sick in camp; April-May 1778. |
| Freeman/ Freemon, Thomas | Private | Seventh/ Third, Young | Feb 16, 1778 enlisted; April 1778 sick present; May-June 1778 |
| French, Alexander | Sergeant | Second, Parker | May-June 1778. |

| | | | |
|---|---|---|---|
| French, Richard | Private | First State, Hamilton | Dec 1777-June 1778. |
| French, Samuel | Ensign/ 2nd. Lt. | First State, Brown | Dec 1777; Jan 15, 1778 promoted to 2nd. Lt.; Jan-April 1778; May 1, 1778 resigned. |
| Frewit see Pruit | | | |
| Frey, George | Private | Fourteenth, Marks | June 1778. |
| Frisquit/ Frisquet, George | Drummer/ Private | Twelfth, Casey | Dec 1777 sent to hospital; Jan 1778 reduced to Private; Jan-May 1778. |
| Frith, John | Private | Fourteenth, Winston | Dec 1777 on command; Jan 1778 on guard; March 1778; May 1778; June 1778 on duty. |
| Froman, Tempel/Temple | Private | Seventh, Webb | Dec 1777-Jan 1778; Feb 8, 1778 discharged. |
| Froud/Stroud, James | Private | First State, Meriwether | Dec 1777-June 1778. |
| Fry, Benjamin | Sergeant | Fourteenth, Marks | Dec 1777-June 1778 on furlough. |
| Fry, Gabriel/ Gabrial | Private | Fourteenth, Marks | Dec 1777-April 1778; May 1778 sick present; June 1778 sick Valley Forge. |
| Fry, George | Corporal | Fourteenth, Marks | Dec 1777-April 1778; May 1778 confined. |
| Fry, Joseph | Private | Fourteenth, Marks | Dec 1777 in hospital; Jan-April 1778; May 1778 confined; June 1778 sick Valley Forge; July 1778 dead. |
| Fryer/Friar, Richard | Private | Second, Harrison | Dec 1777 sick in Country House; Jan-June 1778. |
| Fudrill/Fuddrill Charles | Private | Second, Willis | Dec 1777 hospital; Dec 1777-May 1778; June 1778 sick Correll Ferry. |
| Fugate, Benjamin | Private | Twelfth, Casey | Dec 1777 sent to hospital; Jan-Feb 1778 hospital; March 1778 muster roll shows he died about Dec 20, 1777. |
| Fuglar, William | Private | First State, Crump | Dec 1777-June 1778. |
| Fulk, Peter | Private | Twelfth, Casey | Dec 1777 sent to hospital; Jan-March 1778 at hospital; April 1778 supposed to be dead. |

| Name | Rank | Regiment | Service |
|---|---|---|---|
| Fullins, William | Private | Second State, Lewis | March 15, 1778-May 1, 1778; May-June 1778. |
| Fundemore/Fundament, Frederick | Private | Twelfth, Waggener | Dec 1777-Jan 1778; Feb 1778 on guard; March 1778; April 10, 1778 discharged. |
| Fundemore/Fundament, John | Private | Twelfth, Waggener | Dec 1777; Jan 1778 on guard; Feb-March 1778 on command; April 10, 1778 discharged. |
| Funner, Stephen | Private | Fifteenth, Gregory | June 1778 sick Yellow Springs. |
| Funtress, Valentine | Private | First State, Brown | Dec 1777-May 1778; June 1778 sick absent Valley Forge. |
| Furnish/Furnis, Jacob | Private | Seventh, Spencer | Dec 1777 on guard; Jan 1778; March 2, 1778 discharged. |
| Furnish/Furniss, William | Private | Seventh, Spencer | Dec 1777-Jan 1778 hospital; March 2, 1778 discharged. |
| Furs/Fers, Jonathan | Quartermaster Sergeant | Sixth | Feb 1778. |
| Gabriel, James | Private | Fifteenth, Gray | Dec 1777 sick absent. |
| Gadberry/Gadbeary William | Private | First State, Lee | Dec 1777-June 1778. |
| Gafford, Thomas | Private | Fourteenth, Winston | Dec 1777; Jan 1778 on guard; Feb-June 1778. |
| Gaghanan, Michael | Drummer | Third, Briscoe | Dec 1777 absent with Col. Marshall. |
| Gahagan, John | Private | Twelfth, Waggener | Dec 1777-May 1778. |
| Gaines, Jacob | Private | Seventh, Posey | Feb 27, 1778 enlisted. |
| Gaines/Gains, Richard | Sergeant | Seventh/Third, Spencer/Lipscomb | Feb 13, 1778 enlisted; May 1778 on guard; June 1778, in Lipscomb's Company. |
| Gaines, Thomas | Ensign | First State, Ewell, T. | Dec 1777. |
| Gains/Gaines, William | Private | First State, Camp | Dec 1777 on guard; Jan-June 1778. |
| Gains/Gaines, William | Private | Seventh, Spencer | Dec 1777 on command; Jan 1778 sick present; March 3, 1778 discharged. |

| | | | |
|---|---|---|---|
| Gains, Richard | Private | Seventh, Spencer | Feb 13, 1778 enlisted for 1 year; April 1778. |
| Gainstaf, George | Private | Twelfth, Ashby | Dec 1777; Jan 1778 sick in camp; March-April 1778; May 1778 sick in camp. |
| Gaiveman, Richard | Fleming | Fourteenth, Jones | April 1778. |
| Galaspe/Glaspy, Daniel | Private | Twelfth, Ashby | Dec 1777-March 1778; April 1778 sick at hospital; May 1778 hospital at Yellow Springs. |
| Galaspy/Galespy, George | Private | Fourteenth, Marks | Dec 1777; Jan 1778 on duty; Feb-April 1778; May-June 1778 on command. |
| Galden, Jesse | Private | First State, Crump | Dec 1777-Jan 1778; Feb 1778 deceased. |
| Gale, Thomas | Private | Fifteenth, Edmunds | Dec 1777. This man and the one below may be the same individual. |
| Gale/Gail/, Thomas/Thos. | Musician | Fifteenth, Wills | Jan-May 1778. |
| Galford, Thomas | Sergeant | Twelfth, Bowyer, M. | Dec 1777-May 1778. |
| Gallaway/Galloway, Terry | Private | Seventh/Third, Fleming/Young | Dec 1777 on furlough Virginia; Jan-March 1778 on furlough; April-May 1778; June 1778 in Young's Company. |
| Gallen/Gauling, Samuel | Private | Sixth, Massie | Dec 1777 hospital; Jan 1778; Feb 12, 1778 discharged. |
| Galliway/Galleaway, Geo. | Private | Fifteenth, Hull | Dec 1777 sick absent; Jan 1778 sick in hospital; Feb-March 1778 sick absent; April 1778 muster roll shows him deceased on Feb 2, 1778. |
| Gambell/Gamble, Robert | 1st. Lt. | Twelfth, Bowyer, M. | Dec 1777; Jan-March 1778 on command; April 1778 on command at Lancaster; May 1778 on command; June 1778 on command at Lancaster. |
| Gambel/Gamble, Thomas | Private | Third, Peyton, V. | Dec 1777-Jan 1778 with Col. Morgan. |
| Gammel/Gemmill, Nathan | Sergeant | Second, Jones | Dec 1777-June 1778. |

| Name | Rank | Regiment, Company | Notes |
|---|---|---|---|
| Gammill, John | Private | First, Pelham | Dec 1777 sick at Morristown. |
| Gane/Gain, James | Private | Seventh, Posey | Feb 22, 1778 enlisted; April-May 1778 |
| Garbett/Garbet, Richard | Private | Fourteenth, Marks | Feb 16, 1778 drafted; April-June 1778. |
| Gardiner/Guardiner, Richd. | Private | Fifteenth, Harris | Jan 1778 on guard; Feb 1778 sick present; March 15, 1778 deserted. |
| Gardner, George | Private | Second State, Dudley | March 15, 1778-May 1, 1778; May 1778; June 1778 sick absent; July 1778 sick Valley Forge. |
| Gardner/Gardiner, Henson | Sergeant | Sixth, Apperson | Dec 1777 sick Trenton; Jan-Feb 1778 absent with leave. |
| Gardner, John | Private/Sergeant | Seventh/Third, Hill | Dec 1777-Jan 1778 on furlough; April 1, 1778 promoted to Sergeant; April-June 1778. |
| Gardner, Richard | Private | Fifteenth, Harris | Feb 1778 sick present; March 15, 1778 deserted. |
| Gardner/Guardner, Thomas | Private | First State, Lee | Dec 1777 sick; Jan 1778 sick absent; Feb 1778 put on board galley. |
| Gardner, Thomas | Sergeant/Sergeant Major | Second State, Spiller | March 15-May 1, 1778; May-June 1778. On June 1 he was promoted to Sergeant Major of the regiment. |
| Gardner/Gardnor, William | Private | Second State, Spiller | March 15-May 1, 1778; May-June 1778. |
| Garland, Andrew | Private | First, Cunningham | Dec 1777. |
| Garland, Peter | 1st. Lt./Captain | Sixth, Avery/Garland | Dec 1777 in Avery's company, recruiting; promoted to Captain retroactive to Aug 17, 1777, and took over Major Hopkins' company; Jan 1778 recruiting Virginia; Feb-May 1778 recruiting; June 1778. |
| Garner, Absolom/Absalom | Private | Fifteenth, Hull | Dec 1777-March 1778; April 1778 sick present; May 25, 1778 died. |
| Garner, John | Private | Third, Mercer | Dec 23, 1777 discharged. |

| Name | Rank | Company | Notes |
|---|---|---|---|
| Garner/Gardner, William | Private | First State, Hamilton | Dec 1777-Feb 1778; June 1778. |
| Garnett/Garnet, Henry | Captain | Second State, Garnett | Ensign Collins is the only officer shown in Garnett's company for this period. Garnett himself does not appear on the rolls. |
| Garrat/Gerrard (no first name listed) | Corporal | Twelfth, Waggener | Dec 31, 1777 enlisted in light Horse. |
| Garrett/Garratt, Henry | Private | Third, Blackwell | Feb 18, 1778 drafted; April 1778; May 1778 on guard; June 1778 on command. |
| Garrett, John | Private | First State, Camp | Dec 1777 sick country; Jan-Feb 1778 sick absent; March 20, 1778 died. |
| Garrett, Mark | Quartermaster Sergeant | First State, Brown | Jan 1778. |
| Garrett/Garret, William | Private | Second, Taylor, W. | Dec 1777-Jan 1778; Feb 21, 1778 discharged. |
| Garriott, Mark | Quartermaster Sergeant | First State, Brown | Jan 1778. |
| Garrison, Jeremiah | Private | Seventh, Posey | Dec 1777 on guard; Jan 22, 1778 deceased. |
| Garvey, Henry | Private | Third, Peyton, J. | Dec 1777; Jan 31, 1778 discharged. |
| Gary, James | Private | First State, Brown | Dec 1777; March 1778 reported dead. |
| Gaskin/Ghaskins, Littleton | Private | Fifteenth, Harris | Jan 1778 artificer; Feb-March 1778; April 1778 on command; May 1778 on command at Lancaster. |
| Gaskins, Jesse | Private | Fifteenth, Hull | Dec 1777 sick absent; Jan 1778 sick at hospital; Feb-March 1778 sick absent; April 1778 sick hospital; May 1778 missing [ ]. |
| Gaskins/Garkins, Job/Jab | Private | Fifteenth, Mason/Gregory | Dec 1777-Feb 1778; March-April 1778 sick in camp; May 1778; June 1778 in Gregory's Company. |
| Gasway, James | Corporal | Second, Calmes | Dec 1777-June 1778. |
| Gasway, John | Private | Second, Calmes | Dec 1777-May 1778; June 1778 sick Corryell's Ferry. |

| Name | Rank | Company | Notes |
|---|---|---|---|
| Gates, Samuel | Private | Second, Calmes | Dec 1777-Jan 1778; Feb 1778 deserted when on command. |
| Gates, William | Private | Second, Taylor, W. | Dec 1777 hospital; Jan-March 1778. |
| Gatriy/Guthrey, John | Private | Seventh, Hill | April-May 1778 |
| Gauman/Gawmon, John | Private | Fourteenth, Jones | Jan-Feb 1778; March 1778 on command; May 1778. |
| Gay, John | Private | Sixth | June 1778. |
| Gears/Geares, James | Private | Twelfth, Bowyer, T. | Aug 1, 1777 enlisted; Jan 1778 joined; Jan-Feb 1778; March 1778 sick in hospital; April 12, 1778 deceased. |
| Geast/Geist, Thomas | Private | Fourteenth, Reid | Dec 1777; Jan 1778 at hospital; Feb 1778 sick present; March-June 1778. |
| Geddy, David | Private/Fifer | Fourteenth, Winston | Feb 17, 1778 drafted; May 1778; June 1, 1778 promoted to Fifer; June 1778 sick Valley Forge. |
| Gee, Henry | Private | Fourteenth, Thweatt | Feb 6, 1778 died. |
| Gee, Richard | Private | Twelfth, Casey | Dec 1777 left with baggage; Jan 1778 deserted. |
| Gentry/Gentrey, John | Private | Seventh/Third, Jouett/Hill | Feb 11, 1778 enlisted; May 1778; June 1778 in Hill's Company. |
| George, John | Private | Seventh, Webb | Jan 1778 hopital; Feb 17, 1778 discharged. |
| George, Judethan | Sergeant | Second State, Bernard | May 1778; June 1778 sick Valley Forge. |
| George, Travis | Private | Seventh/Third, Fleming/Heth | Feb 10, 1778 enlisted; April 1778 sick present; May 1778; June 1778 in Heth's Company. |
| Germon/Jarmon, Henry | Private | Twelfth, Bowyer, T. | Nov 1777 left for sea service; March 1778; April 1, 1778 "sent from the Rogaley" April 1778 sick in camp; May 1778 on command. |
| Gee, Henry | Private | Fourteenth, Thweatt | Dec 1777-Jan 1778; Feb 6, 1778 dead. |

| Name | Rank | Regiment | Notes |
|---|---|---|---|
| Gerrard/Jarrard, Moses | Private | Twelfth, Waggener | Dec 1777-Feb 1778 hospital; March 1778 muster roll shows him deceased on Jan 14, 1778. |
| Gibany/Giboney, Richard | Private | Twelfth, Vause | Dec 1777-Jan 1778 sick hospital Allentown; Feb-May 1778. |
| Gibbens/Gibbons, Marcus | Sergeant | Sixth, Hockaday | Feb 12, 1778 drafted; April-June 1778. |
| Gibbons/Gibbins, James | Private | Second, Taylor, F. | Dec 1777-Jan 1778 waiter for Lord Stirling; Jan-Feb 1778; March 20, 1778 discharged. |
| Gibbs, Churchill | Sergeant | First State, Hamilton | Dec 1777-June 1778. |
| Gibbs/Gibs, Edward | Private | Second, Taylor, W. | Dec 1777-Jan 1778; Feb 5, 1778 discharged. |
| Gibbs, Herod/Harrod | 2nd. Lt. | Fifteenth, Harris | Jan 1778 on command; Feb-March 1778; April 1778 on command; May 30, 1778 resigned. |
| Gibbs, Joseph | Private | Second, Jones | Dec 1777; Jan 1778 on command; Feb-June 1778. |
| Gibbs, Miles | Sergeant | Second, Taylor, W. | Dec 1777-Jan 1778; Feb 5, 1778 discharged. |
| Gibbs/Gibs, William/Wm. | Sergeant | First, Pelham | Dec 1777 sick absent; Feb 15, 1778 discharged. |
| Gibson/Gipson, Billingsley/Billingsly | Private | Seventh/Third, Posey/Sayers | Feb 27, 1778 enlisted; April-May 1778; June 1778 with Col. Morgan, in Sayer's Company. |
| Gibson, Elijah | Private | Fourteenth, Thweatt | Feb 14, 1778 enlisted; April 1778 lately joined regiment; May 1778 on command; June 1778. |
| Gibson, George | Colonel | First State | Jan-Feb 1778; March-April 1778 on command; May 1778 command at Lancaster; June 1778. |
| Gibson, John | Sergeant | Second State, Quarles | April-June 1778. |
| Gibson, John | Colonel | Sixth | April 1778 on furlough; May-June 1778 on command at Fort Pitt. Oath at Valley Forge on May 12, 1778, witnessed by Muhlenberg. |

| Name | Rank | Regiment/Company | Service |
|---|---|---|---|
| Gibson, John | Private | Seventh/Third, Lipscomb | Feb 14, 1778 enlisted for 1 year; April-June 1778. |
| Gibson, Robert | Corporal | Second State, Garnett | May-June 1778. |
| Gifford/Gifferd, James | Private | First, Lewis | Dec 1777-Jan 1778; Feb 1778 on furlough; March-May 1778; June 1778 on command Valley Forge. |
| Gilbreath/Gilbreth, Robert | Sergeant | Twelfth, Bowyer, T. | Dec 1777; Feb-March 1778 on command; April 1778 bullock guard; May 1778. |
| Gililien, Marcus | Sergeant | Sixth, Hockaday | April 1778 payroll shows he was drafted on Feb 12, 1778. |
| Gill, Daniel/Danl. | Private | Fifteenth, Harris | Feb-April 1778 sick present; May 1778 sick absent; June 1778 sick at Yellow Springs. |
| Gill, Erasmus | 2nd. Lt. | Second, Calmes | Dec 1777-June 1778. |
| Gillam/Gillem, John | Drummer | Sixth, Apperson | Dec 1777-Jan 1778; Feb 19, 1778 discharged. |
| Gillett/Gillet, John/Jno. | Private | First, Cunningham | Feb 19, 1778 enlisted; April 1778 under inoculation; May 20, 1778 died. |
| Gilliam, Ansolum/Anselm | Private | Fifteenth, Edmunds | Dec 1777-March 1778 sick absent; April 1778 sick hospital. |
| Gilliam, Harris | Private | Fifteenth, Edmunds | Dec 1777-March 1778 sick absent; April 1778 sick hospital. |
| Gilliam, Joseph | Private | Sixth | Feb 5, 1778 enlisted; June 1778. |
| Gilliland/Gillilend, Alexander/Ellock | Private | Seventh/Third, Crockett/Briscoe | March 19, 1778 enlisted for 1 year; April 1778 sick present; May 1778 in room of John Long; June 1778 sick Valley Forge, in Briscoe's Company. |
| Gillock, John | Private | Second, Taylor, W. | Dec 1777 on furlough; Jan-June 1778. |
| Gilmore, Robert | Private | First State, Meriwether | Dec 1777-May 1778; June 1778 sick absent. |
| Gimbo/Gimboe, William | Corporal/Sergeant | Third, Peyton, V./Peyton, J. | Dec 1777-March 1778 on furlough Virginia; April-May 1778; June 1778 on command; in J. Peyton's Company. |

| | | | |
|---|---|---|---|
| Gisbon, John | Private | Second State, Bressie | March 15, 1778-May 1, 1778; May-June 1778. |
| Glascock/ Glascocke, Robert/Robt. | Fifer | Fifteenth, Harris | Jan-May 1778. |
| Glason, Patrick | Private | First State, Hamilton | Dec 1777-May 1778; June 1778 sick absent. |
| Glazer/Glazier, Adam | Private | Seventh/ Third, Crockett/ Powell | March 12, 1778 enlisted; April-May 1778; June 1778 in Powell's Company. |
| Glidwell/ Glidewell, Nash | Private | Fourteenth, Thweatt | Feb 14, 1778 enlisted; April 1778 lately joined regiment; May 1778 sick present in camp; June 1778 sick Valley Forge. |
| Glover, Robert/Robt. | Private | Fifteenth, Mason/ Gregory | Dec 1777; Jan-Feb 1778 sick present; March-April 1778 sick in camp; May 1778; June 1778 on guard, in Gregory's Company. |
| Glover, Samuel | Private | Seventh/ Third, Fleming/ Heth | Feb 19, 1778 enlisted; April 1778 sick present; May 1778; June 1778 in Heth's Company. |
| Glover/Glouver, Thomas | Sergeant/ Quartermaster Sergeant | Second State, Spiller | March 15-May 1, 1778 May-June 1778. In May he was promoted to Quartermaster Sergeant. |
| Glover, Thomas | Private | Third, Blackwell | Feb 18, 1778 drafted; April-May 1778; June 1778 on command. |
| Goatley/Goatly, John | Private | First State, Hamilton | Dec 1777-May 1778; June 1778 sick absent. |
| Godby/Godbey, George | Private | Second State, Dudley | March 15, 1778-May 1, 1778; May-June 1778. |
| Godfrey, Robert | Private | Third, Arell | Dec 1777-February 1778; March-May 1778 on command |
| Goff/Gauff, Abraham/ Abram | Private | First State, Nicholas | Dec 1777; Jan 1778 sick at Red Lyon; Feb 1778 sick present; March 1778; April 1778 on command; May-June 1778. |
| Goff, Abram/ Abraham | Private | Fifteenth, Harris | Jan 1778; Feb-April 1778 sick present; May 1778 sick absent; June 1778 sick Yellow Springs. |

| Name | Rank | Regiment | Dates |
|---|---|---|---|
| Goff/Gough, Adam | Corporal | Second, Harrison | Dec 1777-June 1778. |
| Goff, Daniel/Danl. | Private | Fifteenth, Harris | Sept 1777 enlisted; March-April 1778 sick present; May 1778 sick absent. |
| Goff, John | Private | Fifteenth, Harris | Jan 1778 on command; Feb-April 1778; May 16, 1778 deceased. |
| Goff, Philip/Phill | Fifer | Second, Harrison | Dec 1777 hospital; Jan-June 1778. |
| Gogarty/Gogerty, Thomas | Corporal/Sergeant | Twelfth, Wallace | Dec 1777-Feb 1778; February 4, 1778, promoted to Sergeant; March 1778 on command; April 1778; May 1778 on guard. |
| Goin, John | Private | Seventh/Third, Moseley | Feb 14, 1778 enlisted; April-May 1778; June 1778. |
| Going, David | Private | Sixth, Fox | Jan-April 1778; May 13, 1778 deceased. |
| Going, William | Private | Fourteenth, Lambert | May 1778 on guard. |
| Gold/Goold, James | Private | Twelfth, Waggener | Dec 1777-April 1778; May 1778 sick in camp. |
| Golden, Isom/Isham | Private | Second State, Spiller | March 15-May 1, 1778; May 1778; June 1778 sick Valley Forge. |
| Golden, Jesse | Private | Second State, Garnett | May-June 1778. |
| Golden, Simon | Private | Second State, Garnett | May-June 1778. |
| Goldman, Daniel | Private | First State, Hamilton | Dec 1777-June 1778. |
| Goldman, David | Private | First State, Hamilton | Dec 1777-June 1778. |
| Goldman, Francis | Private | Second, Upshaw | Dec 1777-Jan 1778. |
| Goley/Galey, John | Private | Third, Peyton, V./Peyton, J. | Dec 1777-March 1778 on furlough in Virginia; May 1778 sick present; June 1778 in John Peyton's Company. |

| Name | Rank | Company | Notes |
|---|---|---|---|
| Goode, Archibald/ Archabal | Private | Fourteenth, Thweatt | Dec 1777; Jan-Feb 1778 sick in hospital; March-May 1778; June 1778 sick Valley Forge. |
| Goode/Good, Thomas | Private | Sixth, Garland | Dec 1777 sick in hospital; Jan 1778 hospital; Feb 26, 1778 discharged. |
| Goodrum/ Goodwin, Thomas/Thos. | Corporal | Fifteenth, Mason/ Gregory | Dec 1777 waggoner; Jan 1778 sick absent; Feb 1778 sick present; March 1778 sick in camp; April 1778; May 1778 on guard; June 1778 in Gregory's Company. |
| Goph/Cuff, John | Private | First, Scott | Jan 1778; Feb 1778 sick Bethlehem, Feb 1778 sick hospital; March-May 1778; June 1778 sick at Valley Forge. |
| Gorden/Gordon, John | Private | Twelfth, Ashby | Jan 1778 on command; March 1778; April 1778 on command; May 1778. |
| Gorden, William | Private | Twelfth, Bowyer, M. | April 2, 1778 joined; April 26, 1778 deserted. |
| Gordon/Gorgan, George | Private/ Sergeant | Third, Arell | Dec 1777; Jan 1778 promoted to Sergeant; Feb 26, 1778 died. |
| Gordon, James | Private | First State, Payne | Dec 1777; Jan 11, 1778 deceased. |
| Gordon/Gordan, James | Private | Second, Jones | Dec 1777-Feb 1778 hospital; March-May 1778; June-July 1778 sick at Valley Forge. |
| Gordon/Gorden, John | Private | Fourteenth, Marks | Dec 1777 in hospital; Jan 1778; Feb 1778 on command; March 1778; April 1778 on command; May-June 1778. |
| Gordon, Thomas | Private | Sixth, Avery | Dec 1777-Jan 1778; Feb 8, 1778 discharged. |
| Gordon, William/Wm. | Sergeant Major | Sixth | Feb-June 1778. This man and the two below may be the same individual. |
| Gordon, William/Wm. | Private | Sixth, Avery | Dec 1777 on command; Jan 30, 1778 discharged. |
| Gordon, Wm. Jr. | Sergeant | Sixth, Avery | Aug 29, 1777 enlisted; Jan 1778 appointed Sergeant; Jan-Feb 1778. |
| Goring, David | Private | Sixth, Fox | Aug 21, 1777 enlisted; Jan 1778; May 13, 1778 decd. |

| Name | Rank | Regiment | Service |
|------|------|----------|---------|
| Gorman, John | Drummer | Fourteenth, Winston | Dec 1777-Jan 1778. |
| Gormond/ Gorman/ Gormon, Thomas | Private | Twelfth, Madison | Dec 1777 on guard; Jan 1778; Feb 1778 on command; March 1778; April 1778 on command. |
| Gosdan, Will | Private | Twelfth, Bowyer, M. | April 14, 1778 joined; April 26, 1778 deserted. |
| Goss, James | Corporal | First State, Nicholas | Dec 1777-Feb 1778 sick Bethlehem; March-June 1778. |
| Goudman, John | Private | Fourteenth, Jones | Sept 17, 1777 enlisted; May 1778. |
| Gowan/Gowen, Joseph | Private | Fourteenth, Lambert | Dec 1777-June 1778. |
| Gowan/Gowen, William | Private | Fourteenth, Lambert | Dec 1777-Feb 1778; April 1778; May 1778 on guard; June 1778. |
| Gowden/ Gowdon, William | Corporal | Second, Sanford/ Parker | Dec 1777-June 1778. From April on he appears in Parker's company. |
| Gowin, John | Private | Seventh, Moseley | Feb 14, 1778 enlisted |
| Gowin/Gowen, Sherard/Shead | Private | Fourteenth, Overton | Dec 1777 on command; Jan-March 1778; April 1778 sick present; May-June 1778. |
| Grady/Gradey, Jonathan | Sergeant | Fourteenth, Winston | Dec 1777 on command; Jan 1778 at R. hospital; Feb 1778 on command; March 1778; April 1778 on guard. |
| Grady, John | Private | Fourteenth, Winston | May 1778; June 1778 on command. |
| Grafton, John | Private | First State, Camp | Dec 1777 sick in hospital; Jan 1778; Feb 1778 on guard; March-June 1778. |
| Graham, Arthur | Private | First State, Hamilton | Dec 1777-June 1778. |
| Graham, William | Surgeon's Mate | Second | Dec 1777-Jan 1778. |
| Graham/ Grayham, William | Private | Seventh, Mosely | Dec 1777-Jan 1778 in R. Regt; Feb 21, 1778 discharged. |
| Grant, Adam F./ Adam | Private | First, Lawson | Dec 1777-Feb 1778; March 1778 command; April-June 1778. |

| Name | Rank | Regiment | Service |
|---|---|---|---|
| Grant, David | Corporal | Fourteenth, Thweatt | Jan-March 1778; April 1778 sick Lancaster; May 1778; June 1778 sick Princetown. |
| Grant, James | Private | Seventh, Jouett | Dec 1777; Jan 7, 1778 discharged. |
| Grant, John | Sergeant Major | First | Dec 1777; Feb 15, 1778 discharged. |
| Grant, John/Jno. | Private | Third, Mercer/ Powell | Feb 28, 1778 enlisted; June 1778 on detachment, in Powell's Company. |
| Grant, John | Private | Fourteenth, Marks | Dec 1777 in hospital; Jan 1778 hospital sick; Feb 1778 sick absent; March 1778 sick in hospital; April 1778 Lititz hospital; May 1778; June 1778 sick Corryells Ferry. |
| Grass, Frederick | Private | Twelfth, Bowyer, M. | Feb 7, 1778 enlisted; April 14, 1778 joined; April 1778; May-June 1778 on guard. |
| Gratton/Gratten, Robert/Robt. | Private | Seventh/ Third, Posey/ Young | Feb 27, 1778 enlisted; April-May 1778; June 1778 in Young's company, sick Correll's Ferry. |
| Gravatt, John | Sergeant | Second, Upshaw | Dec 1777-Jan 1778. |
| Graves, Francis | Private | Seventh, Webb | Jan 1778 sick in Virginia; Feb 2, 1778 discharged. |
| Graves, Jeremiah | Private | Second State, Dudley | March 15, 1778-May 1, 1778; May-June 1778. |
| Graves, John | Private | Seventh, Webb | Jan 1778; Feb 13, 1778 discharged. |
| Graves, John | Private | Seventh, Young | Dec 1777-Jan 1778 sick in Virginia; Feb 3, 1778 discharged. |
| Graves, Rice | Private | Seventh, Webb | Dec 1777 hospital; Feb 14, 1778 discharged. |
| Gray/Grey, George | Private | First, Lawson | Dec 1777-March 1778 artificer; April 1778 command; May-June 1778 artificer. |
| Gray, James | Captain | Fifteenth, Gray | Dec 1777-May 1778; June 1778 on command at Valley Forge. |

| Name | Rank | Unit | Notes |
|---|---|---|---|
| Gray, John | Drummer | Second, Upshaw/ Jones | Dec 1777 hospital; Jan 1778; Feb-April 1778. For February and March he is listed in Jones' company. |
| Gray, Joseph | Private | Seventh/ Third, Hill | Feb 16, 1778 enlisted; April-May 1778; June 1778 on guard. |
| Gray, Robert | Private | Twelfth, Bowyer | Aug 30, 1777 enlisted; Jan 1778 joined; Jan-May 1778. |
| Gray, William/Wm. | Private | First, Mennis | Feb 7, 1778 enlisted; April 1778; May 1778 sick present; June 1778 sick Valley Forge. |
| Gray, William | Private | Twelfth, Waggener | Dec 1777 deserted. |
| Green, Anderson | Private | First State, Nicholas | Dec 1777-Feb 1778 sick Bethlehem; March 1778 on fatigue; April 1778; May 1778 on guard; June 1778 on command Valley Forge. |
| Green, Burwell | Ensign | Fourteenth, Jones | Aug 30, 1777 appointed; Jan 1778; Feb-March 1778 on command in Virginia; April-May 1778; June 18, 1778 resigned. Oath at Valley Forge on May 28, 1778, witnessed by Muhlenberg. |
| Green Elijah | Private | First State, Ewell, T. | Dec 1777 sick Bethlehem; Jan-Feb 1778; March 1778 on fatigue; April-June 1778. |
| Green, Forrett | Private | Third, Powell | Dec 1777-Jan 1778; Feb 14, 1778 discharged. |
| Green/Gren, Jesse | Corporal | Seventh/ Third, Posey/ Sayers | Feb 27, 1778 enlisted; April-May 1778; June 1778 sick Valley Forge, in Sayers' Company. |
| Green, John | 1st. Lt. | First, Cunningham | Dec 1777 sick at Bethlehem; Jan-March 1778; April 29, 1778 died. Green had been shot in a duel with Elisha White on February 25. |
| Green, John | Sergeant | First State, Hamilton | April-June 1778. |
| Green, Moses | Private | Second State, Quarles | April-May 1778; June 1778 sick Valley Forge. |

| Name | Rank | Regiment, Company | Notes |
|---|---|---|---|
| Green, Richard/Richd. | Private | Third, Mercer | Dec 1777 on command; Jan 1778 waggoner. |
| Green/Greer, Richard | Private | Twelfth, Bowyer, T. | March 1778; April 1, 1778 "sent from the Rogaley"; April-June 1778 |
| Green, Samuel | Private | Seventh Third, Posey/Sayers | Feb 27, 1778 enlisted; April-May 1778 sick country; June 1778 sick at Wilmington, in Sayer's Company. |
| Green, Simon | Private | Seventh, Young | Dec 1777 on guard; Jan 1778; Feb 1778 muster roll shows he was discharged on Feb 20; Payroll shows discharge date of Feb 7. |
| Green/Greer, Walter | Private | Twelfth, Waggener | Dec 1777-Feb 1778 hospital; March-May 1778. |
| Green, William/Will | Private | First, Lewis | Feb 7, 1778 enlisted; April-June 1778 |
| Green, William | Private | Fourteenth, Lambert | Dec 1777; Jan 1778 on command; Feb 1778; March 1778 deserted. |
| Green/William, Wm. | Private | Fifteenth, Mason/Gregory | Feb 1778 joined since last muster; March 1778 sick in camp; April-May 1778; June 1778 in Gregory's Company. |
| Greene/Green, Chrisopher/Topher | Corporal | Second State, Bernard | May-June 1778. |
| Greenwood, George | Private | Second, Jones | Dec 1777; Jan 3, 1778 deserted. |
| Greenwood, Samuel | Private | Seventh/Third, Hill | April-May 1778; June 1778 on guard. |
| Gregory, Charles | Sergeant | Fourteenth, Winston | Dec 1777 on command; Jan 1778 sick present; Feb 1778 S. H.; March 3, 1778 died. |
| Gregory, George | Private | Third, Peyton, V. | Dec 1777-Jan 1778 sick in hospital; Feb 12, 1778 discharged. |
| Gregory, John | Captain | Fifteenth, Gregory | Dec 1777-April 1778 on furlough; May-June 1778. |
| Gregory, Thomas | Private | Fourteenth, Marks | Jan 6, 1778 enlisted; Jan-April 1778 on furlough; May-June 1778. |
| Gregory, William | Private | Second State, Garnett | March 15, 1778-May 1, 1778; May 1778; June 1778 sick Valley Forge. |

137

| | | | |
|---|---|---|---|
| Gregory/ Grigory, William | Private | Second, Upshaw | April 1778; June 1778. |
| Gregory, Wm | Quartermaster Sergeant | Sixth, Hockaday | April 1778. |
| Gregory/ Gregorey, William | Corporal | Fourteenth, Winston | Dec 1777-Jan 1778; Feb 1778 sick in hospital; March 1778; April 20, 1778 deceased. |
| Gresham/ Grisham, Ambrose | Sergeant | Sixth, Fox | Dec 1777-Jan 1778; Feb 11, 1778 discharged. |
| Gresham, John | Private | First State, Brown | Feb 1778. |
| Gresham/ Grisham, Thomas | Private | Third, Powell | Dec 1777; Jan 1778 sick in hospital; Feb 14, 1778 discharged. |
| Griffen, Lewis | Corporal | First State, Ewell, T. | Dec 1777-Jan 1778 sick Bethlehem. |
| Griffeth/Grifith, Griffin | Private | Sixth, Apperson | Dec 1777-Feb 1778; "Time to serve, March 1, 1778." |
| Griffin, John | Private | Fourteenth, Overton | Dec 1777 on command; Jan 1778 waggoner; Feb 1778; March 1778 waggoner; April-May 1778 on command; June 1778 sick Valley Forge. |
| Griffin/Griffen, Michael/Michl. | Fifer | First, Lewis/ Scott | Dec 1777-April 1778; May 1778 sick present; June 1778 in Scott's Company. |
| Griffin, Thomas | Private | Second State, Garnett | May-June 1778. |
| Griffin/Griffen, William | Private | Second, Upshaw | Dec 1777-Jan 1778. |
| Griffith, David | Chaplain/ Surgeon | Third | Dec 1777; Jan-April 1778 on furlough in Virginia; May-June 1778. He is shown as both Chaplain and Surgeon in all months except June, when he is listed as Surgeon. |
| Griffith, Joseph | Private | First State, Crump | April-May 1778; June 1778 sick absent. |

| Name | Rank | Regiment | Notes |
|---|---|---|---|
| Griggs, John | Private | Twelfth, Wallace | Dec 1777-Jan 1778; Feb 1778 on command; March 1778; April 1778 on guard; May 1778. |
| Griggs, George | Private | Twelfth, Madison | Dec 1777-Jan 1778 on fatigue; Feb 1778; March 1778 on command |
| Griggs, Philip | Private | Seventh/Third, Webb/Young | Feb 16, 1778 enlisted; April 1778 on command; May 1778 on guard; June 1778 in Young's Company. |
| Griggs/Greggs, William | Private | Second State, Quarles | April-May 1778; June 1778 sick Princetown. |
| Grigsby, John | Private | Second, Willis | Dec 1777-Feb 1778; March 1778 deceased, no date given. |
| Grills/Grill, William | Private | Twelfth, Waggener | Dec 1777 on command; Jan 1778 sick in camp; Feb-March 1778; April 10, 1778 discharged. |
| Grimes/Grymes, George | Corporal | First State, Brown | Dec 1777-March 1778; April 17, 1778 discharged. |
| Grimes, James | Corporal/Sergeant/Private | Third, Arell/Briscoe | Dec 1777-March 1778; April 16, 1778 promoted to Sergeant; May 1778 demoted to Private; June 1778 in Briscoe's Company. |
| Grimes/Grymes, Moses | Private | First State, Ewell, T. | April-June 1778. |
| Grimes/Grymes, William | Corporal | First State, Brown | Dec 1777-March 1778; April 17, 1778 discharged; May 1778. |
| Grimes/Grymes, William | Sergeant | First State, Hoffler | Dec 1777-Feb 1778. |
| Grimes, William | Captain | Fifteenth, Grimes | Aug 1, 1777 died. His company was called Grimes Company through May 1778, though commanded by First Lieutenant Thomas Lewis. |
| Grinder, John | Private | Twelfth, Bowyer, T. | May 1778. |
| Grinnage/Grennage, Joshua | Private | Sixth, Garland | Dec 1777-Jan 1778; Feb 19, 1778 discharged. |

| Name | Rank | Regiment/Company | Service |
|---|---|---|---|
| Grinstaff, George | Private | Twelfth, Ashby | Dec 1777-Feb 1778 sick in hospital; March-April 1778; May 1778 sick in camp. |
| Grinton/Grunter | Private | Twelfth, Bowyer, T. | August 8, 1777 recruited; Jan 1778 joined; Jan 1778; Feb 1778 on command; March-April 1778. |
| Grisby, Edward/Frederick | Private | First State, Hoffler | Dec 1777-April 1778. |
| Grisham, John | Private | First State, Brown | Dec 1777-Feb 1778. |
| Grisham/Grisholm, John | Private | Fourteenth, Overton | Dec 1777-Feb 1778; March-April 1778 sick present; May-June 1778. |
| Grisham, Joseph | Private | Fourteenth | Appears only on a muster roll Dated Feb. 23, 1778 at Yorktown with no remarks. |
| Grisham/Gresham, Mitcham | Private | Seventh, Webb | Jan 1778; Feb 16, 1778 discharged. |
| Griskill, Hourence | Private | Fourteenth, Lambert | Feb 13, 1778 enlisted; April 1778; May 1778 on command; June 1778. |
| Grisom/Grisum, Benjamin | Private | Seventh/Third, Spencer/Lipscomb | Feb 18, 1778 enlisted for 1 year; May 1778 on guard; June 1778 in Lipscomb's Company. |
| Grizell/Grizle, David | Private | Second State, Bressie | March 15, 1778-May 1, 1778; May-June 1778. |
| Groce/Grose, Isham | Private | Fifteenth, Wills | Feb 19, 1778 enlisted; April 1778; May 1778 sick present. |
| Groom/Groome, Richard | Private | Seventh/Third, Spencer/Lipscomb | Feb 18, 1778 enlisted for 1 year; April-May 1778; June 1778 in Lipscomb's company. |
| Gross, Thomas | Private | Second State, Bressie | March 15, 1778-May 1, 1778; May 1778; June 1778 wounded Princetown. |
| Groveham, John | Private | Seventh, Lipscomb | Feb 14, 1778 enlisted for 1 year; April 1778; May 1778 sick in camp |

| Name | Rank | Regiment | Notes |
|---|---|---|---|
| Groves, Phillip | Private | Fifteenth, Gray | Dec 1777 deserted; Feb 1778 returned from desertion; March 1778; April 1778 on command; May 1778; June 1778 sick Valley Forge; July 1778 dead. |
| Groves/Growes, William | Private | Third, Lee | Dec 1777-Jan 1778; Feb 14, 1778 discharged. |
| Grubs, Heneeley | Private | Fourteenth, Winston | Oct 1, 1777 drafted; May-June 1778. |
| Guerrant/Guerrante, John | Sergeant | Second, Taylor, W. | Dec 1777 on guard; Jan-June 1778. |
| Guffey, John | Private | Fourteenth, Conway | Dec 1777 on duty; Jan-June 1778. |
| Guffy, Henry | Private | Twelfth, Waggener | Dec 25, 1777 discharged. |
| Guinn/Guin, Francis | Private | Twelfth, Ashby | Dec 1777 joined; Feb 1778 on guard; March-May 1778. |
| Gulley/Gutley, George | Private | Third, Peyton, V./Peyton, J. | Dec 1777-March 1778 on furlough; April 1778; May 1778 on command; June 1778 in J. Peyton's Company. |
| Gunn, Elisha/Elishaw | Private | Second, Upshaw | Feb 14, 1778 drafted; April 1778; June-July 1778 sick Valley Forge. |
| Gunn, George | Private/Corporal | First State, Lee | Dec 1777-Jan 1778 on command; Feb 1778 on guard; March 1778 promoted to Corporal. |
| Gunnell/Ginnel, Joseph | Private | First State, Payne | Dec 1777; Jan 1778 sick; Feb-March 1778 sick present; April-June 1778. |
| Guthrie, James | Sergeant | Second State, Taliaferro | March 15, 1778-May 1, 1778; May-June 1778. |
| Guthrie, John | Fifer | Second State, Taliaferro | March 15, 1778-May 1, 1778; May-June 1778. |
| Guthrie/Guthree, John | Fifer | Third/Seventh, Hill | June 1778. |
| Guy/Guey, Joseph | Private | Seventh/Third, Posey/Sayers | Feb 27, 1778 enlisted; April-May 1778; June 22, 1778 killed, in Sayers' Company. |

| Name | Rank | Regiment/Company | Service |
|---|---|---|---|
| Guy, Wm. | Private | Fifteenth, Harris | Jan 1778 on command. This man and the individual below are probably the same. |
| Guy, William/Wm. | Private | Fifteenth, Wills | June 1, 1777 enlisted; Jan 1778; Feb 1778 on duty; March 1778 on command; April-May 1778. |
| Gwin, Jacob | Private | First State, Hamilton | Dec 1777-March 1778; April 26, 1778 deceased. |
| Gwinn/Quinn, Andrew | Private | Twelfth, Bowyer, M. | Dec 1777-May 1778. |
| Hackett/Hackeld, John/Jno. | Private | Seventh/Third, Posey/Powell | Dec 1777-Jan 1778 on furlough; April 1778 on guard; May 1778 on command; June 1778 in Powell's Company. |
| Hackney, William | Private | Fourteenth, Jones | Jan 1778 on duty; Feb-May 1778. |
| Hacks/Hack, Geo. | Private | Fifteenth, Grimes | Feb 11, 1778 drafted; May 1778. |
| Hackworth, William/Will. | Private | First, Scott | Dec 1777-Jan 1778; Feb 1778 on guard; March-May 1778; June 1778 sick in camp. |
| Hadage/Hardage, William | Private | Fourteenth, Reid | Dec 1777 hospital; Jan 1778 sick Lancaster; Feb 1778 sick absent; March 1778 hospital; April 1778 at Lancaster; May-June 1778 hospital Lancaster. |
| [Haddell], William | Private | First, Pelham | June 1778. |
| Haddox/Hadocks, John | Private | Third/Seventh, Peyton, V./Peyton, J. | Dec 1777-Feb 1778; March 1778 on guard; April-May 1778; June-July 1778 sick Valley Forge, in J. Peyton's Company. |
| Hadley, Joseph | Private | Fifteenth, Wills | June 1778 waggoner. |
| Hagan/Hagin, Barnay/Barna | Quartermaster Sergeant | Twelfth | Dec 1777-Feb 1778. |
| Hagarty/Hagerty, James | Private | Twelfth, Waggener | Dec 1777 on guard; Jan-March 1778; April 10, 1778 discharged. |
| Hagerty, Patrick/Partrick | Sergeant | Second, Calmes | Dec 1777-June 1778. |

| | | | |
|---|---|---|---|
| Haggard, James | Private | Seventh, Jouett | Dec 1777 on furlough Virginia; Jan 1778; Feb 13, 1778 discharged. |
| Hagins/Heagins, Michael | Private | Twelfth, Bowyer, M. | Nov 1777 sick at Reading; Dec 1777-Feb 1778 sick at hospital; March 1778 dead. |
| Hair, George | Private | Fifteenth, Harris | Feb 15, 1778 deserted |
| Haken/Hacken, William | Private | Second State, Quarles | April-May 1778; June 1778 sick Valley Forge. |
| Haldfield, Josia | Private | Fifteenth, Gray | Feb 10, 1778 drafted; April 1778 under inoculation; May 1778. |
| Hale, Willmore | Private | Twelfth, Bowyer, T. | April 15, 1778 joined; April 1778; May 1778 sick in camp. |
| Hall, Charles | Private | Second, Willis | Dec 1777 hospital; Jan-Feb 1778. |
| Hall, Geo. | Corporal | Fifteenth, Grimes | Dec 1777-Jan 1778 sick Virginia. |
| Hall, Henry | Private | Fourteenth, Jones | Jan 1778 deserted in Virginia. |
| Hall, Jeremiah | Private | First, Cummings | Dec 1777. |
| Hall, Jesse | Private | Fifteenth, Foster | Dec 1777-Jan 1778; Feb 1778 on command; March 1778 sick in camp; April 1778; May 1778 on guard. |
| Hall, John | Private | First, Cunningham | Dec 1777-Jan 1778 wounded at Redin; February 13, 1778 died. |
| Hall, John | Sergeant | Second, Harrison | Dec 1777-June 1778. |
| Hall, Mark | Private | Second State, Taliaferro | March 15, 1778-May 1, 1778; May-June 1778. |
| Hall, Peter | Private | Seventh, Lipscomb | Dec 1777 left in Virginia July 1777. |
| Hall, Stephen | Private | Second, Taylor, F. | Dec 1777-Jan 1778. |
| Hall, Thomas | Private | Fourteenth, Jones | Sept 18, 1777 enlisted; Jan-Feb 1778 sick in Alexandria, Virginia. |
| Hall, Thomas | Private | Fourteenth, Lambert | Oct 16, 1777 enlisted; April-June 1778. |

143

| Name | Rank | Unit | Notes |
|---|---|---|---|
| Hall, William | Private | First, Cunningham | First appears May 1778 roll as "Dead since the 13th of April, 1778." |
| Hall, William | Private | Second State, Quarles | June 26, 1778 died. |
| Hall, William | Private | Seventh, Lipscomb | Dec 22, 177 enlisted in Light Horse. |
| Halled, Saul | Private | Twelfth, Bowyer, M. | June 1778. |
| Haller, William | Private | Second State, Taliaferro | March 15-May 1, 1778; May 1778; June 1778 sick Valley Forge. |
| Haly, Matthew | Private | Seventh, Crockett | Dec 1777-Jan 1778. |
| Ham, Stephen | Private | Second, Taylor, F. | Dec 1777-Feb 1778; March 12, 1778 discharged. |
| Hamblin/ Hamlin, John | Private | Fifteenth, Harris | March 1778 on command; April-May 1778; June-July 1778 sick Valley Forge; Aug 1778 dead. |
| Hamersley/ Hammersly, Abraham/ Abram | Fifer | Third/ Seventh, Arell/ Briscoe | Feb-May 1778; June 1778 sick absent, in Briscoe's Company. |
| Hamilton, James | Private | Third, Blackwell | Dec 1777-Jan 1778; Feb 14, 1778 discharged. |
| Hamilton/ Hambleton, John | Private | First State, Payne | Dec 1777; Jan 1778 sick Yellow Springs; Feb 1778; March 1778 "barefutted"; April 1778 on command; May-June 1778. |
| Hamilton/ Hambleton, John | Private | Twelfth, Bowyer, T. | Dec 1777-Feb 1778; March 1778; sick in hospital; April 1778 sick in hospital near camp; May 22, 1778 discharged. |
| Hamilton, Thomas | Captain | First State, Hamilton | Dec 1777-June 1778. Oath as a Captain at Valley Forge on May 12, 1778, witnessed by Muhlenberg. Probably the same man as below |
| Hamilton, Thomas | Paymaster | First State | May-June 1778. |

| Name | Rank | Company | Notes |
|---|---|---|---|
| Hamlet/ Hamblet, Gideon | Private | Sixth, Hockaday | Dec 1777 sick country; Feb 10, 1778 discharged. |
| Hamlin/ Hamblin, Richard/Richd. | Private | Fifteenth, Hull | Dec 1777; Jan 1778 on guard; Feb 1778; March-April 1778 sick present; May 1778. |
| Hampton, Lewis | Private | Seventh, Lipscomb | Dec 1777 hospital; Jan 31, 1778 discharged. |
| Hampton, William | Private | Second State, Bernard | April-June 1778. |
| Hamrick, Benjamin/Benjn. | Private/ Corporal | Third/ Seventh, Blackwell | Dec 1777-March 1778 on furlough; April 1778 promoted to Corporal, on command; May-June 1778. |
| Hancocke/ Hancock, Henry | Private | Fifteenth, Mason | Dec 1777-April 1778 on furlough. |
| Handy, Thos. | Private | Fifteenth, Wills | Dec 1777 sick absent; Jan 15, 1778 died. |
| Hankins, Joseph | Private | Fourteenth, Conway | Dec 1777; Jan-May 1778 on command; June 1778. |
| Hansborough/ Hansbrough, James | Quartermaster | Third | Dec 1777-Jan 1778; Feb 10, 1778 resigned. |
| Hansbrough/ Hansborough, Peter | Private | Third/ Seventh, Powell | Feb 12, 1778 enlisted; June 1778 sick Valley Forge. |
| Hansford, William | Private | First, Cummings | Dec 1777; Jan-Feb 1778 on furlough; March 1778 on furlough Virginia; April 1778 on furlough; May 1778; June 1778 on furlough. |
| Hansha/ Hanshaw, John | Private | Twelfth, Wallace | Dec 1777 on guard; Jan-April 1778; May 1778 sick in camp. |
| Hanslow/ Henslow, Laurence/ Lawrance | Private | Fourteenth, Reid | Dec 1777-Jan 1778; Feb 1778 on guard; March 1778 sick present; April-May 1778; June 1778 on guard. |
| Hanson, John | Private | Twelfth, Madison | Dec 1777-Feb 1778; March-April 1778 on guard. |
| Hanson, Shadrock | Private | Twelfth, Bowyer, T. | Aug 30, 1778 enlisted; Jan 1778 joined; Jan-May 1778. |

| Name | Rank | Company | Notes |
|---|---|---|---|
| Hanson, Thomas | Private | Twelfth, Vause | Dec 1777-March 1778 sick at Reading hospital; April-May 1778. |
| Hanson, William | Private | Seventh, Posey | Dec 1777 in hospital; Jan 1778 in Rifle Battn.; Feb 13, 1778 discharged. |
| Harden/Harding, Charles | Private | Second State, Lewis | March 15-May 1, 1778; May-June 1778. |
| Harden, Enos/Ennis | Private | Twelfth, Ashby | Dec 1777-Jan 1778; March-April 1778; May 1778 on command. |
| Harden/Harding, John | Private | Second State, Lewis | March 15-May 1, 1778; May-June 1778. |
| Hardin, Francis | Private | Second, Calmes | Dec 1777-Jan 1778. |
| Hardin, John | Private | Second, Willis | Dec 1777-Feb 1778; March 1778 Deceased, no date given. |
| Hardin/Harding, James/Jas. | Private | Fifteenth, Edmunds/Gregory | Dec 1777-March 1778 sick absent; April 1778 sick in hospital; May 1778 sick absent; June 1778 absent at hospital, in Gregory's Company. |
| Harding, John | Private | First State, Camp | Dec 1777 sick; Jan-Feb 1778 sick absent. |
| Hardy/Hardey, Charles | Private | Seventh/Third, Jouett/Hill | Dec 1777 on furlough Virginia; Jan-March 1778 on furlough; April-May 1778; June 1778 in Hill's Company. |
| Hardy, John | Private | Corporal, Hoffler | May-June 1778. |
| Hardy, Joseph | Private | Second, Harrison | Dec 1777 hospital; Jan 1778-June 1778. |
| Hardy/Hardin, John | Private | Seventh/Third, Crockett/Sayers | Dec 1777-May 1778 waggoner; June 1778 waggoner in Sayer's Company. |
| Hardy/Hardey, Thomas | Private | Seventh, Jouett | Dec 1777 on furlough Virginia; Jan 1778 off; Feb 9, 1778 discharged. |
| Hardy/Hardey, William | Private | Second, Calmes | Dec 1777-May 1778; June 1778 sick Valley Forge. |
| Hardy, Wm. | Private | Fifteenth, Grimes | Feb 11, 1778 drafted; April 1778; May 1778 sick present. |

| Name | Rank | Regiment/Company | Dates |
|---|---|---|---|
| Hardyman/Hardiman, John | Ensign | Second State, Spiller | March 15-May 1, 1778; May-June 1778. |
| Hardyman/Hardiman, John/Jno. | Corporal | Sixth, Hockaday | Dec 1777 sick at Princetown; Jan 1778; Feb 10, 1778 discharged. |
| Harigan/Haricane, Jeremiah | Private | Second, Calmes | Dec 1777-June 1778. |
| Harkins, John | Adjutant | Third | Dec 1777-March 1778 on command |
| Harkley/Harkeley, Henry | Private | Twelfth, Waggener | Dec 1777-March 1778 hospital; April-May 1778 Princeton hospital. |
| Harlow/Harlough, Joel | Private | Fourteenth, Marks | Dec 1777-Jan 1778 sick in hospital; Feb sick absent; April 1778 Shaefferstown hospital. |
| Harmontee/Harmontau, Harris/Harriss | Private | First, Cunningham | Feb 12, 1778 enlisted; April 1778 under inoculation; May 1778; June 1778 sick at Valley Forge. |
| Harper, Daniel/Danl. | Private | Sixth, Avery | Dec 1777 sick in hospital; Jan 1778; Feb 18, 1778 discharged. |
| Harper, David | Sergeant | Second State, Bressie | March 15-May 1, 1778; May-June 1778. |
| Harper, Griffin | Private | Seventh/Third, Webb/Young | Feb 16, 1778 enlisted; April 1778; June 1778 in Young's Company. |
| Harper, James | Sergeant/Quartermaster Sergeant | First State, Hamilton | Dec 1777-June 1778. In May he was promoted to Quartermaster Sergeant. |
| Harper/Harpor, James | Private | Second, Jones | Dec 1777-April 1778; May 1778 discharged. |
| Harper, John | Corporal | First State, Hoffler | Dec 1777-May 1778; June 1778 sick absent. |
| Harper, John | Private | Fifteenth, Foster/Gray | Dec 1777-Jan 1778 sick absent; Feb 1778 sick, in Gray's Company; March 1778 sick absent; April 1778 dead. |
| Harrigan/Horrogan, William | Private | Seventh, Crockett | Dec 1777-Jan 1778; April 1778. |

| | | | |
|---|---|---|---|
| Harris, Burr | Corporal | Third, Mercer | Dec 1777-March 1778 furlough; April 1778; May 1778 sick absent. |
| Harris, Charles | Private | Seventh, Spencer | March 6, 1778 enlisted for 3 year; April 1778; May 15, 1778 deserted. |
| Harris, Charles | Private | Fourteenth, Reid | Aug 28, 1777 enlisted; March-April 1778; May 1778 sick present; June 1778 sick at Valley Forge. |
| Harris, David | Private | First, Cummings/ Mennis | Feb 7, 1778 enlisted; April-May 1778; June 1778 sick Valley Forge. |
| Harris, David | Private | Second, Taylor, W. | Dec 1777-June 1778. |
| Harris, David | Private | Second, Upshaw | Feb 14, 1778 drafted; April 1778; June 7, 1778 died. |
| Harris, Edward | Drum Major | Third | Dec 1777; Jan-March 1778 on furlough; April 1778 on furlough, sick in Dumfries. |
| Harris, Edward | Sergeant | Fifteenth, Edmunds | Feb-April 1778; June 1, 1778 died. |
| Harris, James | Private | First, Mennis | April-June 1778. |
| Harris, James | Private | Third, Peyton, V. | Dec 23, 1777 discharged. |
| Harris/Haris, James | Private | Fourteenth, Winston | Dec 1777 on guard; Jan-May 1778; June 1778 sick Valley Forge. |
| Harris, James/Jeames | Captain | Fifteenth, Harris | March 1778 muster roll shows he resigned on March 10, 1778. This is the only reference to him during the Encampment. |
| Harris/Horrace, Hugh | Private | Seventh/ Third, Crockett/ Lipscomb | March 12, 1778 enlisted; April-May 1778; June 1778 in Lipscomb's Company. |
| Harris, James | Private | Third, Peyton, V. | Dec 23, 1777 discharged. |
| Harris, John | Volunteer | Second, Taylor, W. | May 20, 1778 joined; June 1778. He is listed as a Volunteer, and received pay as a Private. |
| Harris, John | Private | First State, Brown | Dec 1777-Feb 1778. |

| | | | |
|---|---|---|---|
| Harris, John | Private | Third, Powell | Dec 1777 transferred to the Light Dragoons. |
| Harris, John | Private | Fourteenth, Winston | Feb 17, 1778 drafted; May-June 1778. |
| Harris, John | Private | Fifteenth, Harris | May 1778 absent without leave; June 1778. |
| Harris, Richard | Private | Twelfth, Bowyer, M. | Dec 10, 1777 enlisted; April 14, 1778 joined; May 1778; June 1778 deserted. |
| Harris, Robert | Private | Fourteenth, Reid | Aug 28, 1777 enlisted; April-June 1778. |
| Harris, Thomas | Private | Fourteenth, Jones | Jan 1778; Feb 1778 sick present; March-May 1778. |
| Harris/Haris, Walter | Private | First, Cunningham | Aug 1776 enlisted for duration of war; Dec 1777-Jan 1778; Feb 1778 on command; March-April 1778; May 1778 sick present; June 1778. |
| Harris, William | Private | First, Cummings | May 1778. |
| Harris, William/ Will | Private/ Drummer | Second, Harrison | Dec 1777 on command; Jan-Feb 1778; March promoted to Drummer; March-June 1778. |
| Harris, William | Private | Sixth, Massie | Dec 1777 innoculated. |
| Harris, Zedekiah/ Zedekia | Private | First State, Crump | Dec 1777; Jan 13, 1778 deceased. |
| Harrison, Andrew | Private | Second, Taylor, F. | Dec 1777 on furlough; Jan-May 1778; June 1778 sick English Town. |
| Harrison, Andrew | Private | Seventh, Crockett | Dec 1777-Jan 1778. |
| Harrison/ Harison, James | Private | Second State, Garnett | May 1778; June 1778 sick Valley Forge. |
| Harrison, John | Private | Third, Powell | Dec 23, 1777 discharged. |
| Harrison, John Payton/ John Peyton | Captain | Second, Harrison | Dec 1777-June 1778. |

| Name | Rank | Regiment/Company | Notes |
|---|---|---|---|
| Harrison/ Hariason, Joseph | Sergeant | Second, Calmes | Dec 1777-May 1778; June 1778 sick at Valley Forge. |
| Harrison, Lovell/Lovel | Quartermaster Sergeant/ Sergeant | Second, Hoomes | Jan-March 1778 he appears as Quartermaster Sergeant; April-June 1778 he is listed as a Sergeant in Hoomes', formerly Jones' Company. |
| Harrison, Phil/Philip | Corporal/ Sergeant | Seventh/ Third, Young | Dec 1777-March 1778 on furlough; April-May 1778; June 1778 promoted to Sergeant on June 1. |
| Harrison, Robert/Robt. | Private | Fifteenth, Gray | Dec 1777-Jan 1778 sick absent; Feb 1778 sick; March 1778 sick absent; April 1778 sick Lancaster; May 1778. |
| Harrison, Simon | Fifer/ Fife Major | Second State, Spiller | March 15-May 1, 1778, On May 1 he was promoted to Fife Major; May-June 1778. |
| Harrison, Thomas | Private | Second, Sanford/ Parker | Dec 1777 on command; Jan-June 1778. From April on he appears in Parker's company. |
| Harrison/Harris, Thomas | Fife Major | Seventh | Dec 1777; Jan-April 1778 on furlough. |
| Harrison, Valentine | 2nd. Lt./ 1st. Lt. | Second, Harrison/ Parker | Dec 1777-Jan 1778 he is in Harrison's Company; April promoted to 1st. Lt. in Parker's Company; April-June 1778. |
| Harrison, William | Private | Seventh/ Third, Fleming/ Blackwell | Feb 13, 1778 enlisted; April 1778 sick present; May 1778; June 1778 in Blackwell's Company. |
| Harrod/Harred, Edward | Corporal | Fourteenth, Reid | Dec 1777 hospital; Jan 1778; Feb 1778 deserted. |
| Harrod/ Harwood, John | Private | Third, Powell | Dec 1777; Jan 1778 sick in hospital; Feb 1778 sick absent; March 1778 dead. |
| Harrold, John | Private | Twelfth, Wallace | Feb 15, 1778 deserted; May 10, 1778 rejoined. |
| Harron/Heron, John | Private | Seventh/ Third, Posey/ Briscoe | Dec 1777-Jan 1778 on furlough; April-June 1778 taylor at Lancaster, June in Briscoe's Company. |

| | | | |
|---|---|---|---|
| Harrower/ Harroare, Andrew | Private | Fifteenth, Mason/ Gregory | Dec 1777 on guard; Jan-Feb 1778 on command; March 1778; April-May 1778 sick in camp; June 1778 in Gregory's Company, sick Valley Forge. |
| Harrup, Arthur | Private | First, Cummings/ Mennis | Dec 1777; Jan 1778 sick hospital; Feb 1778 on furlough; March-May 1778; June 1778 in Mennis' Company. |
| Hart, Anthony | Private | Seventh, Hill | Dec 1777-Jan 1778. |
| Hart/Heart, James | Private | Seventh/ Third, Hill | Dec 1777-Jan 1778 on furlough; April-June 1778. |
| Hart/Harte, Thomas | Private | First State, Brown | Dec 1777-May 1778. |
| Hart, Thomas | Private | Seventh, Hill | Dec 1777; Jan 27, 1778 discharged. |
| Hartwell, Isham | Private | Second State, Dudley | March 15, 1778-May 1, 1778; May-June 1778. |
| Harvey, Bernard | Private | First, Cummings | Dec 1777. |
| Harvey, Joseph | Private | Second, Taylor, F. | Dec 1777-Feb 1778; March 4, 1778 discharged. |
| Hassal/Hasoll, William | Private | First, Scott | Dec 1777 with Colonel Morgan. |
| Hasten, John | Private | First, Scott | Dec 1777 with Colonel Morgan. |
| Hastings, John | Private | Third/ Seventh, Peyton, V./ Peyton, J. | Dec 1777-Jan 1778 in the hospital; Feb-March 1778 sick present; April 1778 wagoner; May 1778 on command; June 1778 waggoner, in J. Peyton's Company/ |
| Hatcher, Benjamin | Private | Seventh, Fleming | Dec 1777-Jan 1778; Feb 13, 1778 discharged. |
| Hatcher, Daniel | Sergeant | Seventh, Fleming | Dec 1777 on furlough Virginia; Jan 1778; Feb 16, 1778 discharged. |
| Hatcher, Henry | Private | Seventh, Fleming | Dec 1777 with Artillery; Jan 1778 Artillery; Feb 12, 1778 discharged. |

| Name | Rank | Company | Notes |
|---|---|---|---|
| Hatcher, John/Jno. | Private/Corporal | First, Cunningham | Feb 1778 enlisted for 1 year; April 1778 under inoculation; May-June 1778; appears as a Corporal on June roll. |
| Hater, Wm. | Private | Sixth, Massie | Dec 1777. |
| Hatfield, Josiah | Private | Fifteenth Gray | Feb 10, 1778 drafted for one year; April 1778 under inoculation; May 1778; June-July 1778 sick Valley Forge. |
| Hatfield, Joel | Private | Gray | Feb 10, 1778 drafted for one year; April 1778 under inoculation; May-June hospital at Yellow Springs; July 1778 dead. |
| Hatton/Hatten, Christopher | Private | Second, Sanford | Dec 28, 1777 deserted. |
| Hatton, Samuel | Private | First State, Brown | May-June 1778. |
| Hatton, Solomon | Private | First State, Hoffler | May 1778; June 1778 sick absent. |
| Hattox, Charles | Fifer | First State, Payne | Dec 1777 sick; Jan 1778 sick Princetown; Feb-April 1778 sick absent; April 1778 sick [Princetown]. |
| Hawkins, Benjamin | Private | Seventh/Third, Spencer/Lipscomb | Feb 13, 1778 enlisted for 3 years; April-June 1778 |
| Hawkins, Elisha | Private | Second, Taylor, F. | Dec 1777-Feb 1778; March 12, 1778 discharged. |
| Hawkins, John | Adjutant/Ensign | Third/Seventh, Powell | Dec 1777-March 1778 on command; April-May 1778; June 1778 appears as an Ensign in Powell's Company. |
| Hawkins, John/Jno. | Private | Sixth, Massie | Dec 1777 in hospital; Jan 1778 sick absent; March 11, 1778 discharged. |
| Hawkins, Joseph | Corporal | Second State, Bressie | March 15-May 1, 1778; May 1778; June 1778 sick Valley Forge. |
| Hawkins, Joshua | Corporal | Sixth, Avery | Dec 1777 absent wounded; Jan 1778; Feb 2, 1778 discharged. |

| | | | |
|---|---|---|---|
| Hawks/Halks, James | Private | Second State, Dudley | March 15, 1778-May 1, 1778; May-June 1778. |
| Hawley, Peter | Private | Second State, Lewis | June 1778. |
| Hay/Hays, Ambrose/Ambrus | Private | Fourteenth, Reid | Aug 11, 1777 enlisted; Jan-May 1778; June 1778 on command. |
| Hay, John | Private | Second State, Spiller | March 15-May 1, 1778; May 1778; June 1778 sick Monmouth. |
| Hay, Morning | Private | First State, Hamilton | Dec 1777-Jan 1778. |
| Hay, Richard | Private | Second, Upshaw | Dec 1777-Jan 1778. |
| Hayes, John | Major | Third | April 23, 1778 commissioned. Not on any Valley Forge rolls. |
| Hayes, Thomas | Sergeant | Second State, Bernard | March 15-April 15 1778 stationed at York garrison; May-June 1778. |
| Hayley/Haley, Daniel/Danl. | Private | Third/Seventh, Arell/Briscoe | Dec 1777-February 1778; March 1778 on command; April 1778; May 1778 on guard; June 1778 in Briscoe's Company. |
| Haynes, Griffith | Private | Sixth, Fox | May-June 1778. |
| Haynes/Hayns, Richard | Private | Fourteenth, Conway | Dec 1777-Jan 1778; Feb-March 1778 on command; April-June 1778. |
| Hays, John | Private | First, Cummings | Dec 1777. |
| Hays, Seth | Private | Fifteenth, Mason/Gregory | Dec 1777 sick absent in Virginia; Jan 1778 sick Virginia; Feb 1778 driving Capt Masons wagon in Virginia; May 1778 on his march from Virginia; June 1778 Virginia, in Gregory's Company. |
| Hays, William/Wm. | Private | First, Cunningham | Feb 19, 1778 enlisted for 1 year; April 1778 under inoculation; May 1778 sick in hospital; June 1778 sick at Valley Forge. |

| Name | Rank | Regiment/Company | Notes |
|---|---|---|---|
| Haywood, Eleazor/Eleazer | Private | Seventh/Third, Fleming/Heth | March 1778 on command, omitted in the Muster Rolls since November; April-June 1778 waggoner; June 1778 in Heth's Company. |
| Hazalip/Haslip, Spencer | Private | Fourteenth, Overton | Dec 1777-Feb 1778; March 23, 1778 discharged. |
| Hazard, Baker | Private | Second, Calmes | Dec 1777-June 1778. |
| Hazlenton, John | Private | Twelfth, Bowyer, T. | Dec 1777 on command. |
| Hazlewood, Joseph | Private | Sixth, Apperson | Dec 1777 sick Trenton; Jan 1778 hospital Reding; Feb 1778 sick hospital. |
| Hazlewood, Josh/Joshua | Private | Fifteenth, Gray | Dec 1777-Jan 1778 sick absent; Feb 1778 sick; March 1778 on command. |
| Healey/Hailey, James | Corporal | First State, Meriwether | Dec 1777-June 1778. |
| Healton/Helton, Bryant | Private | Fourteenth, Lambert | Dec 28, 1777 enlisted; April 1778 lately joined regiment. |
| Heanage/Hennage, George | Private | Second State, Garnett | March 15, 1778-May 1, 1778; May-June 1778. |
| Heaten, Thomas | Private | Third/Seventh, Peyton, J. | June 1778 guard. |
| Heath, Abraham | Private | Sixth, Fox | Dec 1777 in hospital; Jan 1778. |
| Heath, Durham/Duram | Corporal | Sixth, Fox | Dec 1777; Feb 11, 1778 discharged. |
| Heath, Joshua | Private | Sixth, Fox | Dec 1777 in hospital; Jan 1778; Feb 11, 1778 discharged. |
| Heath, Thomas | Private | Sixth, Fox | Dec 1777-Jan 1778; Feb 11, 1778 discharged. |
| Heaton, John | Private | Fourteenth, Reid | Dec 1777 hospital; Jan-Feb 1778. This man and the one below are probably the same individual. |
| Heaton, John | Corporal | Fourteenth, Reid | March 1778; April 30, 1778 deceased. |
| Hedgon, Isick/Isaac | Private | First State, Hamilton | Dec 1777. |

| | | | |
|---|---|---|---|
| Heisel, William | Corporal | Second State, Quarles | June 1778. |
| Helton, Abraham | Private | Sixth | June 1778. |
| Henderson, Hugh | Private | Third, Briscoe | Jan 1778 payroll states "Being wounded & taken prisoner at Brandywine since come up though not mustered." |
| Henderson, James | Private | Fifteenth, Mason | Dec 1777 sick absent; Jan-March 1778 at hospital; April 1778 "sent to Envilead Corp" |
| Henderson, John | Corporal | Fifteenth, Gregory | Dec 1777 on command; Jan-Feb 1778; March-April 1778 sick present; May 1778 convalescent; June 1778 sick Yellow Springs. |
| Hendrick, Benjm. | Private | Fifteenth, Foster | Dec 1777-Jan 1778 sick absent. |
| Hendrick, Elijah | Private | Seventh, Moseley | Dec 1777-March 1778 on furlough; April 1778 sick Lancaster |
| Hendricks, James | Colonel | First | Dec 1777 absent with leave; Jan 1778 in Virginia; Feb 1778 on furlough. |
| Henesey/ Henesee, Thomas | Private | Twelfth, Vause | Dec 1777-Jan 1778 sick hospital Trenton; Feb 1778; March 1778 on command; April -May 1778. |
| Henry, Christopher | Private | First State, Meriwether | Dec 1777-June 1778. |
| Henry, Edward | Private | Seventh, Spencer | Enlisted for 3 years; Dec 1777 hospital; Jan 3, 1778 died. |
| Henry, Francis | Private | Fourteenth, Conway | Dec 1777; Jan 1778 on command; Feb 1778 sick in camp; March 1778 sick present; April-June 1778. |
| Henry/Henrey, Lawrence/ Larens | Private | Twelfth, Vause | Dec 1777-May 1778. |
| Hensley/ Hencely, Lewis | Fleming | Fourteenth, Marks | Dec 1777-June 1778. |
| Hensley, William | Private | Seventh, Jouett | Dec 1777-Jan 1778 on command with sick; Feb 18, 1778 discharged. |

| Name | Rank | Regiment/Company | Notes |
|---|---|---|---|
| Henson, Elijah | Fifer | First State, Lee | Dec 1777; Jan 1778 on command; Feb-June 1778. |
| Henson, William | Private | First State, Nicholas | Dec 1777 sick meeting house; Jan-Feb 1778 sick Quaker meeting house; March 1778; April 1778 Bethlehem hospital; May 1778 on command on the lines; |
| Henwood, Elijah | Private | Second, Harrison | Dec 1777-May 1778; June 1778 sick Princetown Hospital. |
| Hermons, Joseph | Private | Fourteenth, Thweatt | Feb 15, 1778 drafted; June 1778. |
| Hern, Ephraim | Private | First, Taylor | Feb 7, 1778 enlisted; April 1778 |
| Hern, Nathl. | Corporal | Fifteenth, Mason | Dec 1777 understood he was dead. |
| Herndon, Benjamin | Private | Second, Upshaw | Dec 30, 1777 enlisted in the horse service. |
| Herndon/Hurndon, Thomas | Private | Seventh, Spencer | Dec 1777-Jan 1778; Feb 17, 1778 discharged. |
| Herndon/Hernden, William | Private | First State, Ewell, T. | Jan 1778 sick Yellow Springs; Feb 1778 at Yellow Springs. hospital. |
| Herring, Jonathan | Private | Seventh/Third, Spencer/Lipscomb | Feb 18, 1778 enlisted for 1 year; May 1778; June 1778 in Lipscomb's Company. |
| Herrin/Hearn, Charles | Sergeant | Twelfth, Casey | Dec 1777-Feb 1778 on furlough; March-May 1778. |
| Herrold, John | Private | Twelfth, Wallace | Dec 1777-Jan 1778; Deserted about February 15, 1778; May 10, 1778 joined again. |
| Heryford/Horryford, John | Sergeant | Second, Harrison | Dec 1777-June 1778. |
| Heryford/Hereyford, James | Private/Corporal | Second, Harrison | Dec 1777-Feb 1778; March promoted to Corporal; March-June 1778. |
| Hessal, Edward | Private | First, Scott | Dec 1777 with Colonel Morgan. |
| Hester, Joseph | Private | Sixth, Hockaday | Dec 1777 waggoner; Jan 1778; Feb 19, 1778 discharged. |

| | | | |
|---|---|---|---|
| Heth/Heath, William | Lt. Col./ Colonel | Third/ Seventh | Dec 1777-March 1778 on furlough; April 30, 1778 promoted to Colonel; April-June 1778. From June on he commanded the combined Third and Seventh Virginia Regiments. |
| Heth/Heath, William | Private | Twelfth, Waggener | Dec 1777-Jan 1778; Feb-March 1778 hospital; April-May 1778. |
| Hewell, William | Corporal | Twelfth, Quarles | June 1778. |
| Hicks, Frederick | Private/ Corporal | Second State, Spiller | March 15-May 1, 1778; May-June 1778; He was promoted to Corporal on June 1. |
| Hicks, John/Jno. | Private | Sixth, Hockaday | Feb 17, 1778 drafted; April-June 1778. |
| Hicks, William | Private | First State, Lee | Dec 1777 sick; Jan 17, 1778 deceased. |
| Hickson, Benjamin/ Benjn. | Private | Third/ Seventh, Briscoe | March 25, 1778 drafted; April-June 1778 |
| Higdon, Isick/Isaac | Private | First State, Hamilton | Dec 1777; March 1778 dead. |
| Higgins/ Higgens, Mathew | Private | First State, Ewell, T. | April 1778; May 1778 on command; June 1778. |
| Hildrup/Hildrap, John | Private | Second, Harrison | Dec 1777 hospital; Jan-June 1778. |
| Hilgebeth, Moses | Private | Sixth | June 1778. |
| Hill, Abraham | Private | Fifteenth, Grimes | Dec 1777; Jan 1778 on guard; Feb-June 1778 waggoner. |
| Hill, Caleb | Private | Fifteenth, Gray | Dec 1777-Feb 1778; March 1778 sick; April-May 1778. |
| Hill, Charles | Private | Second State, Quarles | April-May 1778; June 1778 sick Valley Forge. |
| Hill, George | Private | Second, Sanford/ Parker | Dec 1777-May 1778; June 1778 hospital. From April on he appears in Parker's company. |
| Hill, Harry/Henry | Private | Seventh/ Third, Spencer/ Lipscomb | Feb 13, 1778 enlisted for 1 year; April-May 1778; June 1778 in Lipscomb's Company. |

| | | | |
|---|---|---|---|
| Hill, Henry | Private | First State, Hoffler | Dec 1777-June 1778. |
| Hill, James | Private/ Sergeant | First State, Ewell, T. | April-May 1778; June 1778 promoted to Sergeant, on guard. |
| Hill, James | Private | Seventh/ Third, Hill | Dec 1777-Jan 1778 on furlough; April-May 1778; June 1778 sick present. |
| Hill, John | Private | Second State, Quarles | June 1778 sick Valley Forge. |
| Hill, John | Private | Twelfth, Casey | Dec 1777 on command; Jan 1778-March 1778 at hospital; April 1778 at hospital near camp; May 1778; June-Sept 1778 sick at Valley Forge. |
| Hill, Michal | Private | Fifteenth, Grimes | Dec 1777-Feb 1778 sick absent; March 1778 died some time ago in the hospital. |
| Hill, Robert | Private | Twelfth, Casey | May 1778 muster roll shows he was drafted on Feb 28, 1778 for one year. |
| Hill, Samuel | Private | Third, Powell | Dec 1777-Jan 1778; Feb 13, 1778 discharged. |
| Hill, Shadrach/ Shadrick | Corporal | Second, Taylor, F. | Dec 1777 on furlough; Jan-June 1778. |
| Hill, Thomas | Captain | Seventh/ Third, Hill | Dec 1777-Jan 1778 on furlough; April-June 1778. |
| Hill, Thomas | Private | Seventh/ Third, Spencer/ Lipscomb | Jan 13, 1778 enlisted for 1 year; April-May 1778; June 1778 in Lipscomb's Company. |
| Hill, William | Private | Seventh, Moseley | Dec 1777-Jan 1778 in R. Regt.; Feb 25, 1778 discharged. |
| Hill, William | Private | Twelfth, Ashby | April-May 1778. |
| Hilliard/Hellard, Joseph | Private | Sixth, Fox | Nov 13, 1777 enlisted; Jan-May 1778; June 1778 sick Valley Forge. |
| Hilling, Thomas | Private | First State, Camp | Dec 1777 sick Fishwater Mills; Jan-Feb 1778 sick absent. |
| Hinds, George | Private | Twelfth, Wallace | Dec 1777-May 1778. |

| | | | |
|---|---|---|---|
| Hinds/Hines, John | Private | Third/Seventh, Briscoe | Dec 1777-May 1778; June 1778 on guard. |
| Hines/Hynes, Henry | Private | First, Payne | Feb 7, 1778 enlisted; April-May 1778; June 1778 on guard. |
| Hines/Hynes, James | Private | Fourteenth, Reid | Aug 11, 1777 enlisted; Jan 1778 on command; Feb-April 1778; May 1778 on command; June 1778 sick Valley Forge. |
| Hines, James | Private | Fifteenth, Hull | Dec 1777 on guard; Jan-March 1778 on command; April 1778 sick present; May 1778 on guard. |
| Hines/Hynes, Jesse | Private | Fourteenth, Reid | Aug 12, 1777 enlisted; Jan 1778 on command; Feb-June 1778. |
| Hinge, John | Private | Seventh/Third, Lipscomb | Feb 14, 1778 enlisted; June 1778. |
| Hinson/Horson, William | Private | Third, Peyton, V. | Dec 1777 on command with Morgan; with Col. Morgan. |
| Hinton, Christopher | Private | Fourteenth, Jones | Feb 12, 1778 drafted; April-May 1778; June 1778 on command. |
| Hipkinstall/Hepkinstall, James | Private | Second State, Bernard | May-June 1778. |
| Hitchen, Daniel | Private | Second, Harrison | June 1778 sick Valley Forge. |
| Hite, Abraham | 1st. Lt. | Twelfth, Vause | Dec 1777; Jan-Feb 1778 on command; March 1778; April-May 1778 on command at Virginia State Store. |
| Hite, Joseph | Cadet | Twelfth, Vause | Feb 21, 1778 enrolled as a Cadet by Col. Wood; March-May 1778. |
| Hix/Hickes, Daniel/Danl. | Corporal | First, Cunningham | Aug 1776 enlisted for 3 years; Dec 1777-June 1778. |
| Hix/Hicks, Daniel | Private | Sixth, Massie | Dec 1777; Jan 1778 discharged. |
| Hix, James | Private | First State, Meriwether | Dec 1777-Jan 1778; March 1778 dead. |
| Hix/Hicks, James | Corporal | Second, Jones/Hoomes | Dec 1777-Feb 1778 sick hospital; March-May 1778; June 1778 sick at Valley Forge. |

| Name | Rank | Regiment, Company | Notes |
|---|---|---|---|
| Hoar/Orr, Thomas | Private | Fourteenth, Lambert | Dec 1777 hospital; Jan 1778; Feb 1778 deserted; May 1778; June 1778 sick Valley Forge. |
| Hobbs, Elisha | Private | Sixth, Fox | Dec 1777 in hospital; Jan-Feb 1778 sick absent. |
| Hobbs, Frederick | Private | Second, Jones/Hoomes | Dec 1777-May 1778; June 1778 sick absent. |
| Hobbs, Frederick | Private | Sixth, Fox | Dec 1777 in hospital; Jan 1778; Feb 20, 1778 discharged. |
| Hobbs/Hubs, Hartwell | Private | Fourteenth, Jones | Jan-Feb 1778 sick in Lancaster. |
| Hobbs/Hubbs, Robert | Private | Twelfth, Waggener | Dec 1777-March 1778 on command; April 1778 butcher. |
| Hobday, Richard | Sergeant | Seventh, Young | Dec 21, 1777 to Light Horse. |
| Hobday, Richd. | Private | Fifteenth, Mason | Dec 1777 sick absent; Jan-April 1778 hospital; May 1778 hospital Shaffertown. |
| Hobday/Hobdey, William | Private | Seventh, Young | Dec 1777-Jan 1778 hospital; Feb 3, 1778 discharged. |
| Hobson, Benjamin/Benj. | Private | First, Cunningham | Feb 12, 1778 enlisted for 1 year; May 1778 sick at Frederick Town; June 1778 sick at Valley Forge. |
| Hobson, Edward | Private | Second, Taylor, W. | Dec 1777 sick absent; Jan-Feb 1778. |
| Hobson, Nicholas | Captain | Sixth | Heitman shows he resigned on September 23, 1777. See Hockaday. |
| Hobson, William/Wm. | Private | First, Cunningham | Feb 12, 1778 enlisted for 1 year; May 1778 sick at Frederick Town; June 1778 sick at Valley Forge. |
| Hockaday, John/Jno. | 1st. Lt./Captain | Sixth, Massie/Hockaday | Dec 1777 he appears as a 1st. Lt. in Massie's company; Jan 1778 he appears as the Captain of Hobson's former company; Feb 16, 1778 resigned. Heitman erroneously shows him resigning on July 23, 1777. |
| Hodges/Hogguardes, Samuel | Drummer/Private | Twelfth, Ashby | Dec 1777-Jan 1778; March 1778; April 1778 reduced to private, on guard; May 1778. |

| Name | Rank | Regiment/Company | Notes |
|---|---|---|---|
| Hodges, Williamson/ Wm. | Private | Seventh/Third, Webb/Young | Enlisted for 3 years; Jan-Feb 1778 on furlough; April-May 1778; June 1778 in Young's Company |
| Hodgin/Hodgen, Samuel | Private | Seventh/Third, Spencer/Lipscomb | Dec 1777 hospital; Jan 1778; April-May 1778; June 1778 in Lipscomb's Company. |
| Hodgins, Joseph | Private | First State, Hamilton | Dec 1777-June 1778. |
| Hoffler, William | Captain | First State, Hoffler | Dec 1777-June 1778. |
| Hogan, Francis | Corporal | Third, Arell | Dec 23, 1777 discharged. |
| Hogams/Hogins, Isham | Private/Sergeant | Fourteenth, Jones | Sept 6, 1777 enlisted; Jan-Feb 1778 sick Alexandria, Virginia; April-May 1778; In May he appears as a Sergeant; June 1778 Princetown wounded. |
| Hogg, John | Private | First, Pelham | Dec 1777-Jan 1778; Feb 15, 1778 discharged. |
| Hogg, Samuel | 2nd. Lt. | First, Lawson | Dec 1777-June 1778; he is listed as the regiment's "protemporary" Adjutant for March and April. Oath at Valley Forge on May 18, 1778, witnessed by Muhlenberg. |
| Hogg, William | Private | First, Pelham | Dec 1777-Jan 1778; Feb 15, 1778 discharged. |
| Holaday/Holleday, James | Private | Third/Seventh, Mercer/Powell | Dec 1777; Jan-Feb 1778 sick present; March 1778; April 1778 sick at Church Hospital; June in Powell's Company; June-Aug 1778 sick at Valley Forge. |
| Holdcroft/Holdecroft, Edward/Edwd. | Private | Sixth, Hockaday | Dec 1777-Jan 1778; Feb 10, 1778 discharged. |
| Holderby, William | Private | Seventh, Lipscomb | Dec 22, 1777 enlisted in Light Horse. |
| Holdar/Holder, Benjm. | Private | Sixth, Apperson | Dec 1777 "gone on furlow the first Decr. 1777"; Jan 1778-April 1778 on furlough; June 1778 deserted. |

| Name | Rank | Company | Service |
|---|---|---|---|
| Holland/Hallad, Drury/Drewry | Private | First, Cunningham | Aug 1776 enlisted for 3 years; Dec 1777-Feb 1778; March 1778 fatigue; April 1778; May-June 1778 on command. |
| Holland, George | 1st. Lt. | Fourteenth, Winston | Dec 1777-June 1778. |
| Holland, Joseph | Private | Fifteenth, Foster | Feb 1778 muster roll shows he joined since Oct 1, 1777; Jan 23, 1778 died. |
| Holland, Thomas | Private | Third/Seventh, Arell/Briscoe | Dec 1777-Jan 1778 orderly at the hospital; Feb-March 1778 sick absent; April 1778 on command; May 1778; June 1778 on command, in Briscoe's Company. |
| Holliday/Holaday, Absalom | Private | Fifteenth, Hull | Feb 1778 sick present; March 1778 on guard; April 1778 sick present; May 10, 1778 died. |
| Hollings, John | Private | First State, Crump | Dec 1777; Jan 9, 1778 deceased. |
| Hollinsworth/Hollingworth, William | Private | Fourteenth, Conway | Dec 1777; Jan-Feb 1778 sick in hospital; March 30, 1778 deceased. |
| Holloway/Holoway, Archibald/Archie | Private | Second State, Dudley | March 15, 1778-May 1, 1778; May 1778; June 1778 sick absent. |
| Holloway/Holoway, Charles/Carles | Private | First, Taylor/Lawson | Dec 1777-Jan 1778; Feb-March 1778 waggoner; April-June 1778. |
| Holloway/Hollaway, William | Private | Second State, Quarles | April-June 1778. |
| Holmes/Homes, Bartlet/Bartlett | Private | Fifteenth, Gray | Dec 1777-Jan 1778; Feb 1778 on guard; March 1778 sick in camp; April 1778 sick present; May 1778. |
| Holmes, Isick/Isaac | Ensign | Second State, Bernard | April-May 1778; June 1778 sick Valley Forge. |
| Holmes/Hoomes, James | Private | Second State, Quarles | April-June 1778. |

| Name | Rank | Regiment, Company | Service |
|---|---|---|---|
| Holmes/Holms, James | Private | Twelfth, Wallace | Dec 1777-Jan 1778; Feb 1778 on command; March 1778 on scout and deserted Feb 24, 1778. |
| Holmes/Holms, John | Private | Second, Sanford/Parker | Dec 1777-June 1778. From April on he appears in Parker's company. |
| Holmes/Holms, Lewis | Drummer | Fourteenth, Reid | Dec 1777 hospital; Jan 1778 sick Burlington; Feb 1778 sick absent. |
| Holmes/Holms, William | Private | Second, Sanford/Parker | Dec 1777 hospital; Jan-May 1778; June 1778 hospital. |
| Holt, Etheldred | Corporal | Fifteenth, Gray | Dec 1777; Jan 1778 on furlough; Feb 1778; March-April 1778 on furlough; May 1778 "I have hd. is Discharged". |
| Holt/Holl, James | Ensign | Fifteenth, Mason | Dec 1777-May 1778. |
| Holt, John Hunter | 1st. Lt. | First State, Payne | Dec 1777-April 1778; May 1778 on command; June 1778. |
| Holt, Micajah/Macajah | Corporal | Fifteenth, Gray | Dec 1777-April 1778; May 1778 sick present; June 1778 discharged. |
| Holt, Samuel | Private | Second State, Garnett | March 15-May 1, 1778; May-June 1778. |
| Holt, Thomas | Ensign/2nd. Lt. | First, Cummings/Mennis | Dec 1777-May 1778; June 1778 recruiting, in Mennis's Company. He appears as a Lieutenant on the June roll. Oath at Valley Forge on May 28, 1778, witnessed by Muhlenberg. |
| Holt, Thomas | 1st. Lt. | Fourteenth, Overton | Dec 1777-June 1778. Oath at Valley Forge on May 12, 1778, witnessed by Muhlenberg. |
| Holton/Hotton, Mark | Private | Seventh/Third, Posey/Sayers | Feb 27, 1778 enlisted; April-May 1778; June 1778 in Sayer's Company. |
| Honeywood/Honywood, Arthur/Arther | Private | Second, Calmes | Dec 1777-June 1778. |

| Name | Rank | Regiment/Company | Service |
|---|---|---|---|
| Hood, George | Private | Second State, Garnett | June 1778. |
| Hood, John | Private | First, Pelham | Feb 7, 1778 enlisted; April 1778 under inoculation; May-June 1778. |
| Hood, John | Private | Second, Taylor, W. | Dec 1777-Jan 1778; Feb 5, 1778 discharged. |
| Hood, John | Musician | Sixth, Hockaday | Dec 23, 1777 enlisted in the Light Horse. |
| Hood, Joshua | Private | Second, Taylor, W. | Dec 1777-Jan 1778; Feb 14, 1778 discharged. |
| Hooker/ Hoocker, James | Corporal | Fourteenth, Winston | Dec 1777 sick in hospital; Jan 1778 sick Reading; Feb 13, 1778 died. |
| Hoomes/ Hoames Jr., Benjamin | 1st. Lt./ Captain | Second, Willis/ Hoomes | Dec 1777-March 1778; April 24, 1778 promoted to Captain and assumed command of Jones' Company; April-June 1778. Oath at Valley Forge on May 12, 1778, witnessed by Muhlenberg. |
| Hoomes/ Hooms, Thomas C. | Ensign/ 2nd. Lt. | First State, Payne/ Brown | Dec 1777 on guard; Jan-April 1778; May 2, 1778 promoted to 2nd. Lt. and transferred to Brown's Company. Oath at Valley Forge on May 12, 1778, witnessed by Muhlenberg. |
| Hooper/ Hoopers, James/Jams. | Private | Sixth, Hockaday | Feb 17, 1778 drafted; April 1778; May 1778 on guard; June 1778 sick at Valley Forge. |
| Hooper, Mansfield | Private | Fourteenth, Winston | Dec 1777-Jan 1778; Feb 1778 sick in hospital; March 1778; April 20, 1778 died. |
| Hope, William | Private | Seventh, Third, Posey/Sayers | Dec 1777 waggoner on command; Jan 1778 waggoner; April-May 1778 waggoner; June 1778 waggoner, in Sayer's Company. |
| Hopes, William | Private | Seventh, Hill | Feb 12, 1778 enlisted; April 1778; May 23, 1778 deceased. |

| Name | Rank | Company | Notes |
|---|---|---|---|
| Hopkins, Samuel/Saml. | Captain/Major | Sixth, Hopkins | Dec 1777 sick absent; In January promoted to Major, effective November 29, 1777; Feb 1778; March 1778 on furlough; April-May 1778; June 1778 on command. Oath at Valley Forge on May 28, 1778, witnessed by Muhlenberg. |
| Hopkins, William | Private | First State, Crump | April-May 1778; June 1778 sick absent. |
| Hopkins, William | Private | Second State, Spiller | March 15-May 1, 1778; May 1778; June 1778 sick Valley Forge. |
| Hopper, John | Private | Third, Blackwell | Dec 23, 1777 discharged. |
| Hopson, John | Private | Second State, Spiller | March 15-May 1, 1778; May 1778; June 1778 sick Valley Forge. |
| Hopson, Joseph | 1st. Lt. | Seventh, Moseley | Dec 1777-March 1778 on furlough; April 1778 in R. Regt.; May 26, 1778 resigned. |
| Hopwood, Richard | Private | Second State, Bernard | May 1778; June 1778 sick Valley Forge. |
| Hord, James | Ensign | Seventh, Posey | Dec 1777-Jan 1778. |
| Horigan/Horrigan, William/Wm. | Private | Third/Seventh, Briscoe | June 1778 baggage guard. |
| Horn, Simon | Sergeant | Second, Harrison | Dec 1777-June 1778. |
| Horn, William | Private | Twelfth, Wallace | Dec 1777 wounded absent; Jan 1778 sick in camp; Feb 1778 on guard; March-May 1778. |
| Horton, Robert | Drummer | Third, Peyton, V. | Dec 1777-Jan 1778; Feb 12, 1778 discharged. |
| Horton, William | Private | Second State, Quarles | April-June 1778. |
| Hosier, Joshua | Private | Fifteenth, Gregory | Dec 1777 Baltimore; Jan 1778 sick Baltimore. |

| Name | Rank | Regiment/Company | Notes |
|---|---|---|---|
| Hoskins, James | Private/ Corporal | Fourteenth, Thweatt | Dec 1777; Jan 1778 promoted to Corporal; Jan-April 1778; May 1778 sick present; June 1778 sick Carrells |
| Hoskins, Joseph | Private | First State, Ewell, T. | Dec 1777-Feb 1778 sick in Virginia; April 1778 Yellow Springs; May-June 1778 sick Yellow Springs. |
| Hoskins, Samuel | Sergeant | Seventh, Hill | Dec 1777; Jan 26, 1778 discharged. |
| Hoskins, Thomas | Corporal | Sixth, Avery | Dec 1777-Jan 1778; Feb 8, 1778 discharged. |
| Houchens, Barnett/Barnitt | Private | Seventh, Lipscomb | Dec 1777; Jan 31, 1778 discharged. |
| Hough, Thomas | Private | Third/Seventh, Peyton, J. | June 1778. |
| Howard, Benjamin | Private | Fourteenth, Overton | Dec 1777 sick in hospital; Jan 12, 1778 died. |
| Howard, James | Private | Twelfth, Bowyer, T. | Dec 1777-March 1778 on command; April-May 1778 waggoner. |
| Howard, Peter | Private | Fifteenth, Hull | Feb-March 1778; April 1778 sick present; May 1778. |
| Howard, Samuel | Private | Seventh/Third, Fleming/Heth | Feb 19, 1778 enlisted; April 1778 sick present; May 1778; June 1778 in Heth's Company. |
| Howe/How, Elijah/Eligah | Private | Fourteenth, Reid | Oct 3, 1777 enlisted; April 1778 lately joined regiment; May 1778; June 1778 sick Valley Forge. |
| Howell/Howel, Abner | Private | Fourteenth, Jones | Jan 1778 on duty; Feb 1778 on command; March-May 1778. |
| Howel, Samuel | Private | Fifteenth, Wills | Feb 17, 1778 enlisted; April 1778 sick present; May 1778 sick Yellow Springs. |
| Howell/Howel, Joseph | Private | First State, Payne | Dec 1777-Feb 1778; March 1778 fatigue; April-May 1778; June 1778 guard. |
| Howard, Joseph | Private | Twelfth, Bowyer, T. | Dec 1777-May 1778. |
| Howell, Lewis/Lewes | Private | Twelfth, Ashby | Dec 1777-Jan 1778; Feb 22, 1778 discharged |

| Name | Rank | Regiment, Company | Service |
|---|---|---|---|
| Howell/Howel, Philiston/Philisten | Private | First State, Lee | Dec 1777-Jan 1778; Feb 1778 on guard; March 1778; April 1778 sick present; May-June 1778. |
| Howell, Samuel | Provate | Fifteenth. Wills | Feb 17, 1778 drafted; April 1778 sick present; May 1778 sick Yellow Springs; June 1778 sick Valley Forge; July 1778 sick Yellow Springs; Aug 1778 died Yellow Springs. |
| Howle/Howl, Joseph | Private | First State, Payne | Dec 1777; Jan-Feb 1778 sick Bethlehem; March 1778; April 1778 on guard; May-June 1778. |
| Howlet, Samuel | Private | Fourteenth, Overton | Dec 1777-Feb 1778; March 1778 on command; April-May 1778. |
| Hoye, Alexander | Private | First, Pelham | Dec 1777 guard; Jan-June 1778. |
| Hubbard/Hubard, Elias | Private | Second, Parker | Dec 1777-June 1778. |
| Hubbard, Matthew/Matt. | Private | Fifteenth, Edmunds/Gregory | Dec 1777-March 1778 sick absent; April-May 1778 sick hospital; June 1778 absent at hospital, in Gregory's Company. |
| Hubbard, Obediah | Private | Second, Taylor, W. | Dec 1777-Jan 1778; Feb 14, 1778 discharged. |
| Hubbard, Samuel/Saml. | Private | First, Mennis | Dec 1777; Jan 1778 on furlough; Feb 1778; March 1778 on fatigue; April-June 1778. |
| Hubbard, Thomas/Tho. | Quartermaster | First | Dec 1777-June 1778. |
| Hubbard, William/Wm. | Sergeant | First, Mennis | Dec 1777; Jan 1778 wounded and in hospital; Feb-June 1778 on furlough. |
| Hudein, Moses | Private | Seventh, Young | Dec 21, 1777 to Light Horse. |
| Hudgens/Hudgen, Robert | Private | Second State, Garnett | March 15-May 1, 1778; May-June 1778. |
| Hudson, Henry | Sergeant | First, Lawson | Dec 1777-March 1778 on furlough; April 1778 on guard; May-June 1778. |
| Hudson, Henry | Private | Second State, Quarles | April-May 1778; June 26, 1778 died. |

| | | | |
|---|---|---|---|
| Hudson, John | 1st. Lt. | Second State, Bressie | June 1778. In June he received pay for 3 ½ months. |
| Hudson, John | Drummer | Second State, Bressie | March 15-May 1, 1778; May-June 1778. |
| Hudson, John | Private | Sixth, Hockaday | Feb 17, 1778 drafted; April 1778; May 1778 on fatigue; June 1778 sick at Valley Forge. |
| Hudson/Hutson, John | Private | Seventh, Posey | Dec 1777-Jan 1778 on furlough; April 1778; June-July 1778 sick Valley Forge. |
| Hudson, Reuben | Private | Sixth, Avery | Dec 1777-Jan 1778; Feb 7, 1778 discharged. |
| Hudson, Rush | Private | Second, Upshaw | Dec 1777. |
| Hudson, Thomas | Private | Second State, Bressie | March 15-May 1, 1778; May-June 1778. |
| Hudson, Thomas | Private | Second State, Quarles | April-June 1778. |
| Hudson, Thomas | Private | Fourteenth, Reid | Sept 18, 1777 enlisted; April 1778 lately joined regiment; May-June 1778. |
| Hudson, Vincent/Vincen | Fleming | Seventh, Webb | Jan 1778 sick Virginia; Feb 14, 1778 discharged. |
| Hudson, William | Ensign/ 2nd. Lt. | Sixth, Rose | Dec 1777-May 1778 recruiting; Feb 1, 1778 promoted to 2nd. Lt.; Oath at Valley Forge on May 12, 1778, witnessed by Muhlenberg. |
| Hufman, Joseph | Private | First State, Nicholas | Dec 1777-Feb 1778; March 1778 on guard; April 1778; May 1778 on command; June 1778 sick Valley Forge. |
| Hufman/ Huffman, Reuben/Reubin | Private | First State, Nicholas | Dec 1777; Jan 1778 on guard; Feb 1778; March 1778 sick present; April 1778; May 1778 on command on the lines; June 1778 on command Valley Forge. |

| | | | |
|---|---|---|---|
| Hughes/Huse, Francis | Sergeant | Third/Seventh, Mercer/Powell | Dec 1777-March 1778 sick absent; April 1778 sick present, promoted to Sergeant; May 1778; June 1778 in Powell's Company. |
| Hughes, John | Private | First, Mennis | April 1778. |
| Hughes/Hughs, John | Private | Sixth, Fox | Dec 1777 in hospital; Jan 1778; Feb 11, 1778 discharged. |
| Hughes, Joseph | Corporal | Fifteenth, Edmunds | Dec 1777-April 1778. |
| Hughes/Huse, Luke | Private | Third/Seventh, Briscoe | Feb 10, 1778 drafted; June 1778. |
| Hughes/Hughs, Pratt | Private | First State, Lee | Dec 1777 sick; Jan-June 1778. |
| Hughes, Stephen | Private | First, Mennis | Feb 1, 1778 enlisted; April 1778; May 1778 sick present; June 1778 sick at Valley Forge. |
| Hughes, Thomas | Paymaster | Seventh | Dec 1777; Jan 1778 on command; Feb 1778. |
| Hughes, William | Private | Sixth, Fox | Feb 11, 1778 discharged. |
| Hughey, John | Private | First State, Hamilton | Dec 1777-June 1778. |
| Hughs, Alexander | Private | Second State, Garnett | May 1778; June 1778 sick Valley Forge. |
| Hughs/Hughes, Arthur/Arther | Private | Second, Willis | March-May 1778; June-July 1778 sick at Valley Forge. |
| Hughs/Hughes, Edward | Private | Fourteenth, Marks | Dec 1777-Jan 1778 waggoner; Feb 1778 sick absent; March-May 1778. |
| Hughs, John | Private | Second, Harrison | Dec 1777-June 1778. |
| Hughs, Joseph | Corporal | Fifteenth, Gregory | June 1778. |
| Hughs/Hughes, Silvester | Private | Second, Upshaw | Dec 1777-Jan 1778. |
| Hughs, Stephen | Private | Fourteenth, Marks | Nov 14, 1777 enlisted; April-June 1778. |
| Hughs, Thomas | Private | Second, Sanford/Parker | Dec 1777-May 1778; June 1778 hospital. |

| | | | |
|---|---|---|---|
| Hull/Hulm, Bell | Corporal | First State, Ewell, T. | Dec 1777-Feb 1778 on command. |
| Hull, David | Private | First, Cummings/ Mennis | Aug 9, 1777 enlisted; Jan 1778 "pay omitted" Feb 1778-May 1778; June 1778 waggoner, in Mennis' Co. |
| Hull, Edwin | Captain | Fifteenth, Hull | Dec 1777-April 1778; May 1778 on command. |
| Hull, Hopewell/ Hopel | Private | Twelfth, Vause | Dec 1777-May 1778. |
| Hull, Thomas | Corporal | Twelfth, Vause | Dec 1777; Jan 1778 sick in camp; Feb-May 1778. |
| Hull, William | Fleming | First State, Crump | Dec 1777-June 1778. |
| Hulse/Hules, James | Private | Twelfth, Bowyer, T. | Dec 1777-Jan 1778; Feb 1778 sick in camp; March-April 1778; May 1778 sick in hospital. |
| Humphrey see Umphrey | | | |
| Humphrey, Robert | Private | Second State, Spiller | June 1778. |
| Humphrey/ Humphreys, Thomas | Private | Second State, Dudley | March 15-May 1, 1778; May-June 1778. |
| Humphreys, John | Private | Twelfth, Wallace | Dec 1777-March 1778 on command; April 1778; May 1778 on week command. |
| Humphries/ Humphreys Sr., John | Private | First State, Nicholas | Dec 1777; Jan 1778 on command; Feb 1778 on guard; March 26, 1778 deceased. |
| Humphries/ Humphreys Jr., John | Private | First State, Nicholas | Dec 1777; Jan 1778 sick; Feb-April 1778; May 1778 on command; June 1778 sick Valley Forge. After his father died, Jr. is dropped as part of his name. |
| Humphries/ Humphress, William | Private | First State, Payne | Dec 1777-Jan 1778 sick George Town; Feb 1778 sick absent. |
| Hundley, Anthony/ Anthny. | Private | Sixth, Avery | Dec 1777 sick absent; Jan 1778; Feb 4, 1778 discharged. |

| Name | Rank | Regiment/Company | Notes |
|---|---|---|---|
| Hundley, George | Private | Sixth, Apperson | Dec 1777 sick Trentown; Jan 1778; Feb 22, 1778 discharged. |
| Hundley, John | Private | Seventh, Posey | Dec 1777-Jan 1778 in Rifle Battn.; Feb 22, 1778 discharged. |
| Hundley/ Hundly, John | Private | Fourteenth, Conway | Feb 10, 1778 drafted; May 1778; June 1778 sick Valley Forge. |
| Hundley, Joshua/Josh | Private | Fifteenth, Foster/Gray | Dec 1777 on guard; Jan 1778 on command; Feb 1778 sick, in Gray's Company; March 1778 sick in camp; April 1778 sick present. |
| Hundley, Philip | Private | Seventh, Young | Dec 1777 Comr. Guard; Feb 6, 1778 discharged. |
| Hundley/ Hundly, William | Corporal | Seventh/Third, Moseley/Blackwell | Dec 1777-March 1778 on furlough; April 1778; May 1778 sick in camp; June 1778 in Blackwell's Company. |
| Hundley, William | Private | Seventh, Young | Dec 1777 hospital; Jan 1778; Feb 20, 1778 discharged. |
| Hundrey, Joshia | Private | Fifteenth, Gray | Feb 10, 1778 drafted; April 1778 under inoculation; May 1778. |
| Hungerford, James | Private | Sixth, Avery | Dec 1777-Jan 1778; Feb 8, 1778 discharged. |
| Hungerford/ Hungurford, Thomas | 2nd. Lt. | Third/Seventh, Briscoe/Powell | Dec 1777-Feb 1778; March-April 1778 on command; May 1778 on command in Virginia; June 1778 in Powell's Company. |
| Hunt, George/Geo. | Private/Sergeant | Fifteenth, Gregory | Dec 1777 Virginia; Jan 1778 sick Virginia; Feb-April 1778; May 1, 1778 promoted to Sergeant, on command. |
| Hunt, James | Sergeant | Fourteenth, Thweatt | Dec 1777-June 1778. |
| Hunt, James, Jr. | Private/Fifer | Fourteenth, Thweatt | Sept 30, 1777 enlisted; Jan-Feb 1778 sick at York; March 1778; April 1778 promoted to Fifer; April-May 1778. |
| Hunt, John | Private | Seventh/Third, Posey/Lipscomb | Feb 27, 1778 enlisted; April-May 1778; June 1778 in Lipscomb's Company. |

| Name | Rank | Regiment/Company | Notes |
|---|---|---|---|
| Hunt, Mamucan/Memucan | Drummer | Fourteenth, Lambert | Dec 1777 sick in hospital; Jan-June 1778 |
| Hunt, Presley | Private | Sixth, Hockaday | Dec 1777-Jan 1778 waggoner; Feb 26, 1778 discharged. |
| Hunt/Hunte, Samuel | Private | Second, Taylor, W. | Dec 1777 furlough; Jan-June 1778. |
| Hunter, Anthony/Anthy. | Private | Sixth, Avery/Hockaday | Sept 27, 1777 enlisted; Jan-June 1778. In April he also appears in Hockaday's company. |
| Hunter, John | Private | Fifteenth, Mason/Gregory | Dec 1777; Jan 1778 sick present; Feb-April 1778; May 1778 on guard; June 1778 in Gregory's Company. |
| Hunter/Huter, Joshua | Private | First, Lewis | Dec 1777 sick; Jan-Feb 1778 sick hospital; March 1778 on fatigue; April 1778; May 1778 on command; June 1778. |
| Hunter, Stephen/Stephan | Private | Fourteenth, Overton | Dec 1777-May 1778; June 1778 on guard. |
| Hunter, William | Paymaster | First State | Jan 1778. |
| Hurley, James | Corporal | Twelfth, Madison | Dec 1777-Jan 1778 sick in hospital; Feb 1778 roll shows he deserted on October 15, 1777 from a hospital. |
| Hurley/Hurlay, Thomas/Thos | Private | Seventh/Third, Crockett/Briscoe | March 19, 1778 enlisted; April-May 1778; June 1778 sick Valley Forge, in Briscoe's Company. |
| Hurt, John | Chaplain | Sixth | Dec 1777 absent with leave; Jan 1778 on furlough Virginia;; Feb-March 1778 on furlough; April-June 1778. |
| Hurt, West | Private | Seventh, Lipscomb | Dec 22, 1777 enlisted in Light Horse. |
| Hurt/Hurst, William | Private | Fourteenth, Lambert | Feb 23, 1778 enlisted; June 1778 lately joined, sick Valley Forge. |
| Huskinson, Thomas | Corporal | First, Pelham | Dec 1777-Jan 1778; Feb-March 1778 on furlough; April-June 1778. |

| Name | Rank | Company | Notes |
|---|---|---|---|
| Hust, Armstead/ Amsted | Private | Seventh, Moseley | Dec 1777-Jan 1778 sick in hospital; March 1, 1778 discharged. |
| Hutcherson/ Hutchenson, John | Private | Second State, Garnett | April 15-June 1, 1778; June 1778. |
| Hutcherson/ Hutchinson, Thomas | Corporal | First State, Payne | Dec 1777-Jan 1778 sick Georgetown; Feb 1778 sick absent; June 1778 omitted in April and May. |
| Hutchings, Bozwell/ Boswell | Private | Sixth, Rose | Dec 1777-Jan 1778; Feb 28, 1778 discharged. |
| Hutchinson, Charles | Sergeant | First State, Meriwether | Jan 1778 paid to Sept 16, 1777, being sick in Virginia; Feb-June 1778. |
| Hutchinson/ Hutcherson, William | Private | Sixth, Avery | Dec 1777; Jan 31 1778 discharged. |
| Hutchinson, William | Private | Twelfth, Wallace | Dec 1777-March 1778 on furlough; April-May 1778. |
| Hutchison, John | Private | Twelfth, Wallace | Feb 28, 1778 drafted; May 1778 sick in camp. |
| Hutt/Hull, Read | Private | Second, Sanford/ Parker | Dec 1777-June 1778. From April on he appears in Parker's company. |
| Hutson, John/Jno. | Private | Seventh/ Third, Posey/ Briscoe | April-June 1778, June 1778 in Briscoe's Company. |
| Hyatt, Edward | Private | Second State, Taliaferro | March 15, 1778-May 1, 1778; May 1778; June 1778 sick Valley Forge. |
| Hyatt, John | Private | Second State, Taliaferro | March 15-May 1, 1778; May-June 1778. |
| Hyatt, Pitman, Pitt | Private | Second State, Taliaferro | March 15, 1778-May 1, 1778; May-June 1778. |
| Imfelt/Infelt, Joseph | Private | Fourteenth, Reid | Dec 1777 deserted. |
| Inge, John | Private | Seventh, Lipscomb | Feb 14, 1778 enlisted for 1 year; April-May 1778 |

| Name | Rank | Regiment/Company | Service |
|---|---|---|---|
| Inge, John | Private | Fourteenth, Jones | Feb 12, 1778 drafted; April-May 1778; June 1778 on command. |
| Inglish see English | | | |
| Inglish/English, Charles | Private | Second State, Bressie | March 15-May 1, 1778; May-June 1778. |
| Ingram, Jeremiah/ Jerry | Private | Fifteenth, Mason/ Gregory | Dec 1777-May 1778; June 1778 in Gregory's Company. |
| Innes/Innis, James | Lt. Colonel | Fifteenth | Dec 1777-May 1778 on furlough. |
| Innis see Ennis | | | |
| Irby, James | Private | Sixth, Rose | Dec 26, 1777 reenlisted in Light Horse. |
| Irby/Iaby, William | Corporal | Fourteenth, Thweatt | Dec 1777-June 1778. |
| Irby/Iaby, William, Jr. | Private | Fourteenth, Thweatt | Dec 1777 sick in hospital; Jan-May 1778; June 1778 on guard. |
| Irvin/Irwin, Alexander/ Alexr. | Private | First, Lewis | Dec 1777 sick; Jan-Feb 1778 sick hospital; April 1778 hospital Lancaster; April-May 1778; June 1778 on command. |
| Irvin/Irwin, William | Corporal/ Sergeant | Fourteenth, Lambert | Dec 1777; Jan 1778 promoted to Sergeant; Jan 1778; Feb-March 1778 on command; April-June 1778. |
| Irwin, James | Private | Fourteenth, Winston | May-June 1778. |
| Isaccs, John | Private | First State, Crump | Dec 1777-June 1778; Feb 1778 deceased. |
| Isdell, Thomas | Private | First State, Hoffler | April-May 1778; June 1778 sick absent. |
| Isom/Ison, George | Corporal | Second State, Taliaferro | March 15, 1778-May 1, 1778; May-June 1778; July 1778 sick Valley Forge. |
| Israel, John | Cadet | Twelfth, Bowyer, T. | Dec 1777-Jan 1778; Feb-March 1778 on command. |
| Iverson/Ivison, Edward | Sergeant | Second State, Bernard | April-June 1778. |
| Jackman, Robert | Private | Sixth, Avery | Dec 1777-Jan 1778; Feb 8, 1778 discharged. |

| | | | |
|---|---|---|---|
| Jackson, Burwell | Corporal | Second, Taylor, W. | Dec 1777-Jan 1778. |
| Jackson, Daniel | Private | First State, Payne | Dec 1777 sick in hospital; March-March 1778; May roll shows he deserted on April 19, 1778. |
| Jackson, Edward | Private | Second, Willis | Dec 1777-May 1778; June 1778 sick Valley Forge. |
| Jackson, Francis | Private | Fourteenth, Jones | Sept 6, 1777 enlisted; Jan-Feb 1778; March 23, 1778 deceased. |
| Jackson, Isick/Isaac | Private | Twelfth, Bowyer, T. | Aug 12, 1777 recruited; Jan 1778 joined; Jan-April 1778. |
| Jackson, John | Sergeant | Second, Sanford/Parker | Dec 1777-June 1778. From April on he appears in Parker's company. |
| Jackson, John | Private | Fourteenth, Winston | Feb 17, 1778 drafted; May-June 1778. |
| Jackson, Jonathan/Jona. | Private | Third, Mercer | Dec 1777-Jan 1778. |
| Jackson, Mathew/Matthew | Private | Fifteenth, Foster/Gray | Dec 1777 on guard; Jan 1778; Feb 1778 in Gray's Company; March 1778; April-May 1778 sick present; June 1778 sick Valley Forge. |
| Jackson, Michael | Private | First State, Hoffler | May 1778-June 1778. |
| Jackson, Obediah | Private | Second, Upshaw | Feb 14, 1778 drafted; April 1778; June 1778 sick at Valley Forge. |
| Jackson, Reuben/Reubin | Private | Sixth, Garland | Aug 5, 1777 enlisted; Jan-May 1778; June 1778 on guard. |
| Jackson, Thomas | Private | Fourteenth, Lambert | Dec 1777; Jan 1778 on guard; Feb-April 1778; May-June 1778 on command. |
| Jackson, William | Sergeant | Second State, Dudley | March 15-May 1, 1778; May-June 1778. |
| Jackson, William | Private | Second State, Bressie | March 15-May 1, 1778; May-June 1778. |
| Jackson, William | Private | Second, Upshaw | Feb 16, 1778 drafted; April 1778; June 1778. |
| Jackon, William | Private | Sixth, Hockaday | Dec 1777 sick at Princetown; Jan 1778; Feb 10, 1778 discharged. |

| Name | Rank | Company | Notes |
|---|---|---|---|
| Jackways, Samuel | Private | First, Pelham | Dec 1777 guard; Jan-June 1778. |
| Jacobs, Benjamin | Private | Seventh, Lipscomb | Dec 1777-Jan 1778 hospital; Feb 4, 1778 discharged. |
| Jacobs, Samuel | Private | Second State, Lewis | March 15-May 1, 1778; May-June 1778. |
| James, Christopher | Private | Fifteenth, Mason/Gregory | Dec 1777-Jan 1778 sick in Virginia; Feb-March 1778; April 1778 sick in camp; May Yellow Springs; June 1778 sick Yellow Springs, in Gregory's Company. |
| James, Danl. | Sergeant | Third, Mercer | Dec 1777 on furlough; Jan 1778 sick present. |
| James, Elisha | Private | Second State, Spiller | March 15-May 1, 1778; May 1778; June 1778 sick Monmouth. |
| James, Henry | Private | Seventh, Spencer | Dec 1777 sick present; Jan 1778 hospital; Feb 20, 1778 discharged. |
| James, John/Jno. | Private | Sixth, Massie | Dec 1777 in hospital, "Time to serve, Feb. 10, 1778."; Jan 1778. |
| James, John | Private | Seventh, Lipscomb | Dec 1777-Jan 1778 hospital; March 7, 1778 discharged. |
| James, Peter | Private | Second State, Spiller | March 15-May 1, 1778; May 1778; June 1778 sick Monmouth. |
| James, Richard | Private | Twelfth, Waggener | Dec 1777-March 1778; April 10, 1778 discharged. |
| James, Thomas | Private | Fifteenth, Grimes | Dec 1777-Jan 1778 sick Virginia |
| James, Walter | Private | Second State, Dudley | July 1778 roll shows him "omitted from 15 April." |
| James, William | Private/Corporal | Second State, Dudley | March 15-May 1, 1778; May-June 1778. He was promoted to Corporal on May 1. |
| James, William | Private | Fourteenth, Overton | Dec 1777 on command. |
| Janson, George | Private | Fifteenth, Harris | March 1778 sick present. |

Jarmon see Germon

Jarrard see Gerrard

| Name | Rank | Regiment, Company | Service |
|---|---|---|---|
| Jarrell/Jarrel, John | Private | First State, Nicholas | Dec 1777 on guard; Jan-June 1778. |
| Jarrell, Solomon | Private | First State, Nicholas | Dec 1777-May 1778; June 1778 sick present. |
| Jason/Jesson, Robert | Private | Fourteenth, Winston | Jan 1778 in Commissary employ; June 1778 on duty. |
| Jasper, Edward | Private | First State, Payne | Dec 1777; Jan 5, 1778 deceased. |
| Jean/Jane, William | Private | Fourteenth, Jones | September 18, 1777 enlisted; Jan 1778; Feb 1778 sick present; March 1778 sick in hospital; April 5, 1778 died. |
| Jefferies, William/Wm. L. | Private | Fifteenth, Hull | March 1778; April-May 1778 sick present; June 1778 sick Valley Forge. |
| Jeffers/Jeffries, Elisha | Private | Sixth, Massie | Dec 1777-April 1778 on furlough; May 1778; June 1778 sick at Valley Forge. |
| Jeffres/Jeffrys, Burwell | Private | First State, Ewell, T. | Dec 1777-Feb 1778 sick at New Church; March-April 1778. |
| Jeffrey/Jeffery, George/Geo. | Private | Third/Seventh, Arell/Briscoe | Dec 1777-May 1778; June 1778 sick at Valley Forge, in Briscoe's Company. |
| Jeffries, Booker | Cadet | Third, Peyton, J. | May 15, 1778 appointed; July 1778. This man and the one below appear to be the same individual. |
| Jeffries, Booker/Bowker | 1st. Lt. | Fifteenth, Harris | March-April 1778; May 15, 1778 resigned. |
| Jeffries, John | Private | First State, Ewell, T. | Dec 1777 sick Jersies; Jan-Feb 1778 sick in the Jersies; March 1778 sick present; April-May 1778 on guard; June 1778 on command. |
| Jeffris/Jeffries, William | Private | First State, Lee | Dec 1777 sick; Jan-Feb 1778 sick absent; March 1778 Yellow Springs hospital. |
| Jefries/Jeffris, Isick/Isaac | Sergeant/Commissary | Seventh, Webb | Enlisted for 3 years; Jan-February 1778 on furlough; April-May 1778; June 1778 promoted to Commissary. |

| Name | Rank | Regiment/Company | Notes |
|---|---|---|---|
| Jenkins/Jinkins, Benjamin | Private | Twelfth, Bowyer, T. | August 30, 1777 enlisted; Jan 1778 joined; Jan-Feb 1778; March 1778 sick in hospital; April 1778 sick in hospital near camp. |
| Jenkins/Jinkins, John | Private | Second State, Garnett | March 15-May 1, 1778; May-June 1778. |
| Jenkins/Jinkins, Pressly | Private | Second, Taylor, W. | Dec 1777-Jan 1778; Feb 18, 1778 died. |
| Jenkins/Jinkins, Richard | Sergeant/ Quartermaster Sergeant | Second, Jones | Dec 1777-March 1778 he is listed as a Sergeant in Jones' Company; April-June 1778 he appears as Quartermaster Sergeant. |
| Jenkins, Thomas | Private | Third, Arell | Dec 1777; Jan 15, 1778 dead. |
| Jenkins, William | 2nd. Lt. | Fourteenth, Conway | Dec 1777; Jan-June 1778 on command. Oath at Valley Forge on May 12, 1778, witnessed by Muhlenberg. |
| Jenkins, William/Wm. | Private | Fifteenth, Gray | Dec 1777 dead. However he appears on the rolls for Jan-May 1778. |
| Jennett/Jinnitt, Samuel | Private | Fourteenth, Thweatt | August 27, 1777 enlisted; April-May 1778; June 1778 on guard. |
| Jennings/ Jinning, Augustus/ Augustine | Private | Twelfth, Ashby | Dec 1777; Jan 1778 on guard; March-May 1778. |
| Jennings, Baylor/Baytor | Private | Third, Peyton, V. | Dec 1777 on command with Col. Morgan; Jan 1778 with Col. Morgan. |
| Jennings/ Jinnings, Solomon | Private | First State, Nicholas | Dec 1777 sick in the Jersies; Jan-Feb 1778 sick in ye country. |
| Jett, John | Private | First, Cunningham | Feb 10, 1778 enlisted; July 1778 sick at Valley Forge. |
| Jinnett, John | Private | First, Payne | Feb 5, 1778 enlisted; April 1778; May 11, 1778 died. |
| Jobe/Job, Isick/Isaac | Private | Twelfth, Casey | Dec 1777-March 1778 on command; April-May 1778. |
| Jobe/Job, William | Private | Twelfth, Casey | Dec 1777-May 1778. |

| | | | | |
|---|---|---|---|---|
| Johis, John | Private | Second, Upshaw | Dec 1777 sick hospital. | |
| Johns, George | Private | Third/Seventh, Arell/Briscoe | Dec 1777-March 1778; April 1778 sick present; May 1778 on guard; June 1778 advanced guard, in Briscoe's Company. | |
| Johns, James | Private | Fourteenth, Overton | Oct 1, 1777 drafted; Jan 1778 lately joined the Fourteenth regiment, on command; Feb-March 1778; April 1778 sick present; May-June 1778. | |
| Johns, Jesse | Private | Twelfth, Wallace | Dec 1777-April 1778 sent to hospital. | |
| Johns, William | Private | Fourteenth, Overton | Oct 1, 1777 drafted; Jan 6, 1778 enlisted for two years; Jan-April 1778 on furlough; June 1778 sick Valley Forge. | |
| Johnson, Benjamin | Corporal | First State, Crump | April-June 1778. | |
| Johns, William | Sergeant | Fourteenth, Marks | Jan 6, 1778 enlisted for 2 years; Jan-May 1778. | |
| Johnson/Johnston, Benjamin | Private | Third, Powell | Dec 1777; Feb 2, 1778 discharged. | |
| Johnson, Daniel/Danl. | Private | First, Cummings | Dec 1777. | |
| Johnson/Johnston, Edward | Private | Second State, Garnett | May-June 1778. | |
| Johnson/Johnston, Ellis | Private | Second State, Dudley | March 15-May 1, 1778; May-June 1778. | |
| Johnson, George | Private | Third, Peyton, V. | Dec 23, 1777 discharged. | |
| Johnson, Geo. | Private | Fifteenth, Foster | Dec 1777 in Virginia. | |
| Johnson, Jacob | Private | Sixth, Avery | Dec 1777-Jan 1778; Feb 13, 1778 discharged. | |
| Johnson, Jacob | Private | Sixth, Hockaday | Dec 1777 sick at Princetown. | |
| Johnson, James | Private | Twelfth, Ashby | Dec 1777 sick in camp; Jan-Feb 1778; March 1778 on command; April-May 1778. | |

| Name | Rank | Regiment, Company | Service |
|---|---|---|---|
| Johnson, Jeremiah | Private | Second State, Bernard | June 1778. |
| Johnson, John | Private | First, Cunningham | Enlisted Augst 1777 for 3 years; Dec 1777-April 1778; May 15, 1778 died. |
| Johnson, John | Private | Seventh, Lipscomb | Dec 22, 1777 enlisted in Light Horse. |
| Johnson, John | Private | Seventh, Young | Dec 1777-Jan 1778 Comr. Guard; Feb 1778; March 1, 1778 discharged. |
| Johnson/Jonson, John B. | 2nd. Lt. | Fourteenth, Winston | Dec 1777-Jan 1778 recruiting in Virginia; Feb-May 1778; June 1778 sick absent. Oath at Valley Forge on May 28, 1778, witnessed by Muhlenberg. |
| Johnson, John | Private | Fifteenth, Mason | Dec 1777-Jan 1778; Feb 1778 sick present; March-May 1778 sick in camp; June-Oct 1778 sick Valley Forge. |
| Johnson/Jonston, Joseph | Private/Sergeant | First State, Ewell, T. | Jan 1778 promoted to Sergeant; April-May 1778 on command; June 1778 reduced to Private. |
| Johnson, Joseph | Private | Twelfth, Ashby | Dec 1777-March 1778; April 22, 1778 died. |
| Johnson/Johnston, Martin | Private | Third, Peyton, V. | Dec 1777 rifleman on command with Col. Morgan; Jan 1778 with Col. Morgan. |
| Johnson/Johnsten, Moses | Private | Second, Calmes | Dec 1777-June 1778. |
| Johnson, Nicholas | Corporal | Third, Powell | Dec 1777; Jan 31, 1778 discharged. |
| Johnson, Samuel | Drum Major | Seventh | Dec 1777-Jan 1778; Feb 3, 1778 discharged. |
| Johnson/Jonson, Smith | Sergeant | Fourteenth, Thweatt | Dec 1777 sick at hospital; Jan 1778; Feb 18, 1778 died. |
| Johnson, Stanniss | Private | Seventh, Jouett | April 29, 1778 died. |
| Johnson, Thomas | Private | Sixth, Fox | Feb-May 1778 on furlough; June 1778 deserted. |
| Johnson, William | Private | Fourteenth, Overton | Dec 1777-March 1778; April-May 1778 sick absent; June 1778 sick at Yellow Springs. |

| Name | Rank | Regiment/Company | Notes |
|---|---|---|---|
| Johnston, Archibald | Private | Twelfth, Waggener | Dec 1777-Feb 1778; March 1778 sick in camp; April 10, 1778 discharged. |
| Johnston, Benjamin/Ben | Private | Seventh/Third, Webb/Young | Enlisted for 3 years; Jan 1778-February 1778 on furlough; April-May 1778; June 1, 1778 promoted to Corporal, in Young's Company. |
| Johnston, Bayle/Bailey | Private/Corporal | Twelfth, Waggener | Dec 1777-Feb 1778 hospital; March 1778 on fatigue; April 1778 promoted to Corporal; April-May 1778. |
| Johnston/Johnson, James | Private | Sixth, Hockaday | Feb 17, 1778 drafted; April 1778; May-June 1778 on guard. |
| Johnston, Joel/Stoe | Private | Fourteenth, Jones | Jan 1778 deserted in Virginia |
| Johnston, Joseph | Sergeant | Seventh, Spencer | Dec 1777 sick present; Jan 1778 8; Feb 13, 1778 discharged. |
| Johnston, Richard | Private | Second, Sanford | Dec 1777-April 1778. |
| Johnston, Richard/Richd. | Private | Fifteenth, Wills | June 30, 1777 enlisted; Feb 1778 sick present; March-May 1778. |
| Johnston, Saml. | Private | Sixth, Fox | April 1778. |
| Joiner, Daniel | Private | Fifteenth, Harris | Jan 1778; Feb 1778 on guard; March 30, 1778 dead. |
| Jones, Absalom | Private | First State, Meriwether | Dec 1777-June 1778. |
| Jones, Absolum/Absolem | Private | Sixth, Avery | Dec 1777 sick in hospital; Jan 1778; Feb 15, 1778 discharged. |
| Jones, Adam | Private | Second, Hoomes | June 1778. |
| Jones, Albridston/Albridgeton | Adjutant | Fifteenth | Dec 1777-May 1778. |
| Jones, Benjamin | Private | First State, Crump | April-May 1778; June 1778 absent sick. |
| Jones, Berry | Private | Second, Upshaw | Feb 13, 1778 drafted; April 1778; June 1778 sick Valley Forge. |
| Jones, Binns | 2nd. Lt./Quartermaster | Fifteenth, Mason | Dec 1777-March 1778 on furlough; April 1778; May 1778 sick in the country, designated Regimental Quartermaster; June 1778 recruiting. |

| Name | Rank | Regiment, Company | Notes |
|---|---|---|---|
| Jones, Daniel/Danl. | Private | Fifteenth, Harris | March-April 1778 sick present; May 1778. |
| Jones, Edward | Private | First State, Crump | April-May 1778; June 1778 sick absent. |
| Jones, George/Geo. | Private | Third, Mercer | Dec 1777-Jan 1778. |
| Jones, George | Private | Fourteenth, Winston | Feb 18, 1778 enlisted; June 1778 sick at Valley Forge. |
| Jones, Holmes | Sergeant | Fifteenth, Edmunds | Dec 1777-Feb 1778 sick absent; March 1778 "I have heard he was dead not certain." |
| Jones, James | Private | First State, Camp | Dec 1777; Jan-Feb 1778 sick absent; March 1778 hospital Red Lyon; April 20, 1778 died. |
| Jones, James | Private | Third/Seventh, Lee/Peyton, J. | Feb 27, 1778 enlisted; April-May 1778; June 1778 guard, in J. Peyton's Company. |
| Jones, James | Private | Third, Mercer | Dec 1777 sick present; Jan 1778 on guard. |
| Jones, James | Corporal | Seventh, Lipscomb | Dec 1777; Jan 31, 1778 discharged. |
| Jones, Jesse | Private | Second State, Quarles | April-June 1778. |
| Jones, Jesse | Private | Fifteenth, Grimes | Dec 1777-Jan 1778 sick absent; Feb 1778 sick present; March-April 1778; May 1778 on command. |
| Jones, John | Private | First, Mennis | Dec 1777-March 1778 on furlough; March 1778 on command; May-June 1778. |
| Jones, John | Private | Seventh/Third, Webb/Young | April-May 1778; June 1778 in Young's Company. |
| Jones, John | Sergeant | Fourteenth, Reid | Dec 1777 hospital; Jan 1778 sick in camp; Feb 1778 on guard; March 1778 on command. This may be the same man as below. |
| Jones, John | Private | Fourteenth, Reid | April-May 1778; June 1778 left at Valley Forge. |

| | | | |
|---|---|---|---|
| Jones, John | Private | Fourteenth, Winston | Dec 1777 sick in hospital; Jan 1778 sick absent; Feb 1778 sick in hospital; March-April 1778; May 1778 sick present; June 1778 sick Valley Forge. |
| Jones, John | Private | Fifteenth, Foster | Dec 1777; Jan 9, 1778 discharged for Disability. |
| Jones, John | Private | Fifteenth, Mason/ Gregory | Dec 1777-Feb 1778; March 1778 sick in camp; April 1778; May 1778 sick in camp; June 1778 on guard, in Gregory's Company. |
| Jones, Joseph | Private | First State, Ewell, T. | Jan 12, 1778 enlisted; March 1778; April-May 1778 on command; June 1778. |
| Jones, Josiah | Private | Fifteenth, Wills | Feb 19, 1778 enlisted; April 1778 sick present; May-July 1778 sick Yellow Springs; Aug 1778 died Yellow Springs. |
| Jones, Lunsford | Private | First State, Nicholas | Dec 1777-Jan 1778; Feb 1778 sick Yellow Springs Hospital; March 1778 sick Yellow Springs; April 16, 1778 deceased. |
| Jones, Peter | Captain | Fourteenth, Jones | Jan 1778-Feb 1778 on furlough; March-May 1778. Oath at Valley Forge on May 12, 1778, witnessed by Muhlenberg. |
| Jones, Jr., Richard | Private | Third/ Seventh, Powell | Dec 1777-Feb 1778 sick present; April 1778 on command; May-June 1778. |
| Jones, Sr., Richard | Private | Third/ Seventh, Powell | Jan 1778; Feb 1778 on picket; March 1778 sick present; April 1778; May 1778 on guard; June 1778 sick Brunswick. |
| Jones, Richard/Richd. | Private | Sixth, Avery | Dec 26, 1777 enlisted into the Light Dragoons. |
| Jones, Richard | Private | Seventh/ Third, Spencer/ Lipscomb | Feb 18, 1778 enlisted for 1 year; May 1778; June 1778 in Lipscomb's Company. |
| Jones, Robert | Sergeant | Second, Taylor, W. | Dec 1777-Jan 1778; Feb 5, 1778 discharged. |
| Jones, Rolugh | Private | Seventh, Lipscomb | Dec 1777 left in Virginia July 1777. |

| Name | Rank | Regiment/Company | Service Dates |
|---|---|---|---|
| Jones, Samuel/Saml. | Private | Sixth, | Dec 1777-Jan 1778; Feb 11, 1778 discharged. |
| Jones, Samuel | Private | Twelfth, Waggener | Dec 1777-May 1778 |
| Jones, Samuel/Saml. | 2nd. Lt. | Fifteenth, Foster/Gray | Dec 1777-March 1778; April 1778 sick absent; June 6, 1778 convicted at a court-martial and dismissed from the service. However on June 11, Washington restored him to his place in the Army, on the recommendations of Generals Scott and Woodford, and other officers. |
| Jones, Thomas | Private | Seventh, Hill | Dec 1777; Jan 1778 sick present. |
| Jones, Thomas/Thos. | Private | Fifteenth, Foster/Gray | May 20, 1777 enlisted; Jan-Feb 1778; Feb 1778 in Gray's Company; March 1778 sick in camp; April 1778 sick present; May 1778. |
| Jones, William | Private | Second State, Dudley | March 15-May 1, 1778; May-June 1778. |
| Jones, William | Private | Second State, Garnett | March 15-May 1, 1778; May-June 1778. |
| Jones, William | Private | Third/Seventh, Peyton, V./Peyton, J. | Dec 1777-April 1778; May 1778 command; June 1778 guard. |
| Jones, William/Wm. | Private | Sixth, Apperson | Dec 1777 sick Trenton; jan 22, 1778 discharged. On the Feb 1778 payroll he was paid for 22 days. |
| Jones, William | Quartermaster Sergeant | Seventh | Dec 1777-Jan 1778; Feb 24, 1778 discharged. |
| Jones, William/Wm. | Private | Seventh/Third, Jouett | Feb 16, 1778 enlisted; April-May 1778; June 1778 in Hill's Company. |
| Jones, William | Corporal | Fifteenth/Wills Thirteenth | June 25, 1777 enlisted; Feb-March 1778; April 1778 "in 13th Regt by Prior Enlistment". |
| Jones, Wood | Captain | Second, Jones | Dec 1777-Jan 1778. |

| Name | Rank | Company | Service |
|---|---|---|---|
| Jones, Zackariah/Zaceriah | Private | Fourteenth, Marks | Dec 1777-May 1778; June 1778 sick Valley Forge. |
| Jonns, Thomas | Private | Seventh, Webb | Jan 1778; March 3, 1778 discharged. |
| Jordan, George | Sergeant | Third, Peyton, V. | Dec 1777 sick in hospital; Jan 1778; Feb 10, 1778 discharged. |
| Jordan, Henry | Private | Second State, Taliaferro | March 15-May 1, 1778; May-June 1778. |
| Jordan/Jourdon, James | Private | First State, Hamilton | Dec 1777-June 1778. |
| Jordan/Jordon, Joseph | Private | Second, Sanford/Parker | Dec 1777-June 1778. |
| Jordan/Jordin, Michael | Private | First State, Payne | Dec 1777-Feb 1778; March-May 1778 on guard; June 1778 sick Valley Forge. |
| Jordan/Jordon, Simon/Semond | Private | First, Mennis | Dec 1777 sick at Princeton; Jan 1778 wounded in the hospital; Feb 1778 wounded; |
| Jordon/Jordan, John | Ensign | Sixth, Hockaday | April 1778. |
| Jouett, Mathew | Captain | Seventh, Jouett | Nov 15, 1777 died. His former company continued under his name until absorbed into Captain Hill's. |
| Jouett, Robert | Ensign | Seventh/Third, Jouett/Hill | Dec 1777 on furlough Virginia; Jan-March 1778 on furlough; April-May 1778; June 1778 in Hill's Company. |
| Jude, Benjamin | Sergeant | Second State, Bernard | April 1778; May-June 1778 on command with Col. Morgan. |
| Jude, George | Private | First State, Nicholas | Dec 1777 sick Burlington; Jan-Feb 1778 sick Trenton; April roll shows him as deceased on Jan 16, 1778. |
| Junal, Anthony | Private | Seventh/Third, Moseley/Blackwell | Dec 1777-March 1778 on furlough; April 1778; May 1778 on guard; June 1778 in Blackwell's Company. |

| Name | Rank | Company | Notes |
|---|---|---|---|
| Junal, William | Private | Seventh, Moseley | Dec 1777 on guard; Jan 1778 sick present; Feb 21, 1778 discharged. |
| Kain/Keen, Thos. | Sergeant/ Private | Third, Powell | Dec 8, 1777 enlisted; Dec 1777 on furlough; Jan-April 1778; May 1, 1778 deserted; July 10, 1778 reduced to Private. |
| Kalor see Calor | | | |
| Kave see Cave | | | |
| Kay, Richard | Private | Second, Upshaw | Dec 1777-Jan 1778. |
| Keamer/Kemer, James | Private | Second State, Spiller | March 15-May 1, 1778; April-June 1778. |
| Keamon, James | Private | First, Cunningham | Feb 20, 1778 enlisted; July 1778 sick at Valley Forge. |
| Keane see Cain | | | |
| Keaner/Keener, Richard | Drummer | Fourteenth, Jones | Jan-May 1778. |
| Kearn/Kern, Edward | Private | Fourteenth, Jones | Sept 6, 1777 enlisted; Jan 1778; Feb 1778 sick present; April 1, 1778 died |
| Keath/Keith, Alexander | Private | Second, Calmes | Dec 1777-June 1778. |
| Keath/Keith, Vincent | Private | Second, Calmes | Dec 1777-May 1778; June 1778 sick at Carroles Ferry. |
| Keef/Keith, Daniel | Private | Twelfth, Waggner | Dec 1777-March 1778; April 10, 1778 discharged. |
| Keeling/ Keeleng, Thomas | Private | Seventh, Moseley | Dec 1777 sick in hospital; Jan 1778 sick present; Feb 1778; March 7, 1778 discharged. |
| Keep, James | Private | Second, Jones/ Hoomes | Dec 1777-May 1778; June 1778 sick absent. |
| Keer, David | Private | Fourteenth, Marks | May-June 1778. |
| Keer, John | Private | Fourteenth, Marks | Dec 1777-Jan 1778 waggoner; Feb 1778 on guard; March-April 1778; June 1778. |
| Keeton, James | Private | Seventh/ Third, Hill | Feb 16, 1778 enlisted; June 1778. |
| Keihoe, James | Private | Third, Peyton, J. | Dec 23, 1777 reenlisted in the Light Horse. |

| Name | Rank | Regiment/Company | Notes |
|---|---|---|---|
| Kein/Keene, Thomas | Volunteer | Second, Parker | April-June 1778. |
| Keith, Daniel | Private | Twelfth, Waggener | Dec 1777-March 1778; April 10, 1778 discharged. |
| Keith/Kieth, Green | Corporal | Seventh/Third, Posey/Sayer | Feb 27, 1778 enlisted; April 1778; May 1778 on command; June 1778 in Sayer's Company. |
| Keith/Keath, Isham | 1st. Lt. | Third, Peyton, V. | Dec 1777 on furlough; Jan 1778; Feb-March 1778 sick in Virginia. |
| Keize, George | Private | Twelfth, Ashby | March 1778. |
| Kelley/Kelly, Daniel/Danil. | Private | First, Lewis | Feb 7, 1778 enlisted; April-June 1778; Aug 18, 1778 died. |
| Kelley, James | Private | Sixth, Avery | Dec 1, 1777, on furlough; Jan-May 1778 on furlough; June 1778 discharged. |
| Kelley/Kelly, John | Private | First, Lewis | Feb 7, 1778 enlisted; April 1778; May 1778 sick present; June 1778 sick Valley Forge. |
| Kelley/Kelly, John | Private | First State, Camp | Dec 1777; Jan-Feb 1778 sick absent; March 1778 on furlough; April-June 1778. |
| Kęlley, John | Private | Second State, Quarles | April-May 1778; June 26, 1778 died. |
| Kelley, John | Private | Twelfth, Wallace | Feb 28, 1778 drafted; May 1778; June-July 1778 sick Valley Forge. |
| Kelley, Michael | Private | Fourteenth, Lambert | Sept 20, 1777 enlisted; June 1778 lately joined. |
| Kelly, Thomas/Thom. | Private | Third, Blackwell | Dec 23, 1777 discharged. |
| Kelshaw/Kelsher, John/Jno. | Private | Third/Seventh, Arell/Briscoe | Dec 1777-April 1778; May 1778 on guard; June 1778 sick Valley Forge, in Briscoe's Company. |
| Kem/Keam, John | Private | Fifteenth, Hull | Dec 1777 on scout; Jan 1778; Feb 1778 sick present; March-May 1778. |
| Kemp, George | Private | Twelfth, Bowyer, T. | Dec 1777 sick absent. |

| Name | Rank | Regiment | Service |
|---|---|---|---|
| Kemp, Peter | Private | Second State, Garnett | March 15-May 1, 1778; May-June 1778. |
| Kemp/Camp, Thomas | Private | Second State, Taliaferro | March 15-May 1, 1778; May-June 1778. |
| Kendall/Kindal, Francis | Private | Third, Lee | Dec 1777-Jan 1778; Feb 14, 1778 discharged. |
| Kendall, Jen. | Sergeant | Third, Mercer | Dec 1777; Jan 1778 discharged. |
| Kendrick, Jacob | Private | Twelfth, Casey | Dec 1777-March 1778 at hospital. |
| Kenley, Charles | Private | Sixth, Garland | Sept 23, 1777 enlisted; Feb-March 1778. |
| Kennaday/ Kennedy, Wm. | Private | Fifteenth, Mason/ Gregory | Dec 1777-Jan 1778; Feb 1778 on guard; March 1778; April 1778 on guard; May 1778; June 1778 sick Correls Ferry, in Gregory's Company. |
| Kennedy see Cannady | | | |
| Kennedy/ Canady, Daniel | Private | Third, Peyton, V. | Dec 1777-Jan 1778 sick in hospital; Feb 1778 "supposed to be deserted." |
| Kennedy/ Kennady, James | Sergeant | Seventh/ Third, Jouett/Hill | Dec 1777 on furlough Virginia; Jan-April 1778 on furlough; May 1778; June 1778 in Hill's Company. |
| Kennedy/ Kannedy, Nathan | Private | First State, Lee | Dec 1777 sick; Jan 1778 deceased. |
| Kennedy, William | Sergeant | Seventh, Jouett | Dec 1777 sick in hospital; Jan 25, 1778 discharged. |
| Kennerly, Peter | Private | Second, Willis | Dec 1777; Jan 3, 1778 deserted. |
| Kenney/Keney, Patrick/Patrack | Private | Fourteenth, Conway | Dec 1777; Jan 1778 on command; Feb-April 1778; May 1778 on duty; June 1778. |
| Kennon, James | Private | Second, Upshaw | Feb 14, 1778 drafted; April 1778; June-July 1778 sick at Valley Forge. |

| | | | | |
|---|---|---|---|---|
| Kennon, John | 1st. Lt. | Second, Parker | Dec 1777-June 1778. Oath at Valley Forge on May 12, 1778, witnessed by Muhlenberg. |
| Kennon/Kinnon, John | Paymaster | Sixth | Dec 1777-Feb 1778; March-April 1778 on furlough; May-June 1778. Oath at Valley Forge on May 28, 1778, witnessed by Muhlenberg. |
| Kent, Smith | Corporal/ Sergeant | Seventh, Moseley | Dec 1777-March 1778 on furlough; April 1778 sick Lancaster; April 1, 1778 promoted to Sergeant. |
| Kent, William | Private | Third/ Seventh, Briscoe | Dec 1777-May 1778; June 1778 sick absent Lancaster. |
| Kerns/Kirns, Barney/Barny | Private | Twelfth, Waggener | Dec 1777-March 1778; April 10, 1778 discharged. |
| Kerns/Horns, Ephraim/ Ephraham | Private | First, Payne/ Lawson | Feb 5, 1778 enlisted; April-May 1778; June 1778 in Lawson's Company. |
| Kerr see Carr | | | |
| Kerr, James | Private | Seventh/ Third, Fleming/ Heth | Feb 11, 1778 enlisted; April 1778 sick present; May 1778; June 1778 in Heth's Company. |
| Kerr/Care, John | Private | Second, Sanford/ Parker | Dec 1777 hospital; Jan-June 1778. From April on he appears in Parker's company. |
| Kerr, John | Private | Seventh, Fleming | Dec 1777-Jan 1778; Feb 24, 1778 discharged. |
| Kersey/Kersay, Thomas/Thos. | Private | Fifteenth, Gray | Dec 1777-Jan 1778 sick absent; Feb 1778 sick; March 1778 on command; April 1778 dead. |
| Keyser/Keysor, William | Private | Second State, Taliaferro | March 15-May 1, 1778; May-June 1778. |
| Keyton/Keaton, Thomas | Private | Sixth, Garland | Dec 1, 1777 reenlisted, on furlough; Jan-May 1778 on furlough; June 1778 sick Princeton. |
| Kidd, Henry | Private | Seventh, Webb | Jan 1778 sick Virginia; Feb 3, 1778 discharged. |
| Kidd, James | Private | Second, Harrison | Dec 1777-June 1778. |

| Name | Rank | Regiment | Notes |
|---|---|---|---|
| Kidd, William | Private | Seventh, Webb | Jan 1778 hospital; Feb 5, 1778 discharged. |
| Kilburn, Isick/Isaac | Private | Second, Willis | Dec 28, 1777 deserted. |
| Kimbrough, Benjamin | Private/Sergeant | Fourteenth, Winston | Feb 17, 1778 drafted; May 1778; June 1, 1778 promoted to Sergeant, June 1778. |
| Kimmings, Thomas | Private | Second State, Lewis | March 15-May 1, 1778; May 1778. |
| Kindrick, Jacob | Private | Twelfth, Casey | Dec 1777-Jan 1778 sent to hospital; Feb-March 1778 at hospital. |
| Kiney/Kenny, Richard | Private | Twelfth, Waggener | Dec 1777 on command; Jan 1778; Feb 1778 sick in camp; March 1778 on command; April-May 1778 waggoner. |
| Kinney, John | Private | Fifteenth, Gregory | Dec 1777 Virginia; Jan 1778 sick Virginia; |
| King, Elisha | Sergeant | Fourteenth, Overton | Dec 1777 sick in hospital; Feb-April 1778; May 1778 on command; June 1778. |
| King, Francis | Private | Second State, Bernard | May 1778; June 1778 sick at Princetown. |
| King, Henry | Private | Second State, Bernard | May 1778; June 1778 sick Princetown. |
| King, John | Private | First State, Meriwether | Dec 1777-June 1778. |
| King, John | Sergeant | Third, Mercer | Dec 1777-Jan 1778 sick absent. |
| King, John | Private | Third/Seventh, Peyton, V./Peyton, J. | Dec 1777 sick in hospital; Jan 1778; Feb 1778 sick present; March-May 1778; June-Aug 1778 sick at Valley Forge, in J. Peyton's Company. |
| King, John | Private | Seventh/Third, Fleming/Heth | Feb 11, 1778 enlisted; April 1778 sick present; May 1778; June 1778 in Heth's Company. |

| Name | Rank | Regiment | Notes |
|---|---|---|---|
| King, John | Private/ Sergeant | Seventh/ Third, Lipscomb | Dec 1, 1777 reenlisted for 3 years; Dec 1777-Jan 1778 on furlough; Feb 16, 1778 promoted to Sergeant; April-May 1778; June 1778 sick absent. |
| King, Joseph | Private | Fourteenth, Reid | Dec 1777 hospital; Jan 1778 sick at Trenton; Feb 1778 sick absent; March-May 1778; June 1778 on command. |
| King, Miles | Surgeon's Mate | First | Dec 1777-June 1778. Oath at Valley Forge on May 18, 1778, witnessed by Muhlenberg. |
| King, Saber/ Sabert | Private | Seventh/ Third, Jouett/ Hill | Feb 16, 1778 enlisted; April-May 1778; June 1778 in Hill's Company. |
| King, Valentine/ Volintine | Private | Third, Mercer | Dec 1777-Jan 1778. |
| King, William | Private | Second State, Lewis | March 15-May 1, 1778; May-June 1778. |
| King, William | Private | Third/ Seventh, Peyton, V./ Peyton, J. | Dec 1777-Jan 1778 artificer; Feb-March 1778 artificer at the Bridge; April-June 1778 artificer; June 1778 in J. Peyton's Company. |
| Kinkade, Robert | Private | First, Scott | Dec 1777 with Colonel Morgan. |
| Kinkead, William | Adjutant | Twelfth | December 31, 1777 resigned. |
| Kimmings, Thomas | Private | Second State, Lewis | March 15-May 1, 1778; May 1778. |
| Kinnard, David | Private | First State, Camp | Dec 1777; Jan 1778 sick absent; Feb-June 1778. |
| Kinnerd, Richard | Private | Fourteenth, Conway | Dec 1777. |
| Kinsey/Kinzey, John | Private | Fifteenth, Hull | Dec 1777-Feb 1778; March 15, 1778 discharged. |
| Kinsey/Kensey, Solomon/ Sollomon | Private | Fifteenth, Gregory | March 27, 1778 joined, sick present; April-May 1778 sick present; June 1778 sick Valley Forge. |
| Kirk, John | Private | Third, Blackwell | Dec 1777-Jan 1778; Feb 14, 1778 discharged. |

| Name | Rank | Regiment/Company | Notes |
|---|---|---|---|
| Kirk, Thomas | Private | First, Scott | Dec 1777 with Colonel Morgan. |
| Kirkland, Jesse/Jese | Private | Fifteenth, Mason/Gregory | Feb 1, 1778 drafted; May 1778; June 1778 in Gregory's Company. |
| Kirkland/Kirklin, Rowland/Roland | Private | Second, Jones/Hoomes | Dec 1777-Feb 1778; March 30, 1778 dead. |
| Kirtland/Kirkland, Richard | Private | Fourteenth, Jones | Feb 8, 1778 drafted; April-May 1778. |
| Kitchen, Daniel | Private | Second, Harrison | May 1778; June 1778 sick Valley Forge. |
| Kneebone see Neebone | | | |
| Knight, James | Corporal | Second State, Lewis | March 15-May 1, 1778+; May-June 1778. |
| Knight, John | Private | Twelfth, Madison | Dec 1777-March 1778 sick at hospital. |
| Knight, Wm. | Private | Fifteenth, Wills | Feb 14, 1778 enlisted; April 1778 sick present; May 1778. |
| Knows/Knouse, John | Private | Twelfth, Madison | Dec 1777-March 1778; April 1778 absent without leave; May 1778. |
| Knox, George | Private | Twelfth, Ashby | Dec 1777; Jan 1778 sick in hospital; March 1778 at hospital; April-May 1778. |
| Knox, Jeremiah | Private | Second State, Lewis | March 15-May 1, 1778; May-June 1778. |
| Kyle, William | Private | Twelfth, Bowyer, T. | Dec 1777-Jan 1778; Feb-April 1778 on command. |
| Lacey, Nathaniel/Nathl | Private | Third/Seventh, Peyton, V./Peyton, J. | Dec 1777; Jan 1778 on guard; Feb 1778; March 1778 on guard; April 1778 on command at the Lines; May 1778; June 1778 in J. Peyton's Company. |
| Lacy, Elkanah/Elkaniah | Private | Seventh/Third, Moseley/Blackwell | Dec 1777-March 1778 on furlough; April-May 1778; June 1778 in Blackwell's Company, sick Coryells Ferry. |
| Ladd, James | Private | First State, Crump | Dec 1777-Feb 1778; March 25, 1778 deceased. |

| | | | |
|---|---|---|---|
| Lake, Jeremiah | Private | Seventh/Third, Young | Feb 16, 1778 enlisted; April 1778 sick present; June 1778 |
| Lake, Lewis | Private | Seventh/Third, Young | Feb 16, 1778 enlisted; April 1778 sick present; May-June 1778. |
| Lake, William | Private | Fourteenth, Lambert | Nov 27, 1777 enlisted; April 1778 lately joined regiment; May-June 1778. |
| Lambert, Charles/Chs. | Private | Third, Mercer | Dec 1777-Jan 1778; Feb-March 1778 sick present; April 1778 sick at Church Hospital; May 1778 sick absent; June 1778 sick at Yellow Springs. |
| Lambert, George | Captain | Fourteenth, Lambert | Dec 1777 under arrest; Jan 15, 1778 cashiered. Syrus Roberts was promoted and commanded this company from Jan-June 1778. |
| Lambert, John | Private | First State, Lee | Dec 1777; Jan 1778 sick absent; Feb 1778 Yellow Springs hospital; March 1778 Red Lyon hospital; April-June 1778. |
| Lambeth, Charles | Private | Second State, Taliaferro | March 15-May 1, 1778; May-June 1778. |
| Lampkin/Lampkins, John | Private | First State, Camp | Dec 1777 sick Jersies; Jan-Feb 1778 sick absent; March 1778 on furlough; April-June 1778. |
| Lampkin/Lamkins, Peter | Sergeant | First State, Lee | Dec 1777 sick; Jan 1778; Feb 1778 on command; March 1778 at Meeting House; April-June 1778. |
| Lampkin, William | Private | First State, Camp | Dec 3, 1777 dead. |
| Lancaster, Adam | Private | Twelfth, Ashby | May 17, 1778 joined. |
| Lancaster, William | Corporal | First State, Crump | Dec 1777-May 1778; June roll shows him deceased on May 6, 1778. |
| Land, Charles | Surgeon's Mate | Third/Seventh | Dec 1777-June 1778. |
| Land, John | Private | Seventh, Spencer | Dec 1777-Jan 1778 on command; Feb 28, 1778 discharged. |

| | | | |
|---|---|---|---|
| Land, Lewis | Private | First State, Hoffler | Dec 1777-May 1778; June 1778 sick absent. |
| Lander, Charles | Sergeant | Third, Briscoe | Dec 1777 on guard; Feb 5, 1778 discharged. |
| Landman/ Lanaman, George | Private | First State, Brown | Dec 1777-April 1778. |
| Landrum, Thomas | Private | First State, Crump | April-May 1778; June 1778 sick absent. |
| Landrum/ Londrum, Thomas | Private | Seventh/ Third, Spencer/ Lipscomb | Feb 13, 1778 enlisted for 1 year; April-May 1778; June 1778 in Lipscomb's Company. |
| Lane/Lain, James | Private | Seventh/ Third, Posey/ Sayers | Feb 17, 1778 enlisted; April-May 1778; June 1778 in Sayers' Company. |
| Lane, Nathaniel | Private | Sixth, Massie | Dec 1777 in hospital; Jan 1778 "Time of service, March 11, 1778. |
| Lane, Richard | Private | Seventh, Webb | Jan 1778 hospital; Feb 7, 1778 discharged. |
| Lane/Laine, William | Private | Fourteenth, Overton | Dec 1777 sick in hospital; Jan 1778 sick absent; Feb-June 1778. |
| Langford/ Lankford, Euclid | Private | First State, Meriwether | Dec 1777-June 1778. |
| Langford, Philip | Corporal | Third, Arell | Dec 23, 1777 discharged. |
| Langley/Lankly, James | Private | First, Cummings/ Mennis | Jan 28, 1777 enlisted; April 1778; May 1778 sick present; June 1778 in Mennis' Company, sick Yellow Springs; July 1778 sick Valley Forge. |
| Langley, James/Jas. | Corporal | Sixth, Massie | Dec 1777 in hospital; Feb 16, 1778 discharged. |
| Langstone, George | Private | Seventh, Lipscomb | Dec 1, 1777 reenlisted for 3 years; Dec 1777-Jan 1778 on furlough; April 1778 on furlough; April 10, 1778 deceased. |
| Langstone, Wm. | Private | Fifteenth, Gray | Dec 1777-Jan 1778 sick absent; Feb 1778 dead. |
| Lanier/Lenear, Thomas/Thos. | Corporal | Sixth, Fox | Dec 1777 in hospital; Feb 11, 1778 discharged. |

| Name | Rank | Regiment/Company | Notes |
|---|---|---|---|
| Lanive/Leneve, Samuel/Saml. | Corporal/ Sergeant/ Private | First, Cunningham | Enlisted August 1776 for duration of war; Dec 1777; Jan 1778 promoted to sergeant; Jan-June 1778; June 1778 reduced to private. |
| Lank, John | Private | First State, Payne | Dec 1777 sick C Billet; Jan 1778 sick at Yellow Springs; Feb 1778 sick absent; March-June 1778. |
| Lanthon see Clanton | | | |
| Lanton/Lanter, Peter/Perter | Private | Seventh/ Third, Spencer/ Lipscomb | Feb 13, 1778 enlisted for 1 year; April 1778; May 1778 on guard; June 1778 in Lipscomb's Company. |
| Lankaster, Adom | Private | Twelfth, Ashby | Drafted; May 17, 1778 joined; May 1778. |
| Lanler/Lanles, John | Private | Third/ Seventh, Briscoe | June 1778. |
| Lapeley, John | 2nd. Lt. | Seventh, Posey | Dec 1777 wounded at Reading; Jan 1778 sick at Reading |
| Largent see Sargent | | | |
| Lark, James | Sergeant | Fifteenth, Edmunds | Dec 1777-Feb 1778 sick absent; March 1778 "I have heard he was dead not certain." |
| Larkin/Larkns, Edward | Private | First, Scott | Dec 1777-June 1778.May 17, 1778 joined. |
| Larkins/Larkin, James | Private | Twelfth, Bowyer, M. | Dec 1777 on command; Jan-March 1778; April 1778 on two week command; April 16, 1778 captured. |
| Larrance/ Lawrance, John, Sr. | Private | Fourteenth, Conway | Dec 1777-June 1778; Feb 1778 on command; March-June 1778. |
| Larrance/ Lawrance John, Jr. | Private | Fourteenth, Conway | Dec 1777 on duty; Jan-March 1778; April 1778 on guard; May 1778; June 1778 left at Valley Forge. |
| Larrowe/ Larowe, Abraham | Private | Third, Lee | Dec 1777 waggoner; Jan 20, 1778 discharged. |

| | | | |
|---|---|---|---|
| Larrowe/ Larowe, Peter | Private | Third, Lee | Dec 1777-Jan 1778; Feb 14, 1778 discharged. |
| Lary, John | Private | Third, Peyton, V. | Feb 17, 1778 drafted; April 1778; May 1778 sick present; June 1778 sick Valley Forge. |
| Lassey/Lussey, Shadrach | Private | Second, Taylor, W. | Dec 1777-Jan 1778; Feb 21, 1778 discharged. |
| Lattimer/ Lattemore, Mathew | Private | Seventh/ Third, Posey/ Sayers | Feb 27, 1778 enlisted; April 1778 on guard; May 1778 sick in camp; June 1778 in Sayer's Company. |
| Laurence/ Lawrence, John | Private | Fifteenth, Hull | Dec 1777-Jan 1778; Feb-March 1778 on guard; April 1778 sick present; May 1778. |
| Lawler, John | Private | Third, Arell | Dec 1777-Feb 1778; March 1778 on furlough; April 15, 1778 deserted. |
| Lawler, Thomas L. | Quartermaster Protem | Third | Feb 10, 1778 appointed; Feb-May 1778. |
| Lawrence, Ismael/Ishmael | Private | Fourteenth, Winston | Jan 20, 1778 enlisted; May 1778; June 1778 on guard. |
| Lawrence/ Larrance, Jacob | Private | Seventh/ Third, Posey/ Sayers | Feb 27, 1778 enlisted; April-May 1778; June 1778 in Sayers' Company. |
| Lawrence, John | Private | Fifteenth, Gregory | Dec 1777-March 1778 hospital; April 1778 muster roll shows he died on Jan 17, 1778. |
| Lawrence/ Laurence, Thomas | Sergeant | Fourteenth, Overton | Dec 1777 sick in hospital; Jan 1778 sick absent; Feb 1778; March 1778 sick absent; April 1778 sick present; May 1778; June 1778 sick Valley Forge. |
| Lawrue/Lerew, Abram/ Abraham | Private/ Corporal | Seventh/ Third, Spencer/ Lipscomb | Enlisted for 3 years; Dec 1777-Jan 1778 on furlough Virginia; April 1778; May 1778 promoted to Corporal; June 1778 in Lipscomb's Company. |
| Lawson/ Lowson, Andrew | Private | First State, Ewell, T./ Nicholas | May 1778; June 1778 sick present. |

| Name | Rank | Company | Notes |
|---|---|---|---|
| Lawson, Claiborne/ Claibourn W. | Captain | First, Lawson | Dec 1777; Jan-Feb 1778 absent with leave; March-June 1778. Oath at Valley Forge on May 11, 1778, witnessed by Muhlenberg. |
| Lawson, Eppey | Private | Second State, Quarles | First appears on July 1778 roll with comment "Omitted from 15 March to 1 July 1778." |
| Lawson, John Jr. | Private | Second State, Taliaferro | March 15-May 1, 1778; May-June 1778. |
| Lawson, John Sr. | Private | Second State, Taliaferro | March 15-May 1, 1778; May-June 1778. |
| Lawson, William | 2nd. Lt. | Second State, Quarles | April-June 1778. |
| Layn, Nathl | Private | Sixth, Massie | Dec 1777 in hospital. |
| Layne, Josiah | Private | Second State, Bressie | In June 1778 he was paid for 3 ½ months service. |
| Layten, Reuben | Private | Seventh, Lipscomb | Dec 22, 1777 enlisted in the Lt. Horse. |
| Leach, Richard | Private | Seventh, Spencer | Enlisted for 3 years; Dec 1777-Jan 1778 on furlough in Virginia; April-May 1778 |
| League, James/Jas. | Private | Fifteenth, Foster/ Gray | Dec 1777 in Virginia; Jan 1778 on guard; Feb 1778 in Gray's Company; March 1778 sick in camp; April 1778 sick present; May 1778 on guard. The last name may be Seague. |
| League see Seague | | | |
| Leak, William | Private | Fourteenth, Marks | Feb 16, 1778 drafted; April-June 1778. |
| Leard/Laird, David | Private | Twelfth, Madison | Dec 1777 working in Continental shop; Jan-March 1778 artificer. |
| Learwood, Archibald/Arch. | Private | First, Cunningham | August 1777 enlisted for 3 years; Dec 1777-Feb 1778; March 1778 fatigue; April 1778; May 1778 sick present; June 1778. |

| Name | Rank | Regiment, Company | Notes |
|---|---|---|---|
| Learwood, Josiah/Joseph | Private | First, Cunningham | Feb 1776 enlisted for 3 years; Dec 1777-Jan 1778; Feb 1778 on command; March-April 1778; May 1778 sick present; June 1778. |
| Leary/Larey, John | Private | First, Lewis | Dec 1777 sick; Jan 1778 sick in hospital; Feb 1778; March 1778 sick present; April 1778; May 31, 1778 discharged. |
| Leath, John | Corporal | Fourteenth, Jones | Jan 1778 on command York; Feb 1778 on command. |
| Leatherer, Paul | Sergeant | Third, Peyton, V. | Dec 1777-Jan 1778. |
| Leavatt/Levitt, Thomas | Private | Twelfth, Bowyer, M. | Dec 1777-March 1778 leg broken, in Virginia; April 1778 sick in camp; May 1778 sick in hospital; June 1778 sick at Yellow Springs. |
| Ledbetter/Leadbetter, Drury | Private | Sixth, Fox | Dec 1777-Jan 1778; Feb 11, 1778 discharged. |
| Lee, David | Private | Fourteenth, Jones | Sept 18, 1777 enlisted; Jan 1778 on command; Feb-May 1778. |
| Lee, Edward | Private | First State, Hamilton | Dec 1777-June 1778. |
| Lee/Ley, James | Private | Third/Seventh, Mercer/Powell | Dec 1777-March 1778 on furlough; April 1778-May 1778; June 1778 sick Brunswick, in Powell's Company. |
| Lee, James | Private | Fourteenth, Lambert | Sept 9, 1777 enlisted; April 1778 lately joined regiment; May 1778; June 1778 ogg. |
| Lee, Jesse | Private | Second State, Lewis | March 15-May 1, 1778; May-June 1778. |
| Lee, John | Captain/Paymaster | First State, Lee | Dec 1777 sick in country; Jan-April 1778. He is listed in March and April as Paymaster Protemporary. Captain Thomas Meriwether commands the company in April and May 1778. Oath at Valley Forge on May 12, 1778, witnessed by Muhlenberg. |
| Lee, John | Major | Second State | May-June 1778. |

| Name | Rank | Regiment | Notes |
|---|---|---|---|
| Lee, John | Private | Twelfth, Ashby | Dec 1777; Jan 1778 on guard; Feb-April 1778. |
| Lee, Peter | Private | Twelfth, Ashby | Dec 23, 1777 died. |
| Lee, Philip Richard Francis | Captain | Third. Lee | Dec 1777-Jan 1778 wounded absent. Heitman shows he was mortally wounded at Brandywine in Sept 1777, but he lived until circa 1834. |
| Lee, Reubin | Corporal | Seventh, Webb | Jan 1778; Feb 3, 1778 discharged. |
| Lee/Ley, Richard | Private | Third/ Seventh, Powel | Dec 1777-June 1778. |
| Lee, Richeson/ Richerson | Corporal | First State, Meriwether | Dec 1777-June 1778. |
| Lee, Samuel | Private | Twelfth, Bowyer, T. | Dec 1777 on command; Jan-Feb 1778; March 1778 on command; April 1778 waiter in camp; May 1778 on command |
| Lee, Simmons/ Simons | Corporal | Fourteenth, Jones | Sept 18, 1777 enlisted; Jan-April 1778; May 1778 sick present; June 1778 sick Valley Forge |
| Leech, Richard | Private | Seventh, Spencer | Enlisted for 3 years; April 1778; May 1778 absent; June 2, 1778 deserted. |
| Leers, Silas | Corporal | Fifteenth, Gregory | Dec 1777-Jan 1778 hospital; Feb 9, 1778 dead. |
| Leftwich, Joel | Private | First, Scott | Dec 1777 sick hospital; Feb-June 1778 on furlough. |
| Leftwich, John | Sergeant | First, Scott | Dec 1777-May 1778; June 1778 sick at Valley Forge. |
| Legg, John | Private | Third, Blackwell | Feb 18, 1778 drafted; April 1778; May 1778 on command; June 1778 sick Valley Forge. |
| Lehue/Lahew, David | Private | Second State, Lewis | May 1778 'Virginia last payroll"; June 1778. |
| Lehey/Lehew, Jeremiah | Private | Second State, Lewis | March 15-May 1, 1778; May 1778 "Received pay to 15 April and mustered in May"; June 1778. |
| Leigh, John | Corporal/ Sergeant | Seventh/ Third, Hill | Dec 1777-Jan 1778 on furlough; April 1, 1778 promoted to Sergeant; April-June 1778. |

| | | | |
|---|---|---|---|
| Leigh, Richard | Private | Seventh, Hill | Dec 1777 sick in hospital; Jan 28, 1778 discharged. |
| Lemaster/ Lamaster, Benjamin/ Benjn. | Sergeant | First, Lewis | Dec 1777-June 1778. |
| Lemaster, James | Private | Twelfth, Bowyer, T. | Dec 1777-Jan 1778; Feb 1778 on fatigue; March-May 1778. |
| Lemay, John | Private | Fourteenth, Winston | Dec 1777 on command; Jan 1778; Feb 1778 on command; March-June 1778. |
| Lemmon, William/Wm. | Private | Sixth, Rose | Dec 1777; Feb 27, 1778 discharged. |
| Lenigan/ Lennagan, John | Private | Twelfth, Waggener | Dec 1777-March 1778; April 10, 1778 discharged. |
| Lennard/ Leonard, James | Private | Twelfth, Waggener | Dec 1777-March 1778 sick in hospital; April 1778 baker; May 1778 sick in camp. |
| Lenox, Charles | Private | Third, Peyton, J. | Dec 1777-Jan 1778 wounded absent. |
| Lent, William | Private | Third, Peyton, J. | Dec 1777-Jan 1778. |
| Leonard/Lenard, Michael | Private | Third, Blackwell | Dec 1777-Jan 1778; Feb 14, 1778 discharged. |
| Lepford, Edmd. | Private | Fifteenth, Gray | Feb 1778 sick. |
| Leprad/Leprada, Andrew | Private | Fourteenth, Conway | Dec 1777 hospital; Jan 1778 on command; Feb 1778; March 1778 sick present; April 16, 1778 deceased. |
| Leskelete/ Liskelete, John | Private | Twelfth, Wallace | May 1778 roll show he was drafted on Feb 28, 1778, May 1778. |
| Lester, Benjamin | Private | First, Pelham | Dec 1777; Feb 15, 1778 discharged. |
| Leversage/ Laversage, Wilson | Private | Fifteenth, Grimes | Dec 1777-May 1778. |
| Levingood/ Livinggood, Peter | Corporal | Twelfth, Casey | Dec 1777-May 1778. |
| Levingston, Thomas | Private | Second, Upshaw | Dec 1777-Jan 1778. |

| | | | | |
|---|---|---|---|---|
| Levingston see Sevingston | | | | |
| Levinney, Peter | Private | Sixth | June 1778. | |
| Lewe/Leive, John/Jno. | Private | Sixth, Fox | Jan 1778; Feb 1778 absent with leave; March 1778 on furlough. | |
| Lewis, John | Private | Sixth, Fox | Aug 25, 1777 enlisted; Jan 1778; Feb 1778 absent with leave; March 1778 on furlough. | |
| Lewis, Charles | Colonel | Fourteenth | Dec 1777; Jan-Feb 1778 on furlough; March 1778; April 1, 1778 resigned. | |
| Lewis, Gabriel | Sergeant | First, Pelham | Dec 1777-June 1778. | |
| Lewis, John | Captain | Second State, Lewis | July 1778 payroll states "omitted from 15th March to the first July" and pays him for 4 ½ months. | |
| Lewis, John | Sergeant | Twelfth, Madison | Dec 1777-April 1778 | |
| Lewis, John | Private | Fourteenth, Marks | Dec 1777; Jan 1778 sick; Feb-June 1778. | |
| Lewis, John | Private | Fifteenth, Edmunds | Dec 1777 sick absent. | |
| Lewis, John | Drummer | Fifteenth, Hull | Dec 1777; Jan 1778; Feb 1778 sick present; March 1778; April 1778 sick present; May 1778. | |
| Lewis, Thomas | 1st. Lt. | Fifteenth, Grimes | Dec 1777-May 1778. Lewis was the senior officer in the company throughout the Encampment, but it continued under the name of the dead Captain Grimes for the entire period. | |
| Lewis, William | Captain | First, Lewis | Dec 1777-May 1778; June 1778 on furlough, Brigade Inspector. Oath at Valley Forge on May 18, 1778, witnessed by Muhlenberg. | |
| Lewis, Zackariah/ Zacharias | Sergeant | Fourteenth, Reid | Dec 1777-Feb 1778; March 1778 on command; April-May 1778; June 1778 sick Coryells Ferry. | |
| Lightfoot, Philip/Phillip | Corporal | First State, Camp | Dec 1777 absent with leave; Jan-Feb 1778 sick Virginia; March 1778 on furlough Virginia; April-June 1778. | |

| Name | Rank | Regiment, Company | Notes |
|---|---|---|---|
| Lightfoot, Phil/Philip | Private | Sixth, Hockaday | Dec 1777 sick at Princetown; Jan 1778 sick present; Feb 1778 sick absent; June 1778. |
| Ligon, Blackman/Blackn. | Sergeant | Seventh/Third, Moseley/Blackwell | Dec 1777-March 1778 on furlough; April 1778; May 1778 sick in camp; June 1778 sick Valley Forge. |
| Ligon/Lijon, Thomas | Private | Seventh, Fleming | Feb 11, 1778 enlisted; April 1778 sick present; May 1778 |
| Likens/Likings, John | Private | Second, Calmes | Dec 1777-June 1778. |
| Lilbourn/Lilburn, Andrew | Sergeant | Twelfth, Waggener | Dec 1777-Jan 1778; Feb 1778 on command; May 1778; April 10, 1778 discharged. |
| Liles/Lile, James | Private | Fourteenth, Reid | Dec 1777; Jan 1778 on command; Feb 1778 on guard; March 1778 sick present; May-June 1778. |
| Lind, Arthur | Ensign | Third/Seventh, Arell/Peyton, J. | Dec 1777-May 1778; June 1778 on command, in J. Peyton's Company. |
| Lind, George | Private | Sixth, Rose | April-June 1778. |
| Lindsay/Linsey, David | Private | Sixth, Massie/Hockaday | Dec 1777-March 1778 on furlough; April 1778-June 1778. In April he is also listed in Hockaday's company. |
| Lingoe/Lingo, James | Private | Seventh, Webb | Jan 1778 hospital; Feb 6, 1778 discharged. |
| Linn, James | Private | Fifteenth, Edmunds | Dec 1777-Feb 1778; March 1778 sick present; April 1778; May 1778 sick Yellow Springs. |
| Linn, Jos. | Private | Fifteenth, Gregory | June 1778 sick Yellow Springs. |
| Linne/Lynne, Benson | Sergeant | Third, Peyton, V. | Feb 17, 1778 drafted; April-May 1778; June 1778 sick Princeton. |
| Linsey/Lindsay, Edmund/Edmd. | Private | Sixth, Massie | Dec 1777-Jan 1778; Feb 12, 1778 discharged. |
| Linton/Lynton, Michael/Michl/ | Private | Third, Briscoe | Dec 1777-March 1778 on furlough; April-June 1778. |
| Lipscomb, Benoni | Private | Fifteenth, Gray | Dec 1777 sick absent; Jan 1778 on command; Feb-April 1778; May 1778 waiting on Major. |

| Name | Rank | Regiment | Service |
|---|---|---|---|
| Lipscomb/Lepscomb, Morning | Private | Fifteenth, Gray | Dec 1777 on guard; Jan-March 1778; April 1778 sick present; May 1778. |
| Lipscomb/Liscomb, Reuben/Rueben | Captain | Seventh/Third, Lipscomb | Dec 1777-Jan 1778; April 1778 on command; June 1778. |
| Lipscomb, Thomas/Thos. | Private | Fifteenth, Gray | Dec 1777-Jan 1778 sick absent; Feb-May 1778. |
| Lipscomb, Thomas | Ensign | Seventh, Lipscomb | Dec 1777-Jan 1778 on furlough; April 1778; May 20, 1778 resigned. |
| Lipsford/Sipford, Henry | Private | Fifteenth, Foster/Gray | Dec 1777-March 1778 sick absent, in Gray's Company; April-May 1778. |
| Lister, Benjamin | Private | First, Pelham | Dec 1777; Feb 15, 1778 discharged. |
| Lister, John | Sergeant | First, Pelham | Dec 1777 Virginia recruiting; Feb 15, 1778 discharged. |
| Listton, Henry | Sergeant | Fifteenth, Wills | Jan 1778. |
| Litchworth, Benjamin | Private | Third, Powell | Dec 1777-Jan 1778; Feb 17, 1778 discharged. |
| Litteral/Littrall, Joseph | Sergeant | Twelfth, Waggener | Dec 1777-May 1778. |
| Little, James | Private | First State, Payne | Dec 1777; Jan 10, 1778 deceased. |
| Little, Joseph | Private | First State, Lee | Dec 1777 sick; Jan 1778 deceased. |
| Little, Moses | Private | First State, Brown | Dec 1777-June 1778. |
| Lively, Edward | Private | Second State, Taliaferro | March 15-May 1, 1778; May-June 1778. |
| Lively, William | Private | Second State, Taliaferro | March 15-May 1, 1778; May-June 1778. |
| Livingston, Thomas | Private | Second, Upshaw | Dec 1777 hospital; Jan 1778. |
| Lock, Alexander | Sergeant | Fourteenth, Lambert | Dec 1777 in Commissary Department. |
| Lock, William | Private | Second State, Dudley | May-June 1778. |

| | | | |
|---|---|---|---|
| Lock, William | Private | Second State, Spiller | June 1778. |
| Lockell, James | Private | Seventh, Fleming | Dec 1777 sick in hospital; Jan 1778 hospital; Feb 12, 1778 discharged. |
| Lockett/Lockell, Jacob | Sergeant/ Private | Seventh/ Third, Fleming/ Heth | Dec 1777 on furlough Virginia; Jan-March 1778 on furlough; April 1778; May 24, 1778 reduced to Private; June 1778 in Heth's Company. |
| Lockett, Royal | Private | Seventh, Fleming | Dec 1777-Jan 1778; Feb 6, 1778 discharged. |
| Lockley, Daniel | Private | Second State, Dudley | March 15-May 1, 1778; May 1778; June 1778 sick absent; July 1778 sick Valley Forge. |
| Loden/Loaden, Jesse | Private | First State, Nicholas | Dec 1777 on guard; Jan-April 1778; May 1778 on guard; June 1778. |
| Loden/Loadin, William | Private | First State, Nicholas | April 1778 "payed to the 15th of Mar. 1778 in Virginia"; May 1778; June 1778 sick at Valley Forge. |
| Logan/Logen, James | Private | Twelfth, Casey | Dec 1777-May 1778. |
| Logan, William | Private | Twelfth, Bowyer, T. | April-May 1778. |
| Loggans/ Loggins, Martin | Corporal | Fourteenth, Reid | Dec 1777; Jan 1778 time out. |
| London, Owen/Owin | Private | Seventh, Moseley | Dec 1777; Jan 1778 sick present; Feb 25, 1778 discharged. |
| Long, Andrew | Private | Second, Upshaw | Dec 1777 hospital; Jan 1778. |
| Long, Geo./ Georege | Private | Fifteenth, Grimes | Dec 1777-Feb 1778; March 1778 on command; April 1778; May 1778 orderly. |
| Long, Henry | Private | Seventh/ Third, Posey/ Briscoe | Feb 28, 1777 enlisted; April 1778 sick; May 1778 on command; June 1778 sick present. |
| Long, James | Private | Second, Taylor, F. | Dec 1777-March 1778; April 10, 1778 discharged, term of service expired. |

| | | | |
|---|---|---|---|
| Long, John | Private | First State, Camp | May-June 1778. |
| Long, John | Private | Sixth, Avery | Dec 20, 1777 enlisted into Light Dragoons. |
| Long, Jonathan | Private | Third, Arell | Dec 23, 1777 discharged. |
| Long, Lazrais | Private | Fifteenth, Grimes | Feb 11, 1778 drafted; April 1778; May 1778 sick present. |
| Long, Levi/Leve | Private | Second State, Spiller | April-May 1778; June 1778 sick Valley Forge. |
| Long, Nicholas | Sergeant | Second, Upshaw | Dec 1777-Jan 1778. |
| Long, Reuben | Private | Second State, Garnett | March 15-May 1, 1778; May-June 1778. |
| Long, Richard | Corporal | First State, Camp | Dec 1777-Feb 1778 on furlough; March 1778 on furlough Virginia; April-June 1778. |
| Long, William | Private | Second, Upshaw | Dec 1777 hospital. |
| Long, William | 1st. Lt. | Second State, Lewis | March 15-May 1, 1778; May-June 1778. Oath at Valley Forge on May 18, 1778, witnessed by Muhlenberg. |
| Longest, Reuben/Reuban | Private | Second, Calmes | Dec 1777-June 1778. |
| Longuste/Longest, James | Private | Seventh, Hill | Dec 1777 on furlough; Jan 27, 1778 discharged. |
| Lookado, Isick/Isaac | Private | Seventh, Fleming | Dec 1777 sick in hospital; Jan 1778 hospital; Feb 12, 1778 discharged. |
| Lorden/Soden, John | Private | Fifteenth, Gregory | Dec 25, 1777 taken prisoner. He was exchanged in July 1778. |
| Lornan/Lornon, James | Private | First, Lewis | Dec 1777 sick; Jan 1778 on command; Feb 1778 on guard; March-April 1778; May 1778 on command; June 1778 on guard. |
| Love/Lovi, John | Private | First State, Payne | Dec 1777; Jan 1778 on command; Feb 1778; March 1778 "barefutted" April 1778 sick at Red Lyon; May 1778 on command; June 1778. |

| Name | Rank | Regiment | Notes |
|---|---|---|---|
| Love, John | Private | Fifteenth, Edmunds | Dec 1777 taken prisoner. |
| Love, Samuel | Sergeant | Third, Lee | Dec 1777; Jan 31, 1778, time out. |
| Lovell/Loveill, George/Geo. | Private | Fifteenth, Gray | April 1778 reported deserted from Nov 1, 1777, joined April 16, 1778; May 1778 sick present. |
| Lovesay/Lovsey, John | Private | Fourteenth, Jones | Sept 18, 1777 enlisted; Jan-Feb 1778 sick in hospital; March 8, 1778 died. |
| Lovill/Lovee, Randolph | Private | First State, Camp | Dec 1777-Jan 1778. |
| Lovin/Loving, Presley | Private | Second, Calmes | Dec 1777-Jan 1778. |
| Lowe/Low, Robert | Private/Corporal | Second, Jones/Hoomes | Dec 1777-Feb 1778; March promoted to Corporal; March-June 1778. |
| Lowry, Robert | Private | Seventh, Posey | Dec 1777 on guard; Jan 1778; Feb 12, 1778 discharged. |
| Lowry/Lowrey, Thomas/Tho. | Private | Fifteenth, Wills | Aug 21, 1777 enlisted; Dec 4, 1777 deserted; Jan 1778; April 1778; May–July 1778 sick Yellow Springs; Aug 1778 died Yellow Springs. |
| Loyd/Lloyd, George | Private | Second State, Quarles | April-June 1778. |
| Loyd, Thomas | Private | Fourteenth, Lambert | Dec 1777; Jan-March 1778 on command; April-June 1778. |
| Lucas, Ambrose/Abros | Private | First, Cunningham | Feb 14, 1778 enlisted for 1 year; April 1778 under inoculation; May 1778 sick present; June 1778. |
| Lucas, Charles | Private | Fifteenth, Wills | March 17, 1778 enlisted; April 1778 on duty; May 1778. |
| Lucas, Humphrey | Private | Fourteenth, Reid | Dec 1777 hospital; Jan-June 1778. |
| Lucas, Samuel | Drummer/Fifer | Second State, Quarles | April-June 1778. In April and May he is listed as a Drummer, in June as a Fifer. |
| Lucas, Thomas | Private | First State, Crump | April-May 1778; June 1778 sick absent. |

| | | | |
|---|---|---|---|
| Lucas, William | Private | Second State, Taliaferro | March 15-May 1, 1778; May-June 1778. |
| Lumb/Lunk, Joseph | Private | Fourteenth, Lambert | Sept 30, 1777 enlisted; April 1778 lately joined regiment; May-June 1778. |
| Lumes, William | Private | Second, Taylor, F. | Dec 1777 on furlough. |
| Lumpken/ Lumpkin, Moore | Private | Fifteenth, Foster/ Gray | Aug 22, 1777 enlisted; Jan 1778; Feb 1778 in Gray's Company; March 1778; April 1778 sick present; May 1778. |
| Lumpkin, Wilson | Private | Seventh, Hill | Dec 1777-Jan 1778 sick in hospital |
| Lundey/Lundy, James | Corporal/ Private | Twelfth, Madison | Dec 1777 on guard; Jan-Feb 1778 artificer; Feb 1778 reduced to Private. |
| Lungford. Philip | Private | Third, Arell | Dec 23, 1777 discharged. |
| Lunsdale/ Lumsdale, James | Private | Seventh/ Third, Crockett/ Sayers | March 12, 1778 enlisted; April-May 1778; June 1778 in Sayers' Company. |
| Lush, Sebastan/ Sebaston | Private | Third, Briscoe | Dec 1777 waggoner; Feb 5, 1778 discharged. |
| Lussey/Lufsey, Josiah/Josier | Private | Second, Taylor, W. | Dec 1777-Jan 1778; Feb 14, 1778 discharged. |
| Lynaugh, Philip | Private | Third, Blackwell | Dec 1777-Jan 1778; Feb 14, 1778 discharged. |
| Lynch/Linch, David | Private | First, Cunningham | Feb 14, 1778 enlisted for 1 year; April 1778 under inoculation; May-June 1778. |
| Lynch, Patrick/Parlrich | Corporal | Fifteenth, Gregory | Dec 1777; Jan 1778 on command; Feb 1778 on guard; March 1778 sick present; April-June 1778. |
| Lynch/Linch, Peter | Private | Fifteenth, Mason/ Gregory | Dec 1777; Jan-Feb 1778 sick present; March-April 1778; May 1778 on guard; June 1778 on guard, in Gregory's Company. |
| Lynch/Linch, Thomas | Private | First, Scott | Dec 1777 sick Bethlehem; Jan-Feb 1778 sick hospital; March-June 1778. |

| Name | Rank | Regiment | Notes |
|---|---|---|---|
| Lynch/Linch, Timothy | Private | Second State, Dudley | March 15-May 1, 1778; May-June 1778. |
| Lynd, George | Private | Sixth, Rose | April-June 1778. |
| Lyne/Line, Barna/Barneby | Corporal | Fourteenth, Lambert | Dec 1777-Jan 1778; Feb-April 1778 on furlough; May-June 1778. |
| Lyon/Lion, James | Corporal | First State, Lee | Dec 1777; Jan 1778 at Yellow Springs; Feb 1778 sick at Yellow Springs; March 1778 died sometime in March. |
| Lyon, Thomas | Private | Third/Seventh, Heth | June 1778. |
| Lyons, Patrick | Private | Twelfth, Ashby | Dec 1777-Feb 1778; March-April 1778 on command; May roll shows he was taken prisoner on April 15, 1778. |
| Lyons, William/Wm. | Private | Seventh/Third, Posey/Briscoe | Dec 1777-Jan 1778 on furlough; April 1778 absent; May 1778 advanced guard. |
| Macintire/McTire, Charles | Private | Fifteenth, Wills | Feb 18, 1778 enlisted; April 1778; May 1778 on command. |
| McAdams/McAdam, James | Private | Seventh, Third, Crockett/Powell | Dec 1777-Jan 1778 on furlough; Feb-March 1778; April 1778 on guard; May 1778; June 1778 in Powell's Company. |
| McAllister/McAlister, George | Private | Fourteenth, Lambert | Feb 14, 1778 enlisted; April 1778 lately joined regiment; May 1778; June 1778 sick Valley Forge. |
| McAllister, John | Sergeant | Fourteenth, Lambert | Dec 1777-May 1778; June 1778 on furlough. |
| McAllister, William | Private | Fourteenth, Lambert | May-June 1778. |
| McCall/McCalle, Samuel | Sergeant | Twelfth, Vause | Dec 1777; Jan 1778 taken in G. Commissary Dept. Jan 20; Feb-March 1778; April-May 1778 taylor at Lancaster. |
| McCallister/McCallister, Joseph | Private | Seventh, Posey | Dec 1777-Jan 1778 in Rifle Battn.; Feb 22, 1778 discharged. |

| | | | |
|---|---|---|---|
| McCallough, William | Private | Third, Mercer | Dec 1777 sick present; Jan 1778. |
| McCaslin/ McCashlin, John | Private | Twelfth, Waggener | Dec 1777-March 1778; April 10, 1778 discharged. |
| McCarter, James | Private | Second State, Dudley | March 15-May 1, 1778; May-June 1778. |
| McCarty/ McCarta, Daniel | Private | First State, Lee | Dec 1777 sick; Jan 1778 deceased. |
| McCarty/ McCartey, Daniel/Danl. | Fife Major | Third/ Seventh | Dec 1777-Feb 1778 on furlough; March-June 1778. |
| McCarty, Daniel/Dennis | Private | Twelfth, Casey | Dec 1777 sent to hospital; Jan-Feb 1778 at hospital; March 1778; April-May 1778 on furlough. |
| McCarty, Nicholas | Private | Twelfth, Waggener | Dec 1777 roll shows him as "dead but don't know when." |
| McCarty, Samuel | Private | Twelfth, Ashby | Dec 1777; Jan 1778 sick in hospital; Feb 1778 sick at the hospital; March 1778 at hospital; April-May 1778. |
| McCawley/ McCawlay, Edward | Private | Twelfth, Waggener | Dec 1777-Jan 1778; Feb 1778 on guard; April 10, 1778 discharged. |
| McClanachan, Alexander | Colonel | Seventh | Dec 1777-April 1778 on furlough; March 13, 1778 resigned. |
| McClanahan/ McClanocan, Thomas | Private | Second, Taylor, F. | Dec 1777 enlisted in the Light Horse. |
| McClane, John | Private | Twelfth, Vause | Dec 5, 1777 discharged. |
| McClane/ McClain, Thomas | Private | Twelfth, Waggener | Dec 1777-Feb 1778 hospital; March-May 1778. |
| McClardey see McLardy | | | |
| McClintock, William | Private | Twelfth, Wallace | May 1778 roll shows him as drafted on Feb 28, 1778 and on guard. |
| McCloud, Archibald | Private | Twelfth, Waggener | Dec 1777-Jan 1778 on guard; Feb-May 1778. |

| Name | Rank | Regiment, Company | Service |
|---|---|---|---|
| McCloud/ Mcloud, John | Private | Second, Willis | Dec 1777-June 1778. |
| McCollem/ McColm, William | Private | Twelfth, Waggener | Dec 1777-Feb 1778 hospital; March 1778 on guard; April-May 1778 waggoner. |
| McCollock/ McColock, James | Private | Twelfth, Ashby | Dec 1777; Jan 1778 sick in hospital; March 1778; April 1778 on command; May 1778 on command at Lancaster; June 1778 taylor at Lancaster. |
| McCollem/ McColm, John | Private | Twelfth, Waggener | Dec 1777-March 1778; April 1778 weeks command; May 1778, |
| McCormack/ McCormuk, Adam | Private | Fifteenth, Harris | Jan 1778 on command; Feb-April 1778 sick present; May 1778. |
| McCormack, James | Private | Twelfth, Bowyer, T. | Aug 2, 1777 recruited; Jan 1778 joined; Feb 1778; March 1778 sick in camp; April 1778 sick at hospital near camp; May 10, 1778 died. |
| McCormack, John | Private | Fourteenth, Marks | Jan 6, 1778 enlisted; Jan-April 1778 on furlough; May 1778; June 1778 on command; July 1778 sick Valley Forge. |
| McComack/ McCormac, Nicholas | Private | First State, Nicholas | Dec 1777 sick Bethlehem; Jan-Feb 1778 sick Quaker Meeting House. |
| McCorkle/ McKorkle, Robert | Private | Twelfth, Bowyer, M. | Dec 1777 in hospital; Jan-March 1778 sick in hospital; April 1778 sick at Lancaster; May 1778 sick in hospital; June 1778 orderly at Lancaster. |
| McCormick, William | Private | First, Payne | Dec 1777-March 1778 on furlough. |
| McCown/ McGowan, James | Private | Fourteenth, Reid | Nov 1777 roll shows "Deserted Dec 11, 1777; April 1778; May 1778 on command; June 1778 left at Valley Forge. |
| McCown/ McGowan, John | Private | Third, Blackwell | Dec 1777-Jan 1778 on guard; Feb 14, 1778 discharged. |
| McCown/ McCoun, Patrick/Partrick | Private | Third, Peyton, J. | Dec 1777; Jan 31, 1778 discharged. |

| | | | |
|---|---|---|---|
| McCoy/ McCoye, William | Private | Third/ Seventh, Peyton, J. | Feb 17, 1778 drafted; April 1778; May 1778 on command; June-July 1778 sick at Valley Forge. |
| McCrea/ McCray, Hugh | Private | First State, Payne | Dec 1777 sick in hospital; Jan 1778 sick at Reading; Feb 1778 sick absent. |
| McCullough, William | Private | Third, Mercer | Dec 1777-Feb 1778. |
| McCune/ McCurn, Patrick | Private | First State, Ewell, T. | Dec 1777-Feb 1778 sick in Virginia; March-April 1778; May 1778 sick present; June 1778. |
| McDade, James | Private | Twelfth, Vause | Dec 1777; Jan-March 1778 sick in hospital; April 1778 Flying hospital; May 1778. |
| McDaniel/ McDonald, Colvert | Private | Third, Mercer | Dec 1777-Jan 1778 sick present. |
| McDaniel/ McDonal, John | Private | Seventh/ Third, Jouett/ Hill | Feb 16, 1778 enlisted; May 1778 on command; June 1778 sick present, in Hill's Company. |
| McDaniell, William | Private | Seventh, Spencer | Dec 1777-Jan 1778 hospital |
| McDewell/ McDewel, Mathew/ Matthew | Private | Fifteenth, Grimes | Dec 1777 on guard; Jan-April 1778; May 1778 on command. |
| McDonald, Alexander | Private | First State, Hamilton | Dec 1777-June 1778. |
| McDonald, Andrew | Private | Fourteenth, Winston | Dec 1777 sick in hospital; Jan 1778 sick in Jersey; Feb 1778 sick in hospital. |
| McDonald/ McDanul, Angus/Anguish | Private | Third/ Seventh, Briscoe | Dec 1777-March 1778 on furlough; April-May 1778; June 1778 Genl. Woodfords Gd. |
| McDonald/ McDaniel, Daniel | Private | First State, Meriwether | Dec 1777-June 1778. |
| McDonald, John | Private | Twelfth, Bowyer, T. | Dec 1777; Jan 1778 on command; Feb-April 1778; May 1778 absent without leave; June 1778 orderly for the sick at Valley Forge. |

| Name | Rank | Regiment/Company | Notes |
|---|---|---|---|
| McDonald/ McDonnald, John | Private | Twelfth, Vause | Dec 1777-Jan 1778 sick in camp; Feb-March 1778; April 1778 sick in camp; May 7, 1778 discharged. |
| McDonald/ McDannil, Roderick/ Redrick | Private | Fourteenth, Overton | Dec 1777; Jan 1778 on command; Feb 24, 1778 deserted. |
| McDonald/ McDonold, Robert | Drummer | First State, Hoffler | Dec 1777-Feb 1778; June 1778. |
| McDonald/ McDonal, Uriah | Private | Seventh/ Third, Jouett/ Hill | Feb 16, 1778 enlisted; June 1778 in Hill's Company. |
| McDonald, William | Private | Seventh, Spencer | March 10, 1778 discharged. |
| McDougall/ McDougal, Alexander | Private | First State, Brown | Dec 1777-May 1778. |
| McDougall/ McDougle, John | Drummer | First State, Crump | Dec 1777-May 1778; June 1778 sick absent. |
| McDowel, Robert | Private | Twelfth, Waggener | Dec 1777-Jan 1778; Feb 1778 on guard; March-May 1778. |
| McDowell/ McDowel, James | Private | Twelfth, Waggener | Dec 1777 hospital; Jan 1778; Feb-March 1778 on command; April 10, 1778 discharged. |
| McDowell, John | 2nd. Lt. | Twelfth, Bowyer, M. | Dec 1777-May 1778. |
| McDowell/ McDowel, John | Private | Twelfth, Waggener | Dec 1777; Jan 1778 sick in hospital; Feb-April 1778; May 1778 waggoner. |
| McElheny/ McElhenny, John | 2nd. Lt. | Second State, Spiller | March 15-May 1, 1778; May-June 1778. |
| McEvoy, James | Private | Third, Mercer | April 1778; May 1778 on command. |
| McEwing/ McEvan, Alexander | Private | Fourteenth, Reid | Feb 19, 1778 enlisted; April 1778 lately joined regiment; May-June 1778. |
| McFarland/ McFarling, Benjamin/ Benjn. | Private | Third/ Seventh, Arell/ Briscoe | Dec 1777-Feb 1778; March 1778 on command; April 1778; May 1778 sick present; June 1778 in Briscoe's Company. |

| | | | |
|---|---|---|---|
| McFarlane, Robert/Robt. | Private | Seventh/ Third, Crockett/ Sayers | Dec 1777-Jan 1778 on furlough; April 1, 1778 deserted; June 21, 1778, dead, in Sayers' Company. |
| McFarley/ McFarling, John | Private | First State, Lee | Dec 1777 sick; Jan 1, 1778 deceased. |
| McFarlin/ McFarlan, John | Private | Fourteenth, Thweatt | Sept 20, 1777 enlisted; Jan 1778 lately joined regiment; Feb 1778 sick present; March 21, 1778 died. |
| McFarlin, Mark | Private | Second State, Bernard | April-June 1778. |
| McFarling, Daniel | Private | Seventh Third/ Webb/ Young | Enlisted for 3 years; Jan 1778; February 1778 on guard; April-May 1778 on command; June 1778 on guard; in Young's Company. |
| McGary/Megary, William | Private | Second, Jones | Dec 1777-March 1778. |
| McGee/ McGehe, James | Private | Fourteenth, Marks | Dec 1777 in hospital; Jan 1778 sick hospital; Feb 1778 sick absent; March 27, 1778 discharged. |
| McGehee/ McGee, David | Private | Fourteenth, Reid | Sept 1, 1777 enlisted; Jan 1778 sick; Feb 1778 sick absent; March-June 1778. |
| McGeorge, William | Private | Seventh/ Third, Lipscomb | Feb 14, 1778 enlisted for 1 year; April 1778; May 1778 sick in camp; June 1778. |
| McGill, James | Private | Twelfth, Casey | Dec 1777; Jan-Feb 1778 on command; March-April 1778; May 24, 1778 joined the Eighth Pennsylvania Regiment. |
| McGill, Roger | Private | Twelfth, Bowyer, T. | Dec 1777-Jan 1778; Feb 1778 on command; March 1778 sick in hospital; April-May 1778. |
| McGinnis see Meginnes | | | |
| McGinnis, Andrew | Private | First, Cunningham | Feb 23, 1778 enlisted; July 1778. |

| Name | Rank | Regiment/Company | Service |
|---|---|---|---|
| McGinnis/ M Ginnis, Andrew | Drummer | Seventh/ Third, Moseley/ Blackwell | Dec 1777-April 1778 on furlough; April 1778; May 1778 sick in camp; June 1778 in Blackwell's Company. |
| McGinnis/ McGinness, Edward/Edwd. | Private | Third/ Seventh, Mercer/ Powell | Dec 1777-May 1778; June 1778 in Mercer's Company. |
| McGlaughlin/ McGlocklin, Daniel | Private | Twelfth, Ashby | Dec 1777-Jan 1778; March-May 1778. |
| McGlaughlin, Edward | Private | Seventh, Posey | Feb 27, 1778 enlisted. |
| McGlothan/ McLoughlan, John | Private | Second State, Spiller | March 15-May 1, 1778; May-June 1778. |
| McGloughlen/ McGlothlin, James | Private | Third, Lee/ Peyton, J. | Feb 27, 1778 enlisted; April-May 1778; June 1778 guard, in J. Peyton's Company. |
| McGloughlin/ McLoughlin, Thomas | Private | Twelfth, Madison | Dec 1777-March 1778 sick in hospital; April 1778 sick in camp. |
| McGowan see McCown | | | |
| McGowin/ McGovern, James | Private | Twelfth, Bowyer, T. | Dec 1777-Jan 1778; Feb 1778 sick in camp; March 1778 on command; April-May 1778; June 1778 sick Valley Forge. |
| McGown/ Magowen, Daniel | Private | Second, Calmes | Dec 1777-May 1778. |
| McGray, Thomas | Private | Sixth, Hockaday | Dec 1777-Jan 1778; Feb 19, 1778 discharged. |
| McGuire/ Maguire, Andrew | Private | First, Lewis | Dec 1777-Feb 1778; March 1778 on guard; April-May 1778; June 1778 sick Valley Forge. |
| McGuire, Conner | Private | Third, Blackwell | Dec 1777-April 1778 sick at hospital; April-June 1778 sick Lancaster. |
| McGuire, Dennis | Private | Third/ Seventh, Arell/ Briscoe | Dec 1777; Jan 1778; Feb 1778 sick present; March 1778 on command; April 1778; May 1778 fatigue; June 1778 on guard. |

| Name | Rank | Regiment, Company | Notes |
|---|---|---|---|
| McGuire, James | Private | Seventh, Posey | Dec 1777-Jan 1778 on furlough |
| McGuire/McGuier, Lawrence/Larrance | Private | Fourteenth, Lambert | Dec 1777 hospital; Jan 1778 sick in the country; Feb 1778 hospital; March-June 1778 on furlough; July 15, 1778 discharged. |
| McGuire/Maguire, Patrick | Private | Twelfth, Vause | Dec 1777-March 1778; April 1778 on fatigue; May 1778. |
| McGuriman/McGurisman, Duncan | Private | Sixth, Hockaday | Feb 10, 1778 drafted; April-May 1778; sick at Coryells Ferry. |
| McGuy, Bennet | Private | Fifteenth, Hull | March 1778; April 1778 sick present; May 1778. |
| McHaney/McHanney, John | Private | First State, Hoffler | Dec 1777-June 1778. |
| McIntire, Daniel | Private | First State, Hoffler | Dec 7, 1777 discharged. |
| McIntosh, John | Private | Twelfth, Waggener | Dec 1777-March 1778 hospital; April 10, 1778 discharged. |
| McIntosh/McEntosh, William | Private | First State, Ewell, T. | Jan-March 1778; April 1778 on guard; May 1778; June 1778 on guard. |
| McIntosh/McIntoush, William | Private | Second, Harrison | Dec 1777-June 1778. |
| McKay/MacKay, Fitzhugh/Fitzhew | Chaplain | Fifteenth | Dec 1777-May 1778. |
| McKendley, Alexander | Private | First State, Hoffler | June 1778. |
| McKenley/McKendley, John | Private | First State, Hoffler | Dec 1777-June 1778. |
| McKenny, Daniel | Private | Fourteenth, Thweatt | Dec 1777-Feb 1778 on furlough. |
| McKenney/McKenny, James | Private | Third/Seventh, Briscoe | Dec 1777 waggoner; Jan 15, 1778 discharged. Another roll shows him discharged Feb 5, 1778. |

215

| Name | Rank | Regiment, Company | Service |
|---|---|---|---|
| McKenney/ McKinney, Willington | Private | Fifteenth, Hull | Dec 1777 sick absent; Jan 1778 sick in hospital; Feb 1778 sick absent; April 1778 sick present; May 1778 on command; June 1778 sick Valley Forge. |
| McKennon/ McKannon, Christopher/ Christerfer | Private | First State, Hoffler | Dec 1777-June 1778. |
| McKinley, Alexander | Private | First State, Hoffler | June 1778. |
| McKinnish/ McKennick, John | Private | Fifteenth, Edmunds | Dec 1777-Feb 1778; March 1778 on guard; April-May 1778; June 1778 sick Valley Forge. |
| McKinny/ McKiney, John | Private | Twelfth, Bowyer, M. | Dec 1777-Jan 1778; Feb 1778 absent with leave; March 1778 sick in camp; April 1778; May 1778 sick in hospital |
| McKinsey/ McKinzey, John | Private/ Corporal | Second, Harrison | Dec 1777-Feb 1778; March promoted to Corporal; March-June 1778. |
| McKinsey/ McKinzey, John | Private | Fifteenth, Hull | Dec 1777; Jan 1778 on command; Feb 1778; March-May 1778 on command. |
| McLain/ McClain, Thomas | Private | Third/ Seventh, Blackwell | Dec 1777-June 1778. |
| McLardy/ McClardey, Alexander | Corporal | First, Pelham | Dec 1777-May 1778; June 1778 on guard. |
| McLaughtin/ McLaaghlain, Edward | Private | Seventh. Third, Posey/ Sayers | Feb 27, 1778 enlisted; April-May 1778; June 1778 in Sayers' Company. |
| McLeod/ McCloud, Henry | Private | First State, Camp | Dec 1777 orderly hospital; Jan 27, 1778 died. |
| McMahan/ McMahen, Mike/Michael | Private | Seventh/ Third, Posey/ Sayers | Dec 1777-Jan 1778 on furlough; April-June 1778 sick Virginia, in Sayers' Company |

| Name | Rank | Regiment, Commander | Service Record |
|---|---|---|---|
| McMahan, Patrick | Private/ Corporal | Fourteenth, Reid | Dec 1777 hospital; Jan 1778 sick Reading; Feb 1778; March 1778 sick in hospital; April-May 1778; June 1778 promoted to Corporal, sick Coryell Ferry. |
| McMahon/ McMan, John | Private | Fourteenth, Conway | Dec 1777; Jan-Feb 1778 on command; March 21, 1778 deceased. |
| McMahon, Andrew | Fifer/Private | First State, Hamilton | Dec 1777-March 1778; April 1778 demoted to Private; April-June 1778. |
| McMichael, Robert | Private | Twelfth, Waggener | Dec 23, 1777 died. |
| McMickin/ McMeckan, Robert | Private | Third/ Seventh, Blackwell | Dec 1777-Jan 1778; Feb-March 1778 on command; April 1778 sick present; May 1778 on guard; June 1778. |
| McNabb, Robert | Private | Twelfth, Bowyer, M. | Dec 1777-Jan 1778; Feb-March 1778 on command; April 1778 sick near Wilmington; May 1778 sick at Wilmington. |
| McNeal/ McNeil, Peter | Musician | Seventh/ Third, Posey/ Sayers | Dec 1777-Jan 1778 on furlough; April-May 1778; June 1778 in Sayers' Company. |
| McNealy, Robert | Corporal | Seventh, Posey | Dec 1777-Jan 1778 on furlough; Feb 12, 1778 discharged. |
| McNear, Mark | Private | Second, Sanford | Dec 1777 deserted. |
| McNeely/ McNeal, David | Private | Seventh/ Third, Posey/ Sayers | Feb 27, 1778 enlisted; April-May 1778; June 1778 sick Yellow Springs, in Sayers' Company. |
| McPherson/ McPhershon, Asa | Private | Fifteenth, Grimes | Dec 1777-April 1778 sick absent. |
| McPherson, Duncan/Dan | Fifer | First, Cummings | Dec 1777. |
| McQuellin/ Quellen, Robert | Private | First, Lewis | Dec 1777-Feb 1778; March 1778 on command; April 1778; May 1778 sick present; June 1778. |

| Name | Rank | Regiment | Service |
|---|---|---|---|
| McQuinn/ McQuin, Daniel | Sergeant | First State, Lee | Dec 1777 sick; Jan 1778-Feb 1778 sick absent; March 1778 roll shows he died in February. |
| McSwain, Edward | Private/ Corporal | First State, Brown | Dec 1777-March 1778; March 1778 promoted to Corporal; April 17, 1778 discharged. |
| McVee, John | Private | First, Lewis | Dec 1777 sick; Jan-Feb 1778; March 1778 command; April-June 1778. |
| McWay/ McAway, Daniel | Corporal | Twelfth, Casey | Dec 1777-May 1778. |
| McWilliams, John | Private | Second State, Taliaferro | March 15-May 1, 1778; May-June 1778. |
| McWilliams, Robert | Private | Second, Harrison | Dec 1777 hospital; Jan-May 1778; June 1778 sick Valley Forge. |
| Mabon/ Magleon, James | Ensign/ 2nd. Lt. | Sixth, Garland | Dec 1777 recruiting; Jan-March 1778; April-May 1778 recruiting; June 1778. In Feb he was promoted to 2nd. Lt.; Oath at Valley Forge on May 12, 1778, witnessed by Muhlenberg. |
| Mabrey, Robt. | 1st. Lt. | Fifteenth, Mason | Dec 1777; Jan-March 1778 on furlough; April-May 1778. |
| Mace, Mattox | Private | Sixth, Apperson | Dec 1777-Jan 1778; paid through Feb 24, 1778. |
| Mackie, James | Sergeant | Seventh/ Third, Young | May-June 1778. |
| Mackrell, James | Private | Twelfth, Vause | May 1778 roll shows he was drafted on Feb 27, 1778. |
| Maddes, Ja. | Private | Third/ Seventh, Powell | June 1778. |
| Maddin/ Madden, Samuel | Private/ Corporal | Third, Blackwell | Dec 1777-March 1778 on command; April-May 1778; May 1778 promoted to Corporal.; June 1778. |
| Maddis, John | Private | First State, Meriwether | Dec 1777-May 1778; June 1778 sick absent. |
| Maddison, John | Private | Seventh, Lipscomb | Dec 22, 1777 enlisted in the Lt. Horse. |

| | | | | |
|---|---|---|---|---|
| Maddison, Wm. | Private | Fifteenth, Gray | Dec 1777 on guard; Jan-March 1778 on command; April 1778 sick present; May 1778. |
| Maddox, Alexander | Private | First State, Meriwether | Dec 1777-June 1778. |
| Maden/Madin, Robert | Private | First State, Lee/ Meriwether | Dec 1777 sick; Jan 1778 sick absent; Feb-March 1778 on guard; April-June 1778. |
| Maden, William | Private | Second, Taylor, W. | Dec 1777-Jan 1778; Feb 5, 1778 discharged. |
| Madison/ Maddison, Ambrose | Paymaster | Second | Jan 1778-May 1778. |
| Madison, Rowland | Captain | Twelfth, Madison | Dec 1777-Feb 1778; March 11, 1778 resigned. |
| Madlock, Zachariah | Private | Seventh, Young | Feb 11, 1778 enlisted; June 1778 sick Valley Forge. |
| Madox/Maddix, Claborn | Sergeant | Twelfth, Bowyer, T. | Aug 30, 1777 enlisted; Jan-March 1778; April 1778 sick in camp; May 1778. |
| Mahon/Mohon, Matthias | Private | Second State, Spiller | March 15-May 1, 1778; May-June 1778. |
| Mahone, Dudley | Private | First State, Hoffler | Dec 1777. |
| Mahone/Mahon, Merrit | Private | Second State, Dudley | March 15-May 1, 1778; May-June 1778. |
| Mahone/ Mahoughn, Thomas | Private | Second State, Garnett | March 15-May 1, 1778; May-June 1778. |
| Maiden/Maidon, David | Private | Fifteenth, Foster/ Gray | Dec 1777; Jan 1778 on guard; Feb 1778 in Gray's Company; March 1778; April 1778 sick present; May 1778. |
| Mainard/ Marnard, Nathaniel/Nathl. | Private | First, Cummings/ Mennis | Feb 9, 1778 enlisted; June 1778 in Mennis' Company, sick Valley Forge. |
| Major, Ire Manger | Private | Second State, Taliaferro | March 15-May 1, 1778; May-June 1778. |

| Name | Rank | Regiment/Company | Notes |
|---|---|---|---|
| Major, John | Private | Second State, Quarles | April-June 1778. |
| Major/Majors, William | Private | Fourteenth, Thweatt | Feb 14, 1778 enlisted; April 1778 lately joined regiment; May 1778 sick present camp; June 1778 sick Valley Forge. |
| Majors, Henry | Private | First State, Camp | Dec 20, 1777 died. |
| Majors/Magers, James | Private | Twelfth, Ashby | Dec 1777-Jan 1778; March-May 1778. |
| Malany/Melany, John | Private | First State, Meriwether | Dec 1777-June 1778. |
| Mallory, Francis | Sergeant | Second, Taylor, W. | Dec 1777-Jan 1778; Feb 14, 1778 discharged. |
| Mallory, John | Sergeant | Fifteenth, Grimes | Nov 1777 sick present; Dec 1777 muster roll shows he died Jan 3, 1778. |
| Mallory/Mallorry, Philip | 2nd. Lt. | Fifteenth, Grimes | Dec 1777-March 1778 absent with leave; April-May 1778. |
| Mane/Main, Philip | Private | Twelfth, Waggener | Dec 1777; Jan 1778 on guard; Feb-March 1778; April 1778 on guard; May 1778 on command; June-July 1778 sick Valley Forge. |
| Manes/Maines, Tapla/Tapley | Private | Second State, Dudley | June 1778 sick absent; September 1778 "Omitted in March, April and May 1778." |
| Mangum/Mangen, David | Drummer | Fifteenth, Mason/Gregory | Dec 1777-May 1778; June 1778 in Gregory's Company. |
| Mankins, James | Private | First State, Ewell, T. | Dec 1777; Jan 1778 sick Yellow Springs; Feb-May 1778; June 1778 sick Valley Forge. |
| Mann, Daniel | Private | Second, Taylor, W. | Dec 1777 hospital; Jan-Feb 1778; March 14, 1778 died. |
| Mann, Ephraim | Private | Fifteenth, Harris | Feb-April 1778 sick present; May 1778 sick absent; June 1778 sick Yellow Springs. |
| Mann, Millington/Millinton | Private | Seventh, Moseley | Dec 1777-Jan 1778; Feb 19, 1778 discharged. |

| | | | |
|---|---|---|---|
| Mann, Robert | Private | Second, Taylor, W. | Dec 1777 absent; Jan 1778; Feb 21, 1778 discharged. |
| Mann, Ruebin/ Reuben | Private | Second State, Dudley | March 15-May 1, 1778; May-June 1778. |
| Mann, William | Private | Second, Upshaw | Feb 14, 1778 drafted; April 1778; June-July 1778 sick at Valley Forge. |
| Mansfield, Thomas | Fifer/Private | Second State, Lewis | March 15-May 1, 1778; May-June 1778 sick absent; July 1778 sick Valley Forge. He was demoted to Private in May. |
| Marbury/ Marberry, Francis H. | Adjutant | First State | Jan-Feb 1778. |
| Mardes, James | Private | Third, Powell | Entered service April 5, 1778; June 1778. |
| Marks, John | Captain | Fourteenth, Marks | Dec 1777-Jan 1778 on furlough; Feb 1778; March 1778 on furlough; April 1778 on command; May-June 1778. |
| Marks, William | Private | Fourteenth, Jones | Sept 8, 1777 drafted; April-May 1778. |
| Marr/Mars, Barnabas/ Barney | Corporal | Twelfth, Ashby | Dec 1777; Jan 1778 sick in hospital; March 1778 at hospital; April-May 1778. |
| Marshall, David | Private | First State, Meriwether | Dec 1777-June 1778. |
| Marshall/ Martial, George | Private | Second, Upshaw | Dec 1777 hospital; Jan 1778. |
| Marshall, Isick/Isaac | Sergeant | Fourteenth, Jones | Dec 1777 muster roll shows he was taken prisoner on Oct 4, 177. |
| Marshall, James | Private | First State, Meriwether | Dec 1777-June 1778. |
| Marshall, James | Corporal | First State, Payne | Dec 1777-Jan 1778 sick Lancaster; Feb 1778 sick absent; May-June 1778 sick Yellow Springs. |
| Marshall, Richard | Fifer/Private | First State, Meriwether | Dec 1777-Jan 1778; Feb 1778 reduced to private; Feb-June 1778. |
| Marshall, Thomas | Colonel | Third | Dec 4, 1777 resigned. |

| | | | |
|---|---|---|---|
| Marshall, Thomas | Private/ Sergeant | Seventh/ Third, Webb/ Young | Jan-February 1778 on furlough; April-May 1778; June 1778 promoted to Sergeant, in Young's Company. |
| Marshall/ Marshell, William | Private | Second, Sanford/ Parker | Dec 1777-May 1778; June 1778 hospital. |
| Marthus/ Marthis, Elijah | Private | Second State, Garnett | March 15-May 1, 1778; May 1778; June 1778 sick Valley Forge. |
| Martin, Hugh | Surgeon's Mate | Twelfth | Appointed April 29, 1778; April-May 1778. |
| Martin/Marten, James | Private | First, Cunningham | Feb 14, 1778 enlisted for 1 year; April 1778 under inoculation; May-June 1778. |
| Martin/Martain, James | Corporal | First State, Payne | Dec 1777-Jan 1778 sick Lancaster; Feb 1778 sick absent; May-June 1778 sick Yellow Springs. |
| Martin/Marten, James | Sergeant | Fifteenth, Gregory | Dec 1777-March 1778 hospital. |
| Martin/Martain, John | Private | Second, Jones | Feb-March 1778. |
| Martin/Martain, John | Private | Second, Upshaw | Dec 1777-Jan 1778; April 1778; June 1778. |
| Martin, John | Sergeant/ Quartermaster Sergeant/ Sergeant | Seventh/ Third, Jouett/ Hill | Dec 1777 on furlough Virginia; Jan-March 1778 on furlough; April 1778; May 1, 1778 promoted to Quartermaster Sergeant; May 27, 1778 reduced to Sergeant; June 1778 in Hill's Company. |
| Martin, Thomas | Sergeant/ Private | Twelfth, Casey | Dec 1777; Dec 28, 1777 reduced to private; Jan-Feb 1778; March 1778 on command; April-May 1778. |
| Martin/Martain, William | Private | Second, Taylor, F. | Dec 1777; sick hospital; Jan 1, 1778 Deceased. |
| Martin, William | Private | Seventh, Jouett | Dec 1777 sick in hospital; Jan 1778 sick country; February 1778 discharged. |
| Martin, William (son of Jno) | Private | Seventh, Jouett | Dec 1777-Jan 1778; Feb 14, 1778 discharged. |

| Name | Rank | Regiment | Notes |
|---|---|---|---|
| Martram, Henry | Private | Third, Mercer | Dec 15 or 16, 1777 dead. |
| Mason, David | Colonel | Fifteenth | Dec 1777-May 1778 recruiting. |
| Mason, David | 1st. Lt. | Fifteenth, Gregory/ Edmunds | Dec 1777; Jan-April 1778; May 1778; June 1778 in Edmund's Company. |
| Mason, George | Private | Seventh/ Third, Young | Dec 1777-April 1778 on furlough; May 1778; June 1778 on guard. |
| Mason, Gideon | Private | Fifteenth, Mason | Dec 1777-April 1778 on furlough. |
| Mason, James | Captain | Fifteenth, Mason | Dec 1777-March 1778 on furlough. Colonel David Mason wrote to Washington on March 21, that Captain Mason was resigning from the Army as he had been appointed a Lt. Col. in the "Volunteer Service." |
| Mason, James | Sergeant | Fifteenth, Mason | Dec 1777-Jan 1778; Feb 1778 sick present; March 26, 1778 died. |
| Mason, Littleberry | Paymaster | Fifteenth | Dec 1777-Jan 1778 absent; Feb-May 1778 on furlough. |
| Mason, Samuel | Private | Third/ Seventh, Arell/ Briscoe | Dec 1777-Jan 1778; Feb-March 1778 on furlough; April 1778 sick present; June 1778 in Briscoe's Company. |
| Mason, Thomas | Private | Third, Arell | Dec 1777 sick Virginia. |
| Massey, Dade/Daid | Private | First State, Lee | Dec 1777 sick; Jan-Feb 1778 sick Lancaster; March 20, 1778 died. |
| Massey/Massie Taliaferro/ Talliaferro | Private | First State, Hoffler | Dec 1777-May 1778; June 1778 sick absent. |
| Massie, Edmund | Private | Fifteenth, Gray | March 1778 payroll shows he enlisted on Aug 25, 1777, "returned last month a deserter, since joined"; he was then paid for seven months; April 1778 deserted from Nov 7, joined April 19; May 1778 sick present. |

| Name | Rank | Regiment, Company | Notes |
|---|---|---|---|
| Massie, Thomas | Captain | Sixth, Massie | Dec 1777-Jan 1778 on furlough in Virginia; Feb-April 1778 on furlough; May 1778; June 1778 with Morgan's Corps. Oath at Valley Forge in May 1778, witnessed by Muhlenberg. |
| Mathews, Chichester/Chichister | Sergeant | Third, Blackwell | Dec 1777-Jan 1778; Feb 14, 1778 discharged. |
| Mathews/Matthews, Daniel/Danl. | Private | Third/Seventh, Mercer/Powell | Dec 1777-March 1778 on furlough; April-May 1778; June 1778 sick on march, in Powell's Company. |
| Mathews/Matthews, Edward | Private | First, Mennis | Dec 1777; Jan 1778 on furlough; Feb-1778; March 1778 on furlough; April 1778; May 1778 sick present; June 1778 sick Valley Forge. |
| Mathews, John | Private | Third, Peyton, J. | Dec 1777-Jan 1778. |
| Mathews/Matthews, John | Private | Fifteenth, Edmunds | Dec 1777 sick absent. |
| Mathews/Matthews, William | Sergeant | Third, Peyton, J. | Dec 1777-Jan 1778. |
| Mathias, Griffith | Private | Second, Sanford/Parker | Dec 1777-May 1778; June 1778 hospital. From April on he appears in Parker's company. |
| Mattheus/Matthes, John | Private | Fifteenth, Wills | Jan 1778 sick Virginia; Feb-March 1778 sick absent. |
| Matthews/Mathews, Benjm. | Private | Fifteenth, Edmunds | Dec 1777-April 1778 on command; May 1778; June 1778 sick Valley Forge. |
| Matthews, Brian | Private | Twelfth, Wallace | Dec 1777-May 1778. |
| Matthews/Mathews, William | Private | First State, Meriwether | Dec 1777-June 1778. |
| Matthias, Henry | Private | Fifteenth, Grimes | Dec 1777-Jan 1778; Feb 1778 sick present; March-May 1778. |
| Mattock/Mattox, Thomas/Thos. | Private | Sixth, Fox | Dec 1777 in hospital; Jan 1778; Feb 1778 sick absent. |

| Name | Rank | Regiment | Service |
|---|---|---|---|
| Mattocks, Thomas | Private | Second, Willis | Dec 20, 1777 deserted. |
| Mauffett/Moffet, William | Private | Third, Blackwell | Jan-March 1778 on guard |
| Maunsell/Mauncel, William | Private/Sergeant | First State, Camp | Dec 1777 sick in hospital; Jan 1778 promoted to Sergeant; Feb 1778 on command; March 1778 on furlough, April-June 1778. |
| Maury/Mawry, Abram/Abraham, Jr. | 1st. Lt. | Fourteenth, Marks | Dec 1777-Feb 1778; March-April 1778 on furlough; May-June 1778. Oath at Valley Forge on May 29, 1778, witnessed by Muhlenberg. |
| May, George | Private | Third, Briscoe | Dec 1777 sick in hospital; Feb 5, 1778 discharged. |
| May, Thomas | Private | Seventh/Third, Hill | April 1778; June 1778. |
| May, William | Private | First State, Hamilton | Dec 1777-June 1778. |
| May/William, Wm. | Corporal | Fifteenth, Foster/Gray | Dec 1777-Feb 1778; Feb 1778 in Gray's Company; March-May 1778 on command; June 1778 "Discharged on getting a man in place". |
| Mayfield, Charles | Private | Seventh, Crockett | Dec 1777-Jan 1778 in R. Bat. |
| Maynard, Wm. | Sergeant | Sixth, Hockaday | Dec 1777 sick in the country; Jan 1778 discharged. |
| Maynard, William | Private | Fourteenth, Reid | Sept 3, 1777 enlisted; April 1778 lately joined regiment; May 1778; June 1778 sick Valley Forge. |
| Mayo/Mayho, Benjamin | Private | Fourteenth, Overton | Dec 1777; Jan 1778 sick absent; March 23, 1778 discharged. |
| Mayo/Mayho, Stephen | Private | Fourteenth, Overton | Dec 1777; Jan 1778 sick absent; March 23, 1778 discharged. |
| Meachem, Henry | Private | Fifteenth, Edmunds | Jan 1778 on guard; March 1778 sick present; April 15, 1778 died. |
| Mead/Made, Mahlon/Mahlane | Private | Fourteenth, Lambert | Dec 1777 on command; March 1778 on guard; April 1778; May 1778 on guard; June 1778. |
| Meacham, Henry | Private | Fifteenth, Edmunds | Dec 1777-Jan 1778 on guard; Feb 1778; March 1778 sick present; April 18, 1778 died. |

| Name | Rank | Regiment/Company | Notes |
|---|---|---|---|
| Meade/Mead, John | Private | Sixth | Feb 17, 1778 drafted; May-June 1778 |
| Mead, Minor | Private | Sixth | May-June 1778. |
| Meadow, Meadows, John | Private | Seventh, Spencer | Feb 13, 1778 enlisted for 1 year; April 1778; May 1778 payroll shows him dead on May 24, May 1778 muster roll shows he died on May 30. |
| Meadow, Leroy | Private | Seventh, Webb | Jan 1778; February 1778 deceased. |
| Meadow, Vincent | Private | Seventh, Webb | Jan 1778 hospital; Feb 9, 1778 discharged. |
| Mealer/Mealor, Thomas | Private | Sixth, Garland | Dec 1777-Jan 1778 in hospital; Feb 19, 1778 discharged. |
| Mealey, Martin | Private | Second, Sanford | Dec 1777-March 1778. |
| Mears, James | Sergeant | Seventh, Crockett | Dec 1777-Jan 1778 on furlough. |
| Meck, Andrew | Private | Seventh/Third, Crockett/Sayers | Dec 1777-Jan 1778 on furlough; April 1778 tayloring Lancaster; May 1778 taylor Lancaster; June 1778 taylor in Lancaster, in Sayers' Company. |
| Medings/Mading, William | Sergeant | Twelfth, Madison | Dec 1777-April 1778. |
| Medley, William | Sergeant | Second, Taylor, F. | Dec 1777-Feb 1778; Feb promoted to Sergeant; March 12, 1778 discharged. |
| Medlock, Isom | Private | Seventh, Crockett | Dec 1777 waggoner; Jan 1778. |
| Medlock, Zach/Zachriah | Private | Seventh/Third, Young | May 1778; June 1778 sick Valley Forge. |
| Meginnes/McGinnis, Peter | Private | Fifteenth, Wills | June 25, 1777 enlisted; Feb-April 1778; May 1778 on command. |
| Mellon/Melions, Henry | Private | Twelfth, Bowyer, T. | Dec 1777; Jan 1778 sick in hospital; Feb 1778 sick absent; March-April 1778; May 1778 on command. |
| Melone/Malone, Richard/Richd. | Private | Sixth, Rose | Dec 1777-Jan 1778; March 13, 1778 discharged. |

| Name | Rank | Regiment | Notes |
|---|---|---|---|
| Meloy, James | Private | Twelfth, Wallace | Dec 1777 roll shows him as "On scout and missing 20 December." |
| Melton, John | Private | Sixth | Feb 17, 1778 drafted; May-June 1778. |
| Melton, Thomas | Private | Second, Willis | Dec 1777-June 1778. |
| Menear, Mark | Private | Second, Sandford | Dec 1777. |
| Mennis/Minnis, Benjamin/Benjn. | Private | First, Pelham | Dec 1777 on furlough; Feb 15, 1778 discharged. |
| Mennis/Minnis, Callohill/Calohill | Captain/Brigade Major | First, Mennis | Dec 1777; Jan-March 1778 acting as Brigade Major; April-May 1778; June 1778 Brigade Major. Oath at Valley Forge, 1778, witnessed by Muhlenberg. |
| Mennis/Minnis, Francis | 1st. Lt. | First, Lewis | Dec 1777 Virginia recruiting; Jan-March 1778 on command; April-June 1778. Oath at Valley Forge on May 11, 1778, witnessed by Muhlenberg. |
| Mercer, John Francis | Captain | Third, Mercer | Dec 1777-March 1778 on command; April-June 1778. On June 8, 1778, he was appointed an aide-de-camp to Major General Charles Lee. |
| Meriwether/Merriweather, David | 2nd. Lt. | Fourteenth, Marks | Dec 1777-Jan 1778 on command; Feb-June 1778. Oath at Valley Forge on May 29, 1778, witnessed by Muhlenberg. |
| Meriwether, David Wood | Cadet | Fourteenth, Marks | March 1778; April 1778 on command; May 1778. |
| Meriwether/Merewether, James | 2nd. Lt./Adjutant Protemporary | First State, Nicholas | Dec 1777-June 1778. He is listed as Adjutant Protemporary on March 19, 1778, and remains as such for the months of March-June 1778. Oath at Valley Forge on May 12, 1778, witnessed by Muhlenberg. |

| Name | Rank | Regiment/Company | Notes |
|---|---|---|---|
| Meriwether/Merewether, Thomas | Captain/Major | First State, Meriwether | Dec 1777-March 1778; In May-June 1778, he appears as Captain of what had been Lee's company. In June 1778 he is also listed as Major of the regiment. Oath at Valley Forge on May 11, 1778, witnessed by Muhlenberg. |
| Merrill/Merrel, John | Private | Second, Sanford/Parker | Dec 1777-June 1778. From April on he appears in Parker's company. |
| Merriman, John | Private | First State, Camp | Dec 1777 sick Fishwater Mills; Jan-Feb 1778 sick absent. |
| Merrit/Merritt, Archilas/Archilis | Private | Second State, Dudley | March 15-May 1, 1778; May-June 1778. |
| Merrit, John | Private | Twelfth, Madison | Dec 1777 left behind. |
| Merritt/Merrit, Samuel | Private | Second, Calmes | Dec 1777-June 1778. |
| Merritt, Tarpley | Sergeant | Second, Upshaw | Feb 14, 1778 drafted; April 1778; June 1778; July 1778 sick at Valley Forge. |
| Merry, John | Private | Second State, Lewis | March 15-May 1, 1778; May 1778; June 1778. |
| Merryman/Merriman, Francis | Private | Second, Jones | Dec 1777 on command; Jan-Feb 1778 on furlough; March-June 1778. |
| Merryman, John | Private | First State, Camp | Dec 1777 sick at Fish Water Mills; Jan-Feb 1778 sick absent; March 1778. |
| Merryman/Merriman Thomas | Sergeant | Second, Sanford/Parker | Dec 1777-June 1778. From April on he appears in Parker's company. |
| Merryman/Merriman, William | Private | First State, Camp | Dec 1777 sick in hospital; Jan-Feb 1778 sick absent; March roll shows he died on Feb 3, 1778. |
| Michaux/Messhew, Joseph | Captain | Fourteenth, Michaux | Dec 24, 1777 resigned, "at which time his Co. was annexed to Capt. Reid's." |
| Michie, George | Sergeant | Second State, Lewis | March 15-May 1, 1778; May-June 1778. |
| Micou, Henry | Ensign | Third, Peyton, J. | Dec 1777; Jan-May 1778 on command |

| Name | Rank | Regiment/Company | Notes |
|---|---|---|---|
| Milam, John | Private | Seventh, Moseley | Dec 1777-February 1778; Feb 26, 1778 discharged. |
| Miles, John/Jno. | Corporal | First, Cunningham | Feb 12, 1778 enlisted for 1 year; April-June 1778. |
| Middleton, Basil | Surgeon's Mate | First State | Jan 1778. |
| Middleton, John | Private | Third, Arell | Dec 1777; Jan 1778 waiting on Col. Fitzgerald. |
| Middleton, William/Wm. | Private | Fifteenth, Wills | June 5, 1777 enlisted; Feb 1778 sick present; March-April 1778; May 1778 sick present. |
| Milacan/Millican, John | Private | Twelfth, Waggener | Dec 1777; Jan-March 1778 on command; April-May 1778 with Artificers. |
| Miles, William | Private | Second State, Dudley | July 1778 "omitted from 1 May." |
| Milhousen/Milhousin, Abraham | Private | Third, Peyton, V. | Dec 1777-Jan 1778 on command with Col. Morgan. |
| Millar/Miller, Daniel | Private | Twelfth, Bowyer, M. | March 20, 1778 "returned from the Gallies"; April-May 1778. |
| Miller/Millar, Edward | Private | Fourteenth, Marks | Dec 1777-Jan 1778; March 1778 on command; April 1778; May 1778 on duty; June 1778. |
| Miller/Millar, Gilbert/Guilbart | Private | Seventh/Third, Crockett/Sayers | March 8, 1778 enlisted; April 1778 taylor Lancaster; May 1778 sent from Provost Marshal to Yellow Springs; June 1778 sick Valley Forge, in Sayers' Company. |
| Miller, Henry | Private | Fourteenth, Lambert | Feb 23, 1778 enlisted; June 1778 lately joined, sick Valley Forge. |
| Miller, James/John | Private | First, Lawson | Dec 1777-March 1778 waggoner; May-June 1778 waggoner. |
| Miller, James | Private | Second State, Quarles | April-May 1778; June 1778 sick Valley Forge. |
| Miller, John/Jno. | Sergeant | First, Taylor/Payne | Feb 5, 1778 enlisted; April-June 1778 in Payne's Company. |

| Name | Rank | Regiment/Company | Service |
|---|---|---|---|
| Miller/Millor, John | Private | Third/Seventh, Powell | Dec 1777-May 1778; June 1778 sick Valley Forge. |
| Miller/Millar, John | Private | Seventh/Third, Crockett/Sayers | March 12, 1778 enlisted; April-May 1778; June 1778 sick Valley Forge, in Sayers' Company. |
| Miller/Millar, John | Private | Twelfth, Bowyer, T. | Dec 1777 on command; Jan 1778; Feb-May 1778 on furlough; June 1778 sick in Virginia. |
| Miller, Nathaniel/Nath. | Corporal | First, Taylor/Payne | Feb 5, 1778 enlisted; April-June 1778 in Payne's Company. |
| Miller, Richard | Private | Twelfth, Casey | Feb 28, 1778 drafted for one year; May 1778. |
| Miller, Robert | Private | Fourteenth, Reid | Dec 1777 on duty; Jan 1778 on command; Feb-April 1778; May-June 1778 on guard. |
| Miller, Thomas | Corporal | Fourteenth, Reid | Dec 1777 hospital; Jan 1778; Feb 1778 sick absent. |
| Miller, William | Private | First State, Camp | Dec 1777-Feb 1778; March 1778 sick at Red Lyon; April-June 1778. |
| Millington/Millinton, Nathl. | Private | Fifteenth, Harris | Jan-Feb 1778 on command; March 1778 sick present; April 1778 on command; May 1778 on guard. |
| Millirons, Henry | Private | Twelfth, Bowyer, T. | Jan 1778 sick in hospital; Feb 1778 sick absent; May 1778 on command. |
| Millirons, William | Private | Twelfth, Madison | Dec 1777-March 1778 sick in hospital; April 1778 on fatigue; May 1778 on command. |
| Millison/Milason, Samuel | Private | Second, Calmes | Dec 1777-May 1778; June 1778 sick at Valley Forge. |
| Mills, Armstead/Armsted | Private | First, Mennis | Dec 1777-April 1778 on furlough; May 1778; June 1778 waggoner. |
| Mills, Barnet | Corporal | Seventh, Jouett | Dec 1777 on command with sick; Jan 1778 sick in hospital; Feb 11, 1778 discharged. |

| | | | |
|---|---|---|---|
| Mills, Charles | Private | Fourteenth, Winston | Feb 10, 1777 drafted; May 1778; June 1778 sick Coyrells Ferry. |
| Mills, Francis | Private | First, Mennis | Dec 1777; Jan 1778 on furlough; Feb 1778 fatigue; March-June 1778. |
| Mills, John | Private | Twelfth, Ashby | Dec 1777; Jan 1778 sick in hospital. |
| Mills, Moses | Private | Fourteenth, Thweatt | Dec 1777 sick in hospital; Jan-Feb 1778 on furlough to Virginia; March 1778; April 1778 on furlough; June 1778. |
| Mills, Nathan | Private | Seventh, Jouett | Dec 1777 sick in hospital; Jan 1778; Feb 10, 1778 discharged. |
| Mills, Robert | Private | Twelfth, Ashby | Dec 1777; Jan 1778 sick in hospital; March 1778 hospital. |
| Mills, Wiatt | Corporal | Seventh, Jouett | Dec 1777-Jan 1778 on guard; Feb 11, 1778 discharged. |
| Milton, James | Private | Fifteenth, Gray | Feb 10, 1778 drafted; April 1778 under inoculation; May 1778 sick present. |
| Minnes, Alexander | Surgeon | First | Feb 1778. |
| Minnis, Benjamin | Private | First, Pelham | Dec 1777; Feb 15, 1778 discharged. |
| Minnis/Minis, Holman/ Holeman | 1st. Lt. | First, Scott/ Cunningham | Dec 1777 in Virginia on furlough; Jan-Feb 1778; March 1778 on furlough; April-May 1778; June 1778 in Cunningham's Company. Oath at Valley Forge on May 18, 1778, witnessed by Muhlenberg. |
| Minor, John | Private | Seventh/ Third, Hill | Feb 15, 1778 enlisted; April 1778; June-July 1778 sick Valley Forge; August 1, 1778 died. |
| Minor, William | Private | Seventh, Webb | Jan 1778; Feb 5, 1778 discharged. |
| Minord, Nathaniel | Private | First, Mennis | Feb 1, 1778 enlisted; Only appears on a roll dated September 14, 1778. |
| Minton, Thomas/Thos. | Private | First, Cunningham | Feb 14, 1778 enlisted for 1 year; April 1778 under inoculation; May 23, 1778 dead. |

| | | | |
|---|---|---|---|
| Minzies, George/Geo. | Ensign | Fifteenth, Hull | Roll dated April 14, 1778 shows he commanded a detachment of the 15th Virginia "and of some other Reg'ts (that joined the Detachment on Sunday last) now on their march to Head Quarters." The April 1778 payroll paid him back to April 7, 1777. May 1778 sick in camp. |
| Mitchel/ Mitchell, William/Wm. | Private | First, Lawson | Dec 1777 sick Virginia; April 1778 on command; April payroll pays him for 14 months and reads "Omitted to be drawn for from 1st. Feby 1777 whilst in Virginia." May-June 1778. |
| Mitchell, Archibald/ Archey | Private/ Sergeant | Third/ Seventh, Powell | Dec 1777-March 1778 on furlough; April 1778 promoted to Sergeant; April-May 1778; June 1778 on detachment. |
| Mitchell, James | Private | Third/ Seventh, Blackwell | Feb 18, 1778 drafted; April-June 1778. |
| Mitchell/ Mitchel, James | Private | Fourteenth, Lambert | Dec 1777-March 1778 hospital; April 1778 sick Yellow Springs; May-June 1778. |
| Mitchel/ Mitchell, James | Drummer | Fourteenth, Thweatt | Dec 1777-March 1778; April 1778 sick Y. S. H.; May 1778; June 1778 sick Princetown. |
| Mitchell, John | Private | Second State, Bernard | April-May 1778; June 1778 sick Princeton. |
| Mitchell, Ralph | Private | Seventh, Webb | Jan 1778; Feb 13, 1778 discharged. |
| Mitchell/ Mitchel, Reaps/Repps | Private | Second, Jones | Dec 1777-June 1778. |
| Mitchell, Stephen | Sergeant | Fourteenth, Lambert | Dec 27, 1777 discharged. |
| Mitchell/ Mitchel, William | Corporal | Fourteenth, Overton | Dec 1777; Jan 1778 on duty; Feb-April 1778; May 1778 on command; June 1778. |

| | | | | |
|---|---|---|---|---|
| Mitchel, David | Private | Fourteenth, Overton | Dec 1777-Feb 1778; March 1778 sick present; April-May 1778; June 1778 on command. |
| Mitchem, John | Private | Twelfth, Ashby | Dec 1777-Jan 1778; March-May 1778 on guard. |
| Moderwell, Thomas | Corporal | Third, Arell | Dec 23, 1777 discharged. |
| Moffett/Moffet, William/Wm. | Private | Third/Seventh, Blackwell | Dec 1777; Jan-March 1778 on guard; April-May 1778; June 1778 on command. |
| Monathan, Samuel | Private | First State, Payne | Dec 1777; Jan 10, 1778 deserted. |
| Monday, Edward | Private | First, Cummings/Mennis | Dec 1777; Jan-Feb 1778 on furlough; March 1778 on furlough Virginia; April 1778 on furlough; May 1778 on furlough, in Mennis' Company; June 1778 waggoner. |
| Money, Nicklas | Private | Twelfth, Wallace | Dec 1777-March 1778 on command; April-May 1778 on command at Yellow Springs. |
| Moneys, Henry | Private | Second State, Taliaferro | March 15-May 1, 1778; May 1778; June 1778 sick Valley Forge. |
| Monro, William | Private | Second State, Garnett | April 15-June 1778. |
| Monroe/Monro, Andrew | Private | Third, Arell | Dec 1777; Jan 1778; Feb 1778 on picket; March-May 1778 on command |
| Monroe/Monro, John | Private | Third/Seventh, Arell/Briscoe | Dec 1777-Feb 1778; March-May 1778 on command; June 1778 baggage guard, in Briscoe's Company. |
| Monroe, Peter | Private | Sixth, Apperson | Dec 1777 left at Alexandria; Jan 22, 1778 discharged. |
| Moody, Blanks | Private | Seventh, Crockett | Dec 1777-Jan 1778 on guard; Feb 7, 1778 discharged. |
| Moody, Elijah | Private | Seventh/Third, Webb/Young | April 1778 on command; May 1778; June 1778 on guard, in Young's Company. |

| Name | Rank | Regiment | Notes |
|---|---|---|---|
| Moody, James | 2d. Lt. | Second State, Bressie | In May 1778 he was paid for 1 ½ months; May-June 1778. |
| Moody, John | Private | Seventh/Third, Young | Feb 16, 1778 enlisted; April 1778 sick present; May-June 1778. |
| Moon, Jacob | Paymaster | Fourteenth | Dec 1777-Feb 1778; April-June 1778. Oath at Valley Forge on May 12, 1778, witnessed by Muhlenberg. |
| Mooney, John | Private | Twelfth, Bowyer, T. | Dec 1777-May 1778; June 1778 sick Valley Forge. |
| Money, Nicholas | Private | Twelfth, Wallace | Dec 1777-March 1778 on command; April-May 1778 on command Yellow Springs. |
| Moore, Alexander | 2nd. Lt. | Fourteenth, Reid | Dec 1777 on duty; Jan 11, 1778 resigned. |
| Moore, David | Private | Second State, Lewis | March 15-May 1, 1778; May-June 1778. |
| Moore, David | Private | Sixth, Fox | Dec 28, 1777 reenlisted in Light Horse. |
| Moore/More, George | Private | Second State, Dudley | March 15-May 1, 1778; May-June 1778. |
| Moore/More, George | Private/Corporal | Seventh/Third, Spencer/Lipscomb | Enlisted for 3 years; Dec 1777 on furlough Virginia; Jan 1778 on furlough; April-May 1778; June 1778 in Lipscomb's Company as a Corporal. |
| Moore, James | Private | First State, Crump | Dec 1777-Feb 1778. |
| Moore, James | Corporal | Sixth, Rose | Dec 1777-Jan 1778; Feb 21, 1778 discharged. |
| Moore/More, John | Private | First State, Ewell, T. | Dec 1777-Feb 1778 sick at New Church; March 1778 sick Bethlehem; April-May 1778 Yellow Springs. |
| Moore, John | Private | Second State, Lewis | March 15-May 1, 1778; May-June 1778. |
| Moore/More, John | 2nd. Lt. | Twelfth, Casey | Dec 1777-Feb 1778; March 30, 1778 resigned. |

| Name | Rank | Company | Notes |
|---|---|---|---|
| Moore/Moor, John | Private | Fourteenth, Reid | Dec 1777-Jan 1778; Feb 1778 on guard; March 1778 sick present; May 1778; June 1778 on guard. |
| Moore, Peter | Private | Third, Blackwell | Dec 1777 on furlough; Jan 1778; Feb 14, 1778 discharged. |
| Moore/More, Thomas | Private | First State, Ewell, T. | Dec 1777 sick White Marsh; Jan 1778 sick Yellow Springs; Feb 1778 Yellow Springs hospital. |
| Moore, Thomas | Corporal | Second State, Quarles | April-June 1778. |
| Moore/Moor, William | Private | Second State, Quarles | April-June 1778. |
| Moore, William | Private | Second, Upshaw | Feb 14, 1778 drafted; April 1778; June 7, 1778 dead. |
| Moore/More, William | Ensign | Third, Blackwell | Dec 1777-Jan 1778 on command; Feb 1778; March 1778 on command in Virginia; April 1778; May 1778 on command at the Lines; June 1778 sick at Brunswick. |
| Moores/Mores, Michael | Private | Twelfth, Bowyer, T. | Dec 1777; Jan 1778 on G. fatigue; Feb-April 1778; May 1778 on guard. |
| Morce/Mase, Mattak/Mattox | Private | Sixth, Apperson | Dec 1777-Feb 1778. |
| More, Stephen | Private | First State, Ewell, T. | Dec 1777. |
| Moreland/Morland, John | Corporal | Third, Briscoe | Dec 1777-Jan 1778; Feb 5, 1778 discharged. |
| Moreland, Thomas | Private | First State, Lee | Jan 1778 deserted. |
| Morgan/Morgin, David | Private | Fourteenth, Winston | Dec 1777 on guard; Jan-June 1778. |
| Morgan/Mortgin, James | Private | Second, Jones | Dec 1777-June 1778. |
| Morgan, John | Sergeant | First State, Camp | Dec 1777 sick in hospital; Jan 23, 1778 died. |
| Morgan, John | Private | Seventh, Young | Dec 1777-Jan 1778 hospital; Feb 7, 1778 discharged. |
| Morgan/Morgen, John | Private | Twelfth, Casey | Dec 1777-Jan 1778; Feb 1778 on duty; March-May 1778. |

| Name | Rank | Unit | Service |
|---|---|---|---|
| Morgan/Morgain, Spencer | Sergeant | Fourteenth, Lambert | Dec 1777-Feb 1778; March-April 1778 on command; May 1778; June 1778 on guard. |
| Morgan, Thomas | Private | Second State, Lewis | March 15-May 1, 1778; May-June 1778. |
| Morgan, William | Private | Second State, Bernard | May-June 1778. |
| Morgan/Morgin, William | Private | Twelfth, Bowyer, T. | Dec 1777-Feb 1778 sick absent; March 1778 sick in hospital; April-May 1778. |
| Morley, George | Private | First State, Payne/Ewell, C. | March 1778 on guard; May 1778 on command. |
| Morress/Morriss, Micagh/McCajah | Private | Seventh, Spencer | Dec 1777-Jan 1778; March 7, 1778 discharged. |
| Morris, David | Private | Fourteenth, Reid | Dec 1777-Feb 1778; March-May 1778 on command; June 1778. |
| Morris, Hugh | Private | Twelfth, Madison | Dec 1777; Jan 1778 on Quarters guard; Feb-March 1778; April 1778 taylor. |
| Morriss, Isick/Isaac | Private | Fifteenth, Gray | March-April 1778; May 1778 hospital Yellow Springs. |
| Morris, John | Private | First State, Crump | April-June 1778. |
| Morris, John | Private | Fifteenth, Gray | March 1778. |
| Morris, John | Private | Fifteenth, Harris | Jan-March 1778; April 1778 sick present; May 1778 on guard. |
| Morris/Morriss, Joseph | Private | Second State, Quarles | April-May 1778; June 1778 sick Valley Forge. |
| Morris, Owen | Private | First State, Camp | Dec 1777 sick in ye country; Jan-Feb 1778 sick absent; March-June 1778. |
| Morris, Sanders | Private | Second State, Garnett | March 15-May 1, 1778; May-June 1778. |
| Morris/Morriss, Thomas | Private | Second, Taylor, F. | Dec 1777-Feb 1778; March 7, 1778 discharged. |

| Name | Rank | Regiment/Company | Notes |
|---|---|---|---|
| Morris/Morriss, William | Private | Second, Taylor, F. | Dec 1777-Feb 1778; March 7, 1778 discharged. |
| Morris, William/Wm. | Private | Fifteenth, Harris | March 1778 on command; April 1778; May 1778 absent without leave. |
| Morrison, Hugh | Sergeant | Second, Willis | Dec 1777 hospital; Jan-June 1778. |
| Morrison, James/Jas. | Private | Sixth, Apperson | Dec 1777; March 16, 1778 discharged. |
| Morrison, John/Jno. | Private | Sixth, Apperson | Dec 1777; March 16, 1778 discharged. |
| Morrison, Neal | Private | Twelfth, Bowyer, T. | Dec 1777 on command; Jan-Feb 1778; March 27, 1778 died. |
| Morrison, Reuben/Reubin | Corporal | Second, Willis | Dec 1777-June 1778. |
| Morrison, William | Sergeant | Second, Willis | Dec 1777-June 1778. |
| Morrison, William/Wm. | Private | Sixth, Apperson | Dec 1777-Jan 1778; March 16, 1778 discharged. |
| Morrow, James | Private | Twelfth, Bowyer, T. | Dec 1777 sick in camp; Jan-Feb 1778 sick absent; March-May 1778 sick in hospital. |
| Morrow/Morron, Thomas | Private | Seventh/Third, Crockett/Powell | Dec 1777-Jan 1778 sick in hospital; May 1778; June-Aug 1778 sick Valley Forge, in Powell's Company. |
| Morton, Hezekiah | 1st. Lt. | Twelfth, Bowyer, T. | Feb 3, 1778 joined; Feb-May 1778. |
| Morton, Gerrard | Private | Second, Taylor, F. | Dec 1777 left sick Virginia. |
| Mosby, William | Private | Seventh/Third, Fleming/Heth | Dec 1, 1777 enlisted; Dec 1777 on furlough Virginia; Jan-March 1778 on furlough; April-May 1778; June 1778 in Heth's Company. |
| Moseley, Benjamin/Benjm. | Private/Cadet | Seventh/Third, Moseley/Blackwell | May 1778; June 1778 he is listed as a Cadet, in Blackwell's Company. |
| Mosely, George | Private | Fifteenth, Mason | Dec 1777 sick absent; Jan 22, 1778 died. |
| Moseley, William | Captain | Seventh, Moseley | Dec 1777-April 1778 on furlough; May 1778. |

| Name | Rank | Company | Notes |
|---|---|---|---|
| Mosley/ Moseley, Joseph | Private | Fourteenth, Overton | Dec 1777-Jan 1778 on furlough in Virginia; Feb 1778. |
| Moss, Henry | 2nd. Lt. | Second, Taylor, W./ Upshaw | Dec 1777-June 1778; June transferred to Upshaw's Company. |
| Moss, John | Private | Second, Jones | Dec 1777 on command; Jan-June 1778. |
| Moss, Thomas | Private | Third/ Seventh, Mercer/ Powell | Dec 1777; Jan 1778 on command; Feb 1778; March 1778 on guard; May 1778 on command; June 1778 in Powell's Company. |
| Moss, Vester | Private | Third, Lee | Dec 1777 sick Virginia. |
| Mothersett/ Mothershead, Nathaniel/Natt. | Sergeant | First, Taylor/ Payne | Dec 1777-Feb 1778; March-May 1778 on command; March-June 1778, in Payne's Company. |
| Motley, William | Private | Second State, Taliaferro | July 1778 paid for 3 ½ months "15 April to the 1 of Aug." |
| Mott, Richard | Private | Second State, Quarles | April-June 1778. |
| Mount, Mathias | Private | Twelfth, Bowyer, T. | Dec 1777 on command; Jan 1778 sick in camp; Feb 1778 on command; March-May 1778. |
| Mountjoy, Alvin | 1st. Lt. | Third, Mercer | Dec 10, 1777 resigned. |
| Mountjoy, William | Paymaster | Third | Dec 1777-Jan 1778; Feb-March 1778 on furlough April-June 1778. |
| Mounts/Mountz, Richard | Private | Second, Calmes | Dec 1777-Feb 1778. |
| Moxley, George | Private | First State, Payne | Dec 1777-Feb 1778; March 1778 on guard; April 1778; May 1778 on command; June 1778. |
| Moxley/ Mocksly, Rhodom/ Rhodam | Sergeant/ Quartermaster | Second, Calmes | Dec 1777-Feb 1778; March promoted to Quartermaster; March-June 1778. Oath at Valley Forge on May 12, 1778, witnessed by Muhlenberg. |
| Muir/Muire, James | Private | Second State, Taliaferro | March 15-May 1, 1778; May 1778; June 1778 sick Valley Forge. |

| | | | |
|---|---|---|---|
| Mullen, Richard | Private | Second, Harrison | Dec 18, 1777 deserted. |
| Mullikin/ Mullican, John | Private | Sixth, Avery | Dec 1777; Jan 31, 1778 discharged. |
| Mullin, Daniel/Danl. | Private | Fifteenth, Harris | April 1778 on guard; May 1778. |
| Mullin/Mullen, John | Private | First State, Ewell, T. | Dec 1777-Feb 1778 sick in the Jersies; March 1778 sick present; April 1778 Princeton; May 1778 sick Princeton. |
| Mullin, John | Private | Fifteenth, Harris | March 1778 sick present. |
| Mullins/Mulins, David | Private | Fourteenth, Marks | Dec 1777 on guard; Jan 1778 hospital; Feb 1778 sick absent; March-June 1778. |
| Mullins/Mullin, Samuel | Corporal | First State, Lee | Dec 1777 sick; Jan 1778 sick at Yellow Springs; Feb 1778 roll shows he died in January. |
| Mumford, John | Private | Second State, Garnett | April 15-June 1778. |
| Mumford/ Monfoard, William | Private | Second State, Garnett | March 15-May 1, 1778; May-June 1778. |
| Munro, Mathew | Private | Fifteenth, Gregory | Dec 1777-Jan 1778; Feb 11, 1778 dead. |
| Munrow/ Munroe, John | Private | Twelfth, Bowyer, M. | May 1778 roll shows he was drafted for one year and was sick in the country. |
| Murdin/Murden, John | Private | Fifteenth, Grimes | Dec 1777-Jan 1778 sick Virginia. |
| Murdock, John | Private | Twelfth, Bowyer, M. | Feb 27, 1778 drafted for one year; April-May 1778. |
| Murdock, John | Private | Fifteenth, Mason | Dec 1777; died about Jany 2, 1778. |
| Murfrey, Daniel | Private | Fifteenth, Edmunds | Dec 1777. |
| Murfrey, John | Private | Fifteenth, Edmunds | Dec 1777. |
| Murfrey, Lemuel | Private | Fifteenth, Edmunds | Dec 1777 sick absent. |
| Murphey, John | Private | Third, Blackwell | Dec 23, 1777 discharged. |

| Name | Rank | Regiment, Company | Notes |
|---|---|---|---|
| Murphey/Murfey, John/John M. | Private | Twelfth, Casey | Dec 1777 sent to hospital; Jan-March 1778 at hospital; April-May 1778. |
| Murphey/Murfey, John | Private | Fourteenth, Jones | Jan 1778; Feb 1778 sick present; March 1778 on command; April-May 1778; June 1778 sick Valley Forge. |
| Murphey/Murfrey, John | Private | Fifteenth, Wills | Jan 1778; Feb 1778 on duty; March-April 1778; May 1778 on command. |
| Murphey, Lemuel | Private | Fifteenth, Wills | Jan-March 1778 sick absent; April 1778 on duty; May 1778. |
| Murphey/Murphy, Martain/Martin | Drummer | Twelfth, Wallace | Dec 1777-May 1778. |
| Murphey, Thomas | Private | Fourteenth, Conway | Aug 19, 1777 enlisted; Jan 1778 joined the regiment, sick in camp; Feb 1778 sick in hospital; March 10, 1778 deceased. |
| Murphy/Murpey, Danl./Dannel | Corporal | Fifteenth, Wills | Jan-Feb 1778; March 1778 sick present; April 1778; May 20, 1778 deserted. |
| Murphy/Murfey, Dennis/Deanis | Private | Fourteenth, Winston | Dec 1777-June 1778. |
| Murphy/Murphey, John | Private | Third, Blackwell | Dec 23, 1777 discharged. |
| Murphy, John | Private | Twelfth, Bowyer, T. | Dec 1777-March 1778; April-June 1778 on furlough. |
| Murphy, Lewis | Private | Third, Peyton, J. | Dec 1777-Jan 1778. |
| Murphy/Murfey, Owen | Private | Twelfth, Bowyer, T. | Dec 1777-May 1778 on furlough. |
| Murray/Murry, Duncan | Private | First State, Hamilton | Dec 1777-May 1778; June 1778 mustered deserted by mistake. |
| Murray/Murry, Francis | Private | Second State, Quarles | April-June 1778. |
| Murrah, George | Private | Second, Upshaw | Dec 1777. |
| Murray, James | Private | First State, Camp | Dec 1777 sick in ye country; Jan sick absent; Feb 10, 1778 died. |

| Name | Rank | Company | Notes |
|---|---|---|---|
| Murray, John | Private | Twelfth, Wallace | Dec 1777-March 1778 sent to hospital; April 1778 muster roll shows him deceased on Feb 24, 1778. |
| Murray/Murry, Richard | Private | Second, Sanford/Parker | Dec 1777-June 1778. From April on he appears in Parker's company. |
| Murrell, Thomas | Private | Sixth | May 1, 1778 drafted; June 1778. |
| Murrell, Wm. | Private | Sixth, Hockaday | Dec 1777 sick at Princetown. |
| Murrow, John | Private | Second, Parker | April 1778. |
| Murry/Murrey, James | Private | Third, Briscoe | Dec 1777-Jan 1778 on guard; Feb 5, 1778 discharged. |
| Muse, George | Corporal | Second, Upshaw | Dec 30, 1777 enlisted in the horse service. |
| Muse, George | Private | Twelfth, Ashby | Dec 1777-March sick in hospital; April-May 1778. |
| Muse, Richard/Richd. | 1st. Lt. | Fifteenth, Hull | Dec 1777-March 1778 on furlough; April 1778; May 1778 on command. |
| Musgrove/Musgroves, William | Corporal | Second State, Lewis | March 15-May 1, 1778, May 1778; June 1778 sick absent. |
| Mush, Robert/Robt. | Private | Fifteenth, Gray | Dec 1777 on guard; Jan 1778; Feb 1778 sick; March-April 1778; May 1778 sick present; June-July 1778 sick Valley Forge. |
| Mustoe/Mustor, Anthony | Sergeant | Seventh/Third, Posey/Sayers | Feb 27, 1778 enlisted; April-May 1778; June 1778 in Sayer's Company. |
| Nailor, Davis | Private | First, Cunningham | May 1778. |
| Nance/Nancy, Frederick | Corporal/Sergeant | Fifteenth, Wills | August 5, 1777 enlisted; April 1778; May 1778 promoted to Sergeant. |
| Nance/Nantz, Gibbs | Corporal | Fourteenth, Lambert | Dec 1777-Feb 1778; March 1778 hospital; April 1778 deceased. |
| Nance, Thomas | Private | First, Mennis | Dec 1777 deserted. |

| Name | Rank | Regiment/Company | Notes |
|---|---|---|---|
| Nance, Wm. | Private | Sixth, Massie | Dec 1777 prisoner. |
| Napp/Naph, John | Private | Twelfth, Vause | Dec 1777-May 1778. |
| Napper, John | Corporal | Twelfth, Bowyer, M. | March 1778 returned from the gallies March 20; April-May 1778. |
| Nash, Francis | Private | Third/Seventh, Mercer/Powell | Feb 12, 1778 enlisted; April-May 1778; June 1778 in Powell's Company. |
| Nash, Tarpley | Private | Second, Sanford/Parker | Dec 1777 hospital; Jan-June 1778. From April on he appears in Parker's company. |
| Naught, James | Private | First State, Hoffler | Dec 1777-June 1778. |
| Nauters, David | Private | First State, Camp | Dec 1777 sick Georgetown, Maryland; Jan-Feb 1778 sick absent. |
| Naylor, Samuel | Drum Major | First State, Brown | June 1778. |
| Neal/Neall, Henry/Heney | Private | Twelfth, Ashby | Dec 1777-Feb 1778 sick in hospital; March-May 1778. |
| Neal, John | Private | Second, Sanford | Dec 1777-Feb 1778; March 1778 died. |
| Neal/Neille, Wm. | Private | Fifteenth, Foster/Gray | Dec 1777-Jan 1778 sick absent; Feb 1778 sick, in Gray's Company; March 1778 sick absent; April 1778 sick Lancaster; May 1778. |
| Neaves, Daniel | Sergeant | Seventh, Lipscomb | Jan 1778; Feb 2, 1778 discharged. |
| Neaves, Daniel | Private | Fourteenth, Overton | Dec 1777 sick in hospital; Jan 1778 sick absent; March 1778 sick absent; April 1778. |
| Neebone/Kneebone, Arther/Arthur | Private | Fourteenth, Lambert | Dec 1777-March 1778 hospital; April-June 1778. |
| Neighbours, Nathaniel | Private | First, Cunningham | Feb 27, 1778 enlisted; July 1778 first appears on rolls. |
| Nelson, James | Private | Fourteenth, Winston | Feb 17, 1778 drafted; May-June 1778. |

| Name | Rank | Company | Notes |
|---|---|---|---|
| Nelson, John | 2nd. Lt. | Seventh, Young | Dec 1777-February 1778; March 1778 on furlough; April-May 1778. |
| Nelson, John | Private | Fifteenth, Hull | Dec 1777 on guard; Jan-Feb 1778; March-May 1778 on command; June 1778 "Missing since last March". |
| Nemo/Ninao, James | Private | First State, Brown | Dec 1777-Feb 1778. |
| Nettles, Vicarius/Viccarius | Private | Seventh, Young | Dec 1777 guard; Jan 1778; March 5, 1778 discharged. |
| Nettles, William | Private | Seventh, Young | Dec 1777-Jan 1778; Feb 28, 1778 discharged. |
| Nevill, John | Lt. Colonel | Twelfth | Dec 1777; Jan 1778 on furlough; Feb-May 1778. |
| Nevill, Presley | 1st. Lt. | Twelfth, Waggener | Dec 1777-Jan 1778 on command; Feb 1778 on command with the Marquis; March 1778 resigned Feb 1, 1778; April 1778 reported resigned through mistake; May 1778 on command; June 1778 aide-de-camp to the Marquis de la Fayette. |
| New, Jesse/Jese | Private | Sixth, Fox/Hockaday | April-May 1778; June 1778 on command. In April he appears on the payrolls of both companies. |
| Newberry, Henry | Private | First State, Camp | Dec 1777 sick Georgetown, Maryland; Jan-Feb 1778 sick absent. |
| Newcomb, Charles | Private | Seventh, Fleming | Dec 1777 sick in hospital; Jan 1778 hospital; Feb 18, 1778 discharged. |
| Newcomb, Joseph | Private | Seventh/Third, Hill | Dec 1777-Jan 1778 on furlough; April-June 1778 |
| Newcomb, Peter | Private | Second State, Taliaferro | Appears only on roll for March 15-April 15, 1778. |
| Newcomb, Solomon | Private | Seventh/Third, Fleming/Heth | Feb 17, 1778 enlisted; April 1778 sick present; May 1778; June 1778 sick Slotterdam, in Heth's Company. |

| Name | Rank | Regiment | Notes |
|---|---|---|---|
| Newcomb, Thomas | Corporal | Second State, Taliaferro | March 15-May 1, 1778; May-June 1778. |
| Newel, John | Corporal | Fifteenth, Mason | Dec 1777-Feb 1778; March-April 1778 sick in camp; May 1778. |
| Newell, John | Corporal | Fifteenth, Gregory | March-April 1778 sick in camp; June 1778 sick Valley Forge. |
| Newell, William/Wm. | Private | Sixth, Avery | Dec 1777-Jan 1778; Feb 8, 1778 discharged. |
| Newland, John | Private | Twelfth, Casey | Dec 15, 1777 deserted; April 1778 rejoined. |
| Newman, Edward | Private | Second State, Dudley | March 15-May 1, 1778; May-June 1778. |
| Newman/Numan, Joseph | Private | Fourteenth, Marks | Jan 6, 1778 enlisted; Jan-April 1778 on furlough; May-June 1778. |
| Newton, Benjm. | Private | Fifteenth, Gray | Feb 10, 1778 drafted; April 1778 under inoculation; May 1778 hospital Yellow Springs. |
| Newton, Thomas | Private | Second State, Taliaferro | March 15-May 1, 1778; May-June 1778. |
| Nicholas, Jesse | Private | Fifteenth, Gregory | June 1778 sick Valley Forge. |
| Nicholas, John | Captain | First State, Nicholas | Dec 1777-May 1778; June 1778 command with Col. Morgan. |
| Nicholas, William | Private | Second, Sanford/Parker | Dec 1777-June 1778. From April on he appears in Parker's company. |
| Nichols/Nickhals, Charles | Private | First, Scott | Dec 1777 on command; Jan-May 1778; June 1778 detached with Col. Morgan. |
| Nichols/Nicols, Jesse | Private | Fifteenth, Mason | Dec 1777 sick absent; Jan 1778 hospital; Feb-March 1778 at hospital; April-May 1778; June 1778 sick Valley Forge. |
| Nichols/Nichos, John | Private | Seventh/Third, Lipscomb | Dec 1, 1777 reenlisted for 3 years; Dec 1777-Jan 1778 on furlough; April 1778 on furlough; May-June 1778 |
| Nichols/Nicholes, William | Drummer | First State, Brown | Dec 1777-March 1778; April 17, 1778 discharged; May 1778. |

| Name | Rank | Regiment | Notes |
|---|---|---|---|
| Nichols/Nicholds, William | Private | Fourteenth, Lambert | Dec 1777; Jan-March 1778 hospital; April 1778 deceased. |
| Nicholson/Nickelson, John | Corporal | Third, Mercer | Dec 1777-Jan 1778. |
| Nicholson/Nickelson, Thomas | Private | Twelfth, Waggener | Dec 1777-May 1778 on command. |
| Nicholson, William/Wm. | Sergeant | Fifteenth, Grimes | Dec 1777-Jan 1778; Feb 1778 sick present; March 7, 1778 died. |
| Nixon/Nixen, John | Private | Fourteenth, Reid | Dec 1777; Feb 1778 sick in hospital; March 1778; May-June 1778. |
| Nobdy, Richard | Private | Fifteenth, Gregory | June 1778 Shaferstown. |
| Nocket/Thnocknett, Thomas | Private | First, Mennis | Jan-June 1778 on furlough. |
| Norman/Normond, Henry | Private | Twelfth, Vause | Dec 1777-Jan 1778; Feb 1778 sick in hospital; March-May 1778. |
| Norman, Wm. | Private | Third, Lee | Dec 1777-Jan 1778 absent wounded; paid to Feb 14, 1778. |
| Norrell/Norrel, Henry | Corporal | First, Mennis | Dec 1777-Feb 1778; March 1778 fatigue; April-June 1778. |
| Northcut, John | Private | Seventh, Fleming | Dec 1777 sick in hospital; Jan 1778 hospital; Feb 7, 1778 discharged. |
| Northcut, Terry | Private | Seventh, Fleming | Dec 1777 with Rifle Regt; Jan 1778 R. Regimt; Feb 26, 1778 discharged. |
| Norvell/Norvel, Hugh | Corporal | Fourteenth, Overton | Dec 1777; Jan 1778 sick present; Feb-May 1778; June 1778 on guard. |
| Nugent/Neugent, Jacob | Private/Corporal | First, Mennis | Dec 1777-April 1778; April 1778 promoted to Corporal; May 1778; June 1778 on command. |
| Nuland, John | Private | Twelfth, Casey | December 15, 1777 deserted; April 1778 joined; April-May 1778. |
| Nun, Walter | Private | Twelfth, Casey | April 1778; May 1778 under innoculation. |

| Name | Rank | Regiment, Company | Notes |
|---|---|---|---|
| Nunn, James | Corporal | Seventh, Hill | Dec 1777 on command; Jan 27, 1778 discharged. |
| Nunn, Moses | Private | Seventh, Hill | Dec 1777; jan 27, 1778 discharged. |
| Nunnally/ Nunley, John | Private | First, Cunningham | Feb 14, 1778 enlisted for 1 year; April 1778 under inoculation; May-June 1778. |
| Nunnally/ Nunally, Jos. | Private | Fifteenth, Foster | Dec 1777 sick absent; Jan 1778 dead. |
| Nunnelly/ Nunaley, John | Private | Fifteenth, Gray | Feb 1778; March 1778 sick in camp; April-May 1778 sick present; June-July 1778 sick Valley Forge. |
| Nunnelly/ Nunnalley, John J. | Private | Fifteenth, Harris | Jan 1778; Feb 1778 on guard; March 1778 on command; April 1778; May 1778 sick present; June 1778 sick Yellow Springs. |
| Nunnery/Nunry, Obediah | Private | Second State, Lewis | March 15-May 1, 1778; May-June 1778; July 1778 sick Valley Forge. |
| Oakley/Oajly, Elijah | Private | Seventh, Spencer | Dec 1777-Jan 1778 hospital; Feb 28, 1778 discharged. |
| Oakley/Oakly, George | Sergeant/ Private/ Sergeant | First State, Payne | Dec 1, 1777 reduced to Private; Jan 1778 promoted to Sergeant; Feb-March 1778; April 1778 on command; May-June 1778. |
| Oakley/Oakly, John | Private | Third, Peyton, V. | Dec 1777 waggoner absent; Jan 1778 wagoner; Feb 12, 1778 discharged. |
| Oast/Owst, George | Private | First State, Hoffler | Dec 1777-May 1778. |
| Oast, James/Jas. | Private | Fifteenth, Mason/ Gregory | Dec 1777 sick absent in Virginia; Jan 1778 sick Virginia; April 1778 sick in camp; May 1778; June 1778 at hospital, in Gregory's Company. |
| Oats, Leonard | Private | Twelfth, Madison | Dec 1777; Jan 1778 on command; Feb-March 1778; April 1778 on fatigue. |
| Obanion/ Obenion, Benjamin | Private | Third/ Seventh, Blackwell | Feb 18, 1778 drafted; May-June 1778. |
| Obarr see Auber | | | |

| Name | Rank | Regiment/Company | Notes |
|---|---|---|---|
| Obryant, Thomas | Private | Second, Willis | Dec 1777 deserted. |
| Odall/Odell, Rubin/Rueben | Private | Twelfth, Casey | Jan 24, 1777 enlisted; May 1, 1777 transferred to The Commander-in-Chief's Guard; April 1, 1778 returned from His Excellency's Guard; May 1778 on command. |
| O'Donnel, Frederick | Sergeant | Twelfth, Madison | Dec 1777-April 1778; May 1778 sick in camp. |
| O'Harrah/O'Harra, John | Private | Twelfth, Madison | Dec 1777-March 1778 sick in hospital; April-May 1778 on command. |
| Ogan/O'gan, William | Private | Twelfth, Waggener | Dec 1777-Feb 1778; March 1778 roll shows he deserted on Feb 21, 1778. |
| Ogilby, John | 1st. Lt. | Second, Taylor, W./Jones | Dec 1777; Jan 1778. In January he is in Jones' company; Jan 21, 1778 resigned. |
| Oldham, Conway/Conoway | 1st. Lt. | Twelfth, Waggener | Dec 1777-April 1778; May 1778 on furlough. |
| Oldham, Isick/Isaac | Private | First, Lewis | April 1778 "pay omitted from Sept 15, 1777;" April-June 1778. |
| Olive/Ollive, John | Private | First State, Hockaday | Dec 1777 orderly man hospital; Jan-Feb 1778 sick at Georgetown; April 1778 orderly man at Lancaster; May 1778 on command at Lancaster; June 1778. |
| Oliver/Olliver, James | Corporal | Sixth, Apperson | Dec 1777-Jan 1778 hospital; Feb 1778 "Omitted through mistake when mustered." paid for 22 days. |
| Oliver/Ollover, William | Private | Second State, Bressie | March 15-May 1, 1778; May-June 1778. |
| Oliver, William | Corporal | Third, Mercer | Jan 1778 |
| Ollard, Henry | Corporal/Sergeant | Fifteenth, Hull | Dec 1777; Jan 1778 promoted to Sergeant; Feb 1778 sick present; March 1778; April 1778 sick present; May 1778 sick in hospital; June 7, 1778 died. |

| Name | Rank | Regiment | Notes |
|---|---|---|---|
| Olothin/ Olocklin, John | Private | Second State, Dudley | March 15-May 1, 1778; May-June 1778. |
| Olphen/Olphin, Francis | Private | Second State, Spiller | March 15-May 1, 1778; May 1778; June 1778 sick Valley Forge. |
| Olverson see Alverson | | | |
| Oliver, Drury | 1st. Lt/, | Fourteenth, Reid | Dec 1777-June 1778. |
| Oliver, Will | Corporal | Third, Mercer | Dec 1777-Jan 1778. |
| Olvis see Alvis | | | |
| Olway see Alvey | | | |
| Ominet, Daniel | Private | First State, Nicholas | Dec 1777 orderly at hospital; Jan-Feb 1778 orderly man at hospital. |
| O'Neal, George | Private | Twelfth, Waggener | Dec 1777-Feb 1778 hospital; April 10, 1778 discharged. |
| O'Neal, John | Private | First State, Camp | Dec 1777 sick present; Jan-Feb 1778 sick absent; March 15, 1778 died. |
| Oneal, William | Private | First, Cunningham | Aug 1776 enlisted for 3 years; Dec 1777 sick at hospital; Jan-Feb 1778; March 1778 on guard; April 1778; May 1778. |
| O'Neall/ O'Neeal, George | Private | Twelfth, Waggener | Dec 1777-Feb 1778 hospital; March 1778; April 10, 1778 discharged. |
| Oniel/Onail, John | Private | Seventh/ Third, Crockett/ Sayers | March 19, 1778 enlisted; April 1778 sick present; May 1778 "Room of John Long" sick present; June 1778 with Col. Morgan, in Sayers' Company. |
| Orange/ Orrange, Lewis | Private | Seventh/ Third, Fleming/ Heth | Feb 12, 1778 enlisted; April 1778 sick present; May 1778; June 1778 on guard, in Heth's Company. |
| Ord/Orb, Robert/Robt. | Private | Fifteenth, Harris | Jan 1778 on command; Feb 1778 on guard; March-April 1778; May 1778 on command Lancaster. |
| Orr see Hoare | | | |

| Name | Rank | Company | Notes |
|---|---|---|---|
| Orr/Orre, Robert | Private | First, Cunningham | Aug 1777 enlisted for 3 years; Dec 1777; Jan 1778; Feb 2, 1778 deserted; April-June 1778. |
| Orr/Orre, Samuel | Private | Second State, Lewis | March 15-May 1, 1778, May 1778; June 1778; July 1778 sick Valley Forge. |
| Orr, Thomas | Private | Fourteenth, Lambert | Dec 1777 hospital; Feb 1778 deserted; May 1778; June 1778 sick Valley Forge |
| Orrell, Joseph | Private | Seventh, Lipscomb | Feb 14, 1778 enlisted for 1 year; April 1778. This man and John Orwell may be the same individual. |
| Orwell, John | Private | Seventh, Lipscomb | Enlisted for 1 year, May-June 1778. This man and Joseph Orrell may be the same individual. |
| Osburn, Elisha | Private | Twelfth, Waggener | Dec 1777 missing. |
| Osh/Owst, George | Fifer | First State, Hoffler | Dec 1777-June 1778. |
| Oslin see Aslin | | | |
| Oughterson, Hugh | Sergeant | Twelfth, Waggener | Dec 1777-April 1778 hospital; May 1778 comment illegible. |
| Ounstead/Oumstead, Jno. | Private | Sixth, Massie | Dec 1777 innoculated; Jan 1778 on command; Feb-May 1778; June 1778 guard. |
| Overstreet, John | Private/Corporal | Fourteenth, Lambert | Dec 1777-Feb 1778; March 1778 on guard; April 1778 sick present; May 1778; June 1778 sick Valley Forge. |
| Overton, Charles/Chrs. | Private | First, Lewis | Feb 7, 1778 enlisted; April-June 1778. |
| Overton, Clough | Private | Third, Powell | Dec 1777. |
| Overton, John | Adjutant | Fourteenth | Dec 1777. This may be the same man listed below. |
| Overton, John | Captain | Fourteenth, Overton | Dec 1777-May 1778; June 1778 sick absent. Oath at Valley Forge on May 14, 1778, witnessed by Muhlenberg. |
| Ovirby, Jeremiah | Private | Fourteenth, Jones | Jan-Feb 1778 sick at York. |

| Name | Rank | Regiment/Company | Notes |
|---|---|---|---|
| Owen/Owens, David | Private | Seventh/Third, Jouett/Hill | Feb 16, 1778 enlisted; April-May 1778; June 1778 in Hill's Company. |
| Owen, Godfrey | Private | Sixth, Apperson | March-April 1778; May 1778 sick present; June 1778 in hospital Yellow Springs. |
| Owen/Owin, James | Private | Fourteenth, Jones | Sept 18, 1777 enlisted; Dec 1777; Jan-Feb 1778 sick in hospital; March 8, 1778 died. |
| Owens, Charles | Corporal | First State, Hamilton | Dec 1777-May 1778; June 1778 sick absent. |
| Owens, Christopher | Sergeant | Fourteenth, Conway | Dec 1777; Jan 1778 on command; Feb-June 1778. |
| Owens/Owins, John | Private | First State, Hoffler | Dec 1777-Feb 1778. |
| Owens, Rolly | Private | Third/Seventh, Briscoe | June-Aug 1778 sick at Valley Forge. |
| Owens, William | Private | Second, Calmes | Dec 1777-June 1778. |
| Owings, John | Private | Second State, Quarles | April-June 1778. |
| Owins/Owin, John | Private | Second State, Lewis | March 15-May 1, 1778, May-June 1778. |
| Owins/Owin, Vinson/Vincent | Private | Second State, Lewis | June 1778 sick absent; July 1778 sick Valley Forge, "Omitted from April 15 to July 1." |
| Ownstead/Ounstead, John | Private | Sixth, Massie | Dec 1777-June 1778. |
| Oxford, Godfrey | Private | Fourteenth, Winston | Dec 1777 sick hospital; Jan 1778 sick in Jersey; Feb-March 1778 sick in hospital. |
| Oxford, Peter | Private | Second, Harrison | Dec 1777-June 1778. |
| Ozlen, James | Private | First State, Nicholas | Dec 1777; Jan 1778 sick; Feb 9, 1778 deceased. |
| Pace, Jesse | Private | Fourteenth, Marks | Dec 1777-March 1778; April 1778 Unkland hospital; May-June 1778 |
| Pace, Newsam/Nieusem | Sergeant | Sixth, Apperson | Dec 1777 on command; Jan 22, 1778 discharged; Feb 1778 paid for 22 days. |

| Name | Rank | Regiment, Company | Notes |
|---|---|---|---|
| Padington/ Paddington, John | Private | Fifteenth, Hull | Dec 1777-Feb 1778 on command; March 15, 1778 deserted; April 1778 sick present; May 1778 absent without leave; June 1778 sick Valley Forge. |
| Page, Jessey/Jesse | Private/ Corporal | Twelfth, Madison | Dec 1777; Jan 1778 sick in country; Feb 1, 1778 promoted to Corporal; Feb-March 1778; April 1778 on command. |
| Page, Robert/Robart | Private | First, Cunningham | Feb 12, 1778 enlisted for 1 year; April 1778 under inoculation; May-June 1778. |
| Pailor/Payler, Davis | Private | First, Cunningham | Feb 17, 1778 enlisted for 1 year; April 1778 under inoculation; May 1778 sick present; June 1778. |
| Pailor/Payler, John | Private | First, Cunningham | Feb 17 1778 enlisted for 1 year; April 1778 under inoculation; May 10, 1778 died. |
| Pain, Jacob | Sergeant | Fifteenth, Mason/ Gregory | Dec 1777-Jan 1778 sick absent; Feb-April 1778 hospital; May 1778; June 1778 sick Brunswick, in Gregory's Company. |
| Painter, John | Private | First, Scott | March 1778. |
| Palmer/Parmer, Charles | Fifer | Second State, Bernard | April-June 1778. |
| Palmer/Parmer, Henry/Henray | Private | Second, Harrison | Dec 1777-June 1778. |
| Palmer/Parmer, Jeffrey/Jesse | Private | Fifteenth, Gray | Dec 1777 on furlough; Jan-May 1778 on command. |
| Palmer, Thomas | Private | Fourteenth, Winston | Dec 1777 on baggage guard; Jan 1778 on command; Feb 1778 sick in hospital; April 1778 on command at hospital. |
| Panjay see Fanjoy | | | |
| Parajon, Molliston | Private | Seventh, Crockett | Dec 1777-Jan 1778 in R. Bat. |
| Parham, John | Private | Fifteenth, Edmunds | Dec 1777-March 1778 sick absent; April 1778 sick at hospital. |

| Name | Rank | Company | Notes |
|---|---|---|---|
| Parish/Parrish, William/Wm. | Private | First, Mennis | Dec 1777-March 1778 on furlough; April-May 1778; June 1778 on command. |
| Parker, Alexander | 1st. Lt./ Captain | Second, Sanford/ Parker | Dec 1777 on furlough; Jan-March 1778; April promoted to Captain effective Jan 7, 1778, and assumed command of Sanford's Company; April-June 1778. Oath at Valley Forge on May 12 1778, witnessed by Muhlenberg. |
| Parker, Edward | Private | Second, Harrison | Dec 1777-June 1778. |
| Parker, Edward/Edwd. | Private | Sixth, Hockaday | Dec 1777-Jan 1778; Feb 10, 1778 discharged. |
| Parker, John | Private | Second, Jones | Dec 1777-June 1778. |
| Parker, Matthew | Private | Fifteenth, Gregory | Dec 1777-March 1778 hospital; April 1778 muster roll shows he died Jan 20, 1778. |
| Parker, Richard | Lt. Col./ Colonel | Second/ First | Dec 1777-Feb 1778; March 1, 1778 promoted to Colonel of First Virginia, March-June 1778. Oath at Valley Forge on May 11, 1778, witnessed by Muhlenberg. |
| Parker, Robert | Corporal | Second State, Garnett | April 15-June 1, 1778; June 1778. |
| Parker/Parkis, Starling | Fifer | Fourteenth, Conway | Dec 1777; Jan 1778 sick in hospital; Feb 14, 1778 died. This man and the man below must be the same, but are listed in two different companies. |
| Parker, Sterling | Fifer | Fourteenth, Jones | Dec 1777; Jan 1778 sick in hospital; Feb 14, 1778 died. |
| Parker, Thomas | 2nd. Lt. | Second, Upshaw/ Harrison | Dec 1777-Jan 1778; Feb transferred to Harrison's Company; Feb-June 1778. Oath at Valley Forge on May 12, 1778, witnessed by Muhlenberg. |
| Parker, Thomas | Sergeant | Second, Upshaw | Dec 1777-Jan 1778. |
| Parker, William | Sergeant | First State, Ewell, T. | Dec 1777 sick at New Church; Jan 1778 dead. |

| Name | Rank | Regiment/Company | Notes |
|---|---|---|---|
| Parker, William | Private | First State, Payne | Dec 1777; Jan-Feb 1778 armourer; March-May 1778 on furlough. |
| Parkerson, Jacob | Private | Second State, Dudley | March 15-May 1, 1778; May-June 1778. |
| Parkerson/Parkinson, John | Private | Seventh/Third, Spencer/Lipscomb | March 6, 1778 enlisted for 3 years; April 1778 on scout; May 1778; June 1778 in Lipscomb's Company. |
| Parks, Barna | Private | Fourteenth, Lambert | Feb 23, 1778 enlisted; June 1778 lately joined, sick Valley Forge. |
| Parks/Parkes, Henry | Private | First State, Meriwether | Dec 1777-June 1778. |
| Parr, John | Private/Sergeant | Third, Arell | Feb 14, 1778 drafted; April 1778; May 1778 promoted to Sergeant. |
| Parrish/Parish, Henry | Sergeant | Second, Calmes | Dec 1777-June 1778. |
| Parrish/Parisk, Moses | Private | Seventh/Third, Moseley/Blackwell | Dec 1777-March 1778 on furlough; April-May 1778; June 1778 in Blackwell's Company. |
| Parrish/Parish, Nathaniel | Private | First State, Camp | Dec 1777 sick Fishwater Mills; Jan 5, 1778 died. |
| Parrish, William/Wm. | Sergeant | Sixth, Massie | Dec 1777 on command; Jan 1778; Feb 15, 1778 discharged. |
| Parrish, William/Wm. | Sergeant | Sixth, Hockaday | Dec 1777 reenlisted for 3 years, on furlough Virginia; Jan 1778 on furlough; Feb-May 1778; June 1778. |
| Parriss/Pariss, John | Private | Fifteenth, Hull | Dec 1777-Feb 1778; March 1778 sick present; April-May 1778. |
| Parrott/Parrot, George | Private | Second State, Lewis | March 15-May 1, 1778; May 1778; June 1778 sick absent. |
| Parsley, Hezekiah | Private | Sixth, Rose | Dec 1777-Jan 1778; Feb 1, 1778 discharged. |
| Parsley, Joel/Joseph | Private | Second State, Bressie | March 15-May 1, 1778, May 1778; June 1778 wounded Valley Forge. |
| Parsons/Passons, Abijah | Private | Second State, Bressie | May 1778 "Virginia last payroll;" June 1778. |

| Name | Rank | Regiment, Company | Notes |
|---|---|---|---|
| Parsons/ Passons, Woodson/ Woodron | Private | First, Payne/ Lawson | Feb 5, 1778 enlisted; April-May 1778; June 1778 on command, in Lawson's Company. |
| Pasley, Frederick | Private | Fifteenth, Grimes | Dec 1777-Jan 1778 sick Virginia. |
| Pasley, Thomas/Thos. | Private | Sixth, Massie | Dec 1777 in hospital; Jan 1778; Feb 16, 1778 discharged. |
| Paterson/ Patterson, James | Private | Twelfth, Waggener | Dec 1777-March 1778; April 1778 on fatigue; May 1778 hospital. |
| Paterson/ Patterson, Perry | Private | Second, Taylor, F. | Dec 1777 on furlough; Jan-April 1778. |
| Patman/Patmon, Watson | Private | First, Lewis | Feb 7, 1778 enlisted; April-May 1778; June 1778 sick at Valley Forge. |
| Patterson, Tilman/Tilmon | Private | Sixth, Fox | Dec 1777-Jan 1778; Feb 17, 1778 discharged. |
| Patton/Patten, Alexander | Private | Third/ Seventh, Peyton, V./ Peyton, J. | Dec 1777 on furlough Virginia; Jan-March 1778 on furlough; April 1778 sick in camp; May 1778 sick absent; June 1778 Yellow Springs, in J. Peyton's Company. |
| Patton, George | Sergeant | Third, Mercer | Dec 1777-Jan 1778. |
| Patterson, Philip | Private/ Sergeant | Seventh/ Third, Webb/Young | Enlisted for 3 years. Dec 1777-February 1778 on furlough; April-May 1778; June 1, 1778 promoted to Sergeant, in Young's Company. |
| Patterson, Richard | Private | Seventh, Webb | Jan 1778; February 1778 discharged. |
| Patillo/Pattillo, James | Corporal/ Sergeant | Fourteenth, Reid | Dec 1777 hospital; Jan 1778 sick at Reading; Feb-March 1778; May-June 1778. Promoted to Sergeant in June. |
| Pavery, Herbert | Private | Second, Taylor, W. | Dec 1777-June 1778. |
| Paylor, William | Private | Fourteenth, Reid | Aug 11, 1777 enlisted; Jan 1778 sick in camp. |
| Payne/Paine, Anthony/Anty. | Private | Fifteenth, Gray | Feb-April 1778 on command. |

| Name | Rank | Regiment/Company | Service |
|---|---|---|---|
| Payne/Payn, Nathl | Private | Seventh, Jouett | Dec 1777-Jan 1778 on command with sick; Feb 15, 1778 discharged. |
| Payne, Tarlton | 1st. Lt./ Captain | First, Cummings/ Payne | Dec 1777-Feb 1778; Feb 4, 1778 promoted to Captain and assumed command of Taylor's Company; March-June 1778. Oath at Valley Forge on May 18, 1778, witnessed by Muhlenberg. |
| Payne, William | Captain | First State, Payne | Dec 1777; Jan-May 1778 on command in Virginia. |
| Pea/Pee, Thomas | Private | First State, Meriwether | Dec 1777-June 1778. |
| Peace, John | Private | Seventh, Lipscomb | Jan 1778; Feb 2, 1778 discharged. |
| Peace, Samuel | Sergeant | First State, Brown | Dec 1777-May 1778. |
| Peake/Peek, David | Private | Sixth, Hockaday | Dec 1777-Feb 1778; March 16, 1778 discharged. |
| Pearce, Lovell/Louvil | Sergeant | Second State, Garnett | March 15-May 1, 1778; May-June 1778. |
| Pearce/Pierce, William/Wm. | Drummer | Fifteenth, Edmunds/ Gregory | Dec 1777-March 1778; April 1778 sick in camp; May 1778; June 1778 sick Valley Forge, in Gregory's Company. |
| Pearman, Harrison | Private | Sixth, Garland | April-May 1778; June 1778 on guard. |
| Pearman, William | Sergeant | Third, Peyton | Feb 14, 1778 appointed; April-May 1778; June 1778 on command; July 1778 sick at Valley Forge. |
| Pearson, Jona. | Private | Sixth, Massie | Jan 1778 discharged. |
| Peay, Elius | Sergeant | Fifteenth, Gray | Dec 1777-Jan 1778 sick absent; Feb 1778 dead, time uncertain. |
| Pedeford/ Peddeford, Edward | Private | Seventh/ Third, Fleming/ Young | Feb 13, 1778 enlisted; April-May 1778 sick present; June 1778 on guard; in Young's Company. |
| Pebble, Andrus/Andrew | Private | Fifteenth, Hull | April-May 1778. |

| Name | Rank | Regiment, Company | Service |
|---|---|---|---|
| Peebles/Peables, Stephen | Private | Fourteenth, Jones | Sept 18, 1777 drafted; April-May 1778; July 1778 sick Valley Forge. |
| Peerman/Purman, Michael/Meeheal | Private | First, Payne | Feb 5, 1778 enlisted; April 1778; May 15, 1778 died. |
| Pegram, Baker | Sergeant | Sixth, Fox | Dec 1777-Jan 1778; Feb 11, 1778 discharged, |
| Peirce/Pierce, Edward | Private | First State, Crump | May-June 1778. |
| Peirce/Pearce, Penuel | Private | First, Mennis | Feb 7, 1778 enlisted; April 1778; May 1778 sick present; June 1778 sick at Valley Forge. |
| Pelham, Charles | Captain | First, Pelham | Dec 1777 sick absent; Jan 1778 on command; Feb-June 1778. Oath at Valley Forge on May 11, 1778, witnessed by Muhlenberg. |
| Pemberton, Henry | Corporal | Sixth, Avery | Dec 1777; Jan 31, 1778 discharged. |
| Pemberton, William | Private | First State, Meriwether | Dec 1777-March 1778. |
| Penery/Pennery, Thomas | Private | Twelfth, Madison | Dec 1777-Jan 1778; Feb 1778 on command; March-April 1778 sick in camp. |
| Pengier, Kellin | Drummer | First, Mennis | June 1778. |
| Penington/Penington, Daniel/Danl. | Private | Third, Blackwell | Dec 1777-June 1778 on command. |
| Pennell/Pennill, Thomas | Private | Second, Harrison | Dec 1777-June 1778. |
| Penney/Penny, James/Jas. | Drummer | Sixth, Hockaday | Feb 28, 1778 drafted; April-May 1778; June 1778 in hospital Yellow Springs; Sept 1778 deceased. |
| Penny/Penney, John | Private/Fifer | Second State, Bressie | March 15-May 1, 1778, May-June 1778; promoted to Fifer on June 1. |
| Perkins, Charles | Private | Seventh, Jouett | Dec 1777-Jan 1778 sick in hospital; Feb 11, 1778 discharged. |

| Name | Rank | Company | Service |
|---|---|---|---|
| Perkins/Pirkins, Hardin | 2nd. Lt. | Sixth, Hockaday | Dec 1777-Jan 1778; Feb 1778 recruiting; March 1778 on furlough; April 25, 1778 resigned. |
| Perkins, Joseph | Private | First State, Brown | Dec 1777 drafted. |
| Perkins, Joshua | Private | Fifteenth, Edmunds | Dec 1777 sick present. He and the man below are probably the same individual. |
| Perkins/Purkins, Joshua | Private | Fifteenth, Wills | Jan-Feb 1778; March 1778 on guard; April 1778 on command; May 1778. |
| Perremon/Parimon, Banoni/Bennony | Fleming | Fourteenth, Conway | Dec 1777 on duty; Jan 1778 on command; Feb-March 1778; April 1778 on command; May-June 1778. |
| Perris, George | Private | Fourteenth, Lambert | Aug 1777 roll shows he deserted June 2, 1777 in Virginia; June 1778 sick Valley Forge, |
| Perry, Gregory | Private | Seventh/Third, Webb/Young | Jan 1778; Feb 1778 on command; April-June 1778 waggoner; June 1778 in Young's Company. |
| Perry, Henry | Private | Seventh, Spencer | Enlisted for 3 years; Dec 1777 on command; Jan 1778 sick present; April 1778 Generals guard. He transferred to The Commander-in-Chief's guard on March 19, and served there until Jan 31, 1780. |
| Perry/Perey, John/Jno. | Private | Sixth, Hockaday | Dec 1777 reenlisted for three years; on furlough in Virginia; Jan-May 1778 on furlough; June 1778. |
| Perry, Robert | Private | Second State, Bernard | April-May 1778; June 1778 on guard. |
| Perry, William | Private | Sixth, Garland | April-May 1778; June 1778 sick at Princetown. |
| Perryman, Philip | Private | First State, Crump | Dec 1777-June 1778. |
| Peters/Peaters, Anthony/Anthoney | Private | First State, Ewell, T. | Dec 1777; Jan 1778 sick Yellow Springs; Feb 1778 Yellow Springs hospital; March-June 1778. |

| | | | |
|---|---|---|---|
| Peters, John/Jno. | Private | Sixth, Hockaday | Dec 1777 sick at Bethlehem; Jan-March 1778 sick absent; April-June 1778. |
| Peters/Peeters, Jonas/Jones | Private | Twelfth, Waggener | Dec 1777-March 1778; April 10, 1778 discharged. |
| Peterson, John | Private | Twelfth, Bowyer, T. | Dec 1777 sick absent; Jan 1778 on guard; Feb-May 1778. |
| Pettiford/ Pettyford, Drury/Drewry | Private | Second State, Dudley | March 15-May 1, 1778; May-June 1778. |
| Pettiford/ Petiford, Elias | Private | Second State, Dudley | March 15-May 1, 1778; May-June 1778. |
| Pettigrew/ Pettierew, Mathew | Private | Fourteenth, Lambert | Feb 23, 1778 enlisted; June 1778 lately joined, sick Valley Forge. |
| Pettit, James | Private | Second State, Bernard | April-June 1778. |
| Petty/Petey, William | Private | Fourteenth, Winston | Dec 1777; Jan 1778 on guard; Feb-June 1778. |
| Pettypool/ Petty Pool, Colwell | Private | Sixth, Avery | Dec 1777-Jan 1778; Feb 15, 1778 discharged. |
| Pew, Thomas | Private | Second, Calmes | Dec 1777-March 1778; April 1778 deceased at the hospital. |
| Peyton/Payton, John | Captain | Third/ Seventh, Peyton, J. | Dec 1777; Jan-March 1778 on furlough; April-June 1778. |
| Peyton/Payton, Valentine | Captain | Third, Peyton, V. | Dec 1777-Jan 1778; Feb-March 1778 on command in Virginia; April-May 1778. |
| Phambrough see Farnbrow | | | |
| Pharis see Faris | | | |
| Pharoah/ Farough, Manuel | Private | Fifteenth, Hull | April 1778; May 1778 hospital Yellow Springs. |
| Phears/Phearce, Jonathan/ Jonothan | Sergeant | Sixth, Apperson | Dec 1777 hospital Penns; Jan-Feb 1778. "Time To Serve To March 24, 1778." |
| Phelps, Edward | Private | Third, Peyton, J. | Dec 1777-Jan 1778 sick present. |

| | | | |
|---|---|---|---|
| Phelps, William | Private | Second State, Dudley | April 8, 1778 died. |
| Philberts, Obediah | Private | Third, Lee | Dec 1777-Jan 1778 sick at Reading; paid to Feb 14, 1778. |
| Philips, Isick/Isaac | Private | Seventh/ Third, Crockett/ Young | March 19, 1778 enlisted; April 1778 sick present; May 1778; June 1778 sick Valley Forge, in Young's Company. |
| Philips, Larkin | Private | Second State, Quarles | April-June 1778. |
| Philips/Phillips, Robert | Fifer | Sixth, Hockaday | Dec 1777 in the country waiting upon the sick; Jan 1778; Feb 10, 1778 discharged. |
| Philkins, John | Private | Third/ Seventh, Peyton, J. | June 1778. |
| Phillips, Basdale | Private | Fourteenth, Winston | Oct 1, 1777 enlisted; March 1778 has joined the regiment; April 1778 sick present; May 1778; June 1778 sick Valley Forge. |
| Phillips, John | Private | First, Mennis | Dec 1777 sick at Princeton; Jan 1778 sick in the hospital; Feb 1778 discharged. |
| Phillips, John | Private/ Corporal | Second, Taylor, W. | Dec 1777 hospital; Jan-Feb 1778; March promoted to Corporal; March-June 1778. |
| Phillips, John | Private | Twelfth, Casey | April 1778; May 1778 in hospital near camp. |
| Phillips/Philips, Levi/Levy | Private | Second, Willis | Dec 1777-June 1778. |
| Phillips, Phillip | Private | Fourteenth, Winston | Oct 23, 1777 enlisted; April 1778; May 1778 sick present; June 10, 1778 died. |
| Phillips, Richard | Sergeant | Fourteenth, Overton | Dec 1777 on command; Jan-May 1778; June 1778 on command. |
| Phillips, Thomas | Private | Second State, Dudley | March 15-May 1, 1778; May 1778; June 1778 sick absent; July 1778 sick Valley Forge. |
| Phillyoung/ Fillyoung, George | Private | Second State, Bernard | May 1778; June 1778 sick Valley Forge. |

| Name | Rank | Regiment/Company | Dates |
|---|---|---|---|
| Pickells, Jno. | Private | Sixth, Massie | Dec 1777. |
| Picket/Pickit, Francis | Private | Second State, Spiller | March 15-May 1, 1778; May 1778; June 1778 sick Monmouth. |
| Picket/Pickit, George | Drummer | Second State, Spiller | March 15-May 1, 1778; May-June 1778. |
| Picket/Pickit, John | Private | First, Mennis | Dec 1777; Jan-June 1778 on furlough. |
| Pickett, James | Private | First State, Lee | Dec 1777-Feb 1778; March 11, 1778 discharged. |
| Pickrell/Pickreal, Samuel | Fleming | First State, Ewell, T. | June 1778. |
| Pierce, James | Private | Fifteenth, Gregory | Dec 1777-March 1778 hospital. |
| Pierce/Peirce, John, Sr. | Private | Fifteenth, Gregory | Dec 1777-March 1778 hospital; April 1778 sick present; May 1778 convalescent; June 1778 sick Valley Forge. |
| Pierce/Peirce, John, Jr. | Private | Fifteenth, Gregory | Dec 1777-Feb 1778 hospital; March-April 1778; May 1778 sick present; June 1778 sick Valley Forge. |
| Pierson, Charles | Corporal | First, Taylor/Payne | Dec 1777-Jan 1778; Feb-April 1778 on furlough; May 1778; June 1778 on command, in Payne's Company. |
| Pierson/Pierson, Shadrack/Shadrick | Private | First, Taylor/Payne | Dec 1777-June 1778. In June he is in Payne's company. |
| Pigman, Bean | Private/Sergeant | Twelfth, Wallace | Dec 1777-Feb 1778; March 1778 promoted to Sergeant; March-April 1778 sick in camp; May 1778. |
| Pigman/Piggman, Samuel | Private | Twelfth, Vause | Dec 1777 sick in camp; Jan 1778; Feb 1778 "Dyed 26 of Feb 78". |
| Piles, Richard | Sergeant | Twelfth, Bowyer, T. | Dec 1777; Jan 1778 at hospital; Feb-May 1778; June 1778 Assistant to the Forage Master. |

| | | | |
|---|---|---|---|
| Piles, William | Private | Seventh/Third, Moseley/Blackwell | Dec 1777-March 1778 on furlough; April-May 1778 sick in Virginia; June 1778. |
| Pilkinton/Pelkinton, Drury | Private | Second, Upshaw | Feb 14, 1778 drafted; April 1778; June 1778 sick Coryell's Ferry. |
| Pines, Lewis | Private | Second, Taylor, F. | Dec 1777 hospital; Jan 1778. |
| Pingo, Killing | Drummer | First, Mennis | June 1778. |
| Pinn, Thomas | Private | First State, Crump | Dec 1777; Jan 11, 1778 deceased. |
| Pinner, William | Private | Second State, Lewis | March 15-May 1, 1778; May-June 1778. |
| Pinnig, James | Drummer | Sixth, Apperson | Feb 18, 1778 drafted; April 1778. |
| Piper, John | 2nd. Lt./1st. Lt. | First State, Payne/Hamilton | Dec 1777; Jan 1778 sick absent; Feb 1778; March 1778 on command; April-June 1778. He is listed as Regimental Quartermaster on the June 1778 payroll. H also appears as being promoted to 1st Lt. and moved to Hamilton's company. |
| Piper, William | Corporal | First State, Payne | Dec 1777 sick in hospital; Jan 1778; Feb 1778 on guard; March-April 1778; May 1778 on command. |
| Pitman, Isick/Isaac | Private | Twelfth, Wallace | Dec 1777-March 1778 sent to hospital; April 1778 roll shows him as deceased on Nov 25, 1777. |
| Plant, Williamson | Private | Fourteenth, Winston | Dec 1777-Jan 1778 sick in Virginia; Feb 1778. |
| Plowman/Ploughman, Robert/Robt. | Drummer/Drum Major | First, Cunningham | Aug 1776 enlisted for duration of war; Dec 1777-March 1778; March 1778 promoted to Drum Major; April-May 1778; June 1778 sick Valley Forge. |
| Plummer, Robert | Corporal | Second State, Bernard | May-June 1778. |

| Name | Rank | Unit | Notes |
|---|---|---|---|
| Poe, John | Private | Second State, Garnett | March 15-May 1, 1778, May-June 1778. |
| Poe/Powe, Thomas | Private | First State, Ewell, T. | Dec 1777; Jan 1778 Yellow Springs; Feb 1778 Yellow Springs hospital; March-May 1778 sick Yellow Springs; June 1778. |
| Poe, Virgil | Private | Second, Upshaw | Dec 1777 hospital; Jan 1778. |
| Poe, William | Private | Second State, Garnett | March 15-May 1, 1778, May-June 1778. |
| Poindexter, Jacob | Sergeant | Sixth, Massie | Dec 1777-Jan 1778; Feb 1778 discharged, |
| Poindexter/ Pondexter, Jonathan | Sergeant | Sixth, Garland | Dec 1777-Jan 1778; Feb 19, 1778 discharged. |
| Pointer, William | Ensign/ 2nd Lt. | Fourteenth, Thweatt | Promoted to 2nd Lt. in December; Dec 1777-Jan 1778; Feb 1778 on furlough; March 1778; April 1778 on furlough; May 1778 on command; June 1778. Oath at Valley Forge on May 11, 1778, witnessed by Muhlenberg. |
| Polke, Robert | Private | Seventh, Young | Dec 21, 1777 to Lt. Horse. |
| Pollard, Absalom | Corporal | First State, Camp | Dec 1777 skh; Jan-March 1778 sick absent; April-June 1778. |
| Pollard, Hezekiah/ Hezeki | Private | Fourteenth, Winston | Dec 1777 sick in hospital; Jan 1778 sick absent; Feb-March 1778 S. H. |
| Pollard, James | Private | Seventh, Hill | Dec 1777-Jan 1778; Feb 2, 1778 discharged. |
| Pollard, Samuel | Private | Second State, Taliaferro | March 15-May 1, 1778; May 1778; June 1778 sick Valley Forge. |
| Pollock, James | Private | Third/ Seventh, Briscoe | Jan 3, 1778 drafted; June 1778 bullock guard. |
| Pondexter, Gabriel | Private | Fourteenth, Marks | Dec 1777 taking smallpox; Jan 1778 sick in hospital; Feb 1778 sick absent. |

| Name | Rank | Regiment/Company | Service |
|---|---|---|---|
| Pool, Baxter | Private/Corporal | Fourteenth, Winston | Dec 1777-Jan 1778; Feb 1778 on command; March 1778 promoted to Corporal; March-June 1778. |
| Pool, Dudley | Private | Seventh, Fleming | Dec 1777; Jan 1778 sick present; Feb 28, 1778 discharged. |
| Pool, Edward | Corporal | First State, Hoffler | Dec 1777-June 1778. |
| Pool, Henry | Private | Seventh/Third, Posey/Briscoe | Feb 27, 1778 enlisted; April-May 1778 on guard; June 1778 in Briscoe's Company. |
| Pool, Jacob | Private | Third/Seventh, Peyton, V. | Dec 1777; Jan 1778 on command; Feb-May 1778; June 1778 guard, in J. Peyton's Company. |
| Pool, John | Private | Seventh, Third, Fleming/Heth | Feb 16, 1778 enlisted; April-May 1778 sick present; June 1778 in Heth's Company. |
| Pool/Poul, Leban | Sergeant | Fourteenth, Winston | Dec 1777-April 1778; May 25, 1778 deceased. |
| Poole/Pool, Henry | Private | Seventh, Posey | Feb 27, 1778 enlisted; April 1778 guard; May 1778 on guard |
| Pope, Edmund | Private | Fifteenth, Wills | Jan 1778; Feb-March 1778 sick absent; April 1778 muster roll shows he died on Jan 7, 1778. |
| Pope, Humphrey/Umphrey | Private | Second State, Garnett | April 15-June 1, 1778; June 1778. |
| Pope, Joseph | Private | Sixth | June 1778 |
| Poppin see Toppin | | | |
| Porter, Daniel | Corporal | First State, Crump | Dec 1777-June 1778. |
| Pope, Thos. | Private | Fifteenth, Gray | Dec 1777-Jan 1778 on command; Feb 1778; March 1778 on guard; April 1778; May 1778 hospital Yellow Springs. |
| Porter, Ely/Eli | Private | Twelfth, Vause | Dec 1777-Jan 1778; Feb 1778 on guard; March-May 1778. |
| Porter, John | Corporal | Second, Taylor, W. | Dec 1777 sick hospital; Jan 1778; Feb 5, 1778 discharged. |
| Porter, Thomas | Private/Corporal | Second, Taylor, W. | Dec 1777-June 1778. Promoted to Corporal in March. |

| Name | Rank | Regiment/Company | Notes |
|---|---|---|---|
| Porter, William | Ensign | Third, Taylor, W. | Dec 1777-June 1778. Oath at Valley Forge on May 12, 1778, witnessed by Muhlenberg. |
| Porter, William | Private | First State, Crump | Dec 1777-May 1778; June 1778 sick absent. |
| Porter, William | 2nd. Lt. | Twelfth, Bowyer, T. | Jan 27, 1778 joined; Jan 1778-May 1778. |
| Portis/Pottress, Kirby/Kerby | Private | Fifteenth, Gray | Dec 1777-Feb 1778; March 1778 sick in camp; April 1778; May 1778 sick present; June 1778 sick Valley Forge. |
| Posey, Thomas | Captain/Major | Seventh/Second | Dec 1777-Jan 1778 on furlough; April 30, 1778 promoted to Major of the Second Virginia. |
| Posey, Wm. | Private | Third/Seventh, Mercer Powell | Dec 1777-March 1778 sick present; April 1778 sick at Lancaster; May 1778 sick present; June 1778 left Lancaster, in Powell's Company. |
| Potter, Thomas | Private | Seventh, Moseley | Dec 1777-March 1778 on furlough; March 1, 1778 deserted. |
| Pough, Michael | Private | Twelfth, Vause | Dec 1777-Feb 1778; March 1778 on guard; April-May 1778. |
| Pound, William | Corporal | First State, Camp | Dec 1777 sick Virginia; Jan-March 1778 off Virginia; April-June 1778. |
| Pounds, Samuel | Private | Seventh, Moseley | Dec 1777-Jan 1778 sick in hospital; Feb 11, 1778 died. |
| PowellBenjamin | Private | Third, Peyton, V. | Dec 3, 1777 discharged. |
| Powell/Powel, Francis | Private | First, Mennis | Dec 1777; Jan-March 1778 on furlough; April 1778. |
| Powell/Powel, Richard | Private | Twelfth, Waggener | Dec 1777-Jan 1778 hospital; March 1778; April 10, 1778 discharged. |
| Powell, Robert | Captain | Third, Powell | Dec 1777-Jan 1778; Feb-April 1778 on furlough; May-June 1778. |
| Powell/Powel, Samuel | Private | Twelfth, Waggener | Dec 1777; Jan 1778 sick in camp; Feb 1778 roll shows him as deceased March 6, 1778. |
| Powell, Thomas Sr. | Private | First, Pelham | Dec 1777 sick hospital; Feb 15, 1778 discharged. |

| Name | Rank | Regiment/Company | Notes |
|---|---|---|---|
| Powell/Powel, Thomas Jr. | Private | First, Pelham | Dec 1777 confined in provost; Jan 1778 prisoner; Feb 15, 1778 discharged. |
| Powell, William | Private | Seventh/Third, Lipscomb | Feb 14, 1778 enlisted for 1 year; April-June 1778. |
| Powers, Bernard/Barnett | Private | Seventh/Third, Lipscomb | Feb 14, 1778 enlisted for 1 year; April-June 1778. |
| Powers, John | Private | First State, Hoffler | Dec 1777-May 1778. |
| Powers, John | Private | First State, Meriwether | Dec 1777-Feb 1778; March 14, 1778 died. |
| Powers, Lewis | Private | First State, Camp | Dec 20, 1777 died. |
| Powers, William | Private | Second State, Bressie | March 15-May 1, 1778, May-June 1778. |
| Poythress/Poythross, David | Private | Fifteenth, Foster/Gray | Dec 1777-Jan 1778 sick absent; Feb 1778 sick, in Gray's Company; March-April 1778 sick absent; May 17, 1778 died. |
| Prake, James | Private | Second, Harrison | On April 1778 payroll he was paid from May 1, 1777 to May 1, 1778; May 1778; June 1778 sick Valley Forge. |
| Prather/Prater, John Smith | Private | Twelfth, Bowyer, M. | Dec 1777-March 1778 sick in hospital; April 1778 muster roll shows he died on Jan 6, 1778. |
| Pratt, James | Private | Seventh, Fleming | Dec 1777 on furlough Virginia; Jan 1778 Virginia; Feb 13, 1778 discharged. |
| Pray/Ray, Jesse | Private | Fifteenth, Grimes | Feb 11, 1778 drafted; April 1778; May 1778 sick present; June-July 1778 sick Valley Forge. |
| Prentis/Prentice, John | Private | First, Scott | Dec 1777-Feb 1778; March 1778 sick present; April-May 1778; Jan 1778 on furlough. |
| Preston, Daniel | Private | Third/Seventh, Briscoe | Dec 1777-March 1778 on furlough; April-May 1778; June 1778 on command. |
| Preston, Joel | Private | Fourteenth, Lambert | Feb 23, 1778 enlisted; June 1778 lately joined, sick Valley Forge. |

| Name | Rank | Regiment | Notes |
|---|---|---|---|
| Preston/ Presting, Nathan/Nathing | Private | Fourteenth, Lambert | Dec 1777; Jan 1778 on guard; Feb-April 1778; May 1778 on guard; June 1778. |
| Prewitt/Prewit, Richard | Private | Fourteenth, Reid | Feb 18, 1778 drafted; May 1778 sick present; June 1778 sick Valley Forge; July 15, 1778 deceased. |
| Price, David | Corporal | Third, Mercer | Dec 1777-Jan 1778 sick present. |
| Price, Francis | Private | Fifteenth, Harris | Jan 1778; Feb-April 1778 sick present; May 1778 sick present. |
| Price, George | Private | Second State, Bressie | March 15-May 1, 1778, May-June 1778. |
| Price, Jacob | Private | Seventh, Posey | Dec 1777-Jan 1778 on furlough; Feb 24, 1778 discharged. |
| Price, James | Private | Twelfth, Casey | Dec 1777 sent to hospital; Jan-April 1778; May 1778 in hospital near camp. |
| Price, John | Private | Second, Harrison | Dec 1777-May 1778; June 1778 Princeton Hospital. |
| Price, Richard | Private | Second, Harrison | Dec 1777. |
| Price, Richard | Sergeant | Seventh, Spencer | Dec 1777-Jan 1778 on furlough Virginia; Feb 13, 1778 discharged. |
| Price, Thomas | Private | Fourteenth, Reid | Dec 1777 hospital; Jan 1778 sick; Feb 9, 1778 deceased. |
| Price, William/Wm. | Sergeant/ Quartermaster Sergeant | First, Mennis | April-May 1778; June 1778 promoted to Quartermaster Sergeant. |
| Priddy/Prity, Richard/Richd. | Private | First, Mennis | Jan 1778 on furlough, omitted to be drawn for whilst in Virginia; Feb 1778; March 1778 on command; April-May 1778; June 1778 sick Valley Forge. |
| Pride, Habakuk | Private | First State, Brown | June 1778. |
| Primm, James | Quartermaster Sergeant | Third | Dec 1777-Jan 1778; Feb 1, 1778 discharged. |
| Pritchet/Pritchett, Andrew | Private | Fourteenth, Overton | Dec 1777; Jan 26, 1778 discharged. |

266

| | | | |
|---|---|---|---|
| Pritchet/ Pritchett, Peter | Private | Fourteenth, Jones | Jan-Feb 1778 sick Alexandria; March April 1778 sick present; May 1778. |
| Pritchett/ Pritchet, John | Private | Seventh/ Third, Young | Dec 1777-April 1778 on furlough; May 1778; June 1778 attending Dr. Slaughter. |
| Pritton, Henry | Sergeant | Fifteenth, Edmunds | Dec 1777. |
| Privett, Samuel | Private | Second, Calmes | March 1778. |
| Procter, Christopher | Private | Sixth, Fox | Dec 1777 in hospital; Jan 1778; Feb 6, 1778 discharged. |
| Proctor/Procter, Isick/Isaac | Private | Fifteenth, Hull | Dec 1777-March 1778; April 1778 sick present; May 1778; June 1778 sick Valley Forge. |
| Prosser/Propes, Otey/Oley | Private | Seventh/ Third, Fleming/Heth | Feb 11, 1778 enlisted; April, 1778 sick present; May 1778; June 1778 in Heth's Company. |
| Proton/Pruden, Henry | Sergeant | Fifteenth, Wills | Feb 1778 on guard; March 1778 on command; April-May 1778. |
| Pryor/Pryer, David | Private | Seventh/ Third, Fleming/Heth | Feb 19, 1778 enlisted; May 1778 sick present; June 1778, in Heth's Company. |
| Pryor, Jacob | Private | Twelfth, Bowyer, T. | Dec 1777; Jan-Feb 1778 sick absent; March 1778 sick in hospital; April-May 1778. |
| Pryor/Prior, William/Wm. | Sergeant | Fifteenth, Gregory | Dec 1777 in the country; Jan 1778; Feb 1778 on command; March-June 1778. |
| Pruit/Frewit, Jordan | Private | First, Pelham | Dec 1777 sick hospital; Jan 1778 hospital; Feb 1778 sick at Yellow Springs; March 12, 1778 died at Yellow Springs. |
| Puckett, Richard | Private | Second, Taylor, W. | Dec 1777-June 1778. |
| Pulley/Tulley, Wm. | Private | Sixth, Garland | Dec 1, 1777 reenlisted, on furlough; Jan-June 1778 on furlough. |
| Pulliam, James | Private | Fourteenth, Thweatt | Feb 14, 1778 enlisted; April 1778 lately joined regiment; May 1778; June 1778 sick Valley Forge. |

| Name | Rank | Regiment/Company | Service |
|---|---|---|---|
| Pulling/Pullin, William | Private | Fourteenth, Lambert | Dec 1777-Jan 1778; Feb 1778 on guard; March 1778; April 1778 sick present; May-June 1778. |
| Pugh, John | Private | Second State, Lewis | June 1778; July 1778 shows him "Omitted from 15 March to May 1, 1778." |
| Pugh/Puugh, Lewis | Private | Fifteenth, Hull | March 1778; April-May 1778 sick present; June 1778 sick Valley Forge. |
| Purcell/Pursel, David | Private | Seventh/Third, Crockett/Sayers | March 19, 1778 enlisted; April 1778 sick present; May 1778; June 1778 sick ys, in Sayers' Company. |
| Purcell/Pursell, John | Private | First, Lewis | Dec 1777-Jan 1778; Feb 1778 on command; March-June 1778. |
| Purcell/Pursley, Peter | Sergeant | Seventh, Young | Dec 1777-Jan 1778; Feb 7, 1778 discharged. |
| Pursell/Pursley, Robert | Corporal | Second State, Garnett | March 15-May 1, 1778; May-June 1778. |
| Pursell/Pursley, William | Corporal | Second State, Garnett | March 15-May 1, 1778; May-June 1778. |
| Purser/Pursuer, James | Private | Twelfth, Madison | Dec 1777-March 1778; April 1778 sick in camp. |
| Pursley/Purley, Lawrence/Laurance | Private | First State, Lee | Dec 1777 artificer; Jan-March 1778 on command; April-June 1778. |
| Purvis, James | Ensign | First, Taylor | Dec 1777; Jan 15, 1778 resigned. |
| Purvis, William/Wm. | Private | First, Taylor/Payne | Dec 1777-June 1778. |
| Pushy, Charles | Private | Second, Harrison | May 1778 payroll shows "draught 25 March last." |
| Putney, Lewis | Private | Second, Upshaw | Feb 14, 1778 drafted; April 1778. |
| Putny/Putney, James | Private | Second, Calmes | Feb 14, 1778 enlisted; May 1778; June 1778 sick Valley Forge; July 1778 sick at Yellow Springs. |
| Quail/Quale, John | Private | Third, Blackwell | Dec 23, 1777 discharged. |

| | | | |
|---|---|---|---|
| Quarles/Quales, Abner | Private | Fourteenth, Winston | Dec 1777 on guard; Jan 1778; Feb 1778 on command; March 1778; April 1778 on command at Dunkerstown; May 1778 on command; June 1778. |
| Quarles, James | Captain | Second State, Quarles | April-June 1778. Oath at Valley Forge on May 8, 1778, witnessed by Muhlenberg. |
| Quarles/Quarls, Jno. | Private | Sixth, Rose | Feb-March 1778; April 5, 1778 discharged. |
| Quarles, Nathaniel | Sergeant | Fifteenth, Grimes | Dec 1777-May 1778. |
| Quarles, Thomas | Cadet/ Ensign | Second State, Quarles | May-June 1778; June 1, 1778 promoted to Ensign. Oath at Valley Forge on May 8, 1778, witnessed by Muhlenberg. |
| Quegg/Quigg, Daniel | Fifer | First, Mennis | Dec 1777-June 1778. |
| Quellen see McQuellin | | | |
| Quinn see Gwinn | | | |
| Quinn/Quin, James | Corporal | Second, Taylor, F. | Dec 1777-Feb 1778. |
| Quinn, James | Private | Fifteenth, Harris | Jan 1778 sick; Feb-April 1778; May 1778 on guard. |
| Quinn, John | Corporal | Seventh, Spencer | Dec 1777-Jan 1778; Feb 18, 1778 discharged. |
| Quinn, John | Private | Fifteenth, Gray/ Foster | Jan 1778 joined since Oct 1, 1777; Feb 1778 in Gray's Company; March 1778 sick in camp; April-May 1778. |
| Quinn/Gwine, Owin | Private | Twelfth, Madison | Dec 1777 on guard; Jan 1778 on forage guard; Feb 1778 sick in hospital; March-April 1778. |
| Quirk, Thomas | 2nd. Lt. | Seventh, Crockett | Dec 1777-Jan 1778; April-May 1778 |
| Rabon/ Raiborne, Francis | Private | Second State, Lewis | March 15-May 1, 1778; May-June 1778. |
| Race, Andrew | Private | Third, Briscoe | Dec 1777; Feb 2, 1778 discharged on muster roll, pay roll shows him paid to Feb 5. |

| Name | Rank | Regiment | Notes |
|---|---|---|---|
| Raferty/Rafferty, Richard | Private | Fourteenth, Lambert | Dec 1777-Jan 1778 sick in hospital; Feb-March 1778 hospital; April-June 1778. |
| Rafferty/Rafers, John | Private | Twelfth, Madison | Dec 1777-Jan 1778 on guard; Feb 1778 on command; March-April 1778 on guard. |
| Ragan/Regan, Daniel | Sergeant | First State, Ewell, T. | Dec 1777-Feb 1778 sick Georgetown; June 1778. |
| Ragland/Raglan, Edmond | Private | Fourteenth, Reid | Sept 18, 1777 enlisted; April 1778 lately joined regiment; May-June 1778. |
| Ragland, John | Private | Fourteenth, Fourteenth | Feb 17, 1778 drafted; May 1778; June 1778 sick Valley Forge. |
| Ragsdale, Jesse | Private | Seventh, Moseley | Dec 1777-Jan 1778 sick Virginia |
| Ragsdale, John | Private | Sixth, Avery | Dec 1777-Jan 1778; Feb 8, 1778 discharged. |
| Raiden/Raden, Robert | Private | Second State, Bernard | April-June 1778. |
| Railey, George | Private | First, Scott | Jan 1778 on command; Feb 1778 confined; March-April 1778 on guard; May-June 1778. |
| Raines, Giles | 2nd. Lt. | Fifteenth, Gray | Dec 23, 1777 resigned. |
| Raines/Rains, Richard | Private | First State, Camp | Dec 1777 sick present; Jan 1778 sick absent; Feb 12, 1778 died. |
| Rains, Phill | Private | First State, Camp | Jan 1778 sick absent; Feb 12, 1778 died. |
| Rains/Raines, William | Private | Second, Upshaw | April 1778; June 1778. |
| Ralls, Nathaniel | Sergeant | Second, Willis | Dec 1777-May 1778; June-July 1778 sick Valley Forge. |
| Ralston, John | Private | Twelfth, Wallace | Feb 28, 1778 drafted; May 1778. |
| Ramsay, James | Private | Twelfth, Waggener | Dec 1777-March 1778 on command; April 1778 waggons; May 1778. |
| Ramsey, Thomas | Private | Second, Upshaw | Dec 1777-Jan 1778. |
| Rand, Walter | Sergeant | Fifteenth, Wills | Jan-May 1778; June-July 1778 sick Valley Forge. |

| Name | Rank | Regiment | Notes |
|---|---|---|---|
| Randolph, John | Private | First State, Hoffler | Dec 1777-Jan 1778. |
| Randolph, John | Private | Third, Peyton, J. | Dec 23, 1777 reenlisted in Light Horse. |
| Randolph, John | Private | Fourteenth, Jones | Sept 6, 1777 enlisted; June 1778 sick at English Town. |
| Randolph, Sampson/Samson | Private | First State, Hoffler | Dec 1777-Feb 1778. |
| Raney/Rainey, George | Private | Fourteenth, Overton | Dec 1777 sick in hospital; Jan 1778 sick absent; Feb 1778; March 1778 sick absent; April 1, 1778 died. |
| Raney/Rainey, Lewis | Private | First, Lawson | Dec 1777-March 1778 waggoner; April-June 1778. |
| Rankins, Joseph | Fleming | First State, Brown | Dec 1777-Jan 1778; Feb 1778 died. |
| Ranny, Stephen | Surgeon | Twelfth | Appointed April 21, 1778; April-May 1778; June 18, 1778 taken to the hospital. |
| Ransom/Ransome, James | Corporal | Seventh, Young | Dec 1777 hospital; Jan 1778; Feb 5, 1778 discharged. |
| Ratliff/Ratcliff, George/Geo. | Private | Fifteenth, Gregory | Dec 1777-May 1778 hospital; June 1778 unknown where. |
| Rawleigh/Raulegh, John | Corporal | Sixth, Massie | Dec 1777-Jan 1778; Feb 12, 1778 discharged. |
| Rawson, Charles | Private | Sixth, Massie | Drafted Feb 18, 1778; April-May 1778; sick Yellow Springs. |
| Ray see Pray | | | |
| Ray/Wray, John | Private | First, Lawson | Dec 1777 sick Pennsylvania; Jan 1778 sick hospital; February 1778; March 1778 fatigue; April-May 1778; June 1778 on guard. |
| Ray, Thomas | Private | Sixth | June 1778. |
| Ray, William | Private | Sixth | May-June 1778. |
| Ray, William | Private | Seventh, Crockett | Dec 1777-Jan 1778 on furlough; April 1, 1778 deserted. |
| Read, Abram | Private | Fourteenth, Conway | March 19, 1778 drafted; May 1778; June 1778 sick Valley Forge. |
| Read/Reed, Alexander | Sergeant | Twelfth, Wallace | Dec 1777-April 1778 on furlough; May 1778. |

| Name | Rank | Unit | Service |
|---|---|---|---|
| Read, John/Jno. | Private | First, Taylor/Payne | Dec 1777-Feb 1778; March 1778 time expires Apr, 10, 1778, in Payne's Company. |
| Read/Reed, Lewis | Private | Fourteenth, Thweatt | Feb 15, 1778 drafted; June 1778. |
| Reading/Reding, James | Private | Twelfth, Bowyer, M. | Dec 1777-May 1778. |
| Reagin/Ragon, Denis | Private | Twelfth, Bowyer, M. | Dec 1777-May 1778. |
| Reardon/Raden, George | Sergeant | First State, Payne | Dec 1777-June 1778. |
| Rector/Recter, Maxelem/Maximillian | Private | Third/Seventh, Peyton, V./Peyton, J. | Dec 1777 on furlough Virginia; Jan-March 1778 on furlough; June 1778 guard. |
| Redcross/Readcross, Daniel | Private | Fourteenth, Overton | Dec 1777-March 1778; April 1778 sick at hospital; May-June 1778 sick Yellow Springs. |
| Reddin, Joseph | Private | Second State, Bressie | March 15-May 1, 1778, May-June 1778. |
| Redman, Martin | Private | Second State, Lewis | June 1778; July 1778 roll reads "Omitted from 15 March to the first July." |
| Redford/Radford, William | Private | First, Pelham | Dec 1777-June 1778. |
| Redwood, John | Private | Fifteenth, Gray | Dec 1777 on furlough; Jan-April 1778; May 1778 sick present; June 1778 waiting on the sick at Valley Forge. |
| Reece, Adam | Corporal | Twelfth, Waggener | Dec 1777-March 1778 hospital; April 10, 1778 discharged. |
| Reed/Read, Clem | Private | Fourteenth, Jones | Jan-Feb 1778 sick at Lancaster. |
| Reed/Read, Isham | Private | Fifteenth, Harris | Jan 1778 on command; Feb-April 1778 sick present; May 6, 1778 deceased. |
| Reed/Read, John | Private | Second, Calmes | Dec 1777-June 1778. |
| Reed, Ramond | Private | Fifteenth, Edmunds | April 1778 on command. |

| | | | |
|---|---|---|---|
| Reed/Reid, Thomas | Private | Third/ Seventh, Arell/ Briscoe | Dec 1777-Feb 1778 sick absent; March 1778; April 1778 on command; May 1778; June 1778 sick present, in Briscoe's Company. |
| Reese, Adam | Corporal | Twelfth, Waggener | Dec 1777-March 1778 hospital; April 10, 1778 discharged. |
| Reese, Randolph | Private | Fifteenth, Gray | Feb 10, 1778 drafted; April 1778 under inoculation; May 1778. |
| Reid, Nathan | Captain | Fourteenth, Reid | Dec 1777 sick Burlington; Jan-June 1778. Oath at Valley Forge on May 12, 1778, witnessed by Muhlenberg. |
| Reily/Reyla, James | Private | Twelfth, Waggener | Dec 1777-April 1778; May 1778 on command. |
| Reily/Rilay, Patrick | Private | Seventh/ Third, Crockett/ Sayers | Dec 1777-Jan 1778 on furlough; April 1778; June 1778 sick Valley Forge, in Sayers' Company. |
| Reins, William | Drummer | Second, Upshaw | June 1778. |
| Reisor/Reysor, Philip | Private | Seventh/ Third, Crockett/ Hill | March 19, 1778 enlisted; April-May 1778; June 1778 in Hill's Company. |
| Relley/Rilly, Jesse | Private | Fifteenth, Wills | June 18, 1777 enlisted; Feb 1778; March-April 1778 sick present; May 1778. |
| Renney, Wm. | Private | Sixth, Garland | April 1778 payroll shows he enlisted on Sept 22, 1777. |
| Renolls, Thomas | Private | Seventh, Posey | Dec 1777 on guard; Jan 1778; Feb 15, 1778 discharged. |
| Reppets/Repets, William | Private | Fourteenth, Marks | Dec 1777 hospital; Feb 1778 on guard; April 1778; May 1778 confined; June 1778. |
| Revel, Holida/ Hollida | Private | Fifteenth, Harris | Jan 1778 sick; Feb 1778; March-April 1778 sick present; May 1778 sick absent; June 1778 sick Valley Forge. |
| Reyley, John | Private | Fourteenth, Lambert | Sept 30, 1777 enlisted; April 1778; May 1778 sick in camp; June 1778. |

| Name | Rank | Regiment/Company | Notes |
|---|---|---|---|
| Reyley, Owen | Private | Fourteenth, Lambert | Sept 30, 1777 enlisted; April-May 1778; June 1778 on command. |
| Reynolds/ Runnels, Aaron/Aron | Private/ Corporal | Third/ Seventh, Mercer/ Powell | Dec 1777-March 1778 on furlough; April 1778 promoted to Corporal; May 1778; June 1778 in Powell's Company. |
| Reynolds/ Runnolds, Alexander/ Alexr. | Private | Fifteenth, Harris | Jan-Feb 1778; March 1778 on command; April 1778 on guard; May 1778. |
| Reynolds, Arthur | Private | Fourteenth, Jones | Feb 12, 1778 drafted; April |
| Reynolds/ Rennolds, John | Private | Second State, Bernard | March 15-April 15, 1778 stationed in York garrison; May 1778; June 1778 on guard. |
| Reynolds/ Roynolds, Miles | Private | First State, Meriwether | Dec 1777-June 1778. |
| Reynolds, William | Private | Second State, Bernard | Only reference: March 15-April 15, 1778 stationed in York garrison and paid on April 20. |
| Rhea, Mathew | Quartermaster | Seventh/ Third | Dec 1777-June 1778 |
| Rhoads, Jonathan/John | Private | Sixth, Fox | Jan-June 1778. |
| Rhodes, Thomas | Private | First State, Lee | Dec 1777 on furlough; March 1778 deserted. |
| Rhodes, William/Will | Private | Second, Harrison | Dec 1777-June 1778. |
| Rice, David | Sergeant/ Private | Seventh/ Third, Jouett/Hill | April 1778; June 1778 in Hill's Company. This may have been the David Rice who was in the Commander-in-Chief's Guard. |
| Rice, Edmd. | Private | Sixth, Massie | Jan 1778 discharged. |
| Rice, James | Private | Second State, Lewis | March 15-May 1, 1778. |
| Rice, John | Private | First, Lewis | Jan 1778 roll shows he died on Feb 2, 1778. |
| Rice, Thomas | Private | Third, Powell | Dec 1777-Feb 1778; March 21, 1778 deserted. |
| Rice, William/Wm. | Sergeant/ Quartermaster Sergeant | First, Scott | Dec 1777-May 1778; June 1778 promoted to Quartermaster Sergeant. |

| Name | Rank | Regiment | Notes |
|---|---|---|---|
| Rice, William | Private | Third, Peyton, V. | Dec 1777-Jan 1778 sick in hospital; Feb 12, 1778 discharged. |
| Richards, Boswell/ Bozwell | Private/ Corporal | Second State, Dudley | March 15-May 1, 1778; May 1, 1778 promoted to Corporal, May 1778; June 1778 sick absent. |
| Richards/ Ritchards, John | Private | Twelfth, Casey | Dec 1777 sent to hospital; Jan-Feb 1778 at hospital; March-April 1778; May 1778 on guard. |
| Richards, Richard | Private | Seventh, Webb | Jan 1778; Feb 28, 1778 discharged. |
| Richards, Thomas | Sergeant | Twelfth, Casey | Dec 1777-May 1778. |
| Richardson, James | Private | First, Cummings | Dec 1777. |
| Richardson, William | Private | Second State, Dudley | March 15-May 1, 1778; May-June 1778. |
| Richerson, Richardson, Peter | Private | First State, Nicholas | Dec 1777-Feb 1778 sick Georgetown. |
| Richerson/ Richardson, Robert/Robet | Private | Seventh/ Third, Fleming/ Young | Dec 1777-March 1778 on furlough Virginia; May 1778 on guard; June 1778 in Young's Company. |
| Richeson/ Richerson, Dorian | Private | Seventh, Jouett | Dec 20, 1777 deceased. |
| Richeson/ Richerson, Holt/Holl | Lt. Colonel | Seventh/ Third | Dec 1777-April 1778 on furlough; May 1778 on furlough sick Virginia; June 1778. |
| Richeson/ Richison, John | Private | Seventh, Hill | Dec 1777-Jan 1778 sick in hospital |
| Richey/Rickey, Robert | Sergeant | Twelfth, Bowyer, M. | Dec 1777; Jan-Feb 1778 on furlough; March-May 1778. |
| Richey, Thomas | Sergeant | Seventh, Posey | Dec 1777 in hospital; Jan 1778 sick in hospital; Feb 15, 1778 discharged. |
| Rickets/ Ricketts, William | Private | First State, Hoffler | Dec 1777-June 1778. |
| Riddick, Willis | 2nd. Lt. | Fifteenth, Gregory | Feb-May 1778 Prisoner of War on parole. |

| Name | Rank | Regiment | Notes |
|---|---|---|---|
| Riddle, Benjamin/ Benjm. | Private | Sixth, Avery | Dec 1777 reenlisted; Dec 1777-March 1778 on furlough; April 1778; May 1778 waggoner absent; June 1778 waggoner. |
| Riddle/Riddell, George | Private | Second, Harrison | May-June 1778. |
| Riddle, Millender | Private | Second, Upshaw | Dec 1777-Jan 1778. |
| Riddle/Ridle, Reece/Reas | Private | Fourteenth, Winston | Dec 1777; Jan 1778 at R. hospital; Feb-March 1778 S. H; April 20, 1778 died. |
| Ridley/Rialey, Thomas | Drummer | First, Pelham | Dec 1777; Feb 15, 1778 discharged. |
| Riggan/Regan, William | Private | Second State, Taliaferro | March 15-May 1, 1778; May 1778; June 1778 sick Valley Forge. |
| Riggs, Joshua | Private | Second State, Quarles | August 1778 roll reads "Time of service 4 ½ months." |
| Right see Wright | | | |
| Right, John | Private | Twelfth, Wallace | Dec 1777-March 1778 on command; April-May 1778. |
| Riley/Ryley, Edward | Private | Third, Peyton, V. | Dec 1777 on furlough Virginia; Jan 1778 on furlough; April 1778 sick in Virginia; May 1778 sick present. |
| Riley/Rely, George/Geo. | Private | First, Scott | Dec 1777; Jan 1778 on command; Feb 1778 confined; March-April 1778 on command; May-June 1778. |
| Riley/Reily, John | Private | Second, Sanford | Dec 1777 provost guard; January 10, 1778 executed. |
| Riley/Reiley, John | Private | Third, Blackwell | Feb 18, 1778 drafted; April 1778; May 1778 on guard; June 1778. |
| Riley, John | Private | Fourteenth, Conway | Sept 20, 1777 enlisted; April 1778 lately joined regiment; May 1778 sick present. |
| Riley, Owen | Private | Fourteenth, Conway | Sept 20, 1777 enlisted; April 1778 lately joined regiment, June 1778 on command. |

| Name | Rank | Regiment, Company | Service |
|---|---|---|---|
| Rinds/Rines, Cornelius/Carnelius | Private | Fifteenth, Wills | Jan-Feb 1778; March 1778 on guard; April-May 1778. |
| Ripley, John | Private | Second State, Bernard | March 15-April 15, 1778 stationed in York garrison; May-June 1778. |
| Rippito, William | Private | Fourteenth, Marks | Dec 1777-Jan 1778 sick in hospital; Feb 1778 on guard; May 1778 sick present. |
| Roach, James | Private | Second, Upshaw | Feb 14, 1778 drafted; April 1778; June 1778. |
| Roach, Joseph | Private | Second, Taylor, W. | Dec 1777 sick absent; Jan 1778; Feb 14, 1778 discharged. |
| Roach, Wm. | Private | Sixth, Hockaday | Dec 1777 on furlough in Virginia; Jan-May 1778 on furlough; June 1778. |
| Roadley/Rodly, John | Private | Fourteenth, Winston | Dec 1777-Jan 1778 sick in Virginia; Feb 1778. |
| Roadley, Samuel | Private | Fourteenth, Winston | April-May 1778; June 1778 sick Valley Forge. |
| Roads/Roades, William | Private | Fourteenth, Winston | Dec 1777; Jan 1778 on guard; Feb-March 1778; April 1778 sick present; May 1778 sick; June 1778 sick Valley Forge. |
| Roark, John | Private | Twelfth, Wallace | Feb 28, 1778 drafted; May 1778 sick in camp. |
| Robbins, William | Sergeant | First, Lewis | Dec 1777 prisoner. |
| Robbins/Robins, William | Private | Second State, Taliaferro | March 15-May 1, 1778; May-June 1778. |
| Roberson/Robberson, Joseph/Jos. | Private | Fifteenth, Hull | Dec 1777 sick absent; Jan 1778 sick hospital; Feb 1778 sick absent; March-April 1778; May 1778 sick present. |
| Roberts, Ambrose/Ambrus | Private | Second State, Quarles | April-May 1778; June 26, 1778 died. |
| Roberts, Anthony | Private | First State, Camp | Dec 1777 sick Jerseys; Jan-Feb 1778 sick absent; March 1778 on furlough; April-June 1778. |
| Roberts, Barnard | Private | Second, Taylor, W. | Dec 1777 sick present; Jan 1778; Feb 21, 1778 discharged. |

| Name | Rank | Regiment/Company | Notes |
|---|---|---|---|
| Roberts, Daniel | Private | Fourteenth, Thweatt | Dec 1777 sick at hospital; Jan-Feb 1778 on furlough to Virginia; April 1778 on furlough; May 1778; June 1778 on guard. |
| Roberts, Edward | Private | Twelfth, Ashby | Dec 1777-Jan 1778; Feb 1778 on guard; March-April 1778; May 1778 on guard. |
| Roberts/Roberds, George | Quartermaster Sergeant | Fourteenth | Jan-Feb 1778; April-June 1778. |
| Roberts, Henry/Heney | Private | Twelfth, Vause | Dec 1777-Jan 1778 sick in hospital; Feb-March 1778; April 1778 sick in camp; May 1778. |
| Roberts, Hezekiah/Ezekiah | Private | Second State, Bressie | May 1778 "Virginia last pay roll now sick Valley Forge;" June 1778. |
| Roberts, John | Surgeon | Sixth | Dec 1777 absent with leave; Jan-May 1778; June 1778 "attending wounded officer." |
| Roberts, John | Private | Seventh, Moseley | Dec 1777-Jan 1778 sick in hospital; Muster roll shows he died on February 22, but payroll pays him through March 7, 1778. |
| Roberts, Mourning | Private | Fourteenth, Marks | Jan 8, 1778 discharged. |
| Roberts, Syrus/Cyrus L. | 1st. Lt./Captain | Fourteenth, Conway/Roberts | Dec 1777; In January he was promoted to Captain and transferred to command what had been Lambert's company; Jan 1778 on command; Feb 1778 on guard; March-June 1778. Oath at Valley Forge on May 12, 1778, witnessed by Muhlenberg. |
| Roberts, Thos. | Sergeant | First, Cunningham | August 1776 enlisted for 3 years; Dec 1777-April 1778; May 1778 sick present; June 1778 sick at Valley Forge. |
| Roberts, William | Private | Sixth | June 1778. |
| Roberts, William/Wm. | Private | Seventh/Third, Fleming/Heth | Feb 17, 1778 enlisted; April 1778 sick present; June 1778 in Heth's Company. |

| | | | |
|---|---|---|---|
| Roberts, William | Private | Twelfth, Bowyer, T. | Dec 1777-Jan 1778 on command; Feb 1778 sick absent; March 1778 on command; April 1778. |
| Roberts, William | Private | Fourteenth, Marks | Dec 1777; Jan 1778 hospital. |
| Robertson/ Robinson, Cole/Call | Private/ Sergeant | First, Mennis | Dec 1777; Jan 1778 promoted to sergeant; Jan-March 1778 on furlough; |
| Robertson/ Roberson, Elisha/Elijah | Private | First, Mennis | Dec 1777; Jan 1778 on furlough; Feb 1778; March 1778 on fatigue; April 1778; May 1778 on furlough; June 1778. |
| Robertson, John | Private | Second, Upshaw | Feb 14, 1778 drafted; April 1778; June 1778. |
| Robertson, John | Private | Second, Taylor, W. | Dec 1777 hospital; Jan-June 1778. |
| Robertson/ Robinson, Nathan/ Nathaniel | Sergeant | Second, Jones/ Hoomes | March 1778; April 1778 died. |
| Robertson/ Roberson, William/Wm. | Private | First, Mennis | Dec 1777-March 1778 on furlough; April 1778; May 1778 sick present; June 1778 sick Valley Forge. |
| Robertson, William | Private | Twelfth, Bowyer, T. | Aug 30, 1777 enlisted; Jan 1778 joined; March 1778; April 1778 sick in camp; May 1778. |
| Robins, William | Private | Seventh, Spencer | Dec 1777 sick present; Jan 1778 hospital; March 3, 1778 discharged. |
| Robinson/ Robertson, Benjamin | Private | Second, Upshaw | Dec 30, 1777 enlisted in horse service. |
| Robinson/ Robison, Green | Private | First State, Lee | Dec 1777 sick; Jan-Feb 1778 sick absent; March 1778 Yellow Springs Hospital; June 1778. |
| Robinson/ Roberson, James | Private/ Corporal | Second, Jones/ Hoomes | Dec 1777-Feb 1778; March promoted to Corporal; March-June 1778. |
| Robinson, John/Jno. | Private | First, Cunningham | Feb 14, 1778 enlisted for 1 year; April 1778 under inoculation; May-June 1778. |

| Name | Rank | Regiment/Company | Notes |
|---|---|---|---|
| Robinson/Robertson, John | Private | Fourteenth, Reid | March 19, 1778 drafted; May 1778 joined lately; June 1778. |
| Robinson, Marmaduke | Private | Second State, Garnett | Enlisted February 12, 1778; June 1778. |
| Robinson/Robison, Mordecai | Private | First State, Hoffler | April-May 1778; June 1778 sick absent. |
| Robinson/Robison, Nathaniel | Sergeant | Second, Upshaw/Jones | Dec 1777-Jan 1778; March 1778. In March he is in Jones' company. |
| Robinson/Roberson, Rial/Riul | Private | First, Cunningham | Feb 12, 1778 enlisted for 1 year; April 1778 under inoculation; May 1778 sick in the hospital; June 15, 1778 dead. |
| Robison, William | Private/Corporal | Twelfth, Madison | Dec 1777-Jan 1778; Feb 1, 1778 promoted to Corporal; Feb-April 1778. |
| Rodes/Roads, George | Private | Seventh, Jouett | Dec 1777-Jan 1778 sick in hospital; Feb 10, 1778 discharged. |
| Rodes, Thomas | Private | First State, Lee | Dec 1777 on furlough. |
| Rodgers/Rogers, Jos. | Private | Fifteenth, Hull | Dec 1777 sick absent; Jan 1778 sick at hospital; Feb-March 1778 sick absent; April-May 1778 sick hospital. |
| Rodgers, William/Wm. | Private | First, Mennis | Feb 9, 1778 enlisted; April 1778; May 1778 sick present; June 1778 sick at Valley Forge. |
| Rogers/Rodgers, Andrew | 2nd. Lt. | Fourteenth, Lambert | Dec 1777 sick in Jersey; Jan 1778 sick in country; Feb 1778; March 2, 1778 resigned. |
| Rogers, Henry | Private | Twelfth, Ashby | Dec 1777-Jan 1778; March 1778 at hospital. |
| Rogers, Hosia/Hoshe | Private | Third, Mercer | Dec 1777-Jan 1778. |
| Rogers/Roggers, John | Corporal | Third, Mercer | Dec 1777-Jan 1778. |
| Rogers/Roggers, Michael/Michal | Private | Third/Seventh, Mercer/Powell | Dec 1777-April 1778; May 1778 on command; June 1778 on guard, in Powell's Company. |

| Name | Rank | Company | Notes |
|---|---|---|---|
| Roe, John | Private | Second, Taylor, F. | June 1778. This man and John Rowe in Upshaw's Company may be the same individual. |
| Roe, Joseph | Private | Seventh, Webb | Enlisted for 2 years; Jan 1778 hospital; February 1778 deceased. |
| Rogers, Henry | Private | Twelfth, Ashby | Dec 1777-March 1778 at hospital. |
| Rogers, Ulissus/Ulisis | Private | Sixth, Hockaday | Dec 1777 wounded, in hospital; Jan 1778 hospital; Feb 19, 1778 discharged. |
| Rollins/Roling, James | Private | Seventh Third, Posey/Sayers | Feb 27, 1778 enlisted; May 1778 attending sick; June 1778 sick Yellow Springs, in Sayers' Company. |
| Rollins/Rallings, Thomas | Corporal | Third/Seventh, Peyton, V./Peyton, J. | Feb 17, 1778 drafted; April-June 1778; June 1778 in J. Peyton's Company. |
| Rolls/Ralls, Bethlehem | Private | Third/Seventh, Blackwell | Feb 12, 1778 drafted; May-June 1778/ |
| Ronals/Ronnals, Arthur | Private | Fourteenth, Jones | Drafted Feb 12, 1778; April-May 1778. |
| Rone, Samuel | Corporal/Private | First State, Crump | Dec 1777; Jan 1778 demoted to Private; Jan-Feb 1778 waggoner; March-June 1778. |
| Rooks, Thomas | Private | Fourteenth, Jones | Drafted Feb 11, 1778; April-May 1778. |
| Roney, John | Sergeant Major | Sixth | Dec 1777-Jan 1778. |
| Rooney/Rona, Patrick | Private | Twelfth, Waggener | Dec 1777-May 1778 on command. |
| Ronsafer, Benjamin | Private | First State, Crump | Dec 1777-Feb 1778. |
| Ronsell/Rousell, Henry | Private | Seventh, Hill | Dec 1777 sick in hospital; Jan 27, 1778 discharged. |
| Rose, Alexander | Captain | Sixth, Rose | Dec 1777; Jan-April 1778 recruiting; May-June 1778. Oath at Valley Forge on May 28, 1778, witnessed by Muhlenberg. |
| Rose/Roase, George/Geo. | Private | Fifteenth, Grimes | Dec 1777; Jan 1778 on guard; Feb-March 1778; April-May 1778 on picquet. |

| Name | Rank | Company | Notes |
|---|---|---|---|
| Rose, Isick/Isaac | Private/ Corporal | Third/ Seventh, Mercer/ Powell | Dec 1777-March 1778; April 1778 promoted to Corporal; May 1778 sick present; June 1778 left sick on march, in Powell's Company. |
| Rose, Jesse/Jessey | Private/ Corporal | Third, Peyton, V./ Peyton, J. | Dec 1777-April 1778; April 1778 promoted to Corporal; May 1778 on command; June 1778 in J. Peyton's Company. |
| Rose/Roose, William | Private | Twelfth, Waggener | Dec 1777-Feb 1778 hospital; March 1778 sick in camp; April 10, 1778 discharged. |
| Rose, William/Wm. | Private | Fifteenth, Wills | Aug 16, 1777 enlisted; Feb-April 1778; May 1778 on duty. |
| Ross/Rose, Elijah | Private | Second State, Quarles | April-May 1778; June 1778 sick Valley Forge. |
| Ross, John | Private | Fourteenth, Lambert | Dec 1777-April 1778; May 1778 on guard; June 1778. |
| Ross, Thomas | Corporal | Fourteenth, Lambert | Dec 1777-Feb 1778; March 1778 on guard; April-May 1778; June 1778 with Col. Morgan. |
| Ross/Rose, William | Private | Fourteenth, Lambert | Dec 1777 on command; Jan 1778; Feb-May 1778 on furlough. |
| Rountree, John | Private | First State, Crump | Dec 1777; Jan 16, 1778 deceased. |
| Rouse/Rouze, Peter | Private | Twelfth, Vause | Dec 1777 sent sick with baggage; Jan-March 1778 sick Reading |
| Rousell/ Rowsell, Thomas | Private | First State, Hamilton | Dec 1777-Jan 1778. |
| Routt, Richard | 2nd. Lt. | Twelfth, Ashby | Dec 1777-Jan 1778; Feb-May 1778. |
| Row, Edward | Private | Seventh/ Third, Crockett/ Sayers | March 19, 1778 enlisted; April-May 1778; June 1778 in Sayers' Company. |
| Rowark, John | Private | Twelfth, Wallace | May 1778 roll shows he was drafted on Feb 28, 1778, and was sick in camp. |
| Rowe, Debnam/ Debnum | Private | Seventh, Young | Dec 1777-Jan 1778 sick in Virginia; Feb 3, 1778 discharged. |

| | | | | |
|---|---|---|---|---|
| Rowe, John | Private | Second, Upshaw | Feb 14, 1778 drafted; April 1778. This man and John Roe in F. Taylor's Company may be the same individual. |
| Rowe, John | Private | Seventh, Young | Dec 21, 1777 to Lt. Horse. |
| Rowland, Burrel/Burwel | Private | Fifteenth, Grimes | Dec 1777-May 1778. |
| Rowland, William/Wm. | Private | Fifteenth, Grimes | Dec 1777-March 1778 sick absent; April 1778 discharged March 15 from hospital near camp, reenlisted; May-June 1778. |
| Rowling/Rolling, Howell | Private | Fifteenth, Grimes | Feb 14, 1778 drafted; April 1778; June 5, 1778 died. |
| Rowling, James | Private | Seventh, Posey | Feb 27, 1778 enlisted; April 1778 attending on sick Yellow Springs; May 1778 attending sick |
| Rowling, Jesse | Private | First, Cunningham | Feb 13, 1778 enlisted; July 1778 sick at Valley Forge. |
| Rowlins, Howell | Private | Fifteenth, Grimes | Feb 14, 1778 drafted; April 1778; May 1778 muster roll shows he died on June 5, 1778. |
| Roy, Beverly | Ensign | Third, Powell | Dec 1777-Jan 1778; Feb-March 1778 on command; April-May 1778. |
| Royston/Rosten, Conquest | Private/Fifer | Second State, Lewis | March 15-May 1, 1778; May 1778; June 1778 sick absent. |
| Rucker, Angus | 1st. Lt. | First State, Nicholas | Jan-June 1778 "Omitted in all the muster rolls by being in Virginia." |
| Rucker, Elliott | 2nd. Lt. | First State, Hamilton | Dec 1777-Feb 1778. |
| Rucks/Rux, Benjamin/Benjm. | Corporal | Fifteenth, Harris | Jan-May 1778. |
| Rudder, Alexander | Cadet | First State, Ewell, T. | Dec 1777 sick absent; Jan roll shows he was discharged on Feb 15, 1778. |
| Rudder, Epaphrodites/Epaphraditus | 1st. Lt. | First State, Hoffler | Dec 1777-May 1778; June 1778, in Valentine's, formerly Camp's company. Oath at Valley Forge on May 12, 1778, witnessed by Muhlenberg. |

| Name | Rank | Regiment/Company | Service |
|---|---|---|---|
| Rum, Adam | Private | Second, Harrison | May-June 1778. |
| Rush, Henry | Private | Second, Harrison | Dec 1777 hospital; Jan-March 1778. |
| Russel, Wm. | Private | Third, Arell | Dec 1777-Jan 1778; Feb 20, 1778 deserted. |
| Russell, Albert | 2nd. Lt. | Twelfth, Waggener | Dec 1777-Feb 1778; March 1778 on command; April-May 1778. |
| Russell, Charles | Ensign/ 2nd Lt. | First State, Nicholas/ Lee | Dec 1777-Feb 1778 on furlough in Virginia; Feb 12, 1778 promoted to 2nd. Lt.; March-May 1778 on furlough in Virginia; May 1778 transferred to Lee's former company; June 1778. |
| Russell, George | Private | Third/ Seventh, Blackwell | Dec 1777-April 1778 on furlough; May 1778; June 1778 sick Valley Forge; July 10, 1778 dead. |
| Russell, George | Private | Fifteenth, Mason | In May he was paid back to Feb 11, 1778. |
| Russell, Henry | Private | Second, Taylor, F. | Dec 1777 on furlough; Jan-June 1778. |
| Russell/Russill, Jeffery/Jeffrey | Sergeant | Fourteenth, Winston | Dec 1777 on command; Jan-June 1778. |
| Russell, John | Private | Second State, Lewis | March 15-May 1, 1778; May-June 1778; July 1778 sick Valley Forge. |
| Russell, John | Sergeant | First State, Meriwether | Dec 1777-June 1778. |
| Russell, John | Private | Third, Lee | Dec 1777 attending on Capt. Lee; Jan 1778 on command; paid to Feb 14, 1778. |
| Russell, Matt | Private | Fifteenth, Gregory | June 1778 on guard. He and the man below are probably the same individual. |
| Russell/Russel, Mathew | Private | Fifteenth, Mason | Feb 1, 1778 drafted; May 1778. |
| Russell, Nathan | Private | Seventh/ Third, Fleming/ Heth | Feb 13, 1778 enlisted; April 1778 sick present; May 1778 on command; in Heth's Company. |
| Russel/Rusle, Thomas | Private | Twelfth, Bowyer, T. | Dec 1777; Jan-Feb 1778 sick in camp; March-April 1778; May 1778 confined. |

| | | | |
|---|---|---|---|
| Russey, James | Private | Seventh, Young | Dec 1777-Jan 1778; Feb 9, 1778 discharged. |
| Rust, Geo. | Private | Fifteenth, Hull | Dec 1777 sick absent; Jan 15, 1778 died. |
| Rust, Mathew | Sergeant | Fifteenth, Hull | Dec 1777-Jan 1778 sick at hospital; Feb-March 1778 sick absent; April 1778 sick in hospital; May 1778 on furlough. |
| Rutherford, Archibald | Private | Seventh, Crockett | Dec 1777 waggoner; Jan 1778. |
| Rutherford, Julius | Private | Twelfth, Madison | Dec 1777-Jan 1778; Feb 1778 on command; March 1778 on guard; April-May 1778 on command; June 1778 waggoner. |
| Rutherford/ Rutheford, Thomas/Thos. | Private | Third/ Seventh, Peyton, V. | Dec 1777 on furlough Virginia; Jan-March 1778 on furlough; April 1778 on command at the Lines; May-June 1778. |
| Ruthvins/ Ruthvens, John | Private/ Corporal | Seventh/ Third, Jouett/ Hill | Dec 1777 on furlough Virginia; Jan-March 1778 on furlough; April 1778 on guard; May 1, 1778 promoted to Corporal; May 1778; June 1778 in Hill's Company. |
| Rutter, Adam | Private | First, Lawson | Dec 1777-March 1778 waggoner; April 1778 waggoner Wilmington; May-June 1778 waggoner. |
| Rutter, Thomas | Drummer | Fifteenth, Gregory | Dec 1777-Jan 1778; Feb 1778 sick present; March-April 1778; May 1778 sick present; sick Valley Forge. |
| Ruxton/ Ruckston, David | Private | Third, Peyton, V. | Dec 1777-Jan 1778 waiting on the Doctor; Feb 12, 1778 discharged. |
| Ryalls/Rialls, James | Private/ Corporal | Fifteenth, Hull | Dec 1777-Jan 1778; Feb 1778 sick present, promoted to Corporal; March-April 1778 sick present; May 1778. |
| Ryalls/Rialls, Samuel/Saml. | Private | Fifteenth, Hull | Dec 1777-Feb 1778; March-May 1778 sick present. |

| Name | Rank | Regiment | Notes |
|---|---|---|---|
| Ryan/Ryon, John | Private | Twelfth, Waggener | Dec 1777-Jan 1778; Feb 1778 on guard; March 1778 on furlough; April 1778; May 1778 sick in camp; June-July 1778 sick Valley Forge. |
| Ryce, James | Private | Second State, Bressie | May 1778 payroll states "Virginia last payroll" and pays him for 2 ½ months; June 1778 wounded Valley Forge. |
| Sabastian/Sebaston, Benjamin | Private | Twelfth, Waggener | Dec 1777-Jan 1778; Feb 1778 on command; March-May 1778. |
| Sacket/Sackett, James | Surgeon's Mate | Fourteenth | Dec 1777-Feb 1778; April 1778 arrested; April 24, 1778 resigned. He was court martialed on April 6 and found guilty of "absenting himself and going to the State of New York without leave" and sentenced to be reprimanded by the commander of his regiment. |
| Sacrey/Sacry, Isick/Isaac | Private | Second, Upshaw | Dec 1777 hospital. |
| Sacrey/Sacry, James | Private | Second, Upshaw | Dec 1777 hospital. |
| Saddler/Sadler, Richard | Private | Seventh/Third, Young | Feb 16, 1778 enlisted; April 1778 sick present; May 1778 on guard; June 1778. |
| Sadler, John | Private | Second, Taylor, W. | Dec 1777-Jan 1778; Feb 21, 1778 discharged. |
| Sadler, Robert | Private | Second State, Garnett | March 15-May 1, 1778; May-June 1778. |
| Sage, James | Private | Seventh/Third, Crockett/Sayers | Feb 29, 1778 enlisted; April-May 1778; June 1778 in Sayers' Company. |
| Sage, John | Private | Twelfth, Ashby | Dec 1777; Jan-Feb 1778 sick in hospital; March 1778 at hospital; May 1778. |
| Sale, Leonard | Private | Second, Taylor, F. | Dec 1777-Feb 1778; March 12, 1778 discharged. |

| Name | Rank | Regiment/Company | Notes |
|---|---|---|---|
| Sallard, Eliphat/Eliphate | Private | First State, Camp | Dec 1777 skh; Jan-Feb 1778 sick absent; June 1778 payroll reads "Struck out of 2 last M. Rolls Agreeable to Orders. Therefore omitted in 2 last P. Rolls." |
| Salmetre/Salmeter, Anthony | Private | First State, Lee | Dec 1777 sick; Jan 1778 sick absent; Feb 1778 died. |
| Salmon, Anthony | Private | First State, Lee | Dec 1777 sick; Jan-Feb 1778 sick absent. |
| Salmon, George | Private | First, Lawson | Dec 1777; Jan 1778 guard; Feb-April 1778; May 1778 on command; June 1778. |
| Salmon, Thomas/Thos. | Private | First, Cunningham | Feb 17, 1778 enlisted for 1 year; April 1778 under inoculation; May-June 1778. |
| Salter, John | Private | Third, Powell | Dec 1777-Feb 1778; April-May 1778. |
| Sammonds, John | Private | Fifteenth, Grimes | Nov 1777 sick Virginia; Jan 1778 "Died about 1st Jany." |
| Sammons, Charles/Chas. | Private | Fifteenth, Edmunds Gregory | Dec 1777-March 1778 sick absent; April 1778 sick in hospital; May 1778 sick absent; June 1778 absent at hospital. in Gregory's Company. |
| Sammons, James | Private | Fifteenth, Grimes | Dec 1777-March 1778 sick absent. |
| Sammons, John | Private | First State, Meriwether | Dec 1777-Feb 1778. |
| Sampson/Sumpson, George/Geo. | Private | Fifteenth, Harris | Jan 1778 on command; Feb 1778; March 1778 sick present; April 1778 on guard; May 1778 sick present; June 1778 sick Yellow Springs. |
| Sampson, John | Private | Seventh, Lipscomb | Dec 1, 1777 reenlisted for 3 years; Dec 1777-Jan 1778 on furlough; April 1778 on furlough; May 1778 muster roll shows him as deserted on May 1; May 1778 payroll shows him as deceased on April 10. |
| Sampson, Richard | Private | Third, Arell | Dec 1777-Jan 1778 waggoner. |

| | | | |
|---|---|---|---|
| Samuel, Gray | Sergeant | Second State, Quarles | April-May 1778; June 1778 sick Valley Forge. |
| Samuel/Samual, Henry | Private | Seventh/Third, Hill | Feb 16, 1778 enlisted; April-May 1778; June 1778 sick Valley Forge. |
| Samuel, James | Private | Seventh/Third, Webb/Young | Feb 16, 1778 enlisted; May 1778; June 1778 in Young's Company. |
| Samuel, Jeremiah/Jery | Corporal | Seventh, Moseley | Dec 1777-April 1778 on furlough; April 1778 |
| Samuel, William | Private | Second State, Quarles | April-June 1778. |
| Sanders, Jacob | Private | Seventh, Lipscomb | Dec 1777 left in Virginia July 1777. |
| Sanders, Presley | Sergeant | Second, Sanford/Parker | Dec 1777-June 1778. From April on he appears in Parker's company. |
| Sanders, William | Private | Twelfth, Madison | Dec 1777-Jan 1778 sick in hospital. |
| Sanderson, William | Private | First, Cunningham | Feb 12, 1778 enlisted for 1 year; April 1778 under inoculation; May 1778; June 1778 sick at Valley Forge. |
| Sandridge, Augustine/Austin | Quartermaster | Sixth | Dec 1777 sick absent; Jan-Feb 1778; March 1778 on furlough; April-June 1778. Oath at Valley Forge on May 12, 1778, witnessed by Muhlenberg. |
| Sandridge/Sandidge, Joseph | Corporal | Sixth, Avery | Dec 26, 1778 discharged. |
| Sanford, Thomas | 2nd. Lt. | First State, Ewell, T. | Dec 1777; Jan 14, 1778 resigned. |
| Sanford, William | Captain | Second, Sanford | Dec 1777-March 1778; April 6, 1778 resigned. |
| Sangster, John | Private | Fourteenth, Jones | Jan 1778 deserted in Virginia. |

| Name | Rank | Regiment, Company | Notes |
|---|---|---|---|
| Sansum/Sansom, Philip | Ensign | First, Lewis | Dec 1777 on furlough; Jan-April 1778 on command; May-June 1778 on command in Virginia, |
| Sargent/Largent, James | Private | Twelfth, Vause | Dec 1777; Jan-Feb 1778 on guard; March 1778; April 1778 on fatigue; May 1778. |
| Sargent/Largent, William | Private | Twelfth, Vause | April 1778 roll show he was drafted on Feb 19, 1778; April-May 1778. |
| Sarjant/Sargent, Jeremiah | Private | Twelfth, Waggener | Dec 1777-March 1778 hospital; April 10, 1778 discharged. |
| Satorwhite/Saterwhite, William | Private | Seventh/Third, Hill | Feb 16, 1778 enlisted; April-June 1778. |
| Satter, John | Private | Seventh/Third, Powell | June 1778. |
| Saunders, Jesse | Private | Seventh, Jouett | Dec 1777-Jan 1778 sick in hospital; Feb 18, 1778 discharged. |
| Saunders, John | Private | Seventh, Crockett | Dec 1777-Jan 1778 in R. Bat. |
| Saunders, Robert Hyde | 2nd. Lt. | First State, Crump | Dec 1777-May 1778; June 8, 1778 resigned. Oath at Valley Forge on May 18, 1778, witnessed by Muhlenberg. |
| Saunders/Sanders, Thomas | Private | Fourteenth, Marks | Dec 1777; Jan 1778 on duty; Feb 1778; March 13, 1778 deserted. |
| Saunders, William/Wm. | Private | Seventh/Third, Young | Feb 16, 1778 enlisted; April 1778 sick present; May-June 1778. |
| Savage, Thomas | Private | Seventh/Third, Crockett/Sayers | March 19, 1778 enlisted; April-May 1778; June 1778 June 1778 in Sayers' Company; July 7, 1778 discharged. |
| Sawyers/Sawers, James | Private | Fourteenth, Thweatt | Jan 1778 lately joined regiment, artificer at York; Feb-May 1778 on command at Little York; June 1778 on command. |

| Name | Rank | Regiment/Company | Notes |
|---|---|---|---|
| Sayers, Robert | 1st. Lt. | Seventh/Third, Crockett/Sayers | Dec 1777-Jan 1778 on furlough; April-May 1778. For June 1778 he is shown commanding the Major's Company of the combined Third and Seventh Regiments, but there was no Major for the unit. |
| Scaggs, Richard | Private | Seventh, Crockett | Dec 1777-Jan 1778 in R. Bat. |
| Scanland/Scandlen, John | Private | Second, Upshaw | Dec 1777 hospital; Jan 1778. |
| Scanland, William | Private | Second, Upshaw | Dec 1777-Jan 1778. |
| Scantlin/Scantling, Jeremiah | Private | Fourteenth, Conway | Dec 1777; Jan-May 1778 artificer; June 1778. |
| Scarborough, Isick/Isaac | Private | Fourteenth, Conway | Feb 23, 1778 enlisted; June 1778 lately joined, sick Valley Forge. |
| Scates, John | Private | Fourteenth, Thweatt | Dec 1777; Jan 1778 sick at hospital; Feb 21, 1778 died. |
| Scoggan, Ephraim | Private | Fifteenth, Edmunds | Dec 1777 sick absent; Jan 15, 1778 died. |
| Scott, Abraham | Private | First, Pelham | Feb 1778 enlisted; April 1778 under inoculation; May-June 1778. |
| Scott, Andrew | Private | Twelfth, Ashby | Dec 1777; Jan-Feb 1778 sick in hospital; March-May 1778. |
| Scott, Daniel | Private | Seventh/Third, Fleming/Heth | Feb 11, 1778 enlisted; May 1778 on command; June 1778 in Heth's Company. |
| Scott, George/Geo. | Private | Sixth, Massie | Dec 1777 innoculated; Jan 1778; Feb 1778 on command; March-April 1778; May 1778 on command; June 1778 "prisner." |
| Scott, Isick/Isaac | Private | First State, Brown | Dec 1777; Jan 4, 1778 died. |
| Scott, James | Private | First, Cummings/Mennis | Dec 1777; Jan-Feb 1778 on furlough; March 1778 on furlough Virginia; April 1778 on furlough; May 1778; June 1778 in Mennis' Company. |

| | | | |
|---|---|---|---|
| Scott, Jesse/Jessey | Private | First State, Payne | Dec 1777 on guard; Jan 1778 sick; Feb 1778 sick absent; March 1778 sick present; April 1778 on guard; May 1778 on command. |
| Scott, John | Private | First State, Payne | Dec 1777; Jan 1778 sick; Feb 1778 sick absent; March 1778 deceased. |
| Scott, John | Ensign | Second State, Taliaferro | March 15-April 15, 1778. |
| Scott, John | Private | Third/Seventh, Mercer/Powell | Dec 1777-March 1778 furlough; April-May 1778; June 1778 in Powell's Company, waiting on G. Ley. (Probably General Charles Lee.) |
| Scott, John | Private | Twelfth, Madison | Dec 1777; Jan 1778 sick in hospital; Feb-April 1778. |
| Scott, John | Private | Fourteenth, Winston | Feb 17, 1778 drafted; May 1778; June 14, 1778 died. |
| Scott, John Epps/Eppes | 2nd. Lt. | Fifteenth, Hull | April 1778 sick present; May 1778. In April he receives pay back to July 21, 1777. |
| Scott, Joseph | Captain | First, Scott | Dec 1777 wounded and taken; Jan 1778; Feb 1778 prisoner of war; March 1778 taken prisoner; May 1778 prisoner of war; June 1778 muster roll shows "sick in Philadelphia," payroll shows "on Parole in Virginia." |
| Scott, Joseph Jr. | 2nd. Lt. | First, Pelham | Dec 1777 Virginia recruiting; Jan 1778 on guard; Feb 1778 on command; March-June 1778. Oath at Valley Forge on May 11, 1778, witnessed by Muhlenberg. |
| Scott, Joseph | Private | First State, Payne | June 1778. |
| Scott, Mathew | Sergeant | Twelfth, Madison | Dec 1777; Jan-March 1778 on command; April 1778. |
| Scott, Stephen | Private | Fourteenth, Winston | Oct 1, 1777 enlisted; March 1778 has joined the regiment; May 1778 sick in camp; June 1778 on guard. |
| Scott, William | Private | First State, Hamilton | Dec 1777-June 1778. |

| Name | Rank | Regiment | Notes |
|---|---|---|---|
| Scott, William | Private | First State, Payne | Dec 1777; Jan 1778 sick Bethlehem; Feb 1778; March 1778 sick present; April 1778 sick Yellow Springs. |
| Scott, William, Jr. | Private | First State, Payne | Dec 1777 sick hospital; Jan 1778 sick at Bethlehem; Feb 1778 sick absent; March 1778; May 1778 on guard; June 1778. |
| Scrus/Scrues see Cruse | | | |
| Scurlock, Alexander | Private | Fifteenth, Harris | May 1778 sick present; June 1778 sick Yellow Springs. |
| Seague, Barthw. | Private | Fifteenth, Foster | Dec 1777 sick absent; Jan 1778 dead. The last name may be League. |
| Seabrey, Augustine | Private | Fifteenth/ Grimes | Feb 11, 1778 drafted; June 1778 sick Valley Forge. |
| Sealy/Seely, Charles | Private | Seventh/ Third, Spencer/ Lipscomb | Feb 27, 1778 enlisted for 1 year; April 1778 May 1778 hospital; June 1778 in Lipscomb's Company. |
| Sears/Seears, Thomas | Private | First State, Meriwether | Dec 1777-June 1778. |
| Sears/Seares, William/Wm. | Private | Sixth, Rose | Dec 1777; Jan 1778 on command; Feb 1778; March 13, 1778 discharged. |
| Seay/See, Jacob | Private | Second, Jones | Dec 1777-Feb 1778 hospital; March-June 1778. |
| Seay/See, James | Private | Second, Taylor, W. | Dec 1777-Jan 1778; Feb 21, 1778 discharged. |
| Seayers/Sairs, John | Private | First State, Payne | April-May 1778; June 1778 deserted. |
| Sebastine/ Sebastin, Marin | Sergeant | Fifteenth, Hull | Dec 1777-Jan 1778 sick at hospital; Feb-March 1778 sick absent; April 1778 sick hospital. |
| Sebra/Sebrea, William/Willm. | Private | Fifteenth, Hull | Dec 1777 sick in hospital; Jan 1778 on guard; Feb 1778 sick present; March 1778 on command; April 1778; May 1778 hospital Yellow Springs; June-July 1778 sick Valley Forge. |
| Sebry, Orstean/ Austean | Private | Fifteenth, Grimes | Feb 11, 1777 drafted; April 1778; May 1778 sick present. |

| | | | |
|---|---|---|---|
| Seers, Silas | Corporal | Fifteenth, Gregory | Dec 1777-Jan 1778 sick in the hospital; Feb 9, 1778 dead. |
| Selden/Seldon, Joseph | 1st. Lt. | First State, Lee | Dec 1777 in the country; Jan 1778 sick absent; Feb 1778; March 1778 on furlough; April-June 1778. Oath at Valley Forge in June, 1778, witnessed by Muhlenberg. |
| Selden/Seldin, Samuel | 2nd. Lt. | First, Scott | Dec 1777; Jan 1778 on command; Feb-June 1778. Oath at Valley Forge on May 11, 1778, witnessed by Muhlenberg. |
| Sell, George | Private | Twelfth, Bowyer, T. | Dec 1777-Feb 1778; March 1778 on command; April-May 1778. |
| Sellers/Sellars, William | Private | Second State, Bernard | March 15-April 15, 1778 stationed in York garrison; May-June 1778. |
| Selman/Silman, Joseph | Private | First State, Hoffler | Dec 1777-June 1778. |
| Sennet/Senate, Stephen | Private | First, Lewis | Dec 1777-Jan 1778 on command; Feb-June 1778. |
| Serky/Seerkey, John | Private | Fifteenth, Hull | April-May 1778. |
| Settle/Suttle, Benjamin | Corporal | First State, Lee | Dec 1777 sick; Jan-Feb 1778 sick absent; March-June 1778. |
| Sevingston, Alexr. | Private | Fifteenth, Foster | Dec 1777 sick absent; Jan 1778 dead. The last name may be Levingston. |
| Sewell/Sowill, Thomas | Sergeant/ Quartermaster Sergeant | Twelfth, Wallace | Dec 1777-Jan 1778; Feb 1778 on command; March 1, 1778 promoted to Quartermaster Sergeant; March-May 1778. |
| Sexton, Archer/ Archibald | Private | Fourteenth, Reid | Dec 1777 hospital; Jan 26, 1778 deceased. |
| Sexton, John | Private | Fourteenth, Reid | Dec 1777 hospital; Jan 1778 sick at Reading; Feb 1778 sick absent; March 1778 sick in hospital; April-June 1778. |
| Sexton, Zacharia/ Zacharea | Private | First State, Crump | Dec 1777; Jan 24, 1778 deceased. |
| Sexton, William | Private | Third, Powell | Dec 1777-Jan 1778; Feb 7, 1778 discharged. |

| Name | Rank | Regiment | Service |
|---|---|---|---|
| Sexton, William | Private | Fourteenth, Lambert | Dec 1777-Jan 1778; Feb 1778 on furlough; March-June 1778. |
| Shackelford, Alexander | Private | First State, Crump | April-May 1778; June 1778 sick absent. |
| Shackelford, Richard | Corporal/ Private | First State, Crump | Dec 1777; Jan 1778 demoted to Private; Jan-June 1778. |
| Shackleford, George | Private | Seventh, Young | Feb 16, 1778 enlisted. No further record. |
| Shackleford, William | 2nd. Lt. | Fourteenth, Thweatt | November 23, 1777 died. |
| Shaddox/ Chaddox, Richard | Private | Third/ Seventh, Sayers | May 1778 sick in camp; June 1778 on guard. |
| Shakleford, Leonard | Corporal/ Sergeant | Seventh, Hill | Dec 1777-Jan 1778 on furlough; April 1, 1778 promoted to Sergeant; April-May 1778 |
| Shanks, John | Private | Second, Sanford/ Parker | Dec 1777-June 1778. From April on he appears in Parker's company. |
| Shannon, Pattrick/Patrick | Private | Twelfth, Madison | Dec 1777; Jan 1778 on fatigue; Feb 1778 on command; March-April 1778 on guard. |
| Shannon, Patrick | Private | Twelfth, Wallace | Dec 1777-April 1778 on furlough; May 1778. |
| Sharo, John | Private | Third/ Seventh, Sayers | June 1778. |
| Sharp, John | Sergeant | Second State, Quarles | April-June 1778; June 1778 reduced to Private. |
| Sharp/Sharpe, William/Will | Private/ Drummer | First, Lewis | Feb 7, 1778 enlisted; April-June 1778; June 1778 promoted to Drummer. |
| Sharwood, Lewis | Private | Fifteenth, Gregory | June 1778 unknown where. |
| Shavis see Chavis | | | |
| Shaw, James | Private | Twelfth, Madison | Dec 1777-March 1778 sick in hospital; April 1778 sick in Lancaster. |
| Shaw, John | Private | Seventh, Posey | Feb 27, 1778 enlisted; April-May 1778 |

| Name | Rank | Regiment/Company | Notes |
|---|---|---|---|
| Shaw, John | Private | Twelfth, Bowyer, T. | Dec 1777-March 1778; April 1778 on guard; May 1778. |
| Shaw, William | Private | Fourteenth, Reid | Dec 31, 1777 discharged. |
| Shea/Shay, Dennis | Private/ Corporal | Third/ Seventh, Arell/ Briscoe | Dec 1777 guard; Jan 1778 command; March-April 1778 command; May 1778 promoted to Corporal; June 1778 in Briscoe's Company. |
| Shealds, Charles | Private | Fifteenth, Edmunds | Dec 1777. |
| Shearer/Shurer, Richard | Private | Third/ Seventh, Peyton, V./ Peyton, J. | Dec 1777 on furlough Virginia; Feb-March 1778 on furlough; April 1778 on guard; May 1778; sick Valley Forge, in J. Peyton's Company. |
| Shearlock, James | Private | Fifteenth, Harris | Jan 1778 on command. |
| Sheldon, Thomas | Fife Major | Second | Dec 1777-June 1778. |
| Shelton, Joel | Private | Second, Taylor, W. | Dec 1777-Jan 1778; Feb 14, 1778 discharged. |
| Shelton, Thomas | Corporal | Second, Taylor, F. | Dec 1777-Feb 1778; March 12, 1778 discharged. |
| Shenault/ Shinalt, John | Private | Fourteenth, Marks | Jan 6, 1778 enlisted; Jan-April 1778 on furlough; May 1778; June 1778 on command. |
| Shepherd/ Shepperd, Joseph/James | Private | Third/ Seventh, Mercer/ Powell | Dec 1777-Jan 1778; Feb 1778 Genl Guard; March-May 1778; June 1778 on guard; in Powell's Company. |
| Shepherd/ Shipherd, Richard | Private | Third, Arell | Dec 1777; Jan 15, 1778 dead. |
| Shepperd/ Sheppard, Edward | Private | Seventh, Lipscomb | Dec 1777-Jan 1778 hospital; Feb 22, 1778 discharged. |
| Sherman/ Shearman, Duke/Ducke | Sergeant | Sixth, Hockaday | Dec 1777 sick Bethlehem; Jan-Feb 1778 sick absent. |
| Sherman, Joseph | Private | First State, Crump | Dec 1777; Jan 1778 deceased. |

| Name | Rank | Regiment, Company | Notes |
|---|---|---|---|
| Sherwood, Lewis | Private | Fifteenth, Mason | Dec 1777 wounded absent; Jan-April 1778 hospital; May 1778 "hospital but can't say what." |
| Shield/Shields, John | 1st. Lt./ Captain | First State, Meriwether/ Shields | Dec 1777-June 1778. In April 1778 he was promoted to Captain of Meriwether's former company. |
| Shields/Sheals, Charles | Private | Fifteenth, Wills | Jan-March 1778 sick absent; April-May 1778 sick Lancaster. |
| Shimer, Abraham | Private | Third, Blackwell | The Aug 1778 muster roll, dated Sept 9, 1778, which shows he had enlisted on Feb 12, 1778, and was sick at Valley Forge. |
| Shinalt/Shinnalt, Benjamin | Private | Second, Upshaw | Feb 14, 1778 drafted; April 1778; June 1778. |
| Shirley/Sherly, Micage/Cage | Private | Third/ Seventh, Briscoe | May 1778; June 1778 sick at Valley Forge. |
| Shores/Shors, Thomas | Private | Seventh, Jouett | Dec 1777; Jan 1778 on guard; Feb 12, 1778 discharged. |
| Short, Joshua | Private | Sixth, Apperson | Dec 1777 hospital Penna.; Jan 1778 hospital Reading; Feb 1778 hospital. |
| Shouse, Samuel | Private | Twelfth, Ashby | Jan-March 1778 on guard; April 1778 on commandl May 1778 on command "at Virga State Store". |
| Shuffield, Thomas | Private | Fourteenth, Jones | Jan 1778 deserted in Virginia. |
| Shugars, William | Private | Third, Mercer | Dec 1777-Feb 1778 on furlough. |
| Sidebotham, John/Jno. | Corporal | Third, Briscoe | Dec 1777; Jan 1778 on command; Feb 5, 1778 discharged. |
| Sidebotham/ Sidebothem, Joseph/Jos. | Private | Third, Briscoe | Dec 1777 sick in camp; Jan 1778; Feb 5, 1778 discharged. |
| Silence, William | Private | Second, Sanford/ Parker | Dec 1777 hospital; Feb-May 1778; June 1778 hospital; July 1778 sick at Valley Forge. From April on he appears in Parker's company. |
| Simes/Symes, Cuthbert | Private | First State, Meriwether | Dec 1777-March 1778. |

| | | | |
|---|---|---|---|
| Simmonds/ Simmons, Isick/Isaac | Private | Sixth, Fox | Dec 1777 in hospital; Jan 1778 sick absent; Feb 11, 1778 discharged. |
| Simmons/ Simons, James/Jas. | Private | Fifteenth, Gregory | Dec 1777-March 1778 hospital; June 1778. |
| Simmons/ Simons, Lemuel | Private | Fifteenth, Gregory | Dec 1777 Virginia; Jan 1778 sick Virginia. |
| Simmons, Micajah/ Mecagah | Private | Fourteenth, Marks | Dec 1777; Jan 1778 sick at hospital; Feb 1778 sick; March-May 1778; June 1778 sick Valley Forge. |
| Simmons, Spratley | Sergeant | Fifteenth, Gray | Dec 1777 sick absent; Jan 1778; Feb 1778 sick; March-May 1778. |
| Simmons/ Semmons, Thomas | Private | First, Lewis | Dec 1777-Jan 1778; Feb 1778 sick hospital; March-June 1778. |
| Simmons, Thomas | Sergeant | Fifteenth, Gray | Dec 1777; Jan-March 1778 on furlough; April 4, 1778 discharged. See Bridges, James. |
| Simmons/ Simons, Williamson | Private | Fifteenth, Gregory | Dec 1777; Jan 1778 sick present; Feb-June 1778. |
| Simms/Simmes, Charles | Lt. Col. | Sixth | Dec 1777 on furlough to Jersey; Jan 1778 on furlough Virginia; Feb-March 1778 on furlough; May-June 1778. Oath at Valley Forge on May 12, 1778, witnessed by Muhlenberg. |
| Simms, Micajah/ Mc Jaja | Private | Sixth, Apperson | Dec 1777; Jan 1778 absent with leave; Feb 1778. |
| Simms/Syme, Richard/Richd. | Private | Third, Mercer | Dec 1777-Feb 1778. |
| Simons/ Simonds, Henry | Private | Fifteenth, Grimes | Dec 1777-8; May 1778 on quarters guard. |
| Simons/ Simmons, Thomas | Private | First, Calmes | Dec 1777-May 1778. |
| Simpson/ Simson, Allen | Private | Twelfth, Bowyer, M. | Dec 1777; Jan 1778 on fatigue; Feb-May 1778. |

| Name | Rank | Regiment/Company | Notes |
|---|---|---|---|
| Simpson/Simson, Francis | Private | Twelfth, Casey | Dec 1777 on guard; Jan-May 1778. |
| Simpson, John | Private | Twelfth, Vause | Dec 1777-April 1778; May 1778 on guard. |
| Simpson/Simson, Joshua | Private | First, Pelham | Dec 1777 sick hospital; Jan 1778 on command; Feb 1778 on guard; March 1778 on fatigue; April-June 1778. |
| Sims, Isick/Isaac | Private | Fifteenth, Grimes | Feb 11, 1778 drafted; April 1778; May 1778 sick present; June 1778 sick Yellow Springs. |
| Sims/Simms, William | Sergeant | Seventh/Third, Fleming/Heth | Feb 16, 1778 appointed; April-May 1778; June 1778 in Heth's Company. |
| Simson, James | Private | Seventh, Webb | Jan 1778 hospital; February 1778. |
| Sinah, John/Jno. | Private | First, Taylor/Payne | Dec 1777-Jan 1778; Feb-June 1778 waggoner; May 1778 on in Payne's Company. |
| Singleton, Daniel/Danl. | Sergeant | Twelfth/First, Bowyer, T./Pelham | Aug 30, 1777 enlisted; Jan 1778 on guard; Feb-March 1778; April 1778 sick in camp; May 1778 "joined from the 12th Virginia"; June 1778 on guard. |
| Singleton, Israel/Isreal | Private | Fifteenth. Gray | Dec 1777-Feb 1778 on guard; March 1778 sick in camp. |
| Singleton, John | Private | Fifteenth, Gregory | Dec 1777-June 1778. |
| Sinnet, Jno. | Private | First, Payne | April 1778; May 1778 died. |
| Sipford see Lipsford | | | |
| Sisson, Robert | Private | Second, Sanford/Parker | Dec 1777 hospital; Jan-June 1778. From April on he appears in Parker's company. |
| Skelly/Skulley, William | Private | First, Pelham | Dec 1777-March 1778; April 1778 on command; May-June 1778. |
| Skinner, Alexander | Surgeon | First | Dec 1777 absent with leave; Jan-March 1778 on furlough; April-June 1778. Oath at Valley Forge on May 11, 1778, witnessed by Muhlenberg. |

| Name | Rank | Regiment | Notes |
|---|---|---|---|
| Skirlecks, Alexr. | Private | Fifteenth, Harris | May 1778 sick present. |
| Skirlock/Shirlock, James | Private | Fifteenth, Wills | June 7, 1777 enlisted; Feb 1778; March 10, 1778 deserted. |
| Slate, James | Private | Second, Jones | Dec 1777-June 1778. |
| Slate, John | Corporal | Fifteenth, Mason | Dec 1777-Jan 1778 sick absent; Feb 1778 at hospital; March 1778 sick in camp; April 1778 hospital; May 1778 Yellow Springs; June 1778 sick Yellow Springs. |
| Slaughter, Augustin/Augustine | Surgeon | Seventh | Dec 1777-March 1778 on furlough; April-May 1778; June 1778 sick Valley Forge. |
| Slaughter, Ezekiel | Private | Fourteenth, Thweatt | Dec 1777-Feb 1778 sick at hospital; March 1778. |
| Slaughter, George | Major | Twelfth | Dec 23, 1777 resigned. |
| Slaughter/Slaughtor, John | Private | Third, Peyton, V. | Dec 1777 rifleman on command with Col. Morgan; Jan 1778 with Col. Morgan. |
| Slaughter/Slater, John/Jno. | Private | Sixth, Massie | Dec 1777 innoculated; Jan-June 1778. |
| Slaughter, John | 2nd. Lt. | Twelfth, Bowyer, T. | Dec 1777 sick absent; Jan 1778; Feb 1778 on command; March 1778; April 1778 sick in camp; May 1778. |
| Slaughter, Robert | 2nd. Lt. | Third, Arell | Dec 18, 1777 resigned. |
| Slaughter, Thomas | Quartermaster | First State | Jan-Feb 1778. |
| Slaughter, William | Sergeant | First State, Camp | Dec 1777 sick country; Jan 1778; Feb-March 1778 on furlough; April-June 1778. |
| Slaughter, William/Wm. | Private | Sixth, Massie | Jan 1778; Feb 12, 1778 discharged. |
| Slaughter/Slauter, William | Private | Fourteenth, Winston | Dec 1777 sick in hospital; Jan 1778 sick in Jersey; Feb 1778 sick in hospital. |
| Slavens/Slavins, John | Private | Twelfth, Bowyer, M. | Dec 1777-April 1778; May 1778 sick in camp. |

| Name | Rank | Regiment/Company | Service |
|---|---|---|---|
| Sledd/Selead, Seaton/Seatin | Private/Fifer/ Private | First State, Hamilton | Dec 1777-March 1778; April 1778 demoted to Private; April-May 1778; June 1778 sick absent. |
| Small, Henry | Private | First State, Meriwether | Dec 1777; Jan 1778, died about Jan 15, 1778. |
| Smith, Adam | Musician | Twelfth, Bowyer, M. | March 20, 1778 enlisted; April-May 1778. |
| Smith, Alexander | Drum Major | Second | Dec 18, 1777 deserted. |
| Smith, Ballard | 2nd. Lt. | First, Pelham/ Mennis | Dec 1777 sick absent; Jan-Feb 1778; March 1778 on fatigue; April 1778; May-June 1778 in Mennis' Company. Oath at Valley Forge on May 11, 1778, witnessed by Muhlenberg. |
| Smith, Caleb | Private | Seventh, Moseley | Dec 1777-March 1778 on furlough; April 1778 promoted Fifer with Brother Charles |
| Smith, Charles/Chas. | Fifer | Seventh Third, Moseley/ Blackwell | April 1, 1778 appointed Fifer "in his Brother Calebs place", but Caleb appears as a Private; May 1778 sick in camp; June-July 1778 sick Valley Forge, in Blackwell's Company. |
| Smith, Edward | Private | First State, Ewell, C. | June 1778 sick at Yellow Springs. |
| Smith, Edward | Private | First State, Ewell, T. | Dec 1777-March 1778; April 1, 1778 died. |
| Smith, Elijah | Private | Seventh Third, Fleming/ Heth | Dec 1777; Jan 1778 sick present; Feb-May 1778; June 1778 sick Valley Forge, in Heth's Company. |
| Smith, Frederick | Private/ Corporal | Seventh Third, Fleming/ Heth | Dec 1777 on furlough Virginia; Jan-March 1778 on furlough; Feb 14, 1778 promoted to Corporal; April-May 1778; June 1778 in Heth's Company. |
| Smith, Francis/ Frances | Fifer | Second State, Garnett | March 15-May 1, 1778; May-June 1778. |
| Smith, Francis | Private | Fifteenth, Gray | Dec 1777-Feb 1778; March 1778 on command; April 1778 sick present; May 1778. |

| | | | |
|---|---|---|---|
| Smith, Frederick | Private | Twelfth, Bowyer, M. | Dec 1777 roll shows he died in Nov 1777. |
| Smith, Frederick | Corporal | Seventh, Fleming | Dec 1777-March 1778 on furlough. |
| Smith, George | Private | Second, Calmes | Dec 1777-June 1778. |
| Smith, George | Private | Third, Mercer | Dec 1777-March 1778 sick absent; April 1778 sick at Lancaster. |
| Smith, Gregory | Colonel | Second State | May-June 1778. Oath at Valley Forge on May 18, 1778, witnessed by Muhlenberg. |
| Smith, Henry/Heney | Corporal | Twelfth, Ashby | Dec 1777; Jan 1778 sick in hospital; March-May 1778. |
| Smith, Isick/Isaac | Sergeant | First, Pelham | Dec 1777-June 1778. |
| Smith, Isick/Isaac | Private | Second, Taylor, W. | Dec 1777-June 1778. |
| Smith, Isick/Isaac | Private | Third, Blackwell | Dec 1777 on guard; Jan 1778; Feb 14, 1778 discharged. |
| Smith, James | Private | First, Mennis | Feb 1, 1778 enlisted; June 1778 sick Yellow Springs. |
| Smith, James | Private | First State, Camp | Dec 1777 hospital; Jan-Feb 1778 sick absent; March 1778 rolls show he deserted from hospital, Feb 8, 1778. |
| Smith, James | Private | Third, Mercer | Dec 1777; Jan 1, 1778 discharged. |
| Smith, James | Private | Seventh/ Third, Crockett/ Sayers | Dec 1777-Jan 1778 on furlough; April-May 1778; June 1778 in Sayers' Company. |
| Smith, James | Ensign | Seventh/ Third, Hill/Sayers | Dec 1777; Jan 1778; April 1778 on furlough Virginia; May 1778; June 1778 in Sayers' Company. |
| Smith, James | Private | Twelfth, Bowyer, M. | May 1778 "Joined-Returned from the Enemy"; The Oct 1777 roll shows him "missing October 4 at German Town." |
| Smith, James | Private | Fourteenth, Lambert | Sept 9, 1777 enlisted; April 1778 lately joined regiment; May-June 1778. |

| Name | Rank | Regiment/Company | Service |
|---|---|---|---|
| Smith, James | Private | Fourteenth, Thweatt | Dec 1777; June 1778 sick in hospital; Feb 1778 sick present; March-June 1778. |
| Smith, Jesse | Corporal | Third/Seventh, Peyton, V. Peyton, J. | Feb 17, 1778 drafted; April 1778; May 1778 on command; June 1778 sick Brunswick, in J. Peyton's Company. |
| Smith, John Sr. | Private | First, Cunningham | May 1777 deserted; May 25, 1778 joined since last muster; June 1778. |
| Smith, John | Private | First, Lawson | Dec 1777 sick Princeton; Jan-Feb 1778; March 1778 fatigue; April 1778; May 1778 on command; June 1778. |
| Smith, John | Private | First, Pelham | Dec 1777 sick hospital; Jan-April 1778 sick at Trenton; May-June 1778 sick Princeton |
| Smith, John/Jno. Jr. | Private | First, Scott | Dec 1777; Jan 1778 on command; Feb 1778; March 1778 sick present; April-May 1778; June 1778. |
| Smith, John | Private | Second, Upshaw | Dec 1777 hospital; Jan 1778. |
| Smith, John | Private | Second State, Bernard | May 1778; June 1778 on guard. |
| Smith, John | Private | Seventh Third, Hill | April-June 1778. |
| Smith, John | Private | Seventh, Posey | Dec 1777-Jan 1778 on command |
| Smith, John | Private | Twelfth, Casey | Dec 1777 sent to hospital; Jan-Feb 1778 at hospital; March-May 1778. |
| Smith/Smyth, John | Private/Corporal | Twelfth, Waggener | Dec 1777 on command; Jan 1778; Feb 1, 1778 promoted to Corporal; Feb-May 1778. |
| Smith, John | Corporal | Fourteenth, Conway | Oct 1777 missing at Germantown, Oct. 4; Jan 1778; Feb 1778 on duty; March-April 1778; May 30, 1778 died. |

| | | | |
|---|---|---|---|
| Smith, Joseph | Corporal | Second, Sanford/ Parker | Dec 1777-June 1778. From April on he appears in Parker's company. |
| Smith, Larkin | Private | Seventh/ Third, Fleming/ Heth | Feb 12, 1778 enlisted; April 1778 sick present; May 1778; June 1778 in Heth's Company. |
| Smith, Littleberry/ Littlebury | Private | Second State, Bernard | April-May 1778; June 1778 sick Valley Forge. |
| Smith, Peter | Private | Fourteenth, Winston | Dec 1777 sick in hospital; Jan 1778 on furlough; Feb 1778. |
| Smith, Redman/ Redmd. | Private | First, Lewis | Feb 7, 1778 enlisted; May-June 1778 on guard. |
| Smith, Richard | Corporal | Fourteenth, Thweatt | Died about Dec 20, 1777. |
| Smith, Robert | Private | First State, Meriwether | Dec 1777-June 1778. |
| Smith, Robert | Private | Fourteenth, Reid | March-June 1778. |
| Smith, Robert | Corporal/ Sergeant | Twelfth, Waggener | Dec 1777-Feb 1778; March 1778 promoted to Sergeant; March-May 1778. |
| Smith, Samuel | Private | Twelfth, Madison | Dec 1777-Feb 1778; March 1778 on guard; April 1778. |
| Smith, Stephen | Private | Third/ Seventh, Blackwell | June 1778. |
| Smith, Thomas | Private | First State, Crump | Dec 1777-Feb 1778. |
| Smith, Thomas | Private | Seventh/ Third, Fleming/ Heth | Dec 1777 on guard; Jan 1778 on command; Feb-April 1778; May 1778 on command; June 1778 on guard; in Heth's Company. |
| Smith, Thomas | Sergeant | Seventh, Moseley | Dec 1777 sick in hospital; Jan 1778 sick present; February 1778; March 1, 1778 discharged. |
| Smith, Thomas | Musician | Twelfth, Bowyer, M. | Dec 1777 sick at Lancaster; Jan 1778 sick in hospital; Feb-April 1778. |
| Smith, William/Will | 1st. Lt. | Fifteenth, Harris | May 1778. |

| Name | Rank | Regiment | Notes |
|---|---|---|---|
| Smith, William/Wm. | Private | First, Lawson | Dec 1777 sick Virginia; June 1778 sick Virginia. |
| Smith, William | Private | First State, Hamilton | Dec 1777-May 1778; June 1778 sick absent. |
| Smith, William | Fifer | Twelfth, Casey | Dec 1777-May 1778. |
| Smith, William | Private | Fourteenth, Reid | Dec 1777 on duty; Jan 1778 absent without leave; Feb 1778 deserted. |
| Smith, William, Sr. | Private | Fourteenth, Reid | Dec 1777 hospital; Jan 1778; March-May 1778; June 1778 on command. |
| Smith, William P./Will P. | Private | First, Lewis | Feb 7, 1778 enlisted; April-June 1778; August 4, 1778 died. |
| Smith, William S/Will. S. | Sergeant | First, Lewis | Feb 7, 1778 enlisted; April-June 1778. |
| Smithee/Smitha, Benjamin | Private | Second, Willis | Dec 1777-June 1778. |
| Snape/Snipe, Nathaniel | Private | Third, Mercer | Dec 1777-Jan 1778. |
| Snead/Sneed, Christopher/Christefer | Private | First, Mennis | Dec 1777 sick Princeton; Jan 1778 on furlough; Feb-June 1778. |
| Snead/Sneed, John | Private | Sixth, Avery | Dec 1777 sick in hospital; Jan 1778; Feb 10, 1778 discharged. |
| Snead/Sneed, Philip | Sergeant | Sixth, Avery | Dec 1777-Jan 1778; Feb 8, 1778 discharged. |
| Snelling/Sneling, Enoch | Private | First State, Hoffler | Dec 1777-June 1778. |
| Snethers/Smithers, Stephen | Private | Twelfth, Wallace | Dec 1777-April 1778 on furlough; May 1778. |
| Snively/Shively, George | Private | Seventh, Third, Spencer/Lipscomb | March 26, 1778 enlisted for 1 year; April 1778 sick in camp, May 1778; June 1778 in Lipscomb's Company. |
| Snow, John | Private | Second, Taylor, F. | Dec 1777-March 1778; April 10, 1778 discharged, time of service expired. |

Soden see Lorden

| | | | |
|---|---|---|---|
| Sollers/Sallers, William/Willm. | Private | Third/ Seventh, Arell/ Briscoe | Jan 1778 sick present; Feb 1778; March 1778 on command; April 1778; May 1778 on command; June 1778 bullock guard. |
| Sooleven, Thomas | Private | Seventh, Crockett | Feb 27, 1778 enlisted; April-May 1778 |
| Southall, Stephen/Stavon | Private/ Cadet | Fifteenth, Wills | March 1778; April 1, 1778 promoted to Cadet. |
| Southard/ Suthard, William | Private | Second, Willis | Dec 1777-March 1778; April 27, 1778 dead. |
| Southerland/ Southerlin, Rawleigh/ Raligh | Private | Second, Willis | Dec 1777-June 1778. |
| Southerlin, William | Private | Third, Mercer | Dec 1777-March 1778 on furlough. |
| Southworth, Thomas | Private | First State, Meriwether | Dec 1777-June 1778. |
| Spain, Absolum/ Absalom | Private | Fifteenth, Grimes | Dec 1777-April 1778 on furlough. |
| Spann/Span, James | Private | Seventh, Young | Dec 1777 on command; Jan 1778; Feb 12, 1778 discharged. |
| Speed, John | Private | Second State, Bernard | March 15-April 15, 1778 stationed in York garrison. May-June 1778. |
| Speed, John | Private | Fifteenth, Gregory | Dec 1777 on guard; Jan 1778 on command; Feb 1778 on guard; March 1778 sick in camp; April 1778 sick present; May 1778. |
| Speers/Spears, Robert | Sergeant/ Private | Fourteenth, Reid | Dec 1777 on duty; Jan 1778 on command; Feb 1778; March-May 1778 on command; May 17, 1778 reduced to Private; June 1778 sick English Town. |
| Spence, Henry/Heney | Private | Fifteenth, Hull | Dec 1777-Jan 1778; Feb-April 1778 sick present; May 1778. |
| Spence/Spense, James | Privatep | Fifteenth, Hull | Dec 1777-Jan 1778; Feb 1778 on guard; March 1778; April 1778 sick present; May 1778 hospital Yellow Springs. |

305

| | | | |
|---|---|---|---|
| Spence, John | Private | Fifteenth, Hull | Dec 1777 sick absent; Jan 1778 sick at hospital; Feb 1778 sick absent; March 1778; April 1778 under guard; May 1778; June 1778 sick Valley Forge. |
| Spencer, Abraham | Private | Third/ Seventh, Blackwell | Feb 17, 1778 drafted; June 1778 sick Valley Forge. |
| Spencer, Abraham | Private | Seventh, Moseley | Dec 1777; Jan 1778 absence Leave; Feb 19, 1778 discharged. |
| Spencer, Benjamin | Private | First State, Lee | Dec 1777-Jan 1778; Feb 1778 on guard; March 1778 Red Lyon Hospital; April-May 1778; June 1778 sick absent. |
| Spencer, Elisha | Private | First State, Nicholas | Dec 1777-Feb 1778 sick at Bethlehem; March-June 1778. |
| Spencer, Francis | Private | First, Pelham | Dec 1777 sick absent; Feb 15, 1778 discharged. |
| Spencer, Griffith | Private | Seventh/ Third, Moseley/ Blackwell | Dec 1777-March 1778 on furlough; April-May 1778; June 27, 1778 deceased, in Blackwell's Company. |
| Spencer, John | Private | First, Lawson | Dec 1777 sick Virginia; March 1778; May-June 1778. |
| Spencer, John | Matross | First Artillery, Burwell | Enlisted June 1, 1776, for three years; Muster roll for First Artillery shows May-June 1778 turned over to First Virginia Regiment. |
| Spencer, John | Private | Seventh/ Third, Jouett/Hill | Feb 11, 1778 enlisted; May 1778; June 1778 in Hill's Company. |
| Spencer, John | Private | Seventh, Lipscomb | Dec 1777 hospital; Jan 31, 1778 discharged. |
| Spencer, John | Surgeon's Mate | Fourteenth | Muster roll and payroll show him appointed on April 24, 1778. No other entries. |
| Spencer, Joseph | Captain | Seventh, Spencer | Nov 14, 1777 resigned. The company was referred to as Spencer's through May 1778. |

| | | | |
|---|---|---|---|
| Spencer, Moses | Private | Seventh/Third, Fleming/Heth | Feb 10, 1778 enlisted; April 1778 sick present; May 1778; June 1778 Heth's Company. |
| Spencer, Nathaniel/Nat. | Private | Second State, Quarles | April-May 1778; June 26, 1778 died. |
| Spencer/Spenser, Patrick/Partrick | Fife Major | First, Mennis | Dec 1777; Jan 1778 deserted. |
| Spencer, Thomas | Private | Seventh/Third, Lipscomb | Feb 14, 1778 enlisted for 1 year; April-May 1778; June 1778 hospital. |
| Spencer/Spencere, William/Wm. | Fifer | Sixth, Massie | Dec 1777-April 1778 on furlough; May-June 1778. |
| Spencer, William | Private | Seventh, Moseley | Dec 1777-Jan 1778; Feb 19, 1778 discharged. |
| Spencer, William | Private/Corporal | Twelfth, Waggener | Dec 1777 hospital; Jan-May 1778; promoted to Corporal in May. |
| Spender, William | Private | Third/Seventh, Mercer/Powell | Dec 1777 on duty; Jan 1778 guard; Feb 1778 on picket; March-May 1778; June 1778 in Powell's Company. |
| Spicer, Benjamin | Private | Fourteenth, Winston | Feb 17, 1778 drafted; May 1778 sick in camp; June 11, 1778 died. |
| Spiller/Spillar, Benjamin C./Benj. C. | Captain | Second State, Spiller | March 15-May 1, 1778; May-June 1778. Oath on May 25, 1778, witnessed by Muhlenberg. |
| Spilman, William | Private | Second State, Dudley | July 1778 "Omitted from 1st April." |
| Spindle, Ambrose | Private | Sixth, Avery | Dec 1777 absent wounded; Jan 31, 1778 dead. |
| Spinner, John | Private | Second, Taylor, W. | Dec 1777-Jan 1778; Feb 14, 1778 discharged. |
| Splaune/Splane, Thomas | Private | Second, Harrison | Dec 1777 hospital; Jan-June 1778. |
| Spragans/Spraggans, Thomas | Private | Sixth, Apperson | Dec 1777; Jan 22, 1778 discharged; in Feb 1778 he was paid for 22 days. |

| Name | Rank | Regiment/Company | Service |
|---|---|---|---|
| Sprous/Sprouse, Charles | Private | Seventh// Third, Spencer/ Lipscomb | Feb 11, 1778 enlisted for 1 year; May 1778; June 1778 in Lipscomb's Company. |
| Spruce, John | Private | First, Lewis | Jan-June 1778. |
| Squires, James | Private | Second, Sanford/ Parker | Dec 26, 1777 on command. |
| Stacey, Jeremiah | Private | Third/ Seventh, Peyton, V./ Peyton, J. | Dec 1777-Jan 1778; Feb 1778 on Gl. Woodfords guard; March-May 1778; June 1778 in J. Peyton's Company. |
| Stacey/Stacy, Simon | Private/ Corporal/ Private | Fifteenth, Edmunds/ Gregory | Dec 1777; Jan 1778 promoted to Corporal; Feb 1778 reduced to Private; March-May 1778; June 1778 in Gregory's company. |
| Stacey/Stacy, Stephen | Private | Fifteenth, Gray | Dec 1777; Jan 1778 on command; Feb-March 1778; April 1778 sick present; May 1778. |
| Stackerpole/ Stakerpoll, John | Private | Seventh/ Third, Spencer/ Lipscomb | March 6, 1778 enlisted fpr 3 years; April-May 1778; June 1778 in Lipscomb's Company. |
| Stafford, Joshua | Private | Fifteenth, Grimes | Feb 13, 1778 drafted; April-May 1778. |
| Stafford, Thomas | Private | First State, Hoffler | April-May 1778; June 1778 sick absent. |
| Stagers/ Staggers, Duderick/ Dederick | Private | Twelfth, Wallace | Dec 1777; Jan-March 1778 sent to hospital; April 1778 on guard; May 1778 on weeks command. |
| Stagg, John | Private | Twelfth, Vause | April 1778 roll shows he entered on March 21, 1778; May 1778. |
| Stallions/ Stalions, Richard | Private | Second, Jones | Dec 1777-Feb 1778 hospital. |
| Standley/ Stanley, Jonah | Private | First, Lewis | Dec 1777 sick; Jan-March 1778 sick hospital. |
| Stanley, John | Private | Seventh, Crockett | Dec 1777 on guard; Jan 1778 waggoner. |
| Staples, John | Private | Fourteenth, Jones | Feb 14, 1778 enlisted; Aug 1778. |

| Name | Rank | Regiment, Company | Notes |
|---|---|---|---|
| Staples/Stapels, Joseph | Sergeant | Fourteenth, Marks | Jan 6, 1778 enlisted for two years; Jan-April 1778 on furlough; May-June 1778. |
| Stapleton/Stableton, Andrew | Private | Twelfth, Vause | Dec 1777-Feb 1778; March 1778 sick in camp; April-May 1778. |
| Stapp/Step, Kellis, Killis | Private | Seventh, Spencer | Dec 1777-Jan 1778; March 2, 1778 discharged. |
| Starke/Stark, Richard | Ensign | Seventh/Third, Webb/Young | Jan 1778 on furlough Virginia; February 1778 on furlough; April-May 1778; June 1778 in Young's Company. |
| Stark/Starke, Wm. | 1st. Lt. | Sixth, Garland | Dec 1777-June 1778 on furlough. |
| Starkey, John | Corporal | Seventh, Fleming | Dec 1777-Jan 1778; Feb 15, 1778 discharged. |
| Starling/Sterling, William | Corporal | Twelfth, Wallace | Dec 1777; Jan 1778 roll shows he deserted on Feb 4, 1778. |
| Starne/Sterne, William/Wm. | Private | Seventh, Third, Fleming/Heth | Dec 1777 on furlough Virginia; Jan-March 1778; April-May 1778 on guard; June 1778 in Heth's Company. |
| Steel, John | Private | First State, Meriwether | Dec 1777. |
| Steel, Thomas | Private | Third, Peyton, V. | Dec 1777 sick Virginia; Jan 1778 his name is crossed out. |
| Stephens/Stevens, Charles | Private | Seventh/Third, Fleming/Heth | Feb 19, 1778 enlisted; April 1778 sick present; May 1778 on guard; June 1778 on guard, in Heth's Company. |
| Stephens/Steavens, Hubbard/Hubard | Drummer/Private | Sixth, Fox | Dec 1777 in hospital; Jan 1778 reduced to Private; Jan-April 1778; May 1778 on duty; June 1778. |
| Stephens/Stevens, John | Corporal | First State, Brown | Dec 1777; Jan 2, 1778 died. |
| Stephens/Stevins, John | Private | Second State, Taliaferro | March 15-May 1, 1778; May 1778; June 1778 sick Valley Forge. |
| Stephens/Stevens, Joseph | Private | Fourteenth, Jones | Feb 8, 1778 drafted; April 1778. |

| Name | Rank | Regiment, Company | Service |
|---|---|---|---|
| Stephens, Nathaniel | Private | Second State, Bernard | March 15-April 15, 1778 stationed in York garrison. Paid on April 20, 1778. |
| Stephens/ Stevins, Smith | Private | Fifteenth, Harris | Jan 1778 on command; Feb 1778-May 1778 sick present; June-Oct 1778 sick Valley Forge. |
| Stephens/ Stevens, Warrington/ Warington | Private | First State, Hoffler | Dec 1777-June 1778. |
| Stephinson, James | Private | Fifteenth, Wills | April 1778. |
| Sterling, James | Corporal | Seventh, Posey | Dec 1777-Jan 1778 in Rifle Battn.; Feb 24, 1778 discharged. |
| Stevens, Charles | Private | Seventh, Fleming | Feb 19, 1778 enlisted; May 1778 sick present; June 1778 on guard. |
| Stevens, Jacob | Private/ Corporal | Seventh/ Third, Crockett/ Sayers | March 12, 1778 enlisted; April-May 1778; June 1, 1778 promoted to Corporal, in Sayers' Company. |
| Stevens/ Stephens, James | Private | Second State, Quarles | April-June 1778. |
| Stevens/ Stephens, John | Private | Second State, Dudley | March 15-May 1, 1778; May-June 1778. |
| Stevens/Stivins, William | Private | Fourteenth, Lambert | Aug 15, 1777 enlisted; April 1778 lately joined regiment; May 1778 sick in camp; June 15, 1778 deceased. |
| Stevenson/ Stephenson, Arthur/Arthr. | Sergeant/ Private | Third/ Seventh, Arell/ Briscoe | Dec 1777 listed as a Sergeant, a Private on the later rolls; Dec 1777-Feb 1778 on furlough; April 1778 on guard; May 1778; June 1778 in Briscoe's Company. |
| Stevenson/ Stephenson, John | Private | First State, Hoffler | Dec 1777-June 1778. |
| Steward, Alexander | Private | Second State, Lewis | March 15-May 1, 1778; May-June 1778. |

| Name | Rank | Regiment, Company | Service |
|---|---|---|---|
| Steward/Stewart, Thomas | Private | Sixth, Hockaday | Feb 17, 1778 drafted; April 1778; May on command Fort Pitt; June 1778 on command with Col. Gibson at Fort Pitt. |
| Stewart/Steward, Benjamin | Private | First State, Payne/Ewell, C. | Dec 1777-Feb 1778; March 1778 sick present; April-June 1778. |
| Stewart/Stuard, Charles | Private | First, Mennis | Dec 1777 sick Princeton; Jan 1778 sick hospital; Feb 1778; March 1778 sick present; April-May 1778; June 1778 absent. |
| Stewart/Steward, Charles | Private | First State, Camp | Dec 1777 sick Virginia; Jan-Feb 1778 sick absent; March 1778 on furlough Virginia; April-June 1778. |
| Stewart, Charles | 2nd. Lt. | Fifteenth, Gregory | Dec 1777-March 1778; April 1778 on command; May 1778. |
| Stewart, James | Private | Fifteenth, Grimes | Dec 1777-Feb 1778 sick absent; April 1778 muster roll reads "Died some time ago in the hospital." |
| Stewart, Lewis | Private/Surgeon's Mate | Seventh/Third, Posey | Feb 28, 1778 enlisted; April 1778; May 10, 1778 appointed Surgeon's Mate; May-June 1778. |
| Stewart, Lewis | Private | Fifteenth, Gregory | June 1778. This man and the one below are probably the same individual. |
| Stewart, Lewis | Private | Fifteenth, Mason | Feb 1, 1778 drafted; May 1778. |
| Stewart/Stuart, Mack | Private | First State, Hoffler | April-May 1778; June 1778 sick absent. |
| Stewart/Stuart, Solomon | Private | First State, Hoffler | April-May 1778; June 1778 sick absent. |
| Stewart/Steuart, William | Private | Twelfth, Bowyer, T. | Dec 1777-Feb 1778 on command; March 1778 on guard; April-May 1778. |
| Stewart, William | Private | Fourteenth, Lambert | Dec 1777; April-June 1778 waggoner. |
| Stiff, Jacob | Corporal | Sixth, Massie | Dec 1777 "Time to serve, Feb. 2, 1778."; Jan 1778 discharged. |
| Still, William | Private | First, Cunningham | Feb 23, 1778 enlisted; First appears in Sept 1778 "sick absent, joined." |

| Name | Rank | Regiment | Notes |
|---|---|---|---|
| Stilwell, Samuel | Private | Twelfth, Ashby | Dec 1777-Feb 1778 hospital; March 1778 dead. |
| St. John, Isick/ Isaac/Isacke | Sergeant | Seventh, Webb | Enlisted for 2 years. Jan 1778; February 1778 discharged. |
| St. Lawrence, Patrick | Sergeant Major | Twelfth | Dec 1777-May 1778 |
| Stivers, Edward/ Eadward | Private/Fifer | Seventh, Third, Spencer/ Lipcomb | Enlisted for 3 years. Dec 1777 on furlough Virginia; Jan 1778 on furlough; April 1778 promoted to Fifer; April-May 1778; June 1778 in Lipscomb's Company. |
| Stivers, Peter | Private | Seventh, Spencer | Dec 1777 on guard; Feb 2, 1778 discharged. |
| Stivers, Reuben/ Ruebin | Drummer | Seventh/ Third, Spencer/ Lipscomb | Dec 1777 on furlough Virginia; Jan 1778 on furlough; April-May 1778; June 1778 in Lipscomb's Company. |
| Stoakes/Stokes, Allen | Private | Fifteenth, Grimes | Dec 1777-Feb 1778 sick absent; March 1778 muster roll reads "Died some time ago in the hospital." |
| Stoakes/Stokes, Nathanial/Nathl. | Private | Fifteenth, Grimes | Feb 11, 1778 drafted; May 1778 sick present; June-July 1778 sick Valley Forge; Aug 1778 muster roll shows "Dead July". |
| Stokes/Stocks, Hampton/ Hamton | Private | Fourteenth, Thweatt | Aug 27, 1777 enlisted; Jan 1778 lately joined this regiment; April 1778 sick Yellow Springs hospital; May 1778 sick present; June 1778 sick Carrells. |
| Stokes, John | Private | First State, Crump | Dec 1777-May 1778; June 1778 sick absent. |
| Stokes, John | 1st. Lt. | Sixth, Avery | Dec 1777-Jan 1778; Feb-May 1778 on furlough; June 1778 on guard. Oath at Valley Forge on May 12, 1778, witnessed by Muhlenberg. |
| Stokes, Silvanah/ Silvanus | Private | Seventh/ Third, Moseley/ Blackwell | Dec 1777-March 1778 on furlough; April-May 1778; June 1778 in Blackwell's Company. |
| Stone, Hezekiah | Corporal | Sixth, Garland | Dec 1777-Jan 1778; Feb 16, 1778 discharged. |

| Name | Rank | Regiment/Company | Notes |
|---|---|---|---|
| Stone, Robert | Private/ Sergeant | First State, Brown | Dec 1777-March 1778; April 17, 1778 discharged. |
| Stone, William | Private | First State, Hoffler | Dec 1777-May 1778; June 1778 sick absent. |
| Stone, William | Private | Fourteenth, Reid | Sept 18, 1777 enlisted; April 1778 lately joined regiment; May-June 1778. |
| Story, Daniel | Private | Fifteenth, Gray | Feb 10, 1778 drafted; April 1778 under inoculation. |
| Story, Lewis | Private | Fifteenth, Gray | Feb 10, 1778 drafted; April 1778 under inoculation; May 1778. |
| Stovall/Stovale, Abraham | Private | Seventh/ Third, Fleming/ Heth | Feb 11, 1778 enlisted; April 1778 sick present; May 1778 on guard; June 1778 in Heth's Company. |
| Strange, Archibald | Sergeant | Seventh, Jouett | Dec 1777 on furlough Virginia; Jan 1778 on furlough; Feb 7, 1778 discharged. |
| Stratton, Isick/Isaac | Private | Fourteenth, Overton | Jan 18, 1778 enlisted; May-June 1778. |
| Strauther/ Straughder, James | Sergeant | Second State, Lewis | March 15-May 1, 1778; May-June 1778. |
| Stricklin/ Strigling, Edward | Private | First State, Camp | Dec 1777 confined; Jan-Feb 1778 sick absent; in April 1778 he was paid for March and April, having been struck off the March muster roll; May-June 1778. |
| Striplain/ Streplin, William | Private | Third/ Seventh, Mercer/ Powell | April 1778; May 1778 on command; June 1778 in Powell's Company. |
| Stripling, Samuel | Private | Third, Lee | Dec 1777 sick Virginia. |
| Stripling/ Stribling, Segismund/ Sagismond | 2nd. Lt./ 1st. Lt. | Twelfth, Waggener/ Ashby | Dec 1, 1777 promoted to 1st. Lt. and transferred to Ashby's company; Dec 1777-Jan 1778; March-May 1778. |
| Strong, John | Private | Third, Blackwell | Dec 23, 1777 discharged. |
| Strong, William | Corporal | First State, Nicholas | Dec 1777-Feb 1778; March 1778 on guard; April-June 1778. |

| | | | |
|---|---|---|---|
| Strother, William | Sergeant | Twelfth, Wallace | Dec 1777-March 1778 on furlough; April-May 1778. |
| Stroud, Jesse | Private | Sixth, Massie | Dec 1777 in hospital, "Time to serve, Feb. 1778." |
| Strouse/Strouce, Jacob | Private | Seventh Third, Fleming/ Young | Feb 13, 1778 enlisted; April 1778 on guard; May 1778; June 1778 in Young's Company. |
| Stuart/Stewart, James/Jas. | Private | First, Cummings | Dec 1777. |
| Stuart/Stewart, John/Jno. | Private | Third/ Seventh, Arell | Dec 1777 seaman; March 1778; April 1778 on furlough; May 1778; June-July 1778 sick at Valley Forge. |
| Stuart/Stuard Patrick/ Partrick | Private | Seventh/ Third, Hill | Dec 1777-Jan 1778 on command with General Woodford; May 1778 with General Woodford; June 1778 on command Gnl. Woodford. |
| Stuart, Robert | Drummer | Seventh, Hill | Dec 1777-Jan 1778 sick in hospital; April 1778 hospital not to be heard of. |
| Stubblefield, Beverly | 2nd. Lt. | Sixth, Avery | Dec 1777-April 1778 on furlough; May 1778 recruiting; June 1778. Oath at Valley Forge on May 28, 1778, witnessed by Muhlenberg. |
| Stubblefield, George | Major | Fourteenth | Dec 1777-Jan 1778; Feb 22, 1778 resigned. |
| Stubblefield, Peter | 1st. Lt. | First State, Camp | Dec 1777; Jan 1778; Feb 1778 on guard; March 1778 on furlough Virginia; April-May 1778; June 12, 1778 resigned. Oath at Valley Forge on May 12, 1778, witnessed by Muhlenberg. |
| Stubbs/Stubs, Benjamin | Private | Fourteenth, Winston | Dec 24, 1777 deserted; March-April 1778 sick in hospital; May-June 1778 sick Yellow Springs. |
| Stubbs, John | Private | Fourteenth, Jones | Sept 18, 1777 enlisted; Jan-March 1778 sick in hospital; May 1778 died not known when. |

| | | | |
|---|---|---|---|
| Stunks, Thomas | Private | Seventh/ Third, Moseley/ Blackwell | Dec 1777-March 1778 on furlough; April 1778 sick Lancaster; May-June 1778 sick in Virginia. |
| Sublett/Sublit, Benjamin/ Benjm. | Corporal | Fifteenth, Gray | Dec 1777 sick absent; Jan-April 1778; May 1778 sick present; June 1778 Valley Forge. |
| Sugars/Suggers, Wm. | Private | Third/ Seventh, Mercer/ Powell | Dec 1777-March 1778 on furlough; April 1778 sick in camp; May 1778 on command; June 1778, in Powell's Company. |
| Suggs, George | Private | First, Lewis | Dec 1777-April 1778; May-June 1778 on command. |
| Sullinger/ Sullenger, John | Private | Second, Upshaw | Dec 1777-Jan 1778. |
| Sullivan, Craven | Private | First State, Hamilton | Dec 1777-May 1778; June 1778 sick absent. |
| Sullivan/ Sulavin, James | Private | First State, Lee | Dec 1777 sick; Jan-Feb 1778 sick absent; March 1778 Yellow Springs Hospital. |
| Sullivan, John | Corporal | Twelfth, Bowyer, M. | Dec 1777-April 1778; May 1778 sick in hospital. |
| Sullivan, Matthew/ Mathew | Private | Twelfth, Bowyer, M. | Dec 25, 1777 missing. |
| Sullivan, Timothy | Sergeant | First State, Hamilton | Dec 1777. |
| Sullivan, Thomas/Thos. | Private | Seventh/ Third, Crockett/ Powell | Feb 27, 1778 enlisted; June 1778 on guard, in Powell's Company. |
| Summers, Simon | Adjutant | Sixth | Dec 1777 on furlough; Jan 1778 on furlough Virginia; Feb-March 1778 on furlough; April 1778; May 1778 "On furlough to the Sweet Springs in Virginia;" June 1778 on furlough in Virginia. Oath at Valley Forge on May 12, 1778, witnessed by Muhlenberg. |
| Surber, Joseph | Private | Twelfth, Waggener | Dec 1777-March 1778 on command; April 10, 1778 discharged. |

| Name | Rank | Regiment/Company | Service |
|---|---|---|---|
| Surles/Surrils, Covirton/Covinton | Corporal | Second State, Spiller | June 1778; July 1778 sick Valley Forge. |
| Sutherland/Southerland, Wm. | Private | Third/Seventh, Mercer/Powell | Dec 1777-March 1778; April 1778; May 1778 on command; June 1778, in Powell's Company. |
| Sutton/Stuton, John Jr. | Paymaster | First | Dec 1777-June 1778. Oath at Valley Forge on May 11, 1778, witnessed by Muhlenberg. |
| Sutton, John | Sergeant | First State, Hoffler | Dec 1777-May 1778. |
| Sutton, William | Private | First State, Payne | Dec 1777 waggoner; Jan-Feb 1778; March-June 1778 on command. |
| Sutton, William | Private | Seventh, Posey | Dec 1777-Jan 1778 on furlough. |
| Swan, Ralph/Ralf | Private | Fifteenth, Hull | Dec 1777-Feb 1778; March-May 1778 sick present. |
| Swanscomb/Swanscom, Richard | Private | Seventh/Third, Crockett/Briscoe | March 12, 1778 enlisted; April-May 1778; June 1778 sick at Valley Forge, in Briscoe's Company. |
| Swanson, Thos. | Private | Fifteenth, Hull | Dec 1777 sick absent; Jan 1778 sick at hospital; Feb-March 1778 sick absent; April 1778 muster roll shows him deceased on March 8, 1778. |
| Swarer/Swayer, Anthony | Private | Twelfth, Vause | Dec 1777-March 1778 on command; April 1778 "waits on French Engineer"; May 1778 "wating french Colo". |
| Swearingen/Swiaringen, Joseph | 2nd. Lt. | Twelfth, Bowyer, T. | Dec 1777-Jan 1778; Feb 1778 on command; March 1778; April 1778 on command; May 1778. |
| Sweatman, Richard | Private | Second, Sanford | Dec 1777-Feb 1778; March 1778 died. |
| Sweeny/Sweney, John | Drummer | First, Lewis/Scott | Dec 1777; Jan 1778 sick present; Feb-April 1778; May 1778 sick present; June 1778 sick at Valley Forge, in Scott's Company. |
| Sweeny/Swinnie Peter | Drummer | Sixth, Fox | Sept 24, 1777 enlisted; Jan-May 1778. |

| Name | Rank | Regiment | Service |
|---|---|---|---|
| Sweeny/Sweney, Stephen | Private | First State, Brown | Dec 1777-May 1778. |
| Swift, Thomas | Private | Fourteenth, Winston | Feb 17, 1778 drafted; May 1778; June 1778 on duty. |
| Swiney/Swinnie, Joseph | Private | Sixth, Apperson | Dec 1777 sick hospital; March 4, 1778 discharged. |
| Swisser/Swisher, Philip | Private | Seventh/Third, Posey/Sayers | Feb 27, 1778 enlisted; April 1778; May 1778 on guard; June 1778 on guard, in Sayers' Company. |
| Syphers see Cyphers | | | |
| Sykes, Barnard/Barnerd | Private | Second, Jones | Dec 1777 hospital; Jan 1778 dead. |
| Sykes, George | Private | Second State, Taliaferro | March 15-May 1, 1778; May 1778; June 1778 sick Valley Forge. |
| Sykes, Hubbard/Hubard | Corporal | Sixth, Fox | Dec 1777-Jan 1778; Feb 11, 1778 discharged. |
| Sykes/Sikes, Thomas | Private | Fourteenth, Winston | Dec 1777 sick in hospital; Jan 1778 on command; Feb 1778 sick in hospital; March-June 1778. |
| Sylrey/Silrey, William | Drummer | Second State, Bernard | April-June 1778. |
| Symes/Sims, Edward | Sergeant | First State, Payne | Dec 1777-Jan 1778; Feb 1778 on guard; March-April 1778; May-June 1778 sick Yellow Springs. |
| Syrus see Cyrus | | | |
| Tabbs/Tabb, Augustine | 1st. Lt. | Second State, Bernard | June 1778. |
| Tackett, Benoni/Nen | Private | Sixth, Fox | Dec 1777 in hospital; Jan 1778 "Time to serve Feb. 1778." |
| Tadlock/Tudlock, Joshua | Private | Seventh/Third, Jouett/Hill | Feb 16, 1778 enlisted; May 1778 on guard; June 1778 on command, in Hill's Company. |
| Taff, Peter | Private | Seventh, Webb | Jan 1778; Feb 18, 1778 discharged. |

| | | | |
|---|---|---|---|
| Talbot, Charles M. | Sergeant | Sixth, Apperson | Dec 1777 "clerk to Comecery ye 15 of Jan." This would be either a Commissary of Issues or Commissary of Purchases. |
| Taliaferro, Philip | Captain | Second State, Taliaferro | March 15-April 15, 1778 payroll only. |
| Tandy, Roger | Private | Seventh/ Third, Jouett/Hill | Feb 16, 1778 enlisted; April 1778 sick in camp; May 1778 hopital; June 1778 sick Yellow Springs, in Hill's Company. |
| Tankersly/ Tankersley, Fontaine/ Funtain | Private | Seventh/ Third, Fleming/Heth | Feb 10, 1778 enlisted; April-May 1778 sick present; June 1778 in Heth's Company. |
| Tankersly/ Tankersley, Richard | Private | Seventh/ Third, Fleming/Heth | Feb 10, 1778 enlisted; April 1778 sick present; May 1778; June 1778 in Heth's Company. |
| Tanner/Taner, John | Private | First State, Lee/ Meriwether | Dec 1777 confined; Jan-Feb 1778; March 1778 on guard; April-June 1778 |
| Tanner, Paul | Private/ Corporal | Third, Arell | Dec 1777; Jan 1778 promoted to Corporal; Feb 1778 sick present; March 1778; April-May 1778 on command |
| Tanner, William | Private | Twelfth, Bowyer, T. | Dec 1777-March 1778; April 1778 on guard; May 1778. |
| Tapp, Vincent/ Vinson | Sergeant, Sergeant Major | Twelfth, Ashby | Jan 1778; March-May 1778; May 1778 promoted to Sergeant Major. |
| Tapp, Vincent/ Vinson, Jr. | Private | Twelfth, Ashby | Dec 1777-Jan 1778; March-May 1778. |
| Tart, John | Private | First State, Hoffler | May 1778; June 1778 sick absent. |
| Tate, James | Private | Second, Jones/ Hoomes | Dec 1777-June 1778. |
| Tate/Tait, James | Private | Third/ Seventh, Mercer, Powell | Feb 12, 1778 enlisted; April 1778 on command on the Lines; May 1778 sick present; June 1778 on guard, in Powell's Company. |

| | | | |
|---|---|---|---|
| Tate, John | Private | Third, Mercer | Feb-March 1778 Commissary Guard |
| Tatham/Talham, Charles | Private | Fourteenth, Reid | Jan-May 1778 waggoner. |
| Tatum, William | Private | Third, Peyton, V. | Dec 1777-Jan 1778 sick in the hospital; Feb 1778 sent to the Corp Invaleds. |
| Tawson, Charles | Private | Sixth, Massie | Feb 18, 1778 drafted; April 1778. |
| Taylor, Abraham | Private | Fourteenth, Reid | Dec 1777 sick in Virginia. |
| Taylor/Tayler, Charles | Private | First State, Camp | Dec 1777 sick Lancaster; Jan-Feb 1778 sick absent; March 1778 Hospital Red Lyon; April-June 1778. |
| Taylor/Tylor, Charles | Private | Third, Briscoe | Dec 1777; Muster roll shows him discharged on Jan 29, but he is paid through Feb 5, 1778. |
| Taylor, Edward | Private | Seventh/Third, Hill | Dec 1777-Jan 1778 on furlough; April-June 1778 |
| Taylor, Elijah | Private | Third, Mercer | Dec 1777 sick absent. |
| Taylor, Ferguson | Fifer | Seventh/Third, Fleming/Heth | Dec 1777 on furlough Virginia; Jan-March 1778 on furlough; May 1778; June 1778 sick Springfield, in Heth's Company. |
| Taylor, Francis | Captain | Second, Taylor, F. | Dec 1777 furlough; Jan-June 1778. |
| Taylor, George | Private | Seventh/Third, Fleming/Sayers | March 13, 1778 enlisted; April 1778 sick present; May 1778; June 1778 sick at Delaware. |
| Taylor, George | Private | Third/Seventh, Heth | June 1778. |
| Taylor, George | Private | Twelfth, Wallace | Dec 1777-May 1778. |
| Taylor, Humphrey | Private | Second State, Bernard | June 1778. |

| | | | |
|---|---|---|---|
| Taylor, Isick/Isaac | Private | Sixth, Avery | Dec 1777-March 1778 on furlough. May be the same man shown below. |
| Taylor, Isick/Isaac | Sergeant | Sixth, Hockaday | April 1778. |
| Taylor, James | Drummer | Second State, Lewis | March 15 to May 1, 1778, This man and the man below are probably the same individual. |
| Taylor, James | Drum Major | Second State, Lewis | May-June 1778. |
| Taylor, James | Private | Second State, Quarles | April-June 1778. |
| Taylor, James | Sergeant | Sixth, Massie | Dec 1777 on command; "Time to serve, Jan. 29, 1778." |
| Taylor, James | Sergeant | Seventh/ Third, Fleming/ Heth | Dec 1777 on furlough Virginia; Jan-February 1778 on furlough; Feb-May 1778; June 1778 in Heth's Company |
| Taylor, James | Private | Seventh, Spencer | Feb 13, 1778 enlisted for 1 year; April-May 1778 |
| Taylor/Taler, James | Private | Twelfth, Bowyer, T. | Dec 1777-Jan 1778; Feb 1778 sick absent; March 1778 sick in camp; April 23, 1778 deceased. |
| Taylor, John | Private | First State, Camp | Dec 1777 waggoner; Jan 16, 1778 died. |
| Taylor, John | Private | Seventh/ Third, Fleming/ Heth | Feb 19, 1778 enlisted; April 1778 Unchland hospital; May 1778 sick present; June 1778 sick Valley Forge, in Heth's Company. |
| Taylor, John | Private | Twelfth, Ashby | Dec 1777; Jan 1778 sick in hospital; March 1778 muster roll shows he died Jan 18, 1778. |
| Taylor, Joseph | Private | Fourteenth, Winston | Dec 26, 1777 deceased. |
| Taylor, Peter | Private | Twelfth, Casey | Jan 1778 on command; Feb 1778 at hospital; March 1778 on command; April 1778 orederly at hospital near camp. |

| | | | |
|---|---|---|---|
| Taylor, Richard | Captain/ Major | First/ Thirteenth, Taylor | Dec 1777-Jan 1778; Feb 1778 on furlough; February 4, 1778 promoted to Major of the Thirteenth Virginia. Tarlton Payne took over his company. |
| Taylor, Richard | Private | First State, Lee | Dec 1777 sick; Jan 1778 sick at Yellow Springs hospital; Feb 1778 roll shows he died "sometime in Jany." |
| Taylor, Richd. | 2nd. Lt. | Sixth, Massie | Dec 1777; Jan 1778 recruiting Virginia; Feb-May 1778 recruiting; June 1778. |
| Taylor, Richard/Richd. | Private | Seventh/ Third, Hill | Jan 12, 1778 enlisted; April 1778; June 1778 sick at Valley Forge; July 5, 1778 died. |
| Taylor, Richard/Richd. | Private | Fifteenth, Foster/Gray | Dec 1777-Feb 1778 sick absent; Feb 1778 in Gray's Company; March 1778; April 1778 on command; May 1778. |
| Taylor, Robert | Private | Seventh/ Third, Fleming/ Heth | Feb 10, 1778 enlisted; April 1778 sick present; May 1778; June 1778 sick Correll's Ferry, in Heth's Company. |
| Taylor, Samuel | Private | Second, Upshaw | Dec 1777-Jan 1778. |
| Taylor, Thomas | Private | First State, Hoffler | May 1778; June 1778 sick absent. |
| Taylor, Thomas | Private | Second, Taylor, W. | Dec 1777-Jan 1778; Feb 14, 1778 discharged. |
| Taylor/Talor, Thornton | Ensign | Third, Briscoe | Dec 1777 at the hospital; Jan 1778 sick at hospital; March 1778 sick [ ] Virginia; April 1778 on furlough; May 1778 on furlough Virginia. |
| Taylor, Timothy/Tim | Private | Twelfth, Waggener | Dec 1777-Feb 1778 on guard; March 1778 on command; April 10, 1778 discharged. |
| Taylor, William | Private | First State, Camp | Dec 1777 sick country; Jan 28, 1778 died. |
| Taylor, William | Sergeant | First State, Meriwether | Dec 1777-Feb 1778. |

| | | | | |
|---|---|---|---|---|
| Taylor, William | Private | First State, Payne | Dec 1777 sick in hospital; Jan 1778 sick Reading; Feb 1778 sick absent. | |
| Taylor, William | Private | Second State, Quarles | April-May 1778; June 1778 sick Delaware. | |
| Taylor, William | Captain | Second, Taylor, W. | Dec 1777-June 1778. | |
| Taylor, William | Private | Twelfth, Casey | Dec 1777 sent to hospital; Jan-March 1778 at hospital; April 1778 "No account of". | |
| Taylor, William | Private | Fourteenth, Reid | June 1778. | |
| Tearn/Turn, Joseph | Private | Third/Seventh, Powell | Jan 1778 on guard; Feb 1778 Genl Guard; March 1778 guard; April 1778 on detachment; May-June 1778 on guard. | |
| Templar/Templer, James | Private | Third, Mercer | Dec 1777; Jan 1778 on command; Feb-March 1778; April 1778 on command at the Lines; May 1778. | |
| Tennell/Tennille, Benjamin | Sergeant | Third, Lee | Dec 1777; Jan 1778 on command; paid to Feb 14, 1778. | |
| Tennell/Tennel, George | Private/Sergeant | Third, Peyton, J. | Feb 17, 1778 enlisted; April 1778; May 1778 promoted to Sergeant; June-July 1778 sick at Valley Forge. | |
| Terrell/Terrel, Joseph | Private | Seventh/Third, Fleming/Heth | Feb 10, 1778 enlisted; April 1778 sick present; May 1778; June 1778 in Heth's Company. | |
| Terry, Gideon/Giddeon | Private | Seventh, Lipscomb | Dec 1777; Jan 31, 1778 discharged. | |
| Terry, John | Private | Fourteenth, Lambert | Dec 1777-March 1778 hospital; April 1778 Princetown hospital; May 1778; June 1778 sick Valley Forge. | |
| Terry, Nathaniel | 1st. Lt. | Fourteenth, Thweatt | Dec 1777-June 1778. Oath at Valley Forge on May 11, 1778, witnessed by Muhlenberg. | |
| Terry, Obediah | Private | Sixth, Avery | Dec 1777-Jan 1778; Feb 15, 1778 discharged. | |

| | | | |
|---|---|---|---|
| Terry, Stephen | Private | Third, Powell | Dec 1777. |
| Terry, Stephen | Private | Twelfth, Vause | Dec 1777 sick meeting house hospital; Jan-Feb 1778 sick Reading; March 1778 on command; April 1778 on guard; May 1778. |
| Terry/Terray, Thomas | Sergeant/ Private | Third/ Seventh, Lee/Peyton, J. | Feb 1, 1778 enlisted; April 1778; May 1778 reduced to Private; June 1778 in J. Peyton's Company. |
| Terry, Vincent | Private | Seventh, Lipscomb | Dec 1777-Jan 1778 hospital; Feb 2, 1778 discharged. |
| Terry, William | Private | Third, Powell | April 1778. |
| Thacker, William | Private | First State, Lee | Dec 1777; Jan 1778 deserted. |
| Tharp/Tharper, David | Private | Third, Peyton, V. | Dec 1777 on command with Col. Morgan; Jan 1778 with Col. Morgan. |
| Thaxton, Syrus | Private | Fourteenth, Reid | Aug 11, 1777 enlisted; Jan 1778 on command; Feb 1778; March 1778 on guard; April 12, 1778 died. |
| Thelaball/ Thelable, Robt./Robert | 2nd. Lt. | Fifteenth, Edmunds | Dec 1777-May 1778 on furlough. |
| Thnocknett see Nocket | | | |
| Thomas, Buckner/ Buckner | Private | Fourteenth, Jones | Jan 1778 on duty; Feb-May 1778. |
| Thomas, Daniel | Private | First State, Brown | Dec 1777-June 1778 |
| Thomas, Evan | Private | Third, Briscoe | Dec 1777-Jan 1778; Feb 5, 1778 discharged. |
| Thomas, Frederick | Private | Fourteenth, Jones | Sept 6, 1777 enlisted; Jan 1778; Feb 1778; March 1778 sick present. |
| Thomas, George | Private | First, Taylor/ Payne | Dec 1777-Feb 1778; March 1778 in Payne's Company; time expires April 10, 1778. |

| Name | Rank | Regiment/Company | Notes |
|---|---|---|---|
| Thomas, George | Private | Seventh, Lipscomb | Dec 1777-Jan 1778; Feb 22, 1778 discharged. |
| Thomas, James | Private | Second, Calmes | Dec 1777-Feb 1778. |
| Thomas/Thommas, Jeremiah | Private | First, Mennis | Jan-June 1778 on furlough. |
| Thomas, Jesse | Private | Seventh/Third, Fleming/Heth | Feb 19, 1778 enlisted; April 1778 sick present; May 1778; June 1778 in Heth's Company. |
| Thomas, John | Private | Third/Seventh, Blackwell | Dec 1777-May 1778; June 1778 on guard. |
| Thomas, John F. | Private | Fifteenth, Gray | April 1778 muster roll shows returned deserted; April 19, 1778 joined; April 1778 sick present; May 1778 hospital Yellow Springs. |
| Thomas, Joseph | Private | Second, Taylor, F. | Dec 1777-Feb 1778. |
| Thomas, Joseph | Private | Second, Upshaw | Feb 18, 1778 drafted; April 1778; June 1778. |
| Thomas, Moses | Private | Second, Harrison | May-June 1778. |
| Thomas/Tommos, Peter | Private | Fourteenth, Conway | Dec 1777; Jan-April 1778; May on command. |
| Thomas, Robert | Private | Second, Upshaw | Feb 14, 1778 drafted; April 1778; June-July 1778 sick at Valley Forge. |
| Thomas, Samuel | Private | Fifteenth, Wills | August 16, 1777 enlisted; Feb 1778 muster roll shows he deserted on Oct 1, 1777. |
| Thomas, William | Private | First, Cummings/Mennis | Feb 7, 1778 enlisted; April-May 1778; June 1778 in Mennis' Company. |
| Thomas, William | Private | First State, Meriwether | Dec 1777-June 1778. |
| Thomas, William | Fifer | Second State, Dudley | March 15-May 1, 1778; May 1778; June 1778 sick absent. |

| | | | |
|---|---|---|---|
| Thomasin/ Tommason, George | Private | Third, Powell | Dec 1777; Jan 31, 1778 discharged. |
| Thomason, William | Private | Fourteenth, Marks | Dec 1777 in hospital; Feb-May 1778; June 1778 sick Valley Forge. |
| Thompson, Benjamin/ Benjm. | Private/ Corporal | Sixth, Avery | Dec 1777-June 1778; Feb 1, 1778 promoted to Corporal. |
| Thompson, Brothers | Private | First, Mennis | April 1778; May 1778 sick present; June 1778 sick Valley Forge. |
| Thompson/ Thomson, Daniel | Private | First State, Ewell, T. | Dec 1777 sick New Church; Jan-Feb 1778; March 1778 on command; April-May 1778; June 1778 sick Princetown. |
| Thompson, Flanders | Private | Fourteenth, Thweatt | Dec 1777-March 1778; April 1778 on guard; May-June 1778 on command. |
| Thompson, Francis | Private | Seventh, Lipscomb | Dec 1777 hospital; Jan 31, 1778 discharged. |
| Thompson, George | Sergeant | Seventh, Lipscomb | Dec 1777; Jan 31, 1778 discharged. |
| Thompson, Henry | Corporal | Fourteenth, Thweatt | Dec 1777 sick at hospital; Jan 14, 1778 died. |
| Thompson, John | Private | Second State, Garnett | June 1778. |
| Thompson, John | Corporal/ Sergeant | Second State, Spiller | March 15-May 1, 1778; May-June 1778 |
| Thompson/ Thomson, John | Sergeant Major | Second | Jan-June 1778. |
| Thompson, John/Jno. | Private | Third/ Seventh, Briscoe | Dec 1777 sick in hospital; Jan 1778 sick at hospital; March 1778 sick present; April-June 1778. |
| Thompson, John | Private | Third, Mercer | Dec 1777-Jan 1778. |
| Thompson, John | Private | Sixth, Rose | Feb 17, 1778 drafted; May-June 1778. |
| Thompson, John | Private | Fourteenth, Overton | Dec 1777 on guard; Jan-Feb 1778; March 1778 on command; April-June 1778. |

| | | | |
|---|---|---|---|
| Thompson, Littleberry | Private | First State, Hamilton | April 1778 "Not drawn for since 15 Mar." April-June 1778. |
| Thompson, Richard | Private | Fourteenth, Winston | Feb 17, 1778 drafted; May-June 1778. |
| Thompson, Richard | Private | Fifteenth, Mason | Muster roll shows he died on Dec 10, 1777, pay roll shows date of death as Dec 9. |
| Thompson/ Tompson, Stephen | Private | Sixth, Fox | Dec 1777 hospital; Jan 1778 sick absent; Feb 1778. |
| Thompson, Thomas | Private | Fourteenth, Jones | Feb 8, 1778 drafted; April 1778; May 1778 on duty. |
| Thompson, William | Private | First State, Hamilton | Dec 1777-June 1778. |
| Thompson, William | Private | Fifteenth, Harris | Feb 5, 1778 drafted; March 1778; April 1778 sick; May 1778. |
| Thompson, William/Wm. | Private | Fifteenth, Mason | Feb 11, 1778 drafted; April 1778; May 1778 sick in camp. |
| Thomson/ Thompson, John | Corporal/ Sergeant | Second State, Spiller | March 15-May 1, 1778; May-June 1778. |
| Thomson/ Tomson, John | Corporal | Fourteenth, Winston | Dec 1777-May 1778; June 1778 sick Valley Forge. |
| Thornhill, John | Private | Twelfth, Casey | Feb 28, 1778 drafted; May 1778. |
| Thornton/ Thaunton, Henry | Private | Fourteenth, Winston | Dec 1777; Jan 1778 on guard; Feb-March 1778; April 1778 sick present; May 1778 sick; June 1778 sick Valley Forge. |
| Thornton, Jere/ Jerry | Private | Seventh, Spencer | Dec 1777 on furlough Virginia; Jan 1778 on furlough; Feb 20, 1778 discharged. |
| Thornton, Jesse | Fifer | Seventh, Spencer | Dec 1777-Jan 1778 hospital; April 10, 1778 discharged. |
| Thornton, Ransom | Private | Fourteenth, Winston | Jan 20, 1778 enlisted; May 1778; June 1778 sick at Valley Forge. |
| Thrailkill/ Thrailkild, John | Private | Third, Mercer | Dec 1777-March 1778 on furlough. |
| Threat/Thweat, Drury | Private | Sixth, Rose | Dec 1777-Jan 1778; Feb 10, 1778 discharged. |
| Thrift, Charles | Private | Twelfth, Casey | Dec 1777-March 1778 at hospital; April 1778 sick hospital Lancaster; May 1778 at hospital near camp. |

| Name | Rank | Regiment | Notes |
|---|---|---|---|
| Thrift, John Graves | Private | Fourteenth, Jones | Feb 1778 deserted in Virginia. |
| Thurman, William | Private | Third, Lee | Dec 1777-Jan 1778; paid to Feb 14, 1778. |
| Thurston/Thruston, John | Private | First State, Crump | Dec 1777; Jan 18, 1778 deceased. |
| Thweatt/Thwait, Thomas | Captain | Fourteenth, Thweatt | "Taken prisoner on October 4, and got his Parrole 27 Mar '78." Did not rejoin the regiment. |
| Tibbs/Tibbes, John | 2nd. Lt. | Third, Peyton, J. | Dec 1777-March 1778 on furlough; April-May 1778. |
| Tillar/Tiller, Henry | Sergeant | Fifteenth, Gray | Dec 1777 sick absent; Jan 1778; Feb 1778 sick absent; March-May 1778. |
| Tillery/Tillory, John | Private | Fifteenth, Hull | Dec 1777-March 1778; April 1778 sick present; May 1778 on command. |
| Tillis/Tills, John | Private | Third, Lee | Dec 1777 attending on Capt. Lee; Jan 1778 on command; paid through Feb 14, 1778. |
| Timberlake, Henry | Sergeant | First, Cummings | Dec 1777. |
| Timberlake, John | Private | Seventh, Jouett | Dec 1777 on furlough Virginia; Jan 1778; Feb 10, 1778 discharged. |
| Timmons, John | Sergeant | Twelfth, Ashby | Dec 1777-Jan 1778; March 1778 on guard; April-May 1778. |
| Timmons, Peter | Private | Twelfth, Ashby | Feb 19, 1778 drafted; May 1778. |
| Tipton, Abraham | 1st. Lt. | Twelfth, Casey | Dec 1777 on furlough; Jan-Feb 1778; March 16, 1778 resigned. |
| Todd, Henry | Private | Sixth, Rose | Dec 1777-Feb 1778; March 9, 1778 discharged. |
| Toilar, Anthony | Private | Fourteenth, Overton | Jan 1778 lately joined the Fourteenth Virginia. Could be Tyler, Anton see below |
| Tolbert, Paul | Private | First State, Brown | Dec 1777. |
| Toler, John | Private | Fifteenth, Edmunds | Dec 1777. This man and the one below may be the same individual. |
| Toler, John | Private | Fifteenth, Wills | Jan-Feb 1778; March-May 1778 sick present; June-Aug 1778 sick Valley Forge. |

| | | | |
|---|---|---|---|
| Toles, Reuben | Private | Second State, Lewis | March 15-May 1, 1778; May-June 1778. |
| Tomblen, Wm. | Sergeant | Third, Blackwell | Dec 23, 1777 discharged. |
| Tombling/ Tomblin, James | Private | Second, Sanford | Dec 1777-Jan 1778; Feb 20, 1778 deserted. |
| Tomers, John | Private | Third, Arell | March 1778; April 1778 on command |
| Tomkins/ Tompkins, Charles | Private | First, Pelham | Dec 1777-Feb 1778 sick hospital; March 8, 1778 discharged. |
| Tomlin/ Tomblin, Stephen | Private | Third, Blackwell | Dec 1777; Jan-Feb 1778 on guard; March 1778 sick present; April-May 1778. |
| Tomlin, William | Sergeant | Third, Blackwell | Dec 23, 1777 discharged. |
| Tomlinson/ Tomlenson, George | Private | First State, Brown | April 1778 shows "paid from 15th Aug to 30th of Apr." April-May 1778. |
| Tomlinson, Herbert | Private | Fifteenth, Grimes | Dec 1777-Feb 1778 sick absent; March 1778 muster rolls reads "Died some time ago in the hospital." |
| Tomlinson, Littleberry/ Littlbury | Private | Fifteenth, Edmunds | Dec 1777; Jan 1778 on guard; Feb-March 1778 on command; April 1778; May-June 1778 sick Yellow Springs. |
| Tomlinson, Thomas | Private | Fifteenth, Edmunds | Feb 1778 sick present; March 17, 1778 died. |
| Tomlinson, William/Wm. | Private | Fifteenth, Edmunds | Dec 1777-March 1778; April 1778 sick in camp; May 1778. This man and the one below may be the same individual. |
| Tomlinson, Wm. | Private | Fifteenth, Gregory | June 1778. |
| Tompkins/ Tomkin, Drury | Private | Fifteenth, Mason | Dec 1777-May 1778. |
| Tompkins, James | Private | First, Pelham | Dec 1777-Feb 1778 sick in hospital; March 8, 1778 discharged. |

| | | | |
|---|---|---|---|
| Toney, Archer | Fleming | Fourteenth, Overton | Dec 1777 sick in hospital; Jan 1778 sick absent; March 1778 "returned dead 20 Jany but found out he was sick absent." April-June 1778. |
| Toney, John | Private | Seventh, Jouett | Dec 1777 on furlough Virginia; Jan 1778 on furlough; Feb 12, 1778 discharged. |
| Toney, Reuben/Rubin | Drummer | Fourteenth, Overton | Dec 1777 sick in hospital; Jan-June 1778 |
| Tooley, Jesse | Private | Fifteenth, Grimes | Nov 1777 sick absent; Dec 1777 died. |
| Toone/Toon, Argillon/Argelon | Private | Sixth, Garland | Dec 1777-Jan 1778; Feb 26, 1778 discharged. |
| Toone/Tune, Thomas | Private | Fifteenth, Gregory | Dec 1777-Feb 1778; April 1778; May 1778 sick present; June 1778 sick Valley Forge. |
| Toppin/Poppin, John | Private | Second, Willis | Dec 1777-May 1778. |
| Tosh, Andrew | Private | Twelfth, Waggener | Dec 1777-March 1778 on command; April-May 1778. |
| Towell/Towel, John | Corporal | Seventh/Third, Posey/Young | Feb 27, 1778 enlisted; April 1778; May 1778 sick in camp; June 1778 in Young's Company. |
| Towers, John | Private | Third, Arell | March 1778; April 1778 on command; May 1778. |
| Towers, John | Private | First State, Meriwether | Dec 1777-June 1778. |
| Towers, John | Private | Third/Seventh, Briscoe | June 1778. |
| Towers, John | Private | Third, Peyton, J | Dec 1777 sick absent; Jan 31, 1778 discharged. |
| Towles, Oliver | Major | Sixth | Jan-Feb 1778 prisoner of war. |
| Townsden/Townsend, Ewell | Corporal | Third, Peyton, J. | Dec 23, 1777 reinlisted in Light Horse. |
| Townsen/Townsin, John | Private | First State, Hoffler | April-May 1778; June 1778 sick absent. |
| Townswell/Townsend, John | Sergeant | First State, Brown | Dec 1777-Feb 1778. |

| Name | Rank | Regiment | Dates |
|---|---|---|---|
| Townson/Townsin, George | Private | First State, Hoffler | April-May 1778; June 1778 sick absent. |
| Trador/Trader, Moses | Private | Twelfth, Ashby | Dec 1777 joined; Jan 1778; April-May 1778. |
| Trapp/Trap, Thomas | Private | Second, Calmes | Dec 1777-June 1778. |
| Traxler/Trachslor, John | Private | Twelfth, Bowyer, M. | Dec 1777-May 1778. |
| Treacle/Trecle, Dawson/Doson | Private | Second State, Dudley | March 15-May 1, 1778; May-June 1778. |
| Trent, Henry | Private | First State, Hoffler | Dec 1777-Feb 1778. |
| Trent, Thomas/Thos. | Corporal | Fifteenth, Foster/Gray | Dec 1777-Jan 1778 sick absent; Feb 1778 in Gray's Company; Feb-March 1778; April 1778 on command; May 1778. |
| Trigg, James | Sergeant | Sixth, Avery | Dec 1777; Jan 25, 1778 discharged. |
| Trigg, John | Corporal | Sixth, Avery | Dec 1777 absent wounded; Jan 25, 1778 discharged. |
| Triplett, Daniel | Private/Quartermaster Sergeant | First State, Payne | Dec 1, 1777 promoted to Quartermaster Sergeant; Dec 1777-Feb 1778. |
| Triplett, George | 1st. Lt. | First State, Hoffler | Dec 1777-June 1778. He also appears as "Protemporary" Quartermaster from March-May 1778. Oath at Valley Forge on May 12, 1778, witnessed by Muhlenberg. |
| Triplett/Triplet, Peter | Private | First State, Lee/Meriwether | Dec 1777-March 1778 on furlough; April-June 1778 |
| Triplett, Roger | 1st. Lt. | Second State, Bressie | October 1778 payroll shows he was paid from May 5, 1778 through October 1778. |
| Triplett, William | Corporal | First State, Hoffler | Dec 1777-June 1778. |
| Trivett/Trivet, Samuel | Private | Second, Calmes | Dec 1777-June 1778. |
| Troop, James | Private | Seventh, Moseley | Dec 1777-Jan 1778 in R. Regt; Feb 25, 1778 discharged. |

| | | | | |
|---|---|---|---|---|
| Trotter, John | Private | Twelfth, Waggener | Dec 1777-Jan 1778; Feb 1778 on command; March 1778; April 1778; on guard; May 1778 hospital. |
| Trotter, John Giles | Fifer | Fifteenth, Grimes | Dec 1777 prisoner. |
| True, William | Private | Second State, Quarles | April-May 1778; June 26, 1778 died. |
| Trukle, John | Private | Seventh, Young | Dec 21, 1777 to Lt. Horse. |
| Tuck, Bennet | Private | Seventh, Moseley | Feb 14, 1778 enlisted; April 1778; May 1778 sick in camp; June 19, 1778 deceased. |
| Tucker, John | Private | Second, Taylor, W. | Dec 1777-Jan 1778; Feb 5, 1778 discharged. |
| Tucker, Littleberry | Private | Fourteenth, Jones | Feb 12, 1778 drafted; April 1778; May 1778 sick present. |
| Tucker, Michael/Mikell | Private | First, Cunningham | Dec 1777-Jan 1778 sick at Easton; Feb 1778 sick at hospital. |
| Tucker, Reuben/Reubin | Fifer | Sixth, Fox | Dec 1777-Jan 1778; Feb 11, 1778 discharged. |
| Tucker, William | Ensign/ 2nd. Lt. | Fourteenth, Overton | Dec 24, 1777, promoted to 2nd Lt.; Dec 1777-Feb 1778; March-April 1778 on furlough; June 1778 on command. Oath at Valley Forge on May 14, 1778, witnessed by Muhlenberg. |
| Tuder, John | Private | Fourteenth, Reid | Sept 18, 1777 enlisted; April 1778 lately joined regiment; May-June 1778. |
| Tuder, John | Private | Fifteenth, Gregory | June 1778 on guard. This man and the one below may be the same individual. |
| Tuder/Tudor, John | Private | Fifteenth, Mason | Dec 1777 on guard; Jan 1778 sick present; Feb-May 1778. |
| Tuffnell/ Tufnell, James | Private | Third/ Seventh, Blackwell | Dec 1777-May 1778; June 1778 on guard. |
| Tuggle/Tuggal, Joshua | Private | Fourteenth, Marks | Jan 6, 1778 enlisted; Jan-April 1778 on furlough; May 1778; June 1778 on guard. |

| Name | Rank | Regiment, Company | Notes |
|---|---|---|---|
| Tulley see Pulley | | | |
| Tumbling, James | Private | First State, Hoffler | April-May 1778; June 1778 sick absent. |
| Tunley, John | Private | Sixth, Avery | Dec 1777-Jan 1778; Feb 8, 1778 discharged. |
| Tunstall, Henry/Henary | Sergeant | Fourteenth, Thweatt | Aug 9, 1777 enlisted; Jan 1778 lately joined regiment; Feb 1778 sick present; March-June 1778. |
| Tunstill/ Tunstell, Thomas | Private | Fourteenth, Thweatt | March 1778 "Taken prisoner 4th Oct and had his Parrole the 7th of Mar '78." |
| Turner, Daniel | Private | Third, Powell | Dec 1777; Feb 10, 1778 discharged. |
| Turner, Daniel | Private | Twelfth, Casey | Dec 15, 1777 deserted; April 1778 deserted Dec 15 and returned since; May 1778. |
| Turner, Elkanah/Elkh. | Private | Seventh/Third, Webb/Young | Feb 16, 1778 enlisted; May 1778; June 1778 sick Valley Forge, in Young's Company. |
| Turner, Francis | Private | Third, Lee | Dec 23, 1778 enlisted in the Light Horse. |
| Turner, George/Geo. | Private | First, Mennis | Dec 1777; Jan-March 1778 on furlough; April-May 1778; 1778 sick Valley Forge. |
| Turner, George | Private | Seventh/Third, Lipscomb | Dec 1777-Jan 1778; April 1778 on furlough; May-June 1778. |
| Turner, Henry | Private | First, Cummings | Dec 1777. |
| Turner, Isham | Private | Fourteenth, Thweatt | Dec 1777 sick in Virginia; Jan 1778; Feb 1778 on guard; March-June 1778. |
| Turner, John | Sergeant | First State, Crump | Dec 1777-June 1778. |
| Turner, John | Private | Second State, Bressie | March 15-May 1, 1778; May-June 1778. |
| Turner, John | Private | Seventh, Lipscomb | Dec 1777; Jan 31, 1778 discharged. |

| | | | | |
|---|---|---|---|---|
| Turner, Stephen | Private | Fifteenth, Edmunds | Dec 1777 sick absent; Jan 1778 on guard; Feb 1778 sick present; March-April 1778; May-June 1778 sick Yellow Springs. |
| Turner, Thomas | Private | Fourteenth, Thweatt | May 11, 1777 enlisted; Jan 1778 lately joined regiment; Feb 1778 sick present; March-June 1778. |
| Turner, William | Private | Second, Taylor, F. | Dec 1777-on furlough; Jan-March 1778. |
| Turner, William/Wm. | Private | Sixth, Apperson | Feb 28, 1778 drafted; April 1778; May 11, 1778 decd. |
| Turner/Turnor, William/Wm/ | Private | Sixth, Avery | Dec 1777-Jan 1778; Feb 8, 1778 discharged. |
| Turner, William | Private | Seventh/Third, Spencer/Lipscomb | Enlisted for 3 years; April-May 1778; June 1778 in Lipscomb's Company. |
| Turner, William | Private | Fourteenth, Winston | Dec 1777 sick in hospital; Jan 1778 sick at Lancaster; Feb-March 1778 sick in hospital; April 1778 on command, Lancaster; June 1778 sick Valley Forge. |
| Turpin, Horatio | Ensign | Fifteenth, Harris | March 11, 1778 resigned. |
| Turvy/Turvey, Wm. | Private | Third/Seventh, Blackwell | Dec 1777-May 1778 sick at hospital; April-June 1778 sick Lancaster. |
| Tyler, Anton | Private | Fourteenth, Overton | Drafted Oct 1, 1777; Jan 1778. May be Anthony Toilar shown above. |
| Tyler, Arthur | Private | Fourteenth, Overton | Oct 1, 1777 drafted; Jan-May 1778 sick absent; June 1778 sick at Yellow Springs. May be same guy as A. Toliar and A. Tyler above |
| Tyler/Tylor, Bartlett/Bartlet | Private | First State, Camp | Dec 1777; Jan 1778 sick present; Feb 1778 sick absent; March 1778 hospital Red Lyon; April 13, 1778 died. |
| Tyler, Charles | Private | Third, Briscoe | Jan 29, 1778 discharged. |
| Tyler, Johnston | Private | Seventh, Moseley | Dec 1777-Jan 1778 in R. Regt; Feb 20, 1778 discharged. |

| Name | Rank | Regiment, Company | Notes |
|---|---|---|---|
| Tyler, Nathaniel/Nathl. | Sergeant | Third, Lee | Dec 1777; Jan 31, 1778 time out, paid to Feb 1, 1778. |
| Tyler, William | Private | First State, Brown | Dec 1777-June 1778. |
| Tyree/Tiree, John | Corporal | Fourteenth, Winston | Dec 1777; Jan 1778 on guard; Feb-March 1778; April 1778 on guard; May 1778; June 1778 on duty. |
| Underhill, Rowell | Private | Fifteenth, Grimes | Feb 14, 1777 drafted; April-May 1778. |
| Underwood, Gideon | Sergeant | First State, Nicholas | Dec 1777 sick Bethlehem; Jan-June 1778. |
| Underwood, James | Private | Fifteenth, Grimes | Feb 11, 1778 drafted; May 1778 sick present; June-July sick Valley Forge; Aug 1778 muster roll shows "Dead in July". |
| Umphrey/Humphrey, Ralph/Realph | Private | Second State, Spiller | March 15-May 1, 1778; May-June 1778. |
| Upham, Thomas/Thos. | Private | Third/Seventh, Sayers | Feb 27, 1778 enlisted; June 1778 on guard. |
| Upshaw, James | Captain | Second, Upshaw | The rolls of this company show it as Captain James Upshaw's through June 1778. However Upshaw himself is not listed. |
| Usher, William | Private | First State, Payne | Dec 1777-Feb 1778 sick Bethlehem; Feb 1778 sick absent; March-June 1778. |
| Valentine/Volentine, Isham | Private | Fourteenth, Jones | Sept 6, 1777 enlisted; Jan 1778 on duty; Feb 1778 on command; April 1778 sick present; June 1778 sick Valley Forge. |
| Valentine/Vallentine, Jacob | 1st. Lt./Captain | First State, Lee | Dec 1777 in the country sick; Jan-Feb 1778; March 1778 in the country sick. In April he is promoted to Captain and assumes command of what had been Camp's Company. April-June 1778. Oath at Valley Forge on May 29, 1778, witnessed by Muhlenberg. |

| Name | Rank | Company/Regiment | Notes |
|---|---|---|---|
| Valentine/ Vallentine, Josiah/Joseph | Quartermaster Sergeant/ Quartermaster /Ensign | First, Lawson | Dec 1777-April 1778; May 1, 1778 appointed Regimental Quartermaster; May-June 1778. In June he also appears as an Ensign. |
| Vanbuskirk/ Vanbuskerk, Isick/Isaac | Private | Seventh/ Third, Posey/ Sayers | Feb 27, 1778 enlisted; May-June 1778 on guard, June 1778 in Sayers' Company. |
| Vance, John/Jno. | Private | Sixth, Apperson | Dec 1777 sick Trenton; Jan 1778; Feb 1778 sick present "Time to serve March 1, 1778." |
| Vance, Joseph | Private | Twelfth, Bowyer, M. | Dec 1777-Jan 1778; Feb 1778 on fatigue; March-May 1778. |
| Vanderwall/ Vanduvall, Marks/Markis | 2nd. Lt./ 1st. Lt. | First, Cummings/ Mennis | Dec 1777-May 1778; Feb 4, 1778; promoted to 1st. Lt.; June 1778 in Mennis' Company. Oath on May 11, 1778, witnessed by Muhlenberg. |
| Vanmeter, Joseph | Sergeant | Twelfth, Vause | Dec 1777-Feb 1778; March-April 1778 on furlough; May 1778. |
| Vansickle/ Vansakle, Abraham | Private | Twelfth, Bowyer, T. | Dec 1777-Feb 1778; March 20, 1778 Joined the Life Guards. |
| Vass, Vincent | Private | First State, Camp | Dec 1777 sick Georgetown, Maryland; Jan-Feb 1778 sick absent; in April 1778 he was paid for March and April, having been struck off the March muster roll; May 1778; June 1778 sick absent. |
| Vasser, Daniel/Danl. | Corporal/ Sergeant | Fifteenth, Foster/ Hull | Dec 1777; Jan 1778 on guard; Feb 1778 promoted to Sergeant, in Hull's Company; Feb 15, 1778 joined Hull's Company; March-April 1778 sick present; May 1778. |
| Vasser/Varser, George | Private | Second, Taylor, W. | Dec 1777-Feb 1778; March 5, 1778 discharged. |
| Vasser/Vassor, Joel | Private | Fifteenth, Foster/ Gray | Dec 1777-Jan 1778 sick absent; Feb 1778 sick, in Gray's Company; March 1778 sick in camp; April-May 1778. |
| Vaughan, Claiborne | Surgeon's Mate | Sixth | Dec 1777; Jan-March 1778 on furlough; April-June 1778. |

| | | | | |
|---|---|---|---|---|
| Vaughan, Jesse | Private | Sixth, Fox | Dec 1777-Jan 1778; Feb 11, 1778 discharged. | |
| Vaughan, John | Private | Second, Upshaw | Dec 1777 hospital; Jan 1778. | |
| Vaughan/Vaughn, Listra/Lister | Corporal | Third, Powell | Dec 1777-March 1778 on furlough; April-June 1778. | |
| Vaughan/Vaughn, Shadrack/Shadrach | Private | Fifteenth, Gray | Feb 10, 1778 drafted to served one year; April 1778 under inoculation; May 1778 sick present; June 1778 sick Valley Forge; July 1778 dead. | |
| Vaughan, Thomas | Private | First State, Camp | Dec 1777-Jan 1778; Feb 1778 sick present; March-June 1778. | |
| Vaughn/Vaughan, Ambrose | Private | Fourteenth, Jones | Feb 12, 1778 drafted; April 1778; May 1778 sick present; June 1778 sick Valley Forge. | |
| Vaughn, Hugh | Private | First, Lewis | Dec 1777; Jan 1778 on command; Feb 1778 deserted. | |
| Vause, William | Captain | Twelfth, Vause | Dec 1777-Feb 1778 on furlough; March-May 1778. | |
| Vauter/Vawter, Bartholomew | Private | Seventh/Third, Webb/Young | Feb 16, 1778 enlisted. April-May 1778; June 1778 in Young's Company. Muster rolls for June-Sept 1778 show him sick at Valley Forge, but the Oct 1778 muster and pay rolls show he died July 10, 1778. | |
| Vauter, William | Private/Sergeant | First State, Nicholas | Dec 1777; Jan 1778 on command; Feb 7, 1778 promoted to Sergeant; Feb 1778; March 1778 on guard; April 1778; May 1778 on guard; June 1778. | |
| Vauters, David | Private | First State, Camp | Dec 1777 sick Georgetown; Jan-Feb 1778 sick absent. | |
| Vawter/Vewter, Benjamin | Private | Second State, Garnett | March 15-May 1, 1778; May-June 1778. | |
| Veitch, Peter | Private | Third, Arell | Jan 1778 waiting Dr. Brown. | |
| Verey, Wm. | Private | Third, Mercer | May 1778 sick absent. | |

| Name | Rank | Regiment | Notes |
|---|---|---|---|
| Vernon/Varnon, Richard | Private/ Corporal | Fourteenth, Reid | Dec 1777 hospital; Jan 1778 sick at Reading; Feb 1778 sick absent; March 1778 sick in hospital; April-June 1778. |
| Vernon/Varnon, Thomas | Private | Fourteenth, Reid | Dec 1777 on duty; Jan-Feb 1778 artificer; March 1778; May-June 1778. |
| Vertner/ Vertorer, Jacob | Private | Twelfth, Waggener | Dec 1777-March 1778 hospital; April 1778 "Sepos to be Dead." |
| Vest, Samuel | Private | Second State, Lewis | June 1778. |
| Via, Benjamin | Private | Fourteenth, Reid | Sept 1, 1777 enlisted; Jan 1778; March 1778 on guard; June 1778 on guard. |
| Vickers/Vicars, John | Fifer | First State, Ewell, T. | Dec 1777 sick Bethlehem; Jan-Feb 1778 sick at Lancaster; March-June 1778. |
| Vickers/ Vickeas, William/Will. | Private | Twelfth, Bowyer, M. | March 5, 1778 "Returnd. from the Gallies"; April 1778 on picket; May 1778. |
| Vigor, John | Private | Third, Mercer | Dec 1777-Jan 1778 sick present. |
| Vincent, Jonathan | Private | Seventh, Posey | Feb 28, 1778 enlisted; April 1778; May 1778 sick in camp |
| Vowles/Vawles, Henry | Adjutant/ Ensign | Seventh/ Third, Lipscomb | Dec 1777; Jan-April 1778 on furlough; May 1778; June 1778 is listed as regimental Adjutant, and as an Ensign in Lipscomb's Company. |
| Waddle, Mordecai/ Mordica | Private | Seventh, Young | Dec 1777-April 1778 on furlough; May 1778 roll shows he deserted on April 13. |
| Waddey, Samuel | Corporal | Third/ Seventh, Powell | Dec 1777 on furlough; Feb 1778 discharged. |
| Waddil/ Waddell, James | Private | Sixth, Massie | Dec 1777-Jan 1778; Feb 15, 1778 discharged. |
| Wade/Waid, David | Private | Second State, Bernard | April 1778; May-June 1778 sick Valley Forge. |
| Wade, Hampton | Sergeant | Fourteenth, Thweatt | Feb 14, 1778 enlisted; April 1778 lately joined regiment; May-June 1778. |

| Name | Rank | Company | Notes |
|---|---|---|---|
| Wade, Isick/Isaac | Private | Fourteenth, Lambert | Dec 1777. |
| Wade/Waid, Moses | Private | Fourteenth, Winston | Dec 1777-March 1778; April 1778 waiting on the Colonel; May-June 1778. |
| Wager, John | Private | First State, Brown | Dec 1777-Feb 1778. |
| Waggener, Andrew | Captain | Twelfth, Waggener | Dec 1777; Jan 1778 on furlough; Feb-March 1778 on furlough in Virginia; April-May 1778; June 28, 1778 wounded at the Battle of Monmouth. |
| Waites/Waits, John | Private | Third, Peyton, V. | Dec 1777-Jan 1778; Feb 12, 1778 discharged. |
| Walden, Charles | Private | Seventh, Third, Hill | April 1778 on guard; June 1778. |
| Walden/Walding, George | Corporal | Second State, Dudley | March 15-May 1, 1778; May 1778; June 1778 sick absent; July 1778 sick Valley Forge. |
| Walden/Wolden, James | Private | First State, Ewell, T. | Feb 1778; April 1778 "Not drawn for since 15th March." May 1778; June 2, 1778 discharged. |
| Walden/Woldon, John | Private | Second State, Spiller | March 15-May 1, 1778; May-June 1778. |
| Walden/Waldon, Spencer/Spence | Private | First State, Hamilton | Dec 1777-Jan 1778. |
| Walden/Waldon, Thomas | Private | First State, Hamilton | Dec 1777-Feb 1778; died about March 15, 1778. |
| Walden, Zachariah/Zackaria | Private | Second State, Lewis | March 15-May 1, 1778; May-June 1778; July 1778 sick Valley Forge. |
| Waldron/Walden, Peter | Private | Seventh/Third, Crockett/Young | May 1778 "in room of John Long."; June 1778 sick Corrells Ferry, in Young's Company. |
| Waldrop/Waldrope, James/Jas. | Private | Sixth, Apperson | Dec 1777; Jan-Feb 1778 on command; March 2, 1778 discharged. |

| Name | Rank | Regiment, Company | Notes |
|---|---|---|---|
| Walker, David | 2nd. Lt. | Fourteenth, Jones | Jan 1778; Feb 1778 on command; Feb-May 1778. Oath at Valley Forge on May 12, 1778, witnessed by Muhlenberg. |
| Walker, James | Private | First State, Hoffler | Dec 1777-March 1778. |
| Walker, John | Drummer | First State, Nicholas | Dec 1777; Jan 1778; Feb 1778 sick in ye Country; March-June 1778. |
| Walker, John | Private | Third/Seventh, Blackwell | Dec 1777-Feb 1778 sick at hospital; April-June 1778 sick Lancaster. |
| Walker, John | Private | Seventh/Third, Lipscomb | Feb 14, 1778 enlisted for 1 year; April-May 1778; June 1778 hospital. |
| Walker, Langford | Private | Sixth, Avery | Dec 1777 sick in hospital; Jan 31, 1778 dead. |
| Walker, Levin | Ensign/2nd. Lt. | Second State, Bressie | March 15-May 1, 1778; May-June 1778; July 1778 pays him as a 2nd. Lt. from April 27, 1778. Oath taken as an Ensign at Valley Forge on May 18, 1778, witnessed by Muhlenberg. |
| Walker, Moses/Mosses | Private | Twelfth, Bowyer, T. | Dec 1777 on command; Jan-April 1778; May-June 1778 on command. |
| Walker, Richard | Private | Seventh, Spencer | Dec 1777 hospital |
| Walker, Tandy | Private | Sixth, Avery | Dec 1777 sick in hospital; Jan 1778; Feb 8, 1778 discharged. |
| Walker, Willaby | Private | Fifteenth, Hull | May 31, 1778 died. This man and Willoby Walker are probably the same individual. |
| Walker, William | Private | First State, Nicholas | Dec 1777 on guard; Jan-Feb 1778; March 1778 on duty; April-June 1778. |
| Walker, William | Fifer | Sixth, Avery | Dec 1777-Jan 1778; Feb 8, 1778 discharged. |
| Walker, William | Private | Seventh, Jouett | Dec 1777-Jan 1778 sick in hospital; Feb 10, 1778 discharged. |

| | | | |
|---|---|---|---|
| Walker, Willoby | Private | Fifteenth, Harris | Jan 1778 sick; Feb 1778 on guard; March 1778 sick present. This man and Willaby Walker are probably the same individual. |
| Walkins, William | Private | Seventh, Hill | April-May 1778 |
| Wall, Charles | Private | Second State, Lewis | March 15-May 1, 1778; May-June 1778. |
| Wall, James | Private | First State, Brown | Dec 1777-June 1778. |
| Wall, Jesse | Private | Fourteenth, Thweatt | Dec 1777 sick at hospital; Jan 5, 1778 died. |
| Wallace, Adam | 1st. Lt. | Seventh, Posey | Dec 1777-Jan 1778 on furlough; April-May 1778. |
| Wallace, Andrew | Private | Twelfth, Wallace | Dec 1777-May 1778 on command. |
| Wallace, Gustavus B. /Gustus B. | Major | Fifteenth | Dec 1777 sick absent; Jan 1778 sick present; Feb-May 1778. |
| Wallace, James | Private | First, Mennis | Feb 1, 1778 enlisted; June 1778 sick Yellow Springs; July 1778 sick Valley Forge. |
| Wallace, James | Surgeon | Second | Jan-June 1778. |
| Wallace, John | Private | First State, Payne | Dec 1777 sick in hospital; Jan 1778 sick Reading; Feb 1778 sick absent; March-April 1778; May 1778 on command; June 1778. |
| Wallace, Nathaniel | Private | Fourteenth, Winston | Aug 30, 1777 enlisted; May 1778; June 1778 sick near Rocky Hill. |
| Wallace/Wallis, William | Private | Fourteenth, Jones | Jan 1778; Feb 1778 on duty; March-May 1778. |
| Wallace/Wallis, William/Wm. Gibs/Gibbs | Private | Third/ Seventh, Arell/ Briscoe | Dec 1777-May 1778; June 1778 in Briscoe's Company. |
| Waller, Anthony P. | Private | Fifteenth, Gray | Feb 10, 1778 drafted; May 1778 on command. |
| Waller, Daniel | Private | Second State, Dudley | March 15-May 1, 1778; May 1778; June 1778 sick absent. |
| Waller, Thomas | Private | Sixth, Avery | Dec 1777; Jan 25, 1778 discharged. |

| | | | |
|---|---|---|---|
| Waller, William/Wm. | Private | First, Mennis | Dec 1777; June 1778 wounded in the hospital; Feb-May 1778; June 1778 on guard. |
| Waller, William | Private | Second State, Taliaferro | June 1778 sick Valley Forge. |
| Wallis, Joseph | Private | First, Cunningham | July 1778 sick Valley Forge. |
| Walsh/Welsh, James | Private/ Volunteer/ Private | First, Taylor/ Payne | Dec 1777-Feb 1778; March 1778 roll shows his time expires on April 10, 1778; Appears as a Volunteer in April-May 1778 in Payne's Company; June 1778 a Private in Payne's Company. |
| Walsh, William | Private | Third, Mercer | Feb 8, 1778 enlisted; April 1778; June-July 1778 sick at Valley Forge. |
| Walter/Walker, Benjamin | Private | First, Mennis | April 1778; May 1778 sick present; June 1778 sick at Valley Forge; Aug 15, 1778 died. |
| Walters, John | Private | First State, Brown | Dec 1777-Feb 1778. |
| Walters, John | Private | Twelfth, Wallace | Dec 1777-Jan 1778; Feb 1778 on guard; March-May 1778. This man and the soldier below may be the same individual. |
| Walters, John | Sergeant | Fifteenth, Gregory | June 1778. |
| Walters/Walter, John | Sergeant | Fifteenth, Mason | Dec 1777-March 1778; April 1778 hospital; May 1778 Yellow Springs. |
| Walton, John | Private | Third, Blackwell | Dec 1777-March 1778 on furlough; April 10, 1778 deserted. |
| Wammock/ Womack, Ephraim | Private | Fourteenth, Jones | Sept 17, 1777 enlisted; Feb 1778-May 1778. |
| Ward, George | Private | Twelfth, Vause | Dec 1777-May 1778. |
| Ward, James | Private | Seventh/ Third, Crockett/ Sayers | March 19, 1778 enlisted; April-May 1778; June 1778 sick Valley Forge, in Sayers' Company. |

| | | | |
|---|---|---|---|
| Ward, John | Private | First, Mennis | April 1778; May 1778 on furlough; June 1778. |
| Ward, Larrence/ Lawrence | Private | Fifteenth, Wills | Feb 1778 sick present. |
| Ward, Lawrence | Private | Second, Sanford | Dec 1777 hospital; Jan-Feb 1778. |
| Ward, Levy/Levey | Private | Sixth, Rose | Dec 1777-May 1778; April 5, 1778 discharged. |
| Ward, Thomas | Private | Sixth, Avery | Jan 25, 1778 discharged. |
| Ward, William | Private | Second, Taylor, F. | Dec 1777-Jan 1778; Feb 12, 1778 discharged. |
| Ward, William | Private | Fourteenth, Jones | Jan-Feb 1778 sick in Alexandria, Virginia; June 1778 lately joined regiment. |
| Ward, William/Wm. | Private | Fifteenth, Mason | Dec 1777-Jan 1778 on guard; Feb 1778; March-April 1778 sick in camp; May 1778. |
| Warday, Joseph | Private | Second State, Bernard | March 15-April 15, 1778, stationed at York garrison. Paid April 20, 1778. |
| Wardon/ Warden, William | Private | Second, Willis | Dec 20, 1777 deserted. |
| Ware, James | Private | Second State, Lewis | March 15-May 1, 1778; May-June 1778; July 1778 sick at Valley Forge. |
| Ware, Richard | Private | Seventh, Hill | Dec 1777-Jan 1778 sick in hospital; Jan 31, 1778 discharged. |
| Ware, Samuel | Sergeant | Seventh, Lipscomb | Dec 22, 1777 enlisted in the Lt. Horse. |
| Ware, Samuel | Sergeant | Seventh/ Third, Lipscomb | May-June 1778. May be same man as above. |
| Ware/Wair, William/Wm. | Private | First, Mennis | March-June 1778. |
| Waring, Henry | 2nd. Lt. | Seventh/ Third, Webb/Young | Jan 1778; February 1778 on command; April-May 1778; June 1778 on command Valley Forge, in Young's Company. |

| Name | Rank | Company | Record |
|---|---|---|---|
| Warner, Frederick | Private | Seventh/Third, Crockett/Sayers | Dec 1777-Jan 1778; April-May 1778; June 1778 on guard, in Sayers' Company. |
| Warner, John | Private | Second, Harrison | Dec 1777-June 1778. |
| Warren, Peter | Private | Twelfth, Bowyer, T. | Dec 1777-Feb 1778 on command; March 1778 on guard; April-May 1778 on command. |
| Warren, Samuel | Private | Second, Taylor, F. | Dec 1777 left sick Virginia. |
| Warton, Sam | Private | Third, Mercer | Dec 1777-Jan 1778. |
| Waterfield, John | Private | First State, Meriwether | Dec 1777-June 1778. |
| Waters, James | Private | Seventh/Third, Crockett/Sayers | March 19, 1778 enlisted; April-May 1778; June 1778 sick Valley Forge, in Sayers' Company. |
| Waters, Thomas | Private | Third/Seventh | Only record, dated Sept 9, 1778, shows he enlisted on March 19, 1778, and was sick at Valley Forge. |
| Waters/Watters, William | Private | Twelfth, Bowyer, M. | Dec 1777-April 1778; May 22, 1778 dead. |
| Waterson/Watterson, Robert/Robt. | Corporal | Fifteenth, Grimes | Dec 1777-Jan 1778 sick absent; Feb 1778; March 1778 sick absent; April-May 1778; June 1778 on bullock guard. |
| Watkins, Joseph | Private | Sixth, Avery | Dec 25, 1777 discharged. |
| Watkins/Wadkins, Robert/Robt. | Private/Corporal | First, Mennis | Dec 1777; Jan-March 1778 on furlough; April 1 promoted to corporal; April-May 1778; June 1778 sick Valley Forge. |
| Watkins, Thomas | Sergeant | Seventh/Third, Moseley/Blackwell | Dec 1777-March 1778 on furlough; April-June 1778 on command Virginia by order of Colo. Mason; June 1778 in Blackwell's Company. |
| Watkins, William/Wm. | Private | Seventh, Hill | Feb 16, 1778 enlisted; June 1778. |

| Name | Rank | Company | Service |
|---|---|---|---|
| Watkins, William | Private | Seventh, Moseley | Dec 1777 sick in hospital; Jan 1778 muster roll shows him deceased on Dec 15, 1777. |
| Watkins, William | Private | Fourteenth, Jones | Feb 12, 1778 drafted; April 1778-May 1778. |
| Watson/Whatson, Charles | Private | Seventh/Third, Posey/Sayers | Feb 27, 1778 enlisted; April 1778 on guard; May 1778; June 1778 in Sayers' Company. |
| Watson, William | Corporal | First State, Hamilton | Dec 1777-June 1778. |
| Watson, Wm. | Private | Fifteenth, Mason/Gregory | Dec 1777; Jan 1778 on command; Feb-April 1778 waggoner; May 1778 on command; June 1778 waggoner, in Gregory's Company. |
| Watts, Aaron | Private | Fourteenth, Lambert | Dec 1777-Jan 1778; Feb 1778 on command; March-June 1778 on furlough. |
| Watts, John | Private | Seventh, Spencer | Dec 1777; Jan 1778; Feb 18, 1778 discharged. |
| Watts, Robert | Private | Seventh, Spencer | Feb 13, 1778 enlisted for 3 years; April-May 1778 |
| Watts, William | Fifer | Second State, Bressie | March 15-May 1, 1778; May 1778; June 1778 wounded at Valley Forge. |
| Waucitt/Waucett, Samuel | Private | Seventh, Moseley | Dec 1777-February 1778 on ammunition guard; March 1778 on furlough; April 1778; March 12, 1778 deserted. |
| Waugh, James | Private | Second State, Lewis | March 15-May 1, 1778; May-June 1778. |
| Wayne/Whane, Benjamin | Private | Seventh/Third, Hill | Dec 1777-Jan 1778 on furlough; April 1778; May 1778 on command; June 1778 sick Valley Forge. |
| Wayne, Charles | Private | Seventh, Hill | Dec 1777-Jan 1778 sick in hospital; Jan 27, 1778 discharged. |
| Wayne, Humphrey | Private | First State, Camp | Dec 1777 sick in hospital; Jan 12, 1778 died. |
| Wayne, Japeth | Private | Seventh, Hill | April 1778; June-July 1778 sick Valley Forge. |
| Weakly, Thomas | Private | Seventh, Crockett | Dec 1777-Jan 1778 in R. Bat. |

| Name | Rank | Regiment/Company | Service |
|---|---|---|---|
| Weathers/Wethers, James | 2nd. Lt. | First State, Brown | Dec 1777; Jan 15, 1778 resigned. |
| Weathers/Wethers, John | Corporal | First State, Hoffler | Dec 1777-May 1778; June 1778 sick absent. |
| Weaver/Wever, Zachariah | Private | Second State, Garnett | March 15-May 1, 1778; May 1778; June 1778 sick Valley Forge. |
| Webb, Henry | Private | Third, Lee | Dec 1777; Jan 1778 time out 31st Jany. |
| Webb, Isick/Isaac | 2nd. Lt. | Seventh/Third, Hill | Dec 1777-Jan 1778; April-May 1778 |
| Webb, James | Private | Third/Seventh, Peyton, V./Peyton, J. | May 1778 sick present; June 1778 sick Valley Forge. |
| Webb, John | Captain | Seventh/Third, Webb | Jan-February 1778; April-May 1778 on furlough Virginia |
| Webb, John | Private | Fifteenth, Hull | Dec 1777 sick absent; Jan 1778; Feb 1778 sick absent; March-April 1778. |
| Webb, Motley/Mutt | Private | Fifteenth, Hull | Dec 1777 sick absent; Jan 1778 sick at hospital; Feb-March 1778 sick absent; April 1778; May 1778 sick in hospital. |
| Webb, Thomas/Thos. | Private | Seventh/Third | Nov 27, 1777 deserted; April-May 1778; June 1778 on guard; in Sayers' Company. |
| Webber, John | Private | Twelfth, Casey | Feb 28, 1778 drafted; Only appears on May roll which shows he deserted on May 31, 1778. |
| Webley, John | Sergeant | Seventh, Hill | Dec 1777-Jan 1778; Feb 19, 1778 discharged. |
| Weedon/Weeden, Augustine/Augusteen | Private/Sergeant | Second State, Garnett/Quarles | April 15-May 1, 1778; May-June 1778. June 1, 1778 promoted to Sergeant and transferred to Quarles' company. |
| Welch, Edward | Private | Second, Willis | Dec 1777; Jan 3, 1778 deserted. |
| Welch/Welsh, James | Sergeant | Second, Taylor, F. | Dec 1777-Feb 1778. |

| Name | Rank | Regiment/Company | Notes |
|---|---|---|---|
| Welch/Welsh, John | Private | Seventh/Third, Fleming/Heth | Feb 13, 1778 enlisted; April-May 1778; June 1778 on guard, in Heth's Company. |
| Welch, John | Private | Fourteenth, Marks | Jan 8, 1778 enlisted; Jan-May 1778 on furlough; June 1778 deserted. |
| Welch/Welsh, Joshua | Sergeant/Private | Fourteenth, Reid | Aug 28, 1777 enlisted; Jan 1778 sick at York; Feb 1778; March 1778 sick present; April-June 1778; June 1778 reduced to Private. |
| Welch, Nathaniel | 2nd. Lt./1st. Lt. | Second State, Dudley | March 15-May 1, 1778; May-June 1778. Oath taken as a 2nd. Lt. on June 8, 1778, witnessed by Muhlenberg, but appears on rolls as a 1st. Lt. |
| Welch, Patrick/Partrick | Private | Second, Calmes | April-June 1778. |
| Welch, Thomas | Private | Second, Parker | April 1778; June 1778 hospital; July 1778 sick at Valley Forge. |
| Welch, Thomas | Private | Seventh, Posey | Dec 1777-Jan 1778 on command; Feb 12, 1778 discharged. |
| Wells, Anthony | Private | Fourteenth, Winston | Dec 1777 sick in hospital; Jan-Feb 1778 at R. hospital; Feb 10, 1778 died. |
| Wells/Wills, Edward | Private | Fourteenth, Thweatt | Dec 1777-Jan 1778; Feb 1778 sick present; March-June 1778. |
| Wells, James | Private/Sergeant | Third, Mercer | May 1778 promoted to Sergeant, sick at the Church [ ]. |
| Wells, James | Private | Fourteenth, Winston | Dec 1777-March 1778; April 1778 on command, Stedman; May-June 1778. |
| Wells, Jeremiah | Private | Twelfth, Casey | Feb 28, 1778 drafted; May 1778. |
| Wells, John G. | Private | First, Cummings | Dec 1777. |
| Wells, John | Private | Third, Mercer | Dec 1777-March 1778 on furlough; April 1778 sick; May 31, 1778 dead. |
| Wells, Laban/Labon | Private | Sixth, Fox | Dec 1777 in hospital; Feb 11, 1778 discharged. |

345

| | | | |
|---|---|---|---|
| Wells, Lemuel | Private | Fifteenth, Gregory | Dec 1777 Virginia; Jan 1778 sick Virginia. |
| Wells, Samuel/Sam | Private | First, Cummings | Dec 1777. |
| Wells, William | Private | Third, Peyton, V. | Dec 1777 deserted. |
| Wells, William/Wm. | Private | Sixth, Fox | Dec 1777-Jan 1778; Feb 22, 1778 discharged. |
| Welsh/Welh, Wm. | Private | Third/Seventh, Mercer | April 1778; May 1778 sick present; June 1778 sick Valley Forge. |
| Welsh/Welch, Thomas | Private | Second, Sanford/Parker | Dec 1777-May 1778; June 1778 hospital. From April on he appears in Parker's company. |
| West, Charles | Major | Third/Seventh | Dec 1777-Feb 1778; March 1778 on furlough; April-May 1778 on furlough Virginia; July 6, 1778 resigned. |
| West, Randolph/Randal | Private | Fifteenth, Edmunds/Wills | Dec 1777; Jan 1778 in Wills' Company; Feb 1778 sick present; March-May 1778. |
| Westal, Henry | Fifer | Third, Lee | Dec 1777 sick in Virginia. |
| Westfall, Abraham | Private | Twelfth, Vause | Feb 19, 1778 drafted; May 1778. |
| Westmoreland/Wesmorland, Jesse | Private | Second State, Dudley | March 15-May 1, 1778; May 1778; June 1778 sick absent. |
| Westmoreland/Wesmorland, Joseph | Private | Second State, Dudley | March 15-May 1, 1778; May-June 1778. |
| Westmoreland, Joseph | Private | Fourteenth, Jones | Sept 6, 1777 enlisted; Jan 1778-March 1778; April 1, 1778 died. |
| Westney/Westeney, John | Private | Fourteenth, Reid | Oct 23, 1777 enlisted; April 1778 lately joined regiment; May 1778; June 1778 wounded, Monmouth. |
| Weston/Wirston, Thomas | Private | Seventh, Young | Dec 1777-Jan 1778; Feb 20, 1778 discharged. |
| Westphall, Peter | Private | Fourteenth, Lambert | Dec 1777 supposed to be dead. |

| Name | Rank | Company | Notes |
|---|---|---|---|
| Westwood, William | Private | Twelfth, Madison | Dec 1777; Jan 1778 on weeks command; Feb 1778; March 1778 on guard; April 1778. |
| Weymouth, John | Private | First, Cummings | Dec 1777. |
| Whale, George | Private | First State, Camp | Dec 1777 sick in ye country; Jan-Feb 1778 sick absent; March 13, 1778 died. |
| Whaley, William/Wm. | Private | Fifteenth, Mason | June 1777 enlisted; Feb 1778 joined since last muster; March 1778; April 1778 on guard; May 1778. |
| Wharton/Whorton, Ben/Benj. | Private | Fifteenth, Gregory | Dec 1777; Jan 1778 on guard; Feb-April 1778; May 1778 sick present; June 1778 sick Valley Forge. |
| Wharton, Samuel | Private | Third, Mercer | Dec 1777-Feb 1778. |
| Wharton, Thomas | Sergeant | First, Lewis | Dec 1777; Jan-Feb 1778 sick hospital; March-April 1778; April reduced to private; May-June 1778. |
| Whealer, Mathew | Private | Fifteenth, Harris | Jan-Feb 1778 on guard; March-April 1778 sick present; May 17, 1778 deceased. |
| Whealey/Wheely, Thomas | Private | Seventh/Third, Hill | April-June 1778. |
| Wheeler/Whealer, John/Jno. | Private | Sixth, Fox | Sept 27, 1777 enlisted; Dec 1777-Jan 1778; Feb 1778 absent with leave; March-June 1778. |
| Wheeler, Samuel | Corporal | First State, Hamilton | Dec 1777-June 1778. |
| Wheeley, Thomas | Private | Seventh, Hill | Feb 16, 1778 enlisted. |
| Wheelor/Wheeler, Ambrose | Private | Twelfth, Bowyer, T. | Dec 1777-April 1778; May 1778 on command. |
| Wheely/Wheeley, John | Private | Second State, Dudley | May 1778; June 1778 omitted in April, absent sick; July 1778 sick Valley Forge. |
| Wherley/Whirley, Peter | Private | First State, Nicholas | Dec 1777-May 1778; June 1778 on guard. |

| Name | Rank | Regiment | Notes |
|---|---|---|---|
| White, Abraham/ Abram | Private | Second State, Taliaferro | March 15-May 1, 1778; May 1778; June 1778 sick Valley Forge. |
| White, Armisted/ Armsted | Sergeant | Third, Peyton, V. | Dec 1777-Jan 1778. |
| White, Benjamin | Private | Fifteenth, Gray | May 25, 1778 died. |
| White, Charles | Private | Second, Jones | Dec 18, 1778 deserted. |
| White, Charles | Private | Seventh/ Third, Moseley/ Blackwell | Feb 14, 1778 enlisted; April-May 1778; June 1778 sick Correll's Ferry, in Blackwell's Company. |
| White, Dudley | Private | Second, Jones | Feb 1778; March 15, 1778 dead. This man and the one below may be the same individual. |
| White, Dudley | Private | Second, Upshaw | Jan 1778 payroll shows "pay not drawn for since the 13 Aug 1777." |
| White, Elisha | 1st. Lt. | First, Mennis | Dec 1777-March 1778; April 1778 absent without leave. White had mortally wounded John Green in a duel on April 25. |
| White, James | Private | Second State, Garnett | June 1778 "Omitted from 15 March." June 1778. |
| White, James | Private | Third/ Seventh, Peyton, V./ Peyton, J. | Dec 1777-Feb 1778 on furlough; March 1778 on command; May 1778; June 1778 waggoner, in J. Peyton's Company. |
| White, James | Private | Seventh, Young | Dec 1777-Jan 1778 sick Baltimore; Feb 3, 1778 discharged. |
| White, John | Fleming | Second, Sanford/ Parker | Dec 1777 hospital; Jan-June 1778. From April on he appears in Parker's company. |
| White, John | Private | Third, Blackwell | Dec 1777-Jan 1778 on guard; Feb 14, 1778 discharged. |
| White, John | Ensign/ Paymaster | Seventh/ Third, Fleming | Dec 1777-March 1778; April 1778 on command Country Store; May 1778 muster roll shows him as both Ensign and Paymaster. |

| Name | Rank | Unit | Notes |
|---|---|---|---|
| White, Joseph | Drummer/ Private | Fourteenth, Winston | Dec 1777 Color Man; Jan 1778 sick present; Feb 1778; March 16, 178 died. |
| White, Robert | Private | Second, Taylor, F. | Dec 1777 on furlough; Jan-April 1778; April 1778 "Deserted when on furlow." |
| White, Robert/Robt. | Private | Sixth, Garland | Dec 1, 1777 reenlisted; Jan-May 1778 off; June 1778. |
| White, Robert | 1st. Lt. | Twelfth, Madison | Dec 1777-March 1778 sick in Jersies; April 1778. |
| White, Robert | Private | Fifteenth, Gray | Feb 1778 sick; March 1778 sick in camp; April-May 1778 sick present; June 1778 sick Yellow Springs. |
| White, Tarpley/Tarplay | 2nd. Lt. | Seventh/ Third, Jouett/ Lipscomb | Dec 1777-May 1778. As Captain Jouett had died in Nov 1777, White was the senior officer in the company for this period. June 1778 in Lipscomb's Company. |
| White, Thomas | Sergeant | First State, Lee | Dec 1777-May 1778; June 1778 sick absent. |
| White, Thomas | Private | Third, Arell | Jan 1778. |
| White, William | Private | First, Pelham | Dec 1777 sick hospital; Feb 15, 1778 discharged. |
| White, William | Private | First State, Ewell, T. | April 1778 "Not drew for since March 15th"; May 1778; June 1778 sick at Valley Forge. |
| White, William | Sergeant | First State, Meriwether | Dec 1777-June 1778. |
| White, William | 2nd. Lt | Seventh/ Third, Spencer | Dec 1777-Jan 1778; April 1778 on command in Virginia; May 1778. |
| Whiteen/Whele, John | Paymaster | Seventh/Third | May-June 1778. |
| Whitefield, Edward | Private | First State, Ewell, T. | Dec 1777; Jan 1778 sick at Yellow Springs; Feb 20, 1778 deceased. |
| Whitehorn/ Whitehorne, Thomas | Private | Fifteenth, Mason | Dec 1777-Feb 1778; March 30, 1778 discharged. |
| Whitehurst, Jonathan | Private | Fifteenth, Gregory | Dec 1777; Jan 1778 on guard; Feb-May 1778. |

| Name | Rank | Company | Notes |
|---|---|---|---|
| Whitehurst/ Whirthurst, Levy/Levi | Private | Fifteenth, Grimes | March 27, 1778 joined from [ ]; March 1778 payroll pays him to Aug 1, 1777, "Omitted for being absent"; April-May 1778. |
| Whiteman/ Whitman, Charles | Private/ Quartermaster Sergeant | Third/ Seventh, Powell | Dec 1777; Jan 1778 on guard; Feb 1778; March 1778 promoted to Quartermaster Sergeant; April-May 1778. |
| Whitfield, William/Wm/ | Private | Sixth, Fox | Dec 1777-Jan 1778; Feb 20, 1778 discharged. |
| Whiting, John | Private | Third/ Seventh, Briscoe | Feb 5, 1778 enlisted; June 1778. |
| Whiting, Beverley/ Beverly | Ensign | Seventh/ Third, Moseley | Dec 1777-April 1778 on furlough; May 1778 absent without leave. |
| Whitlock/ Whellock, John | Private | Third, Powell | Dec 1777; Feb 14, 1778 discharged. |
| Whitlock, Reuben/ Reubin | Sergeant Major | Second State, Dudley | March 15-May 1, 1778. This man and the man below are probably the same individual. |
| Whitlock, Reuben | Ensign | Second State, Lewis | May-June 1778. |
| Whitlock, Thomas | Sergeant | Seventh, Spencer | Dec 1777 hospital; Jan 1778; April 1778 muster roll shows him discharged on May 1. |
| Whitlock, William/ Wm. H. | Private | Sixth, Avery | Dec 1777-Jan 1778; Feb 8, 1778 discharged. |
| Whitloe/ Whitlow, Francis | Private | Second State, Dudley | June 1778. |
| Whitloe/ Whitlow, Thomas | Private | Second State, Dudley | June 1778. |
| Whitlow/ Whatloe, John | Private | Fourteenth, Thweatt | Deserted April 14, 1777; Jan 1778 deserter returned, left sick Virginia; Feb 1778 sick Alexandria. |
| Whitlow, Michael/ Mike | Private | Seventh/ Third, Moseley | Dec 1777-April 1778 on furlough; May 1778. |

| Name | Rank | Regiment/Company | Service |
|---|---|---|---|
| Whitmore, Wm. | Private | Third/Seventh, Powell | Dec 1777. |
| Whitt, Shadrach/Shadrack | Private | Fifteenth, Foster/Gray | Dec 1777 on command; Jan 1778 waiting on sick; Feb 1778 sick; March 1778 sick absent; April 1778 dead. |
| Whorley, Mathew/Matthew | Private/Corporal | Seventh/Third, Fleming/Heth | Dec 1777 on furlough Virginia; Jan-March 1778 on furlough; Feb 16, 1778 promoted to Corporal; April-May 1778; June 1778 in Heth's Company. |
| Whorton, Benjamin | Private | Fifteenth, Gregory | May 1778 sick present; June 1778 sick Valley Forge. |
| Wiatt/Wiatte, Richard | Private | Seventh, Hill | Dec 1777-Jan 1778. |
| Wibling/Wiblin, William | Private | Second State, Dudley | March 15-May 1, 1778; May 1778; June 1778 sick absent. |
| Wickleff/Wicklift, David | Private | Third, Peyton, J. | Dec 1777-Jan 1778 wounded absent. |
| Wilborn/Willbourn, William/Wm. | Private | Sixth, Garland | Dec 1777 in hospital; Jan 1778 sick absent; Feb, 19, 1778 discharged. |
| Wilbourn, John | Private | Third, Powell | Dec 1777. |
| Wilcocks/Willcocks, William/Wm. | Private | Fifteenth, Hull | March 1778; April-May 1778 sick present; June 9, 1778 died. |
| Wilcox/Willcox, Samuel | Private | Twelfth, Waggener | Dec 1777-Feb 1778 hospital; March 1778 on guard; April 1778. |
| Wilder/Welder, Reuben | Private | Third, Blackwell | Dec 1777-Jan 1778; Feb 14, 1778 discharged. |
| Wildy/Wilday, Mott/Motley | Private | Fifteenth, Hull | Dec 1777 sick absent; Jan 1778 sick at hospital; Feb 1778 sick absent; March-May 1778. |
| Wiley/Willey, George/Geo. | Sergeant/Sergeant Major | First, Mennis | Dec 1777-April 1778; May promoted to Sergeant Major; May-June 1778. |

| Name | Rank | Regiment, Company | Service |
|---|---|---|---|
| Wilkerson/ Wilkinson, Barnard/Barna | Private | Fifteenth, Mason/ Gregory | Dec 1777-March 1778; April 1778 sick in camp; May 1778; June 1778 on guard, in Gregory's Company. |
| Wilkerson/ Wilkinson, Benjamin | Private | Second State, Dudley | March 15-May 1, 1778; May-June 1778. |
| Wilkerson, John/Jno. | Private | First, Cunningham | Feb 17, 1778 enlisted for 1 year; April 1778 under inoculation; May 9, 1778 died. |
| Wilkerson/ Wilkenson, John | Corporal | Sixth, Avery | Dec 1777 sick in hospital; Jan 1778; Feb 8, 1778 discharged. |
| Wilkerson/ Wilkonson, Weedon | Private | Third, Mercer | Dec 1777-Jan 1778; Feb 18, 1778 discharged. |
| Wilkes/Wilks, Burrell/Burwel | Private/ Corporal/ Sergeant | Fifteenth, Mason/ Gregory | Dec 1777 on guard; Jan 1778 on guard; promoted to Corporal; Feb 1778 sick present; March 1778 sick in camp; April 1778; May 1, 1778 promoted to Sergeant; June 1778 in Gregory's Company. |
| Wilkes/Wilks, James | Private | Third, Arell | Dec 1777-Jan 1778; Feb-March 1778 sick present; April 15, 1778 dead. |
| Wilkey, John | Private | Fifteenth, Wills | Aug 16, 1777 enlisted; Feb 1778 sick at York; March 1778 sick absent. |
| Wilkins, Robert | Private | First State, Lee | Dec 1777 on duty; Jan 1778 sick absent; Feb 1778 "died sometime in Jany." |
| Wilkins, Robert/ Ruber | | Seventh/ Third, Posey/Sayers | Dec 1777-Jan 1778 "Gon to Virginia with Doctor Shppes Lady"; April 1778; May 1778 "Respeted"; June 1778 sick [ ], in Young's Company. |
| Wilkins, Thomas | Private | Third/ Seventh, Blackwell | Feb 18, 1778 drafted; April-June 1778. |
| Wilkins, Thomas | Drummer | Fourteenth, Winston | Dec 1777 on command; Jan-June 1778. |

| | | | |
|---|---|---|---|
| Willeby, Edlin | Private | Third/Seventh, Lipscomb | June 1778. |
| Willeley, William | Corporal | Third/Seventh, Lipscomb | June 1778. |
| Willeroy/Willeray, James | Sergeant | Seventh/Third, Lipscomb | Feb 14, 1778 enlisted for 1 year; May 1778 sick in camp; June 1778 sick present. |
| Willey, Thomas | Private | First State, Hoffler | May-June 1778. |
| Williams, Benjamin | Drummer | Second State, Lewis | May-June 1778. |
| Williams, Benjamin/Benjm. | Private | Sixth, Rose | Dec 1777-Feb 1778; March 4, 1778 discharged. |
| Williams, David | Private | Seventh, Spencer | Dec 1777-Jan 1778; March 10, 1778 discharged. |
| Williams/Williamson, David | Private | Twelfth, Bowyer, M. | Feb 27, 1778 drafted for one year; April-May 1778. |
| Williams, David | 2nd. Lt. | Twelfth, Vause | Dec 1777-April 1778; May 1778 on 3 days command. |
| Williams, Edward | Sergeant | Twelfth, Vause | Dec 1777-March 1778; April 1778 on fatigue; May 1778. |
| Williams, Elaz. | Private | Fifteenth, Hull | Dec 1777 sick absent in Virginia. |
| Williams, Frederick | Private | Sixth, Rose | Dec 15, 1777 discharged. |
| Williams, George | Private | Second, Jones/Hoomes | Dec 1777-May 1778; June 1778 sick absent. |
| Williams, George | Private | Second, Harrison | Dec 1777-May 1778; June 1778 sick Valley Forge. |
| Williams, Henry | Private | Fifteenth, Mason Gregory | Dec 1777-Feb 1778; March-April 1778 sick in camp; May 1778; June 1778 sick Correls Ferry, in Gregory's Company. |
| Williams, James | Drummer | First, Lawson | Dec 1777; Jan 1778 sick hospital; Feb-June 1778. |
| Williams, Jarret/Jarrett | Private | Sixth, Garland | Dec 1777; Jan 1778; Feb 14, 1778 died. |

| | | | | |
|---|---|---|---|---|
| Williams, Jesse | Private | Fourteenth, Jones | Sept 18, 1777 enlisted; July 1778. |
| Williams, John | Private | Second, Upshaw | Feb 14, 1778 drafted; April 1778; June 1778. |
| Williams, John/Jno. | Private | Sixth, Avery | Dec 1777-Jan 1778 sick in hospital; Feb-March 1778 in hospital; April 1778 at the Shoe Factory; May 1778 absent supposed to be dead. |
| Williams, John | Private | Twelfth, Casey | Dec 1777 sent to hospital; Jan-March 1778 at hospital; April 1778 "No account of". |
| Williams, John | Private | Fifteenth, Mason | Dec 1777 sick absent; Jan-May 1778. |
| Williams, Joseph | Private | Twelfth, Bowyer, T. | April-May 1778 sick hospital Lancaster. |
| Williams, Jonathan | Private | Third, Peyton, J. | Dec 1777 wounded absent; Jan 1778. |
| Williams, Joshua | Sergeant | Sixth, Fox | Dec 1777-Jan 1778; Feb 11, 1778 discharged. |
| Williams, Lewis | Private | Second, Willis | June 1778 sick Valley Forge. |
| Williams, Lewis/Lewes | Private | Seventh/Third, Jouett/Hill | Feb 16, 1778 enlisted; April 1778 on guard; May-June 1778 on command; June 1778 in Hill's Company. |
| Williams, Peter | Private | Fourteenth, Jones | Feb 12, 1778 drafted; April-May 1778; June 1778 sick Valley Forge; Oct 1778 roll shows he died June 26, 1778. |
| Williams, Rice | Private | Second State, Lewis | March 15-May 1, 1778; May-June 1778; July 1778 sick Valley Forge. |
| Williams, Roger | Sergeant | Sixth, Massie | Dec 1777-Jan 1778; Feb 15, 1778 discharged. |
| Williams, Ruben/Rubin | Sergeant/Private | First, Scott | Dec 1777; Jan 1778 on command; Feb-April 1778; May reduced to Private; May-June 1778 on command. |
| Williams, Seth | Private | Fifteenth, Grimes | Feb 11, 1778 drafted; April 1778; May 1778 sick present. |
| Williams, Thomas | Private | Second State, Spiller | March 15-May 1, 1778; May-June 1778. |

| Name | Rank | Regiment | Notes |
|---|---|---|---|
| Williams, Thomas | Corpotal | Fifteenth, Gray | Dec 1777 sick absent; Jan 1778 sick; Feb-March 1778; April 1778 on guard; May-June 1778 sick Yellow Springs; June 30, 1778 died. |
| Williams, William | Private | Second State, Bernard | March 15-April 15, 1778 stationed in York garrison; May 1778; June 1778 on guard. |
| Williams, William/Wm. | Private | Third, Arell | Dec 1777-Jan 1778; Feb 1778 on duty; March 8, 1778 deserted. |
| Williams, William | Private | Third, Mercer | Dec 1777 on command; Jan 1778 waggoner. |
| Williams, William | Private | Sixth, Fox | Dec 1777-Jan 1778; Feb 11, 1778 discharged. |
| Williams, Wm. | Private | Sixth, Hockaday | Dec 1777-Jan 1778; Feb 10, 1778 discharged. |
| Williams, William | Private | Sixth, Massie | Feb 15, 1778 discharged. |
| Williams, William | Private | Seventh, Young | Dec 1777-Jan 1778; March 1, 1778 discharged. |
| Williams, William | Private | Fourteenth, Jones | Sept 6, 1777 enlisted; Jan-Feb 1778 sick at Lancaster. |
| Williams, Zebedee | Private | First State, Hoffler | Dec 1777-March 1778. |
| Williamson, Jacob | Private | Seventh, Moseley | Dec 1777-Jan 1778 sick in hospital; February 1778; March 7, 1778 discharged. |
| Williamson, James | Private | First State, Hamilton | Dec 1777-Jan 1778; Died about Feb 15, 1778. |
| Williamson/ Williams, John | Private | Fourteenth, Thweatt | Dec 1777 sick in hospital; Jan-Feb 1778; May 1778 on command; April-June 1778. |
| Williamson, Roger/Rodger | Private | Second State, Bressie | March 15-May 1, 1778; May-June 1778. |
| Williamson, Thomas/Thos. | Sergeant | First, Lewis | Feb 7, 1778 enlisted; April-May 1778; June 1778 muster roll sick at Valley Forge; payroll shows "Genl. Scotts Corps". |
| Williamson, Vincent | Private | Seventh/ Third, Webb/ Young | Feb 16, 1778 enlisted. April-May 1778; June 1778 in Young's Company. |

356

| | | | |
|---|---|---|---|
| Williamson, William/Wm. | Private | Third, Arell | Dec 1777-Jan 1778; Feb 20, 1778 died. |
| Willis, George | Private | First, Lawson | Dec 1777 sick Pennsylvania; Jan 1778 sick hospital; Feb-June 1778. |
| Willis, John | Captain | Second, Willis | September 11, 1777 captured at the Battle of Brandywine. He was not exchanged until 1780. |
| Willis, John | Private | Second State, Bernard | April-May 1778; June 1778 sick Valley Forge. |
| Willis, John | Private | Seventh/ Third, Jouett/Hill | Feb 16, 1778 enlisted; April 1778 sick present; May 1778 hospital; June 1778 sick Yellow Springs, in Hill's Company. |
| Willis, John | Private | Third/ Seventh, Young | June 1778. |
| Willmon/ Willmond, Jarret | Private | Twelfth, Waggener | Dec 1777-March 1778 hospital; April 1778 supposed to be dead. |
| Willowby/ Willobey, Edlin/Eadlin | Private | Seventh, Spencer | Enlisted for 3 years. Dec 1777 on furlough Virginia; Jan 1778 on furlough; April-May 1778 |
| Willowby/ Willobey, Eadward/ Edward | Private | Seventh, Spencer | Enlisted for 3 years. Dec 1777 on furlough Virginia; Jan 1778 on furlough; April-May 1778. |
| Wills, Henry | Sergeant | First, Cummings/ Mennis | Feb 4, 1778 enlisted; April 1778; May 1778 sick present; June 1778 sick Philadelphia, in Mennis' Company. |
| Wills/Wells, Thomas | Captain | Fifteenth, Wills | Jan-May 1778. |
| Willson/Wilson, Edward | Private | Twelfth, Bowyer, M. | Dec 1777-Jan 1778; Feb 1778 on duty; March 1778 on guard; April 1778; May 1778 on command. |
| Willson, William/Wm. | Private | First, Mennis | Dec 1777; Jan-June 1778 on furlough. |
| Wilmon, Jerad | Private | Twelfth, Waggener | Dec 1777-March 1778; April 1778 "Sepos to be dead". |
| Wilson/Willson, Archer | Private | Sixth, Hopkins | Dec 1777 wounded; Jan 1778 hospital; Feb 1778 in hospital; Feb 19, 1778 discharged. |

| Name | Rank | Company | Dates |
|---|---|---|---|
| Wilson, Daniel | Sergeant | Sixth, Hopkins | Dec 1777-Jan 1778; Feb 19, 1778 discharged. |
| Wilson/Willson, David | Private | Twelfth, Waggener | Dec 1777-Jan 1778; Feb 1778 on guard; March 1778 on command; April 10, 1778 discharged. |
| Wilson, Ephraim | Private | First, Pelham | Dec 1777 sick hospital; Jan 1778; Feb 15, 1778 discharged. |
| Wilson, Isick/Isaac | Corporal/ Sergeant | Second State, Spiller | March 15-May 1, 1778; May-June 1778; June 1, 1778 promoted to Sergeant. |
| Wilson, Jeremiah | Private | Third/ Seventh, Peyton, V./ Peyton, J. | March 25, 1778 enlisted; May 1778; June 1778 in J. Peyton's Company. |
| Wilson/Willson, John | Private | First, Mennis | Dec 1777; Jan-March 1778 on furlough; April 1778; May 1778 sick present; June 1778 sick Valley Forge. |
| Wilson, John | Private | First, Cummings | Dec 1777; April-May 1778. |
| Wilson, John | Private | Second, Willis | Dec 1777; Jan 3, 1778 deserted. |
| Wilson/Willson, John | Private | Twelfth, Ashby | Dec 1777; Jan 1778 sick in hospital; March 1778 at hospital; April-May 1778. |
| Wilson/Willson, Mahlon | Corporal | Second, Harrison | Dec 1777-June 1778. |
| Wilson, Peter | Private | Second State, Lewis | May-June 1778; July 1778 payroll states he was "omitted from 15th April to 1st of July" and pays him for 3 ½ months. |
| Wilson, Richard | Corporal | Fourteenth, Winston | Dec 1777; Jan 1778 at Reading Hospital; "Dead 8 day of Feb 1778." |
| Wilson/Willson, Stacy | Corporal | Second, Calmes | Dec 1777-June 1778. |
| Wilson, Thomas | Corporal | Seventh, Crockett | Dec 1777-Jan 1778 on furlough. |
| Wilson, William | Private | Second State, Spiller | May-June 1778. |
| Wilson/Willson, William | Private | Second, Sanford | Dec 1777-Jan 1778; Feb 1778 deceased. |

| | | | |
|---|---|---|---|
| Wilson, Wm. | Private | Fifteenth, Gray | Feb 10, 1778 drafted; April 1778 under inoculation; May 1778 hospital Yellow Springs. |
| Wilson, Willis | Sergeant | Fifteenth, Foster/Gray | Dec 1777; Jan 1778 on guard; Feb 1778 in Gray's Company; March-May 1778. |
| Wilton/Willen, Samuel | Private | Third/Seventh, Peyton, V. Peyton, J. | March 10, 1778 enlisted; April 1778 waiting on Lt. Col. Flenby; May 1778 on command; June 1778 waiter Col. Fluray, in J. Peyton's Company. |
| Wimbish, John | Sergeant | Fourteenth, Thweatt | Dec 1777 sick in hospital; Jan-June 1778. |
| Winfrey, Austin | Sergeant | Seventh, Lipscomb | Dec 1777-Jan 1778 hospital; Feb 2, 1778 discharged. |
| Winfrey/Winfree, Isick/Isaac | Private | Seventh/Third, Fleming/Heth | Feb 11, 1778 enlisted; April 1778 sick present; May 1778; June 1778 in Heth's Company/ |
| Winfrey, John | Private | Seventh/Third, Lipscomb | Feb 14, 1778 enlisted for 1 year; April-May 1778; June 1778 with Col. Richeson, Virginia. |
| Wingfield, John, Sr. | Private | Fourteenth, Winston | Feb 17, 1778 drafted; May-June 1778 |
| Wingfield, John, Jr. | Private | Fourteenth, Winston | Feb 17, 1778 drafted; May-June 1778 |
| Wingo/Wengo, William | Private | First, Pelham | Feb 7, 1778 enlisted; April 1778 under inoculation; May-June 1778. |
| Winn, Elisha | Corporal | Sixth, Avery | Dec 1777-Jan 1778; Jan 1778; Feb 12, 1778 discharged. |
| Winn, James | Sergeant | Sixth, Avery | Dec 1777 sick in hospital; Feb 8, 1778 discharged. |
| Winn/Wynne, Samuel See Wynn | Private | Fourteenth, Jones | Jan 1778 on duty; Feb 1778 on command; March-May 1778; June 1778 sick Valley Forge. |
| Winniferd/Winniford, David | Corporal | Seventh, Fleming | Dec 1777-Jan 1778; Feb 19, 1778 discharged. |
| Winston, John | Captain | Fourteenth, Winston | Dec 1777 sick absent; Jan 1778; Feb-June 1778 on furlough. |
| Winston, Robert | Private | First State, Lee | Dec 1777 on duty; Jan 1778 on command; Feb-June 1778. |

| | | | |
|---|---|---|---|
| Winston, William | Corporal | Third, Powell | Dec 1777. |
| Wiott/Weatt, Cader/Cuder | Private | Fifteenth, Harris | Jan 1778; Feb 1778 sick present; March 31, 1778 dead. |
| Wiott/Weatt, Elisha | Private | Fifteenth, Harris | Jan 1778 artificer; Feb-March 1778; April 1778 on command; May 1778 on command Lancaster; June 1778 on command. |
| Wiott, William/Wm. | Private | Fifteenth, Harris | Feb-March 1778; April 1778 sick present; June 1778 sick present. |
| Wire, Timothy | Fifer | Twelfth, Waggener | Dec 1777-Jan 1778 sick in camp; Feb 1778 hospital; March-May 1778. |
| Wise, Edward | Private | Seventh, Young | Dec 1777-Jan 1778 hospital; Feb 20, 1778 discharged. |
| Wishart, Thomas | 1st. Lt. | Fifteenth, Gregory | Dec 1777-March 1778 on furlough; April 20, 1778 resigned. |
| Wislow, Diggs | Private | Seventh, Young | Dec 21, 1777 to Lt. Horse. |
| Witt, Jesse/Jessy | Private | Fourteenth, Lambert | Dec 1777-June 1778. |
| Wood, David | Private | Seventh, Jouett | Dec 1777-Jan 1778 sick in hospital; Feb 10, 1778 discharged. |
| Wood, James/John | Private | Seventh, Spencer | Feb 13, 1778 enlisted for 1 year; April-May 1778 |
| Wood, James | Colonel | Twelfth | Dec 1777; Jan 1778 on furlough; Feb-May 1778. |
| Wood, John | Private | First State, Nicholas | Dec 1777 on furlough; Jan 1778; Feb 1778; sick in ye country; March-May 1778; June 1778 sick present. |
| Wood, John | Private | Third/ Seventh, Peyton, J. | Dec 1777-March 1778 sick absent; April –May 1778; June 1778 on command. |
| Wood, Joseph | Private | First, Lawson | Dec 1777 sick Cross Road; Jan 1778 waggoner; Feb 1778 sick at the hospital; March 1778, June 1778 sick at Lancaster, |
| Wood, Mathew/Matt | Private | First, Mennis | Dec 1777; Jan-March 1778 on furlough. |
| Wood, Robert | Private | Third, Blackwell | Feb 18, 1778 drafted; April-May 1778; |

| | | | |
|---|---|---|---|
| Wood, Thomas | Private | Seventh/Third, Spencer/Lipscomb | Feb 11, 1778 enlisted for 1 year; May 1778; June 1778 in Lipscomb's Company. |
| Wood, Timothy | Private | Fifteenth, Grimes | Dec 1777-March 1778 sick absent; April 1778 Heidle Hospital; May-June 1778. |
| Woodard, Peter | Fifer | Fifteenth, Gregory | Dec 1777-March 1778 hospital. |
| Woodcock, John | Private | First, Lawson | Dec 1777; Jan 1778 on guard; Feb-March 1778; April 1778 on guard; May-June 1778. |
| Woodley, Thomas | Sergeant | Second, Taylor, W. | Dec 1777 command; Jan 1778; Feb 14, 1778 discharged. |
| Woodly/Woodley, Henry | Corporal | First, Lewis | Dec 1777-May 1778; June 1778 sick on the road. |
| Woodridge/Wouldridge, Daniel/Danl. | Private | First, Cunningham | July 1777 enlisted for 3 years; Dec 1777 confined; Jan 1778 sick at hospital; Feb 1778 sick present; March-April 1778 sick absent; May 1778 on guard; June 1778 sick at Valley Forge. |
| Woodrough, Jesse | Private | Second, Upshaw | Dec 1777 hospital; Jan 1778. |
| Woods, Alexander | Private | Twelfth, Wallace | Dec 1777-May 1778. |
| Woods, Mathew | Private | Twelfth, Wallace | Dec 1777; Jan 6, 1778 deserted; May 17, 1778 rejoined; May 1778. |
| Woods, Robert | Private | Third/Seventh, Blackwell | June 1778 sick present. |
| Woodson, Frederick | 2nd. Lt./1st. Lt. | First State, Hamilton/Valentine | Dec 1777-May 1778; June promoted to 1st. Lt. and transferred to formerly Crump's company, now Valentine's. Oath at Valley Forge on May 11, 1778, witnessed by Muhlenberg. |
| Woodward, Charles | Private | First State, Hoffler | May 1778; June 1778 deceased. |
| Woodward/Woodard, James | Private | First State, Hoffler | April-May 1778; June 1778 sick absent. |

| Name | Rank | Company | Notes |
|---|---|---|---|
| Woodward/ Woodard, Micajah | Private | Sixth, Massie | Dec 1777 in hospital; Jan 1778; Feb 12, 1778 discharged. |
| Woodward/ Woodard, William/Wm. | Private | Sixth, Massie | Dec 1777 in hospital; Jan 1778; Feb 12, 1778 discharged. |
| Woody/ Wooddy, William | Private | Second, Jones/ Hoomes | Dec 1777 hospital; Jan-June 1778. |
| Wooldridge, Abram | Corporal | Fifteenth, Harris | Jan 1778; Feb 1778 on command; March 1778 sick present; April 1778; May 1778 sick in camp. June 1778. |
| Woolridge/ Wooldridge, Joseph | Private | Second State, Bernard | |
| Wooley, Richard | Private | First State, Payne | Jan-March 1778 on command; April 1778 deserted. Feb payroll shows he deserted on Feb 14, 1778. |
| Woolford/ Wolford, Solomon | Private | Twelfth, Wallace | Dec 1777; Jan-March 1778 on command; April-May 1778. |
| Wooton, Samuel | Private | Seventh/ Third, Fleming/ Young | Feb 11, 1778 enlisted; April 1778 sick present; May 1778 absent; June 1778 in Young's Company. |
| Worsham, Henry | Private | Second, Taylor, W. | Dec 1777-Feb 1778; March 5, 1778 discharged. |
| Worsham/ Warsham, John | 1st. Lt./ Adjutant | Second, Jones/ Taylor, W. | Dec 1777; Jan transferred to W. Taylor's Company; Jan-March 1778; April promoted to Adjutant; April-June 1778. Oath at Valley Forge on May 18, 1778, witnessed by Muhlenberg. |
| Worsham, Joshua/Joseph | Private | Second, Taylor, W. | Dec 1777-March 1778. |
| Worsham/ Warsham, Richard | 2nd. Lt. | Fourteenth, Reid | Jan-June 1778. Oath at Valley Forge on May 14, 1778, witnessed by Muhlenberg. |
| Wray see Ray | | | |
| Wright, Daniel/Danl. | Private | Third, Arell | Dec 1777-Feb 1778; March 15, 1778 deserted. |

| Name | Rank | Regiment/Company | Service |
|---|---|---|---|
| Wright/Write, Jarrett/Gorrot | Corporal | First State, Ewell, T. | Dec 1777-Feb 1778 sick Bethlehem; April-June 1778. |
| Wright/Right, James | Private | First State, Nicholas | Dec 1777-Jan 1778 on guard; Feb-June 1778. |
| Wright, James | Private | Seventh, Moseley | Dec 1777; Jan 1778 on command; Feb 26, 1778 discharged. |
| Wright, James | Private | Seventh, Posey | Dec 1777; Jan 1778 sick present in camp; Feb 24, 1778 discharged. |
| Wright, James | Private | Third/Seventh, Sayers | June 1778 on guard. |
| Wright, James | Private | Twelfth, Waggener | Dec 1777; Jan 1778 on command; Feb 1778; March-April 1778 on command; May 1778. |
| Wright/Right, James | Private | Fourteenth, Marks | Dec 1777-Jan 1778 in hospital sick; Feb 1778 sick absent; March 1778 sick in hospital; April-June 1778. |
| Wright, Parsons | Private | Sixth, Avery | Dec 1777-Jan 1778; Feb 12, 1778 discharged. |
| Wright/Right, Richard | Private | Second State, Spiller | March 15-May 1, 1778; May-June 1778. |
| Wright, Robert | Corporal/Private | Fourteenth, Winston | Dec 1777-Jan 1778 sick in Virginia; March 1778 reduced to Private; March-June 1778. |
| Wright, Thomas | Private | Sixth, Avery | Dec 1777-Jan 1778 sick in hospital; Feb-June 1778. |
| Wright, Thomas | Private | Seventh, Moseley | Dec 1777-Jan 1778; Feb 24, 1778 discharged. |
| Wright, William/Wm. | Corporal/Sergeant | Third/Seventh, Arell/Briscoe | Dec 1777-Jan 1778; Feb 1778 promoted to Sergeant; March-May 1778; June 1778 in Briscoe's Company. |
| Wright, William/Wm. | Corporal | Sixth, Hockaday | Dec 1777 sick at Princetown; Jan 1778; Feb 20, 1778 discharged. |
| Wroe, Samuel | Private | First State, Brown | Jan 10, 1778 died. |
| Wyall, Henry | Private | Seventh, Hill | April-May 1778 |

| | | | |
|---|---|---|---|
| Wyatt, Edward | Private | Second State, Taliaferro | June 1778 sick Valley Forge. |
| Wyatt, Henry | Private | Seventh/Third, Hill | Feb 16, 1778 enlisted; June 1778 on guard. |
| Wyatt, John | Private | Second State, Taliaferro | March 15, 1778-June 1778. |
| Wyatt, Pitman | Private | Second State, Taliaferro | March 15, 1778-June 1778. |
| Wynn, Samuel | Private | Fourteenth, Conway | Dec 1777. This man and Samuel Winn may be the same individual. |
| Yancey, Absolam | Private | Fourteenth, Overton | Oct 1, 1777 drafted; Jan 1778 on command; Feb 1778; March 1778; April 1778 sick present. |
| Yarborough/Yarbrough, John | Private | Second, Jones | Feb on furlough; March 1778. |
| Yarbrough/Yarborough, Charles | 1st. Lt. | First State, Meriwether | Dec 1777-June 1778. Oath in June 1778, witnessed by Muhlenberg. |
| Yarbrough, John | Private/Corporal | Second, Upshaw | Dec 1777 on furlough Jan 1778; April he appears as a Corporal; April 1778; June 1778. |
| Yarbrough Yarborough, Joseph | Sergeant | Sixth, Rose | Dec 1777-Jan 1778; Feb 19, 1778 discharged. |
| Yarington, John | Private | Seventh, Webb | Jan 1778 hospital; Feb 15, 1778 discharged. |
| Yates, Ed | Private | Twelfth, Madison | Dec 23, 1777 missing. |
| Young, Henry | Captain | Seventh/Third, Young | Dec 1777-February 1778; March 1778 on furlough. April-June 1778. |
| Young, James | Private | Twelfth, Waggener | Dec 1777-May 1778. |
| Young, Lewis | Sergeant | Third, Powell | Dec 1777; Jan 31, 1778 discharged. |

| | | | |
|---|---|---|---|
| Young, Samuel | Private | Third/Seventh, Mercer/Powell | Dec 1777-May 1778; June 1778 on detachment, in Powell's Company. |
| Young, Tinsley | Sergeant | Sixth, Rose | Dec 1777-Jan 1778 in hospital; Feb 21, 1778 discharged. |
| Young, Walter | Fifer | Third/Seventh, Peyton, V./Peyton, J. | Dec 1777 on furlough Virginia; Jan-March 1778 furlough. April-May 1778; June 1778 in J. Peyton's Company. |
| Younger/Yonger, Joshua | Private | Twelfth, Vause | Dec 1777 on command; Jan 1778 waggoner; Feb 1778 drives a waggon; March 1778; April 1778 on furlough; May 1778 6 months furlough. |

## BIBLIOGRAPHY

The following publications were not used in compiling the above lists. However they can provide additional information for researchers on the Valley Forge Encampment, and the Virginia men in the American Revolution. Many of these are available on HathiTrust and other on-line sites.

Alexander, Arthur J. "Exemptions from Military Service in the Old Dominion during the War of the Revolution." *Virginia Magazine of History and Biography*, 53 (1945): 163-171.

Alexander, Arthur J. "Desertion and Its Punishment in Revolutionary Virginia." *William and Mary Quarterly*, 3d Ser., 3 (1946): 383-397.

Alexander, Arthur J. "A Footnote on Deserters from the Virginia Forces During the American Revolution." *Virginia Magazine of History and Biography*, 55 (1947): 137-146.

Anonymous. "Captain Thomas Baytop's Company." *Tyler's Quarterly Historical and Genealogical Magazine*, 8 (1926): 270.

Beale, Robert. "Revolutionary Service of a Virginia Soldier." *Southern Magazine*, 17 (): 602-607.

Beale, Robert. "Revolutionary Experiences of Major Robert Beale." *Northern Neck of Virginia Historical Magazine*, 6 (1956): 500-506.

Benninghoff, Herman O. III. *Valley Forge: A Genesis for Command and Control.* Gettysburg, Pa: Thomas Publications, 2001.

Bockstruck, Lloyd DeWitt. *Revolutionary War Bounty Land Grants Awarded by State Governments.* Baltimore: Genealogical Publishing Co., 1996.

Bodle, Wayne K. The *Valley Forge Winter: Civilians and Soldiers in War.* University Park, Pa: Penn State University Press, 2002.

Bodle, Wayne K. "Generals and 'Gentlemen': Pennsylvania Politics and the Decision for Valley Forge" *Pennsylvania History: A Journal of Mid-Atlantic Studies*, 62 (1995): 59-89.

Bodle, Wayne K. "The Vortex of Small Fortunes: The Continental Army at Valley Forge, 1777-1778." Ph. D. Dissertation, University of Pennsylvania, 1987.

Bodle, Wayne K. and Jacqueline Thibaut. "Valley Forge Historical Research Report." 3 vols., unpublished, (1980).

Booger, William Fletcher, comp. *Gleanings of Virginia History. An Historical and Genealogical Collection, Largely from Original Sources.* Washington: Privately printed, 1903

Boyd, Julian P. *The Papers of Thomas Jefferson* Princeton: Princeton University Press, 1950-2017, 43 volumes to date.

Boyle, Joseph Lee. *Writings From the Valley Forge Encampment of the Continental Army* Maryland: Heritage Books, 8 volumes to date, 2000-2017.

Brumbaugh, Gaius Marcus. *Revolutionary War Records: Volume I, Virginia. Virginia Army and Navy Forces with Bounty Land Warrants for Virginia Military District of Ohio, and Virginia Military Script; From Federal and State Archives.* Washington: Privately printed, 1936.

Burgess, Louis A., comp. *Virginia Soldiers of 1776: Compiled from Documents on File in the Virginia Land Office Together with Material found in the Archives Department of the Virginia State Library, and other Reliable Sources.* 3 vols. Richmond: Richmond Press, 1927-1929.

Cecere, Michael. *Captain Thomas Posey and the Seventh Virginia Regiment.* Westminster, Md.: Heritage Books, 2007.

Cecere, Michael. *They Behaved Like Soldiers: Captain John Chilton and the Third Virginia Regiment, 1775-1778* Westminster, Md.: Heritage Books, 2004.

Chadwick, Bruce. *George Washington's War: The Forging of a Revolutionary Leader and the American Presidency.* Naperville, Ill.: Sourcebooks, Inc., 2004.

Chase, Philander D. et al. eds. *The Papers of George Washington: Revolutionary War Series* Charlottesville, Va: University of Virginia Press, 1985-, 26 volumes to date.

"Colonel Francis Taylor," *Tyler's Quarterly Historical and Genealogical Magazine* 2 (1920): 335-37.

"Continental Soldiers. Abstract of Men raised under the former laws passed for raising soldiers for the Continental Service--November 1782." *Tyler's Quarterly Historical and Genealogical Magazine*, 9 (April 1928): 230-245.

Copeland, Peter F., and Marko Zlatich. "The Minute Battalion of Culpeper County, Virginia 1775-1776." *Military Collector and Historian*, 17 (1965): 52-54.

Copeland, Peter F., and Marko Zlatich. "Joseph Crockett's Western Battalion, Virginia State Troops, 1780-1782." *Military Collector and Historian*, 17 (1965): 82.

Copeland, Peter F., and Marko Zlatich. "2nd Virginia Regiment of the Continental Line, 1779-1781." *Military Collector and Historian*, 17 (1965): 86.

Copeland, Peter F., and Marko Zlatich."13th/9th Virginia Regiment at Fort Pitt-1777-1780." *Military Collector and Historian*, 18 (1966): 120-122, 130.

Copeland, Peter F. and Donald M. Londahl-Smidt. "2nd Regiment, Virginia Continental Line, 1775-1778." *Military Collector and Historian*, 25 (1973): 24-26.

Cropper, John. "Memoir of General John Cropper of Accomack County, Virginia." Ed by Barton Hextall Wise. *Virginia Historical Society Collections*, 11 (1892): 273-315. [Reprinted Onancock: Eastern Shore of Virginia Historical Society, 1974.]

Dabney, Charles William. "Colonel Charles Dabney of the Revolution: His Service as a Soldier and Citizen." *Virginia Magazine of History and Biography*, 51 (1943),: 186-199.

Davidson, Nora F. M. "Revolutionary Services of Robert Bolling, of Petersburg, Va." *Virginia Magazine of History and Biography*, 12 (1904): 154-156.

Eckenrode, H. T. *List of Revolutionary Soldiers in Virginia* Richmond: Virginia State Library and Archives, 1912.

Edwards, William Waller. "Morgan and His Riflemen." *William and Mary Quarterly*, 1st Ser., 23 (1914): 73-106.

Eggleston, J. D. "Officers of the Virginia Line at Winchester, 1783." *William and Mary Quarterly*, 2d Ser., 7 (1927): 61.

Element, N. E. "Revolutionary Pension Declarations from Pittsylvania County, Virginia." *Virginia Magazine of History and Biography*, 25 (1917): 149-160.

Flagg, C. A., and W. O. Waters. "A Bibliography of Muster and Pay Rolls, Regimental Histories, Etc., with Introductory and Explanatory Notes." *Virginia Magazine of History and Biography*, 19 (1911): 402-414; 20 (1912): 52-68, 181-194, 267-281; 22 (1914): 57-67.

Fleming, Thomas. *Washington's Secret War: The Hidden History of Valley Forge*. N. Y.: HarperCollins, 2005.

https://www.fold3.com. has scans of many thousand of pages of military records.

founders.archives.gov. has letters of Thomas Jefferson, George Washington and others.

Gallup, Andrew John. "The Equipment of the Virginia Soldier in the American Revolution, Ph. D. diss., The College of William and Mary, 1991.

Gallup, Andrew. *A Sketch of the Virginia Soldier in the Revolution*. Bowie, Md.: Heritage Books, 1999.

Gibson, John B. "General Gibson." *Western Pennsylvania Historical Magazine*, 5 (1922):. 298-310.

Gilmer, George. "Papers, Military and Political, of George Gilmer, M.D., of 'Pen Park,' Albemarle County, Va." Edited by R. A. Brock. *Virginia Historical Society Collections*, New Ser., 6 (1887): 69-140.

Godfrey, Carlos E. *The Commander-in-Chief's Guard: Revolutionary War*. Washington, D.C.: Stevenson-Smith Co., 1904; reprint, Baltimore: Clearfield Co., 1995.

Goldenberg, Joseph A.; Eddie D. Nelson; and Rita Y. Fletcher. "Revolutionary Ranks: An Analysis of the Chesterfield Supplements." *Virginia Magazine of History and Biography*, 87 (1979): 182-189.

Goodwin, Edmund P. *Colonel William Fleming of Botetourt, 1728-1795*. Roanoke: Roanoke Valley Historical Society, 1976.

Goodwin, Mary R. M. "Clothing and Accoutrements of the Officers and Soldiers of the Virginia Forces 1775-1780. From the Records of the Public Store at Williamsburg." Unpublished research report, Colonial Williamsburg Foundation, 1962.

Graham, James. *The Life of General Daniel Morgan of the Virginia Line of the Army of the United States, with portions of his Correspondence.* New York: Derby & Jackson, 1856.

Gwathmey, John H. *Historical Register of Virginians in the Revolution: Soldiers, Sailors, Marines 1775-1783*. Richmond: Dietz Press, 1938.

Hanko, Charles William. *The Life of John Gibson, Soldier, Patriot, Statesman*. Daytona Beach: College Publishing Co., 1955.

Hart, Freeman H. *The Valley of Virginia in the American Revolution, 1763-1789*. Chapel Hill: University of North Carolina Press, 1942.

Heitman, Francis. *Historical Register of Officers of the Continental Army during the War of the Revolution, April 1777 to December 1783*. Washington, D.C: Rare Book Shop Publishing Co., 1932; reprint, Baltimore: Clearfield Co., 1997.

Herrera, Ricardo A. "Foraging and Combat Operations at Valley Forge February-March 1778." *Army History*, 79 (2011): 6-29.

Herrera, Ricardo A. "'[T]he Zealous activity of Capt. Lee': Light-Horse Harry Lee and Petite Guerre." *The Journal of Military History* 79, (2015): 9-36.

Heth, William. "Orderly Book of Major William Heth of the Third Virginia Regiment, May 15-July 1, 1777." *Virginia Historical Society Collections*, 11 (1892): 319-376.

Higginbotham, Don. *Daniel Morgan: Revolutionary Rifleman*. Chapel Hill: University of North Carolina Press, 1961.

Hocker, Edward W. *The Fighting Parson of the American Revolution: A Biography of General Peter Muhlenberg....* Philadelphia: Privately printed, 1936.

Hunt, Gaillard, ed. *Fragments of Revolutionary History: Being Hitherto unpublished writings of the men of the American Revolution, collected and edited under the authority of the District of Columbia Society, Sons of the Revolution*. Brooklyn: Historical Printing Club, 1892.

*Index of Revolutionary War Pensions*. Washington, D.C.: National Genealogical Society, 1966.

Jackson, John W. *Valley Forge: Pinnacle of Courage*. Gettysburg, Pa: Thomas Publications, 1992.

Jackson, Luther P. "Virginia Negro Soldiers and Seamen in the American Revolution." *Journal of Negro History*, 27 (1942): 247-287.
Jefferson, Thomas. *The Papers of Thomas Jefferson*. Edited by Julian P. Boyd et al. 43 volumes to date. Princeton: Princeton University Press, 1950-2018.
Johnston, Henry P. "Christian Febiger Colonel of the Virginia Line of the Continental Army." *Magazine of American History*, 5 (1881): 188-203.
Johnston, Ross B. *West Virginians in the Revolution*. 1939-1947; reprint, Baltimore: Clearfield Co., 1998.
Joynes, Thomas R. "Ninth Virginia Regiment of the Revolutionary Army." *Historical Magazine*, 7 (1863): 172-175.
Joynes, Thomas R. "Ninth Virginia regiment of the Revolutionary Army, with a list of officers, January 1777." *Pennsylvania Magazine of History and Biography*, 22 (1898): 122-124.
Lender, Mark Edward, and Garry Wheeler Stone. *Fatal Sunday: George Washington, the Monmouth Campaign, and the Politics of Battle* Norman: University of Oklahoma Press, 2016.
Loane, Nancy K. *Following the Drum: Woman at the Valley Forge Encampment*. New York: Barnes & Noble. 2009.
Lockyard, E. Kidd. "Some Problems of the Draft in Revolutionary Virginia." *West Virginia History*, 37 (April 1976): 201-210.
Londahl-Smidt, Donald M. "2nd Virginia Regiment 1775." *Military Collector and Historian*, 28 (1976): 156-157.
McAllister, J. T. *Virginia Militia in the Revolutionary War; McAllister's Data*. Hot Springs, Va.: McAllister Publishing Co., 1913.
McAllister, J. T. "Depositions of Revolutionary Soldiers." *Virginia Magazine of History and Biography*, 4 1897): 411-415; 5 (1897): 53-158.
McAllister, J. T. "Summary of Statements Made by Soldiers who Service in the Revolutionary War from Virginia-Either in the Continental Line or the Virginia State Line." *Virginia Magazine of History and Biography*, 22 (1914): 177-186.
McBarron, H. Charles, and Frederick P. Todd. "6th Virginia Regiment, Continental Line, 1776." *Military Collector and Historian*, 2 (1950): 23-24.
McBride, John David. "The Virginia War Effort, 1775-1783: Manpower Policies and Practices." Ph.D. Dissertation, University of Virginia, 1977.
Michael A. McDonnell, "'Fit for Common Service?' Class, Race, and Recruitment in Revolutionary Virginia," in Resch, John and Walter Sargent, eds. *War and Society in the American Revolution: Mobilization*

*and Home Fronts* (DeKalb: Northern Illinois University Press, 2007), 103-131.

McDonnell, Michael A. "The Politics of Mobilization in Revolutionary Virginia: Military Culture and Political and Social Relations, 1774-1783" (D. Phil. Thesis, Baliol College, Oxford University, 1995.

McGuire, Thomas J. *The Philadelphia Campaign Volume I: Brandywine and the Fall of Philadelphia.* Mechanicsburg, Pa.: Stackpole, 2006.

McGuire, Thomas J. *The Philadelphia Campaign: Volume 2: Germantown and the Roads to Valley Forge.* Mechanicsburg, Pa.: Stackpole, 2007.

McIlwaine, Henry Read, ed. *Journals of the Council of the State of Virginia.* 2 vols. Richmond: Virginia State Library, 1931-1952.

McIlwaine, Henry Read, ed. *Official Letters of the Governors of the State of Virginia.* 3 vols. Richmond: Virginia State Library, 1926-1929.

Mason, George. *The Papers of George Mason 1725-1792.* Edited by Robert A. Rutland. 3 vols. Chapel Hill: University of North Carolina Press, 1970.

Morris, Robert L. "Military Contributions of Western Virginia in the American Revolution." *West Virginia History,* 23 (1962): 86-99.

Morton, W. S. "Revolutionary Soldiers of Amelia County." *William and Mary Quarterly,* 2d Ser., 15 (1935):. 397-402.

Muhlenberg, John P. G. "Orderly Book of Gen. John Peter Gabriel Muhlenberg, [May] March 26-December 20, 1777." *Pennsylvania Magazine of History and Biography,* 33 (1909): 257-278, 454-474; 34 (1910): 21-40, 166-189, 336-360, 438-477; 35 (1911: 59-89, 156-187, 290-303.

Newcomb, Benjamin H. "Washington's Generals and the Decision to Quarter at Valley Forge. *The Pennsylvania Magazine of History and Biography,* 117 (1993): 309-329.

Palmer, William P., editor. *Calendar of Virginia State Papers and Other Manuscripts.* 11 vols. Richmond: Virginia State Library, 1875-1893.

Pennypacker, Samuel W., ed. *Valley Forge Orderly Book of General George Weedon of the Continental Army under the Command of Genl. George Washington, in the Campaign of 1777-8.* New York: Dodd, Mead and Co., 1902.

Peterson, Clarence S. *Known Military Dead during the Revolutionary War.* Baltimore, 1959; reprint, Baltimore: Genealogical Publishing Co., 1967.

Pierce's Register. *Register of the Certificates Issued by John Pierce, Esquire, Paymaster General and Commissioner of Army Accounts for the United States, to Officers and Soldiers of the Continental Army Under Act of July 4, 1783.* 1915; reprint, Baltimore: Genealogical Publishing Co., 1987.

Porterfield, Charles. "Diary of a Prisoner of War at Quebec." Edited by J. A. Waddell. *Virginia Magazine of History and Biography*, 9 (October 1901): 144-152.

Posey, John Thornton. "'The Turbulent Spirit': A Virginia Battalion in the Southern Campaign of 1782." *Virginia Cavalcade*, 40 (Summer 1990): 4-13.

Post, Todd. "2nd Virginia Regiment, September 1775-March 1776." *Military Collector & Historian.* 62 (2010): 316-317.

Powell, Robert C. *A Biographical Sketch of Col. Levin Powell, Including His Correspondence During the Revolutionary War.* Alexandria: G. H. Ramey & Son, 1877.

"Revolutionary Army Orders for the Main Army under Washington, 1778-1779." *Virginia Magazine of History and Biography*, 13-22 (1906-1914), various pages.

"Revolutionary Letters." *Tyler's Quarterly Historical and Genealogical Magazine*, 8 (1927): 176; 9 (1928): 245-248.

Reynolds, William W. "Virginia State and Continental Regiments at the Siege of Yorktown." *Military Collector & Historian* 68, (2016): 345-350.

Sanchez-Saavedra, E. M. *A Guide to Virginia Military Organizations in the American Revolution, 1774-1787.* Richmond: Virginia State Library, 1978.

Schmucker, George W., editor. "Letters of Generals Daniel Morgan and Peter Muhlenberg." *Pennsylvania Magazine of History and Biography*, 21 (1897):. 488-492.

"Second Virginia Battalion, 1777." *Virginia Magazine of History and Biography*, 6 (1898): 124-127.

Selby, John E. *The Revolution in Virginia, 1775-1783.* Charlottesville: University Press of Virginia, 1988.

Sellers, John Robert. *The Virginia Continental Line.* Williamsburg: Virginia Independence Bicentennial Commission, 1978.

Sellers, John Robert. "The Virginia Continental Line, 1775-1780." Ph.D. Dissertation, Tulane University, 1968.

Stephen, Adam. "Letters of General Adam Stephen to R. H. Lee." *Historical Magazine*, 1st Ser., 9 (1865): 118-122.

Stewart, Mrs. Catesby Willis. *The Life of Brigadier General William Woodford of the American Revolution.* 2 vols. Richmond: Whittet & Shepperson, 1973.

Sweeny, Lenora H. *Amherst County, Virginia in the Revolution Including Extracts From the "Lost Order Book" 1773-1782.* 1951; reprint Baltimore: Clearfield Company, 1998.

Sydnor, William. "David Griffith-Chaplain, Surgeon, Patriot." *Historical Magazine of the Protestant Episcopal Church*, 44 (1975): 247-256.

Taliaferro, Benjamin. *The Orderly Book of Captain Benjamin Taliaferro: 2d Virginia Detachment*, Charleston, South Carolina, 1780. Edited by Lee A. Wallace, Jr. Richmond: Virginia State Library, 1980.

"Colonel Francis Taylor." *Tyler's Quarterly Historical and Genealogical Magazine*, 2 (1920): 335-337.

Taylor, P. Fall, editor. "Fourth Virginia Regiment in the Revolution." *Virginia Magazine of History and Biography*, 1 (1893): 202-207.

Thomas, William H. B. *Patriots of the Upcountry: Orange County, Virginia in the Revolution.* Orange: Orange County Bicentennial Commission, 1976.

Tyler, Lyon G. "The Old Virginia Line in the Middle States During the American Revolution." *Tyler's Quarterly Historical and Genealogical Magazine*, 12 (July, October 1930; January, April 1931): 1-42, 90-141, 198-203, 283-289.

Trussell, John B. B., Jr., *Birthplace of an Army: A Study of the Valley Forge Encampment.* Harrisburg: Pennsylvania Museum and Historical Commission, 1976.

U. S. Congress, Walter Lowrie and Walter S. Franklin, eds. *American State Papers; Documents, Legislative and Executive, on the Congress of the United States, from the First Session of the First to the Second Session of the Seventeenth Congress, inclusive; Commencing March 4, 1789, and Ending March 8, 1823. Class IX Claims.* Washington, D.C.: 1834. Contains much information on thousands of Revolutionary War service claims filed in Congress. See McMullin, Phillip W. *Grassroots of America*, for a thorough index.

U. S. House of Representatives. *Resolutions, Laws, and Ordinances, Relating to the Pay, Half Pay, Commutation of Half Pay, Bounty Lands...Officers and Soldiers of the Revolution...and to Funding Revolutionary Debt.* 1838; reprint, Baltimore: Genealogical Publishing Co., 1998.

U. S. War Department. *Letter from the Secretary of War, Communicating a Transcript of the Pension List of the United States - June 1, 1813.* Washington, D.C., 1813; reprinted as *Revolutionary Pensioners; a Transcript of the Pension List of 1813.* Baltimore: Genealogical Publishing Co., 1959.

U.S. War Department. *Letter from the Secretary of War, Transmitting a Report of the Names, Rank and Line of Every Person Placed on the Pension List, in Pursuance of the Act of 18th March 1818.* Washington, D.C., 1820; reprint, Baltimore: Genealogical Publishing Co., 1955.

Van Atta, John R. "Conscription in Revolutionary Virginia: The Case of Culpeper County, 1780-1781." *Virginia Magazine of History and Biography*, 92 (1984): 263-281.

Van Schreevan, William J., et al., editors. *Revolutionary Virginia: The Road to Independence.* 7 vols. Charlottesville: University Press of Virginia for the Virginia Independence Bicentennial Commission, 1973-1983.

"Virginia Officers and Men in the Continental Line," *Virginia Magazine of History and Biography* 2 (1895): 241-58; 357-70.

Ward, Harry M. *Charles Scott and the "Spirit of '76".* Charlottesville, Virginia: University Press of Virginia, 1988.

Ward, Harry M. *Duty, Honor of Country: General George Weedon and the American Revolution.* Philadelphia: American Philosophical Society, 1979.

Wilson, Samuel M., comp. *Catalogue of the Revolutionary Soldiers and Sailors of the Commonwealth of Virginia to Whom Land Bounty Warrants Were Granted by Virginia for Military Services in the War for Independence* 1913. Report, Baltimore: Genealogical Publishing Co., 1967.

Wood, James. "Correspondence of Col. James Wood." *Tyler's Quarterly and Genealogical Magazine* 3 (1921); 28-44.

Woodford, William. "Unpublished Letters of General Woodford, on the Continental Army, 1776-1779 *The Pennsylvania Magazine of History and Biography*, 23, (1899): 453-463

www.southerncampaign.org. This website has thousands of pension applications filed by Virginia soldiers.

Wright, Robert K. Jr., *The Continental Army* Washington, D.C.: Center of Military History, 1986.